Shojo Beat

BABY & Me™

Vol.2

Story & Art by Marimo Ragawa

Baby & Me™ **Table of Contents**

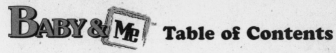

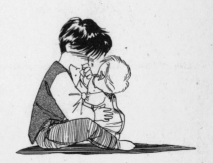

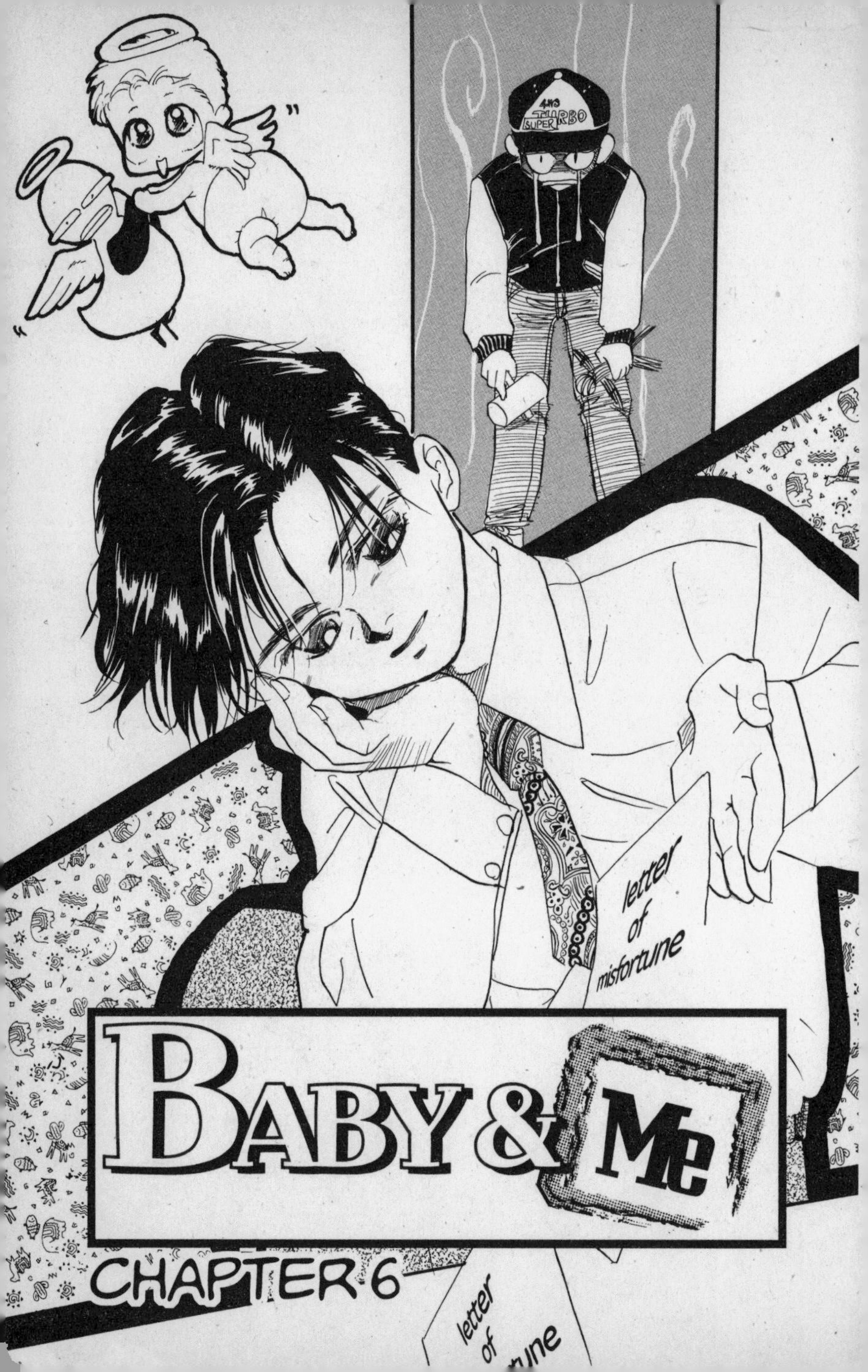
4WS SUPER TURBO
letter of misfortune
BABY & Me
CHAPTER 6
letter of

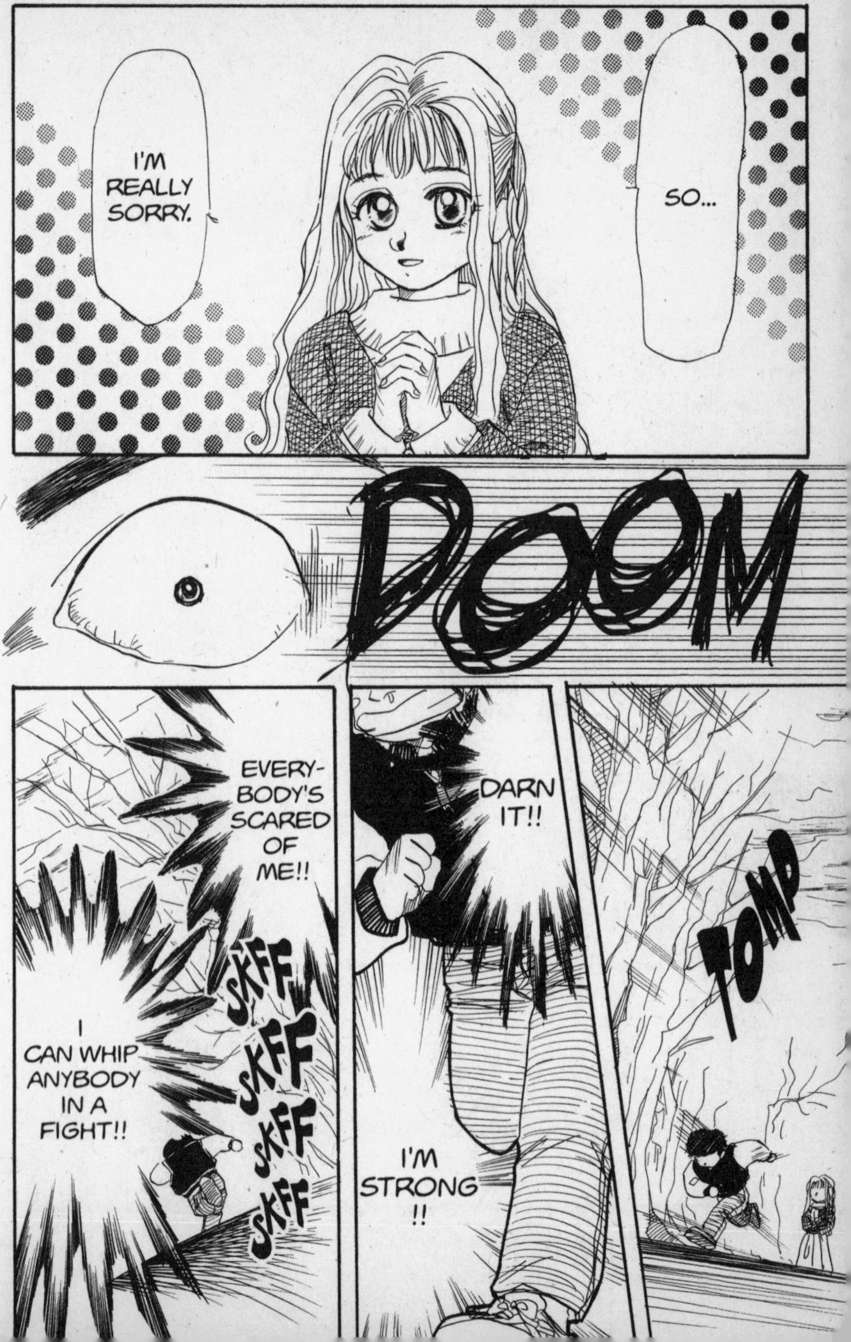

SO...
I'M REALLY SORRY.
DOOM
TOMP
DARN IT!!
I'M STRONG!!
EVERY-BODY'S SCARED OF ME!!
SKFF SKFF SKFF SKFF SKFF
I CAN WHIP ANYBODY IN A FIGHT!!

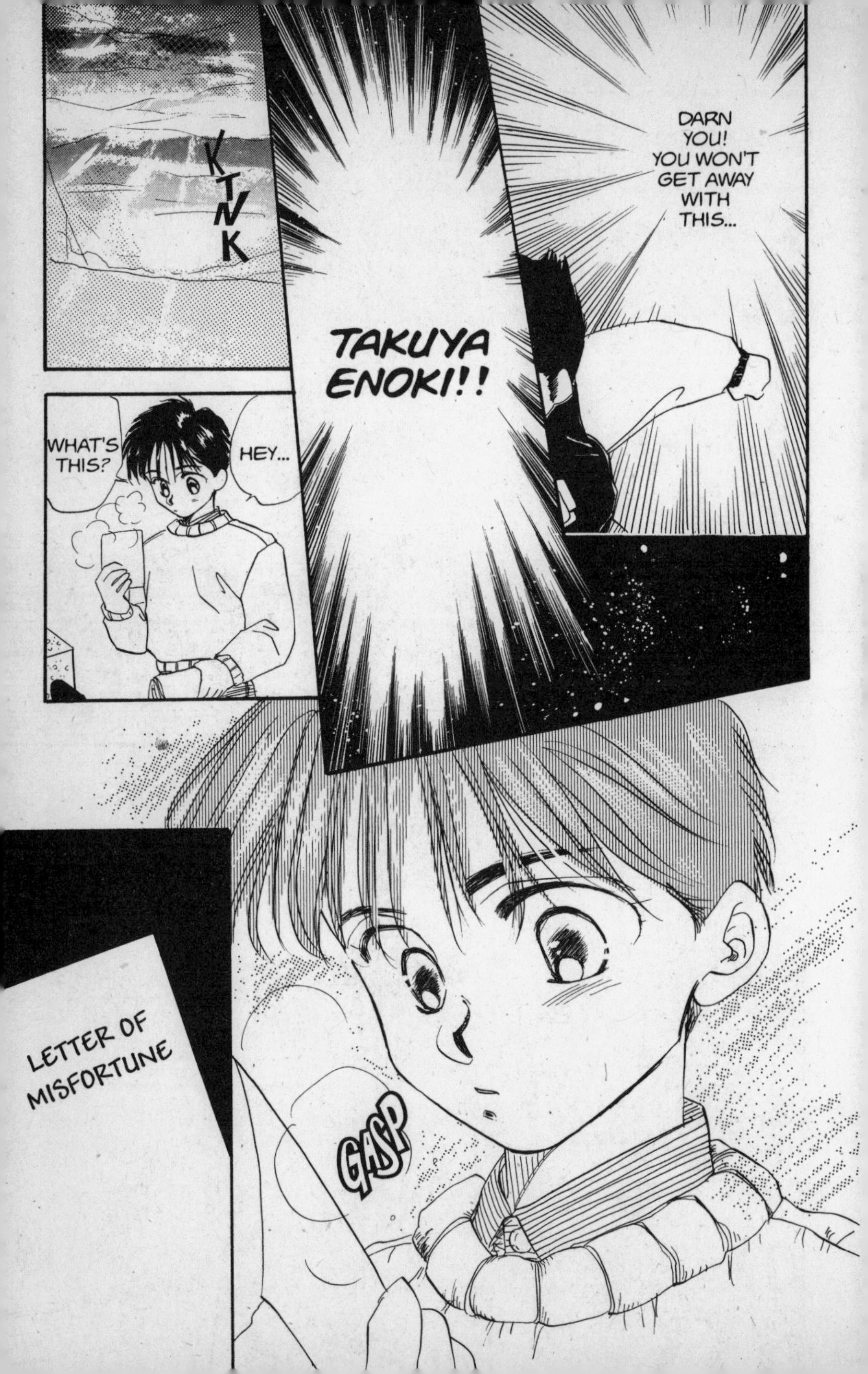
DARN YOU! YOU WON'T GET AWAY WITH THIS...
TAKUYA ENOKI!!
KTNK
HEY...
WHAT'S THIS?
GASP
LETTER OF MISFORTUNE

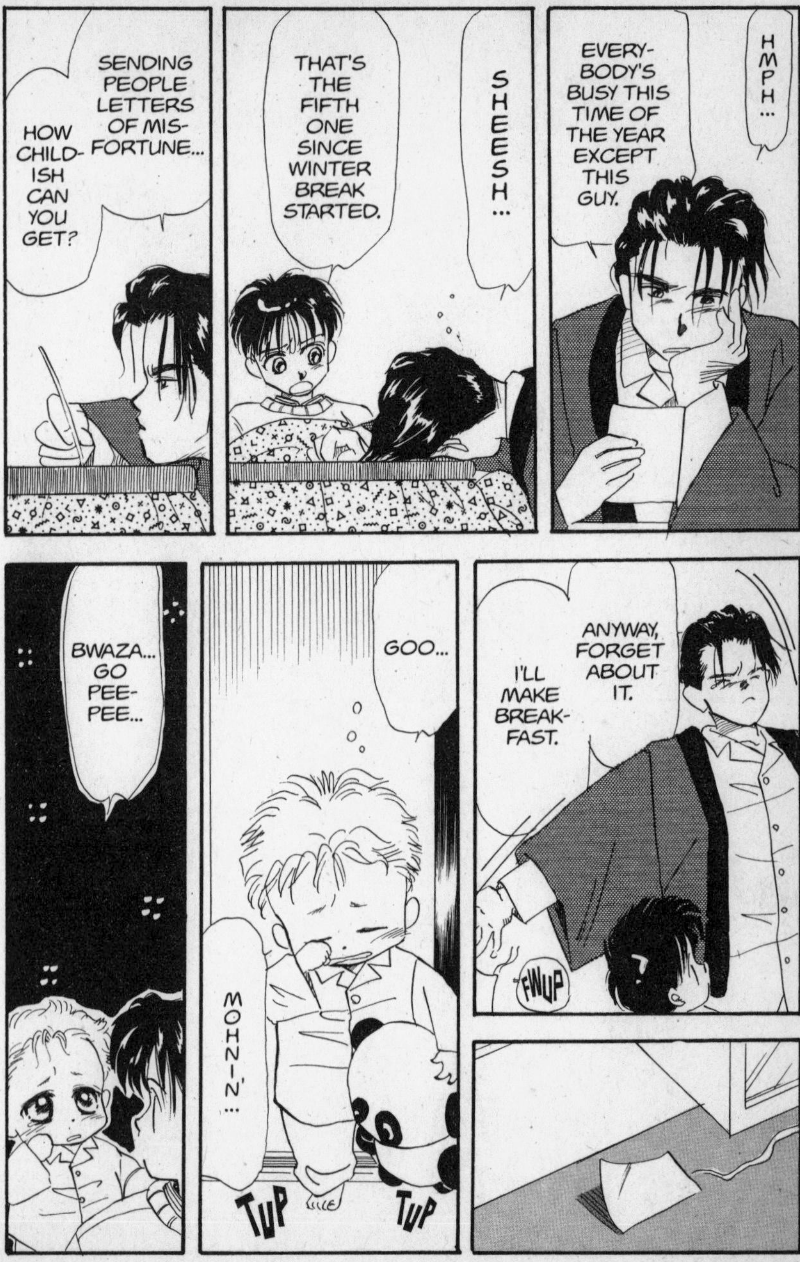
HMPH...
EVERYBODY'S BUSY THIS TIME OF THE YEAR EXCEPT THIS GUY.
SHEESH...
THAT'S THE FIFTH ONE SINCE WINTER BREAK STARTED.
SENDING PEOPLE LETTERS OF MISFORTUNE...
HOW CHILDISH CAN YOU GET?
ANYWAY, FORGET ABOUT IT.
I'LL MAKE BREAKFAST.
FWUP
GOO...
MOHNIN'...
TUP
TUP
BWAZA... GO PEE-PEE...

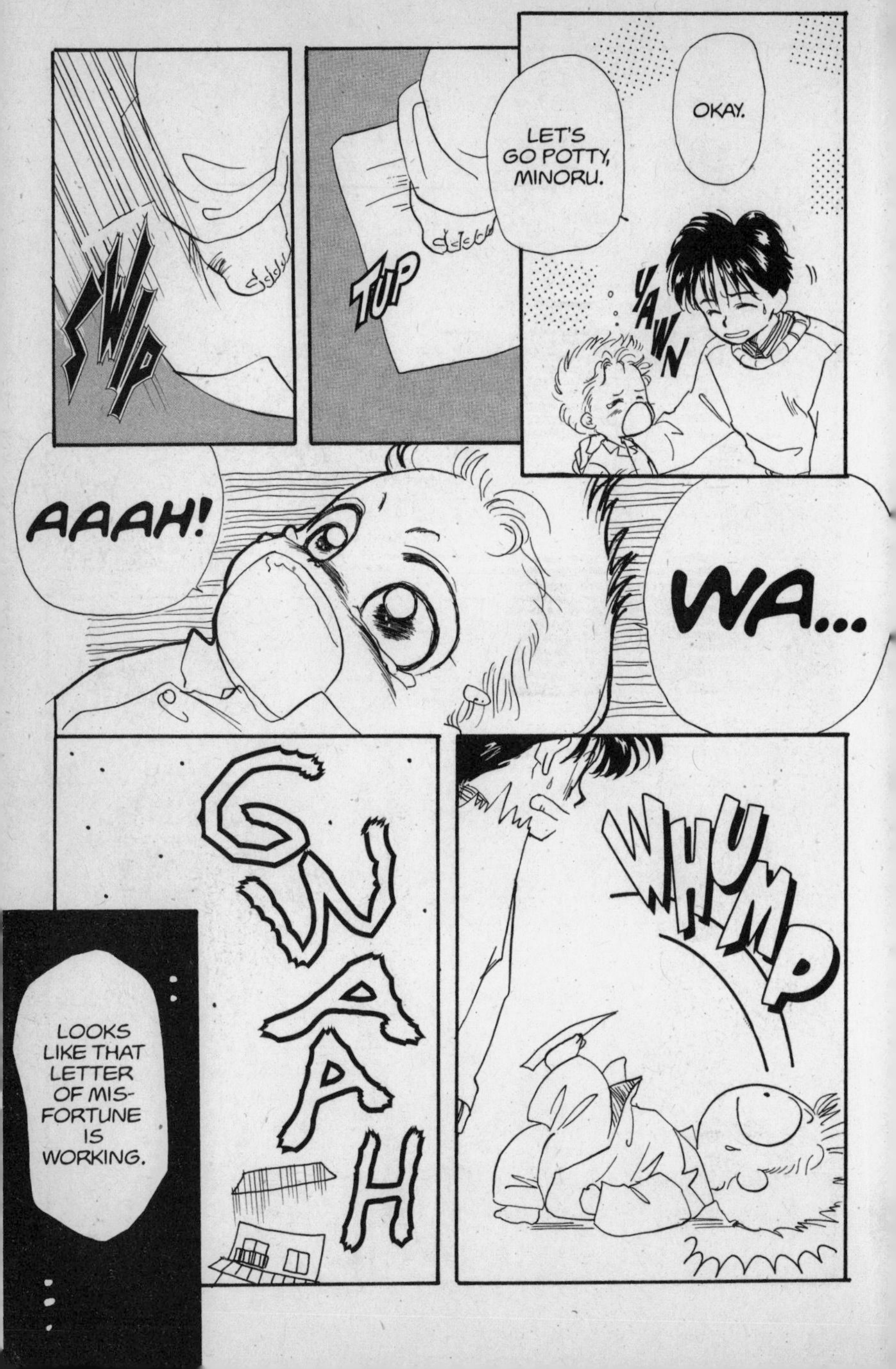
OKAY.
LET'S GO POTTY, MINORU.
YAWN
TUP
SWIP
WA...
AAAH!
WHUMP
GWAAH
LOOKS LIKE THAT LETTER OF MIS-FORTUNE IS WORKING.

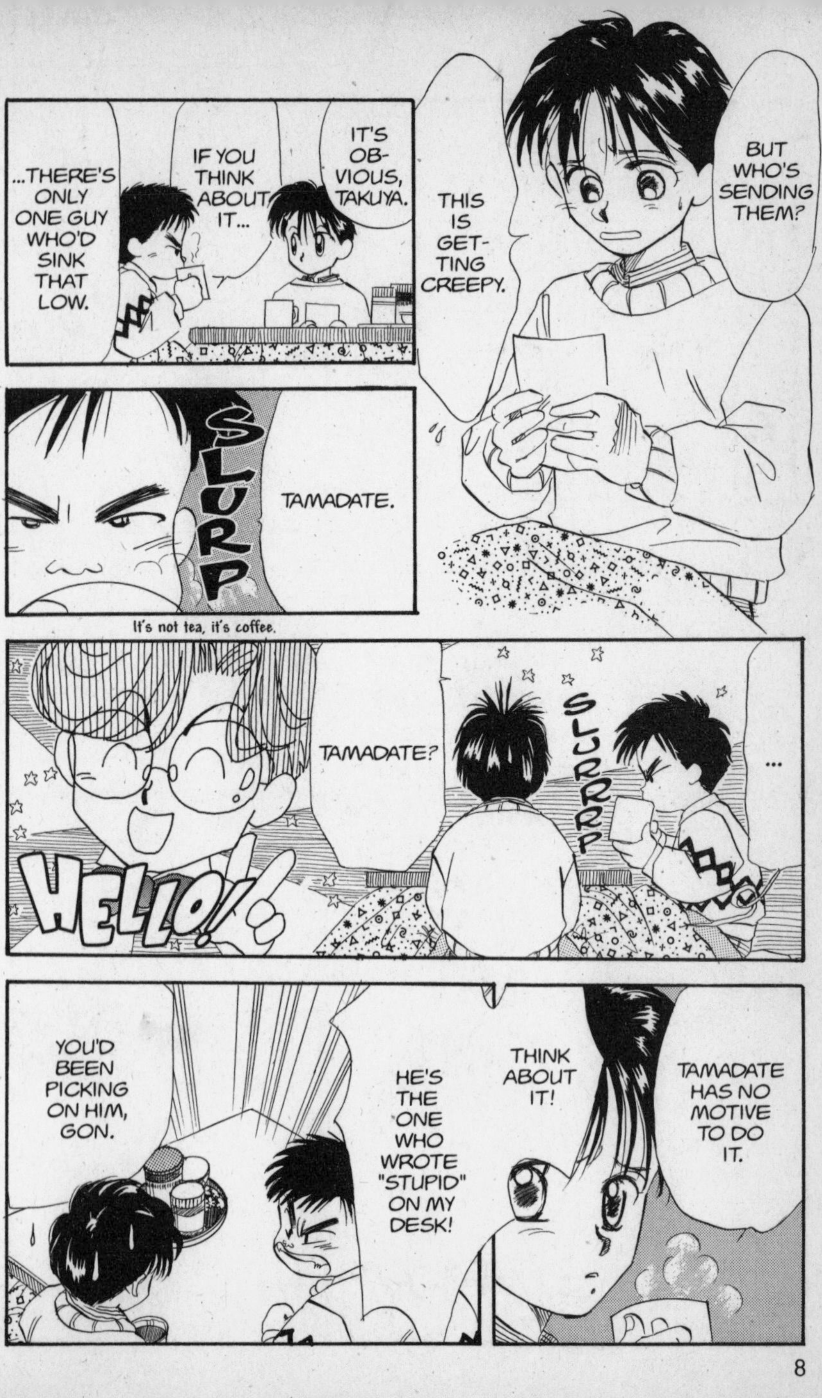
BUT WHO'S SENDING THEM?
THIS IS GETTING CREEPY.
IT'S OBVIOUS, TAKUYA.
IF YOU THINK ABOUT IT...
...THERE'S ONLY ONE GUY WHO'D SINK THAT LOW.
SLURP
TAMADATE.
It's not tea, it's coffee.
...
SLURRRP
TAMADATE?
HELLO!
TAMADATE HAS NO MOTIVE TO DO IT.
THINK ABOUT IT!
HE'S THE ONE WHO WROTE "STUPID" ON MY DESK!
YOU'D BEEN PICKING ON HIM, GON.

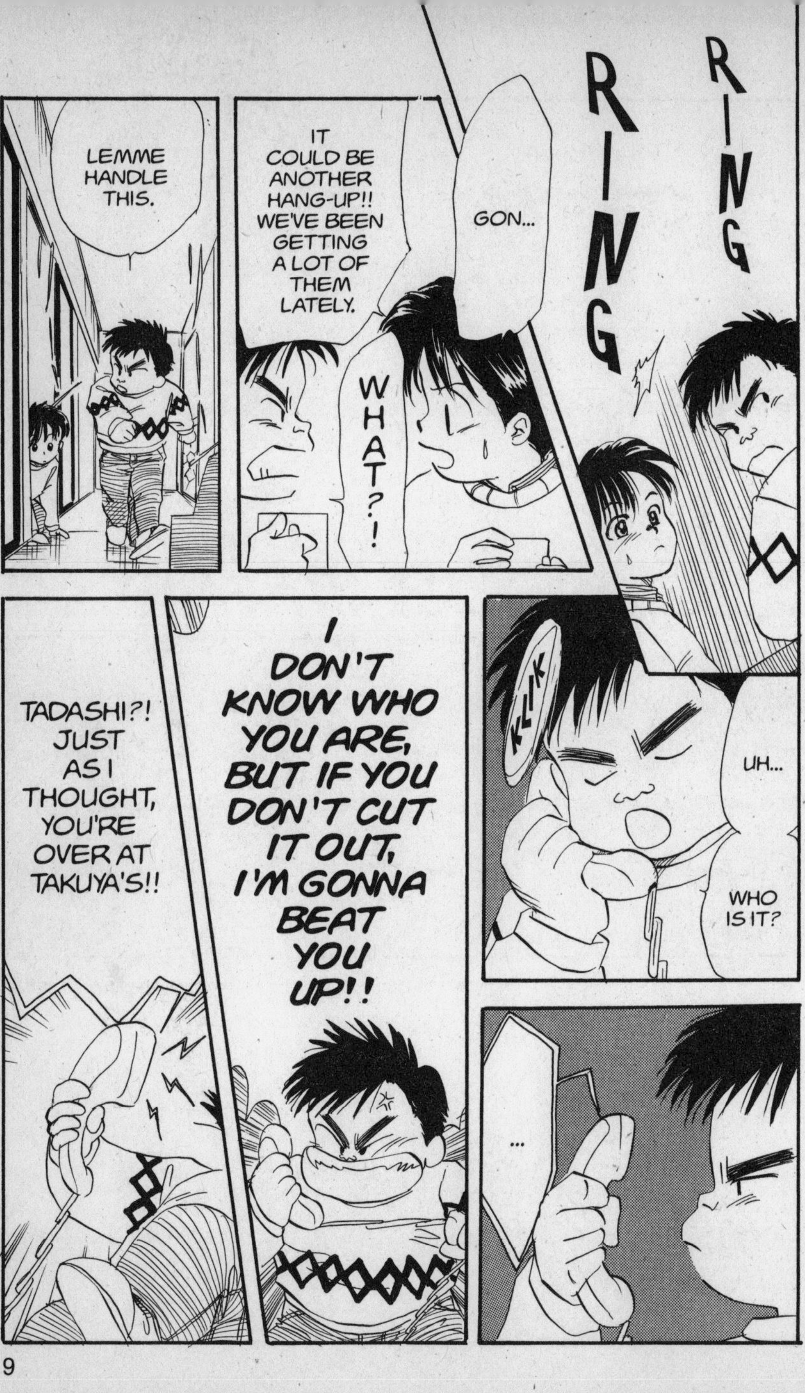
RING RING
GON...
IT COULD BE ANOTHER HANG-UP!! WE'VE BEEN GETTING A LOT OF THEM LATELY.
WHAT?!
LEMME HANDLE THIS.
KLIK
UH...
WHO IS IT?
...
I DON'T KNOW WHO YOU ARE, BUT IF YOU DON'T CUT IT OUT, I'M GONNA BEAT YOU UP!!
TADASHI?! JUST AS I THOUGHT, YOU'RE OVER AT TAKUYA'S!!

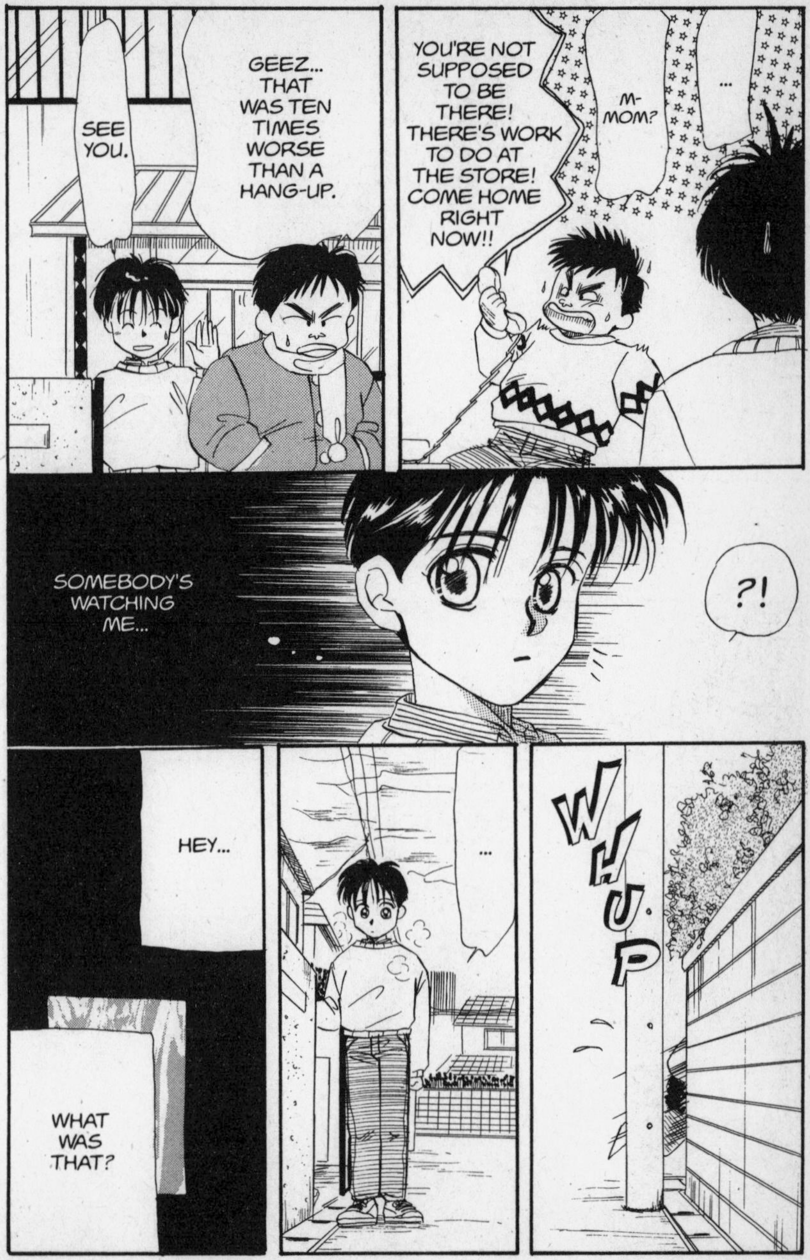
...
M-MOM?
YOU'RE NOT SUPPOSED TO BE THERE! THERE'S WORK TO DO AT THE STORE! COME HOME RIGHT NOW!!
GEEZ... THAT WAS TEN TIMES WORSE THAN A HANG-UP.
SEE YOU.
?!
SOMEBODY'S WATCHING ME...
WHUP
...
HEY...
WHAT WAS THAT?

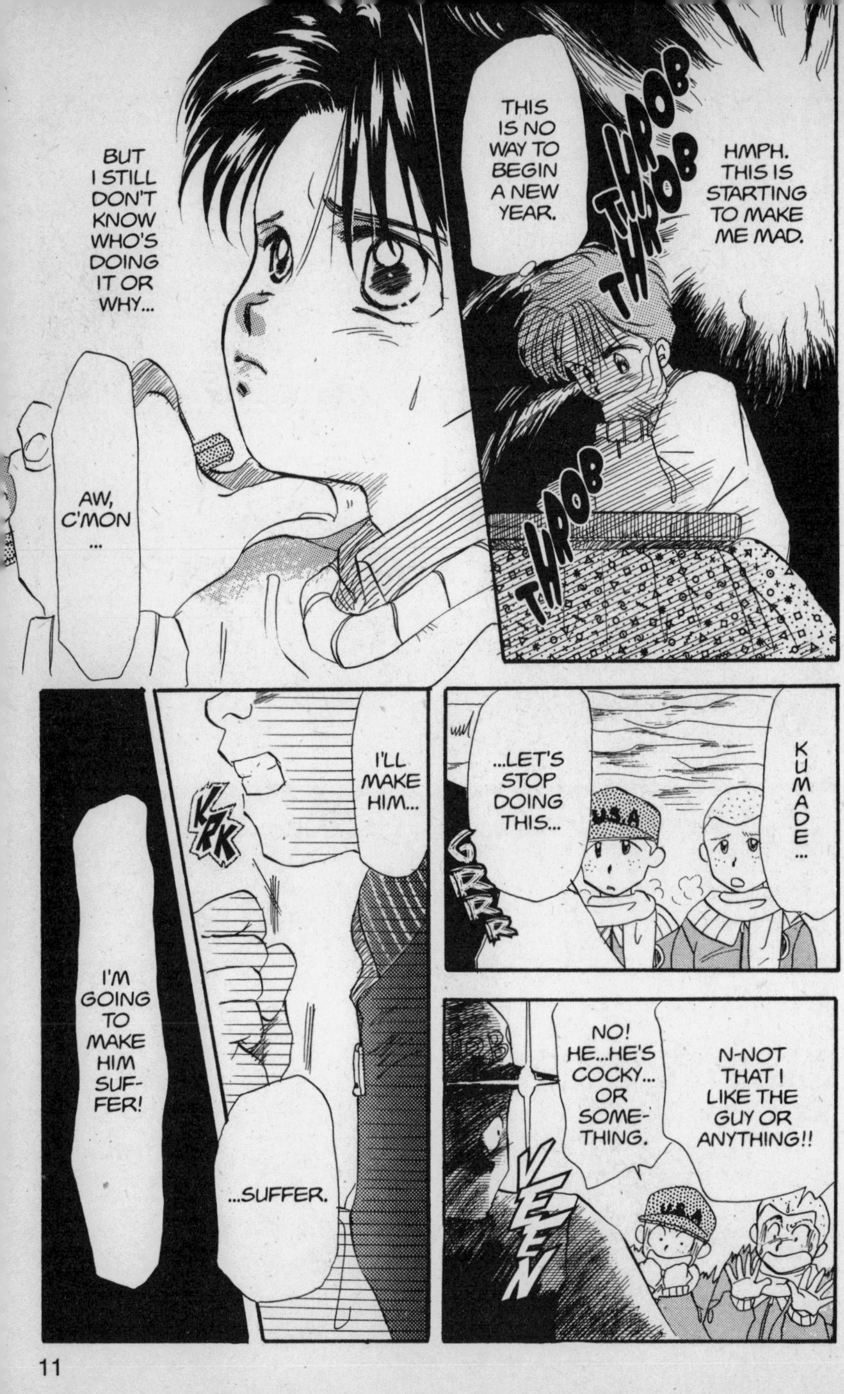
HMPH. THIS IS STARTING TO MAKE ME MAD.
THROB THROB
THIS IS NO WAY TO BEGIN A NEW YEAR.
THROB THROB
BUT I STILL DON'T KNOW WHO'S DOING IT OR WHY...
AW, C'MON ...
KUMADE ...
...LET'S STOP DOING THIS...
GRRR
N-NOT THAT I LIKE THE GUY OR ANYTHING!!
NO! HE...HE'S COCKY... OR SOME-THING.
VEEEN
I'LL MAKE HIM...
KRK
...SUFFER.
I'M GOING TO MAKE HIM SUF-FER!

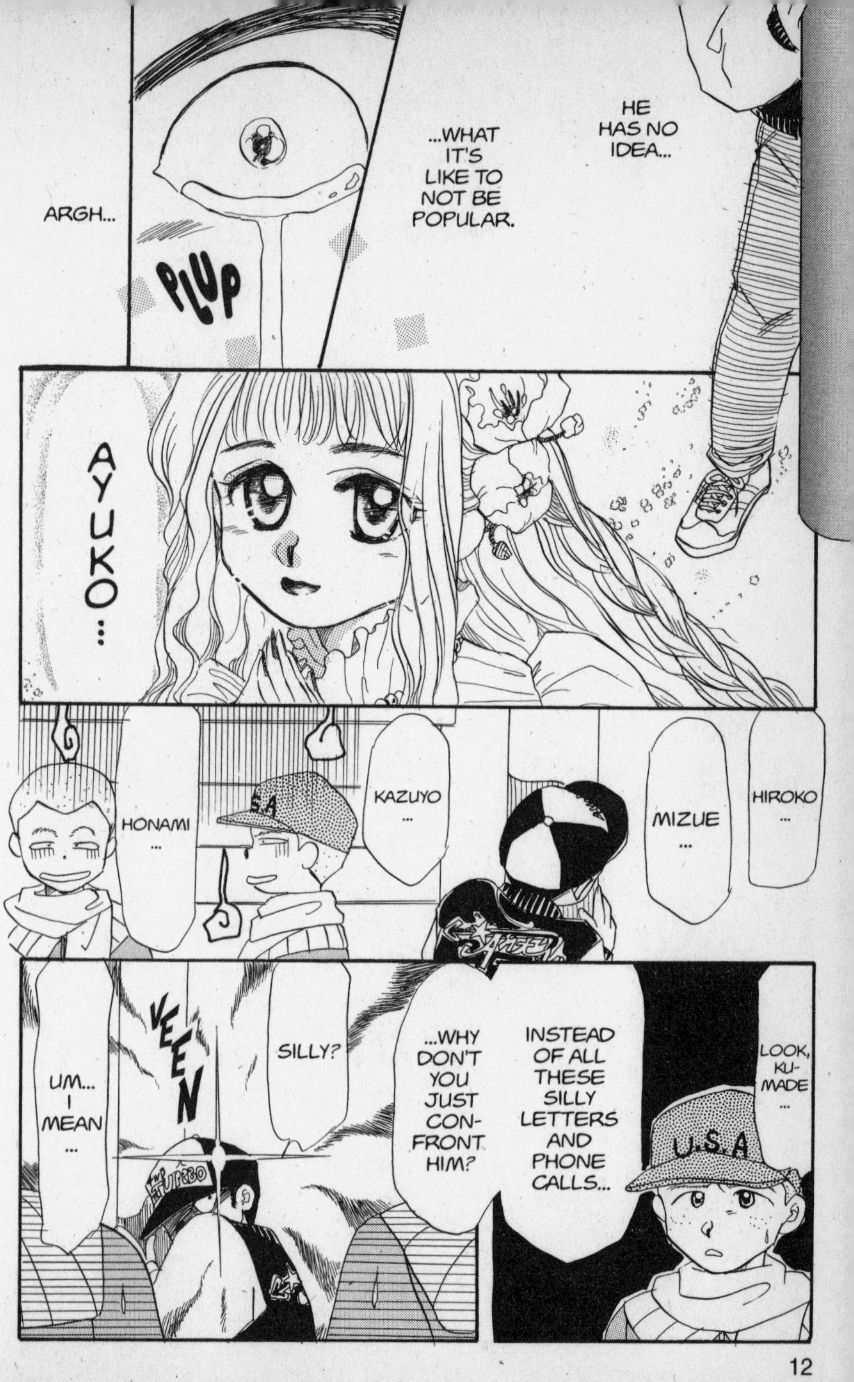
HE HAS NO IDEA...
...WHAT IT'S LIKE TO NOT BE POPULAR.
ARGH...
PLUP
AYUKO...
HIROKO...
MIZUE...
KAZUYO...
HONAMI...
LOOK, KU-MADE...
INSTEAD OF ALL THESE SILLY LETTERS AND PHONE CALLS...
...WHY DON'T YOU JUST CON-FRONT HIM?
SILLY?
VEEN
UM... I MEAN...

KUMADE!!

I'M SORRY!! AAAH!!

GASP

*KRAK

WHAM

POW

STARE

THAT'S ENOKI'S LITTLE BROTHER!!

HEY...

STARE

BA-BUMP

WAAATAH!!

SMIRK

HEH.

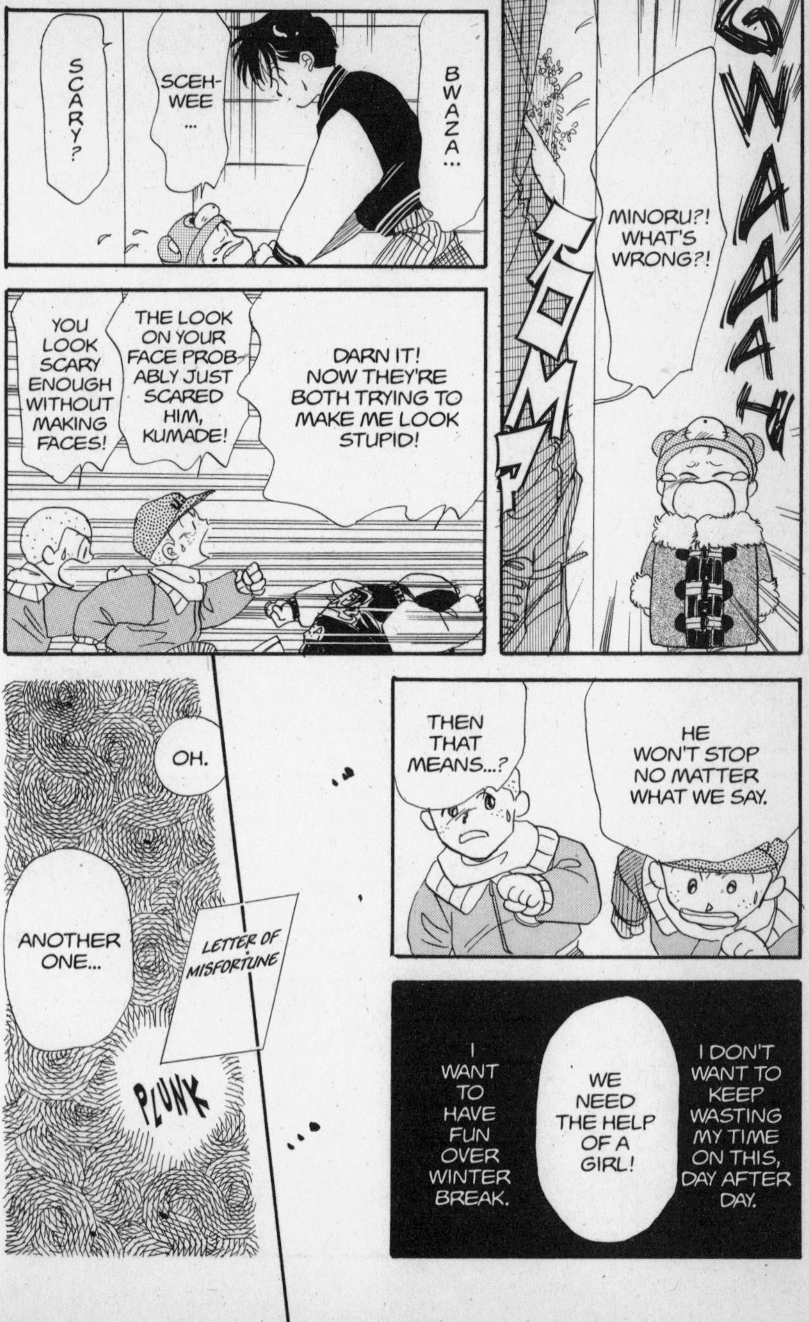

GWAAAH
MINORU?! WHAT'S WRONG?!
TOMP
BWAZA...
SCEH-WEE...
SCARY?
DARN IT! NOW THEY'RE BOTH TRYING TO MAKE ME LOOK STUPID!
THE LOOK ON YOUR FACE PROBABLY JUST SCARED HIM, KUMADE!
YOU LOOK SCARY ENOUGH WITHOUT MAKING FACES!
HE WON'T STOP NO MATTER WHAT WE SAY.
THEN THAT MEANS...?
I DON'T WANT TO KEEP WASTING MY TIME ON THIS, DAY AFTER DAY.
WE NEED THE HELP OF A GIRL!
I WANT TO HAVE FUN OVER WINTER BREAK.
OH.
ANOTHER ONE...
LETTER OF MISFORTUNE
PLUNK

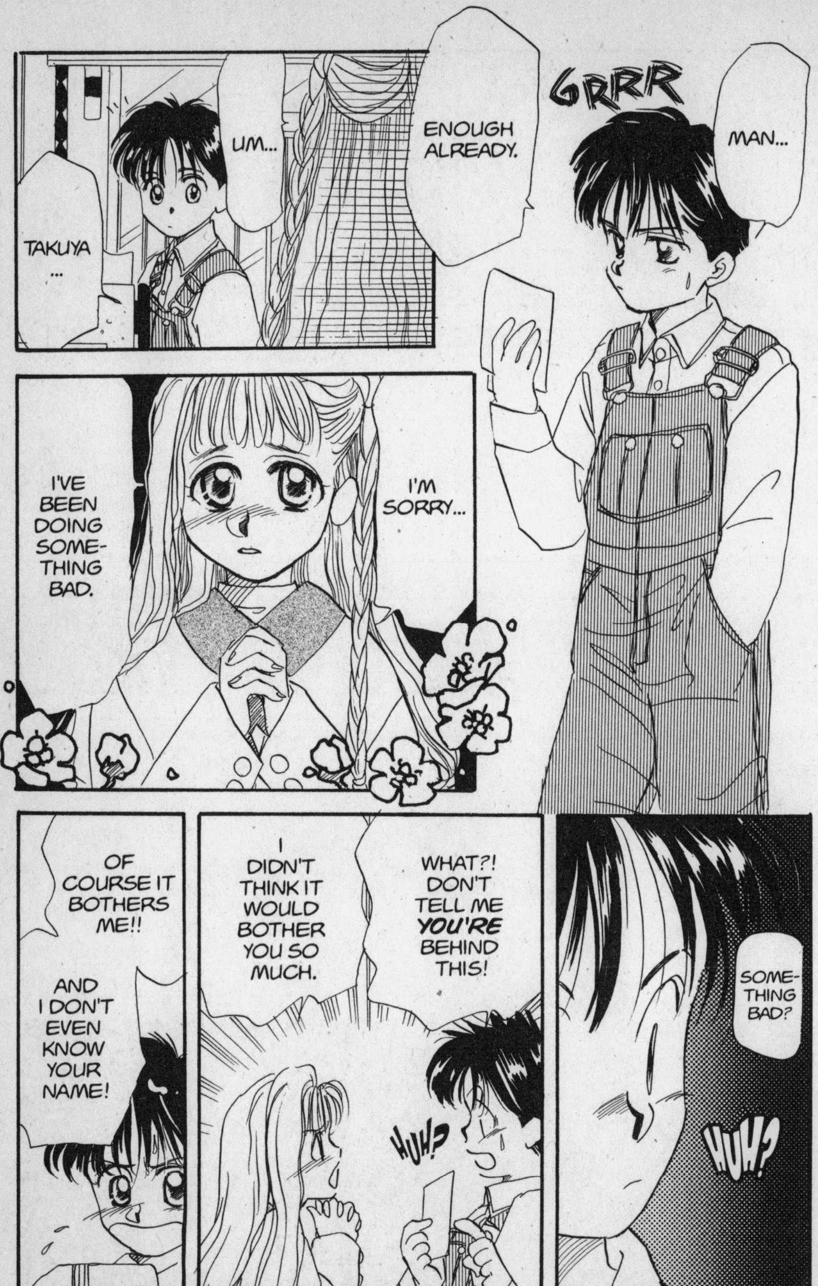
GRRR
MAN...
ENOUGH ALREADY.
UM...
TAKUYA ...
I'M SORRY...
I'VE BEEN DOING SOME-THING BAD.
SOME-THING BAD?
HUH?
WHAT?! DON'T TELL ME *YOU'RE* BEHIND THIS!
I DIDN'T THINK IT WOULD BOTHER YOU SO MUCH.
HUH?
OF COURSE IT BOTHERS ME!!
AND I DON'T EVEN KNOW YOUR NAME!

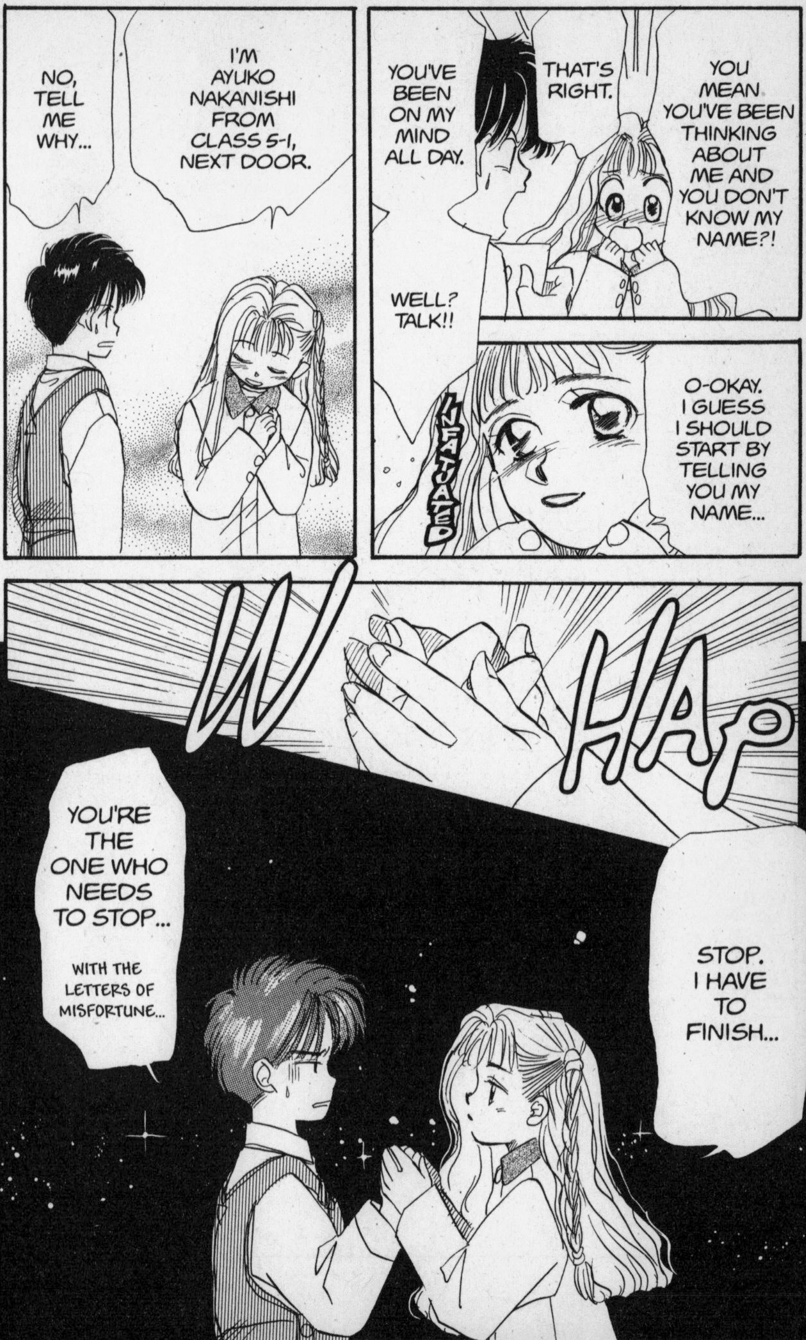
YOU MEAN YOU'VE BEEN THINKING ABOUT ME AND YOU DON'T KNOW MY NAME?!
THAT'S RIGHT.
YOU'VE BEEN ON MY MIND ALL DAY.
WELL? TALK!!
INFATUATED
O-OKAY. I GUESS I SHOULD START BY TELLING YOU MY NAME...
I'M AYUKO NAKANISHI FROM CLASS 5-1, NEXT DOOR.
NO, TELL ME WHY...
WHAP
STOP. I HAVE TO FINISH...
YOU'RE THE ONE WHO NEEDS TO STOP...
WITH THE LETTERS OF MISFORTUNE...

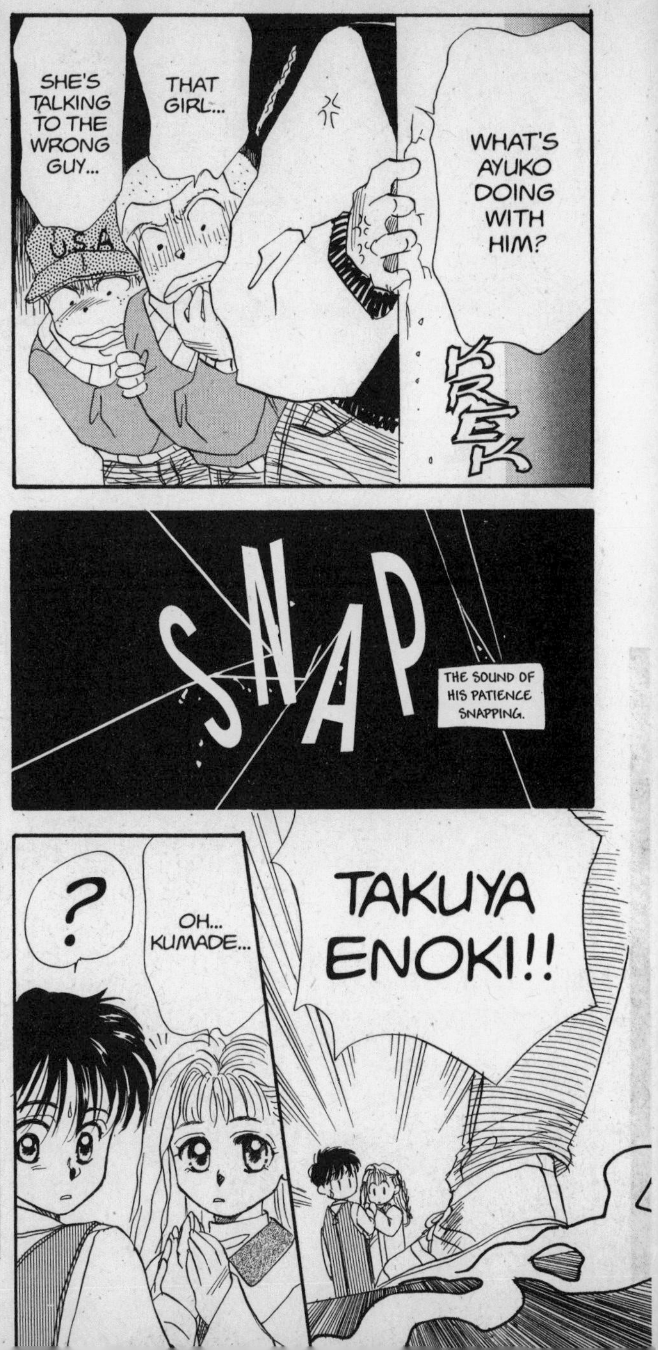
WHAT'S AYUKO DOING WITH HIM?
KREK
THAT GIRL...
SHE'S TALKING TO THE WRONG GUY...
SNAP
THE SOUND OF HIS PATIENCE SNAPPING.
TAKUYA ENOKI!!
OH... KUMADE...
?

THE 3-3-7 CHEER
[MUSIC]

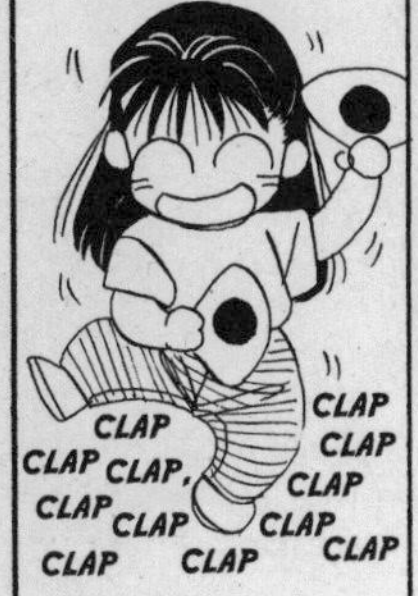
CLAP CLAP
CLAP CLAP, CLAP
CLAP CLAP CLAP
CLAP CLAP
CLAP CLAP CLAP

MY SECOND VOLUME IS FINALLY OUT! THIS CALLS FOR A CELEBRATION! YOUR LETTERS HAVE TAUGHT ME A LOT ABOUT THE POWER OF COMICS. THE MANUSCRIPTS FOR ALL OF THE CHAPTERS IN THIS VOLUME WERE SO LATE THAT MY EDITOR HAD TO COME AND PICK THEM UP IN THE MIDDLE OF THE NIGHT. I WAS SO STRESSED OUT, I ACTUALLY THREW UP. I CRIED GIANT TEARS. SO MY MANUSCRIPT WAS A MESS. IT WAS REALLY DISGUSTING. THEN, WHEN I ASKED FOR THE SCRIPT BACK IN ORDER TO MAKE SOME CORRECTIONS, THE EDITOR HAD WRITTEN A NOTE FOR THE PRINTERS ON THE ENVELOPE WITH A RED MAGIC MARKER, "EXTREMELY URGENT," IN HUGE LETTERS. EVEN THOUGH I KNEW I'D CAUSED MY EDITOR A LOT OF HEADACHES, I COULDN'T HELP LAUGHING.

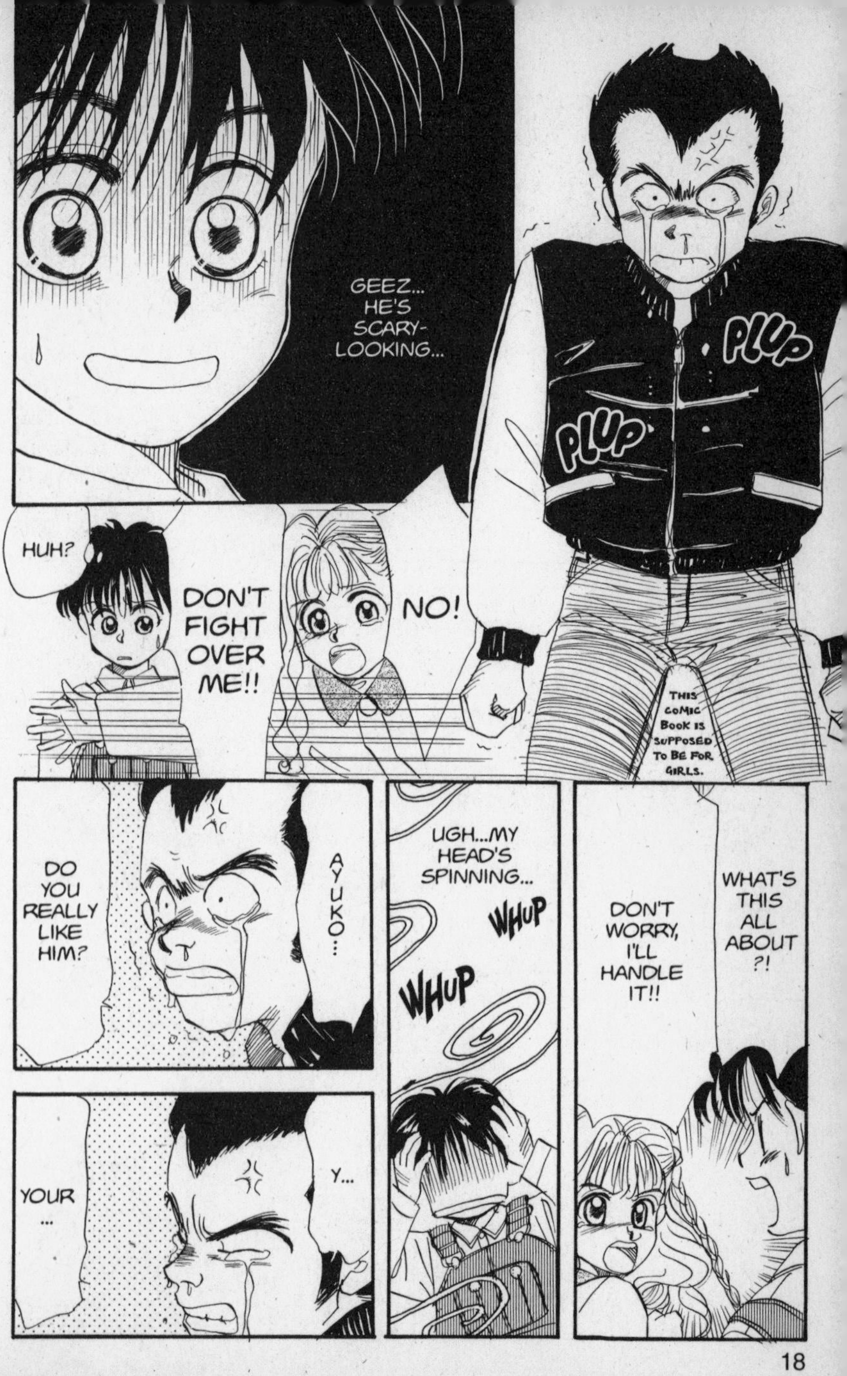
PLUP
PLUP
GEEZ... HE'S SCARY-LOOKING...
NO!
DON'T FIGHT OVER ME!!
HUH?
THIS COMIC BOOK IS SUPPOSED TO BE FOR GIRLS.
WHAT'S THIS ALL ABOUT ?!
DON'T WORRY, I'LL HANDLE IT!!
UGH...MY HEAD'S SPINNING...
WHUP
WHUP
AYUKO...
DO YOU REALLY LIKE HIM?
Y...
YOUR ...

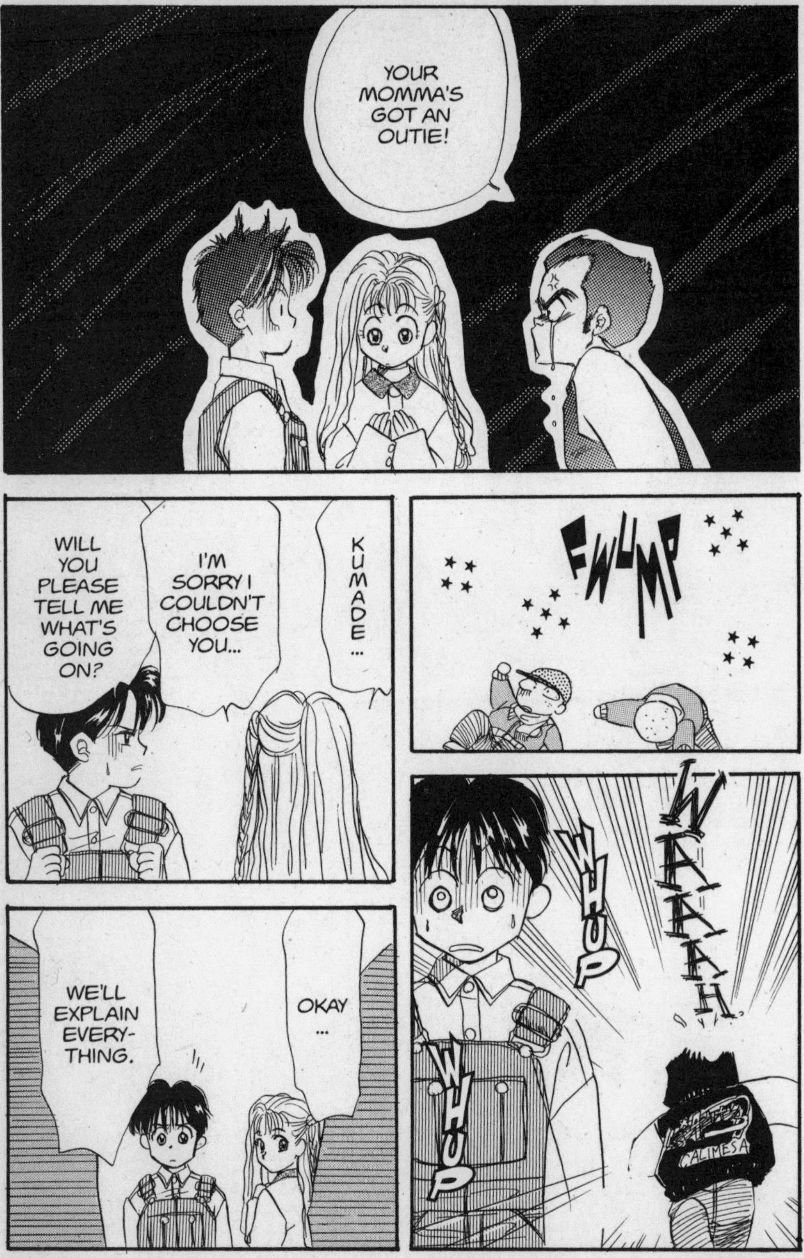
YOUR MOMMA'S GOT AN OUTIE!
FWUMP
KUMADE...
I'M SORRY I COULDN'T CHOOSE YOU...
WILL YOU PLEASE TELL ME WHAT'S GOING ON?
WAAAAH
WHUP
WHUP
CALIMESA
OKAY...
WE'LL EXPLAIN EVERY-THING.

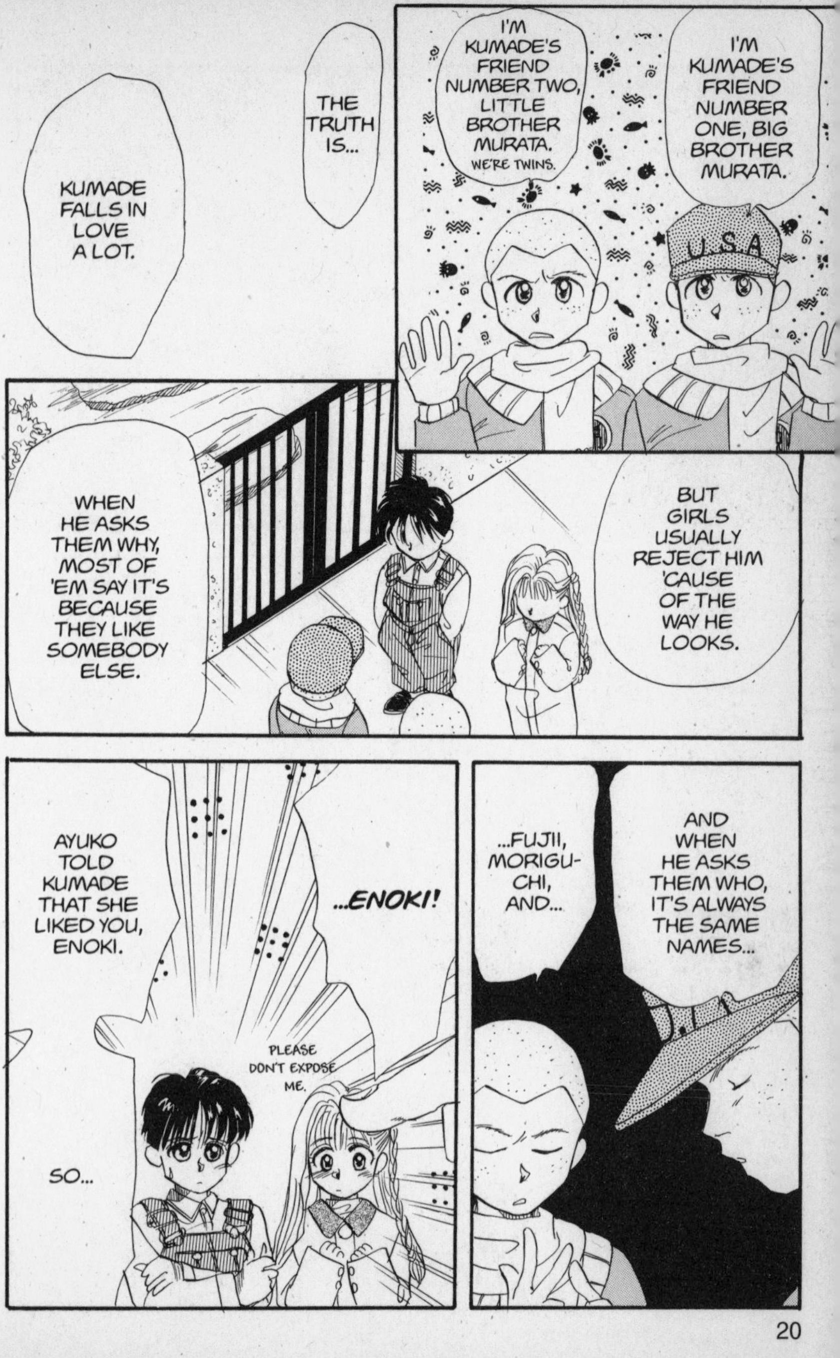
I'M KUMADE'S FRIEND NUMBER ONE, BIG BROTHER MURATA.
I'M KUMADE'S FRIEND NUMBER TWO, LITTLE BROTHER MURATA. WE'RE TWINS.
THE TRUTH IS...
KUMADE FALLS IN LOVE A LOT.
BUT GIRLS USUALLY REJECT HIM 'CAUSE OF THE WAY HE LOOKS.
WHEN HE ASKS THEM WHY, MOST OF 'EM SAY IT'S BECAUSE THEY LIKE SOMEBODY ELSE.
AND WHEN HE ASKS THEM WHO, IT'S ALWAYS THE SAME NAMES...
...FUJII, MORIGU-CHI, AND...
...ENOKI!
AYUKO TOLD KUMADE THAT SHE LIKED YOU, ENOKI.
PLEASE DON'T EXPOSE ME.
SO...

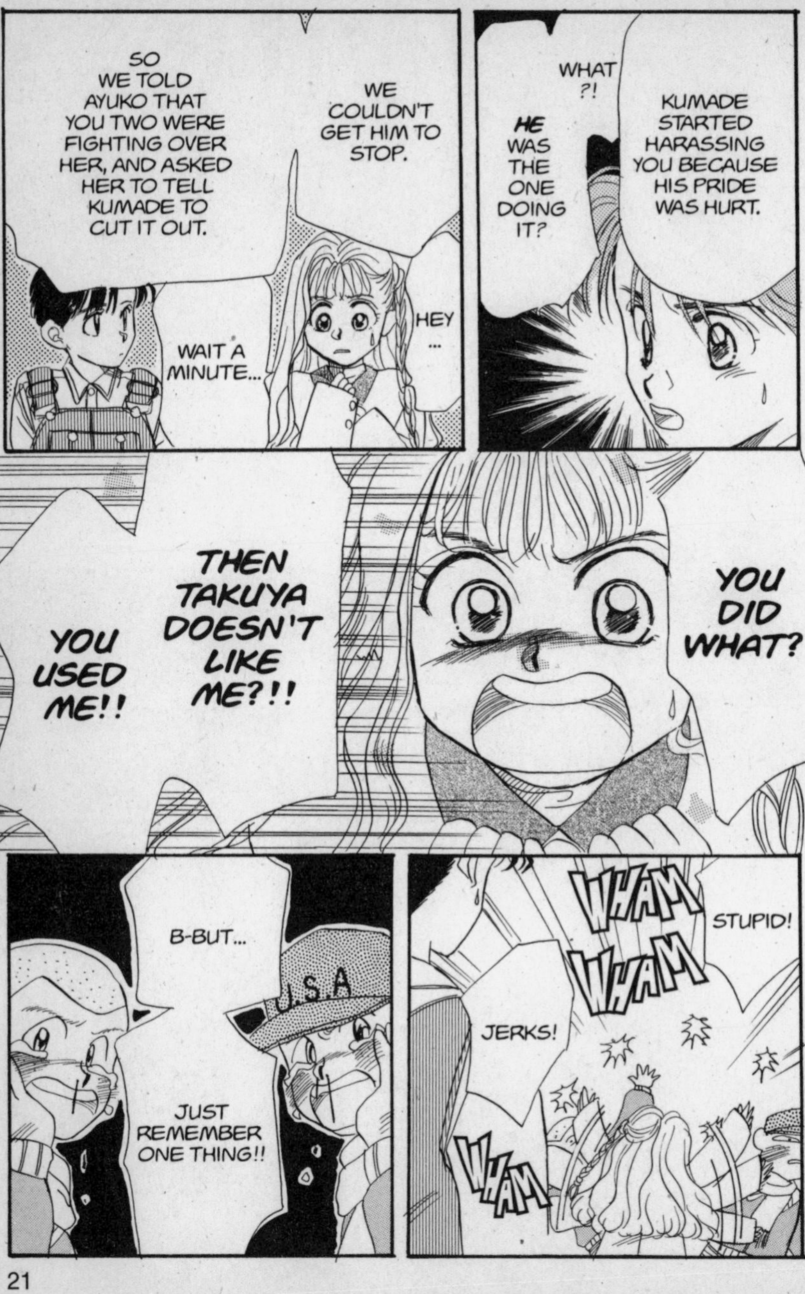
KUMADE STARTED HARASSING YOU BECAUSE HIS PRIDE WAS HURT.
WHAT ?!
HE WAS THE ONE DOING IT?
WE COULDN'T GET HIM TO STOP.
SO WE TOLD AYUKO THAT YOU TWO WERE FIGHTING OVER HER, AND ASKED HER TO TELL KUMADE TO CUT IT OUT.
HEY ...
WAIT A MINUTE...
YOU DID WHAT?!
THEN TAKUYA DOESN'T LIKE ME?!!
YOU USED ME!!
WHAM
STUPID!
WHAM
JERKS!
WHAM
B-BUT...
U.S.A
JUST REMEMBER ONE THING!!

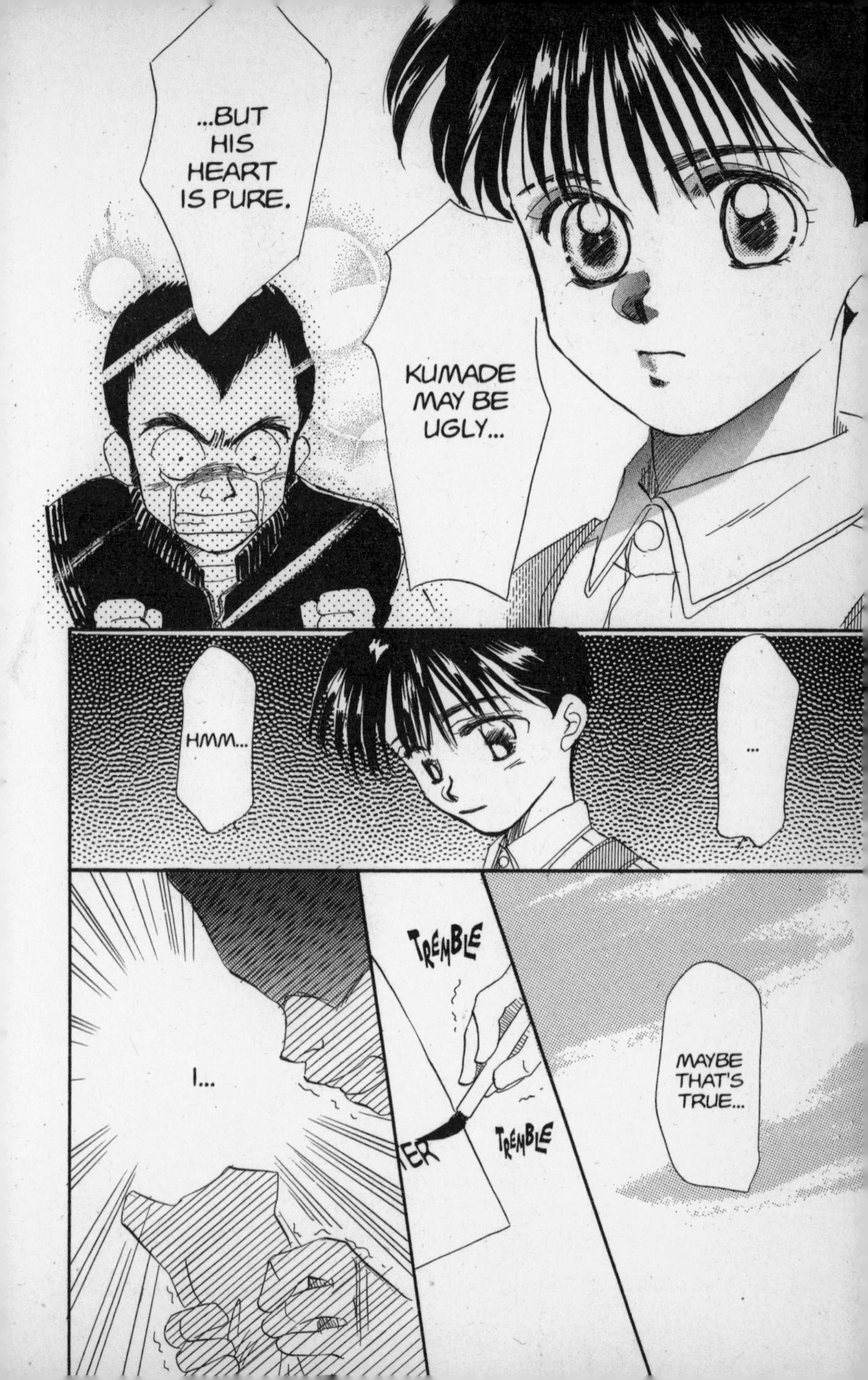
KUMADE MAY BE UGLY...
...BUT HIS HEART IS PURE.
...
HMM...
MAYBE THAT'S TRUE...
TREMBLE
TREMBLE
I...

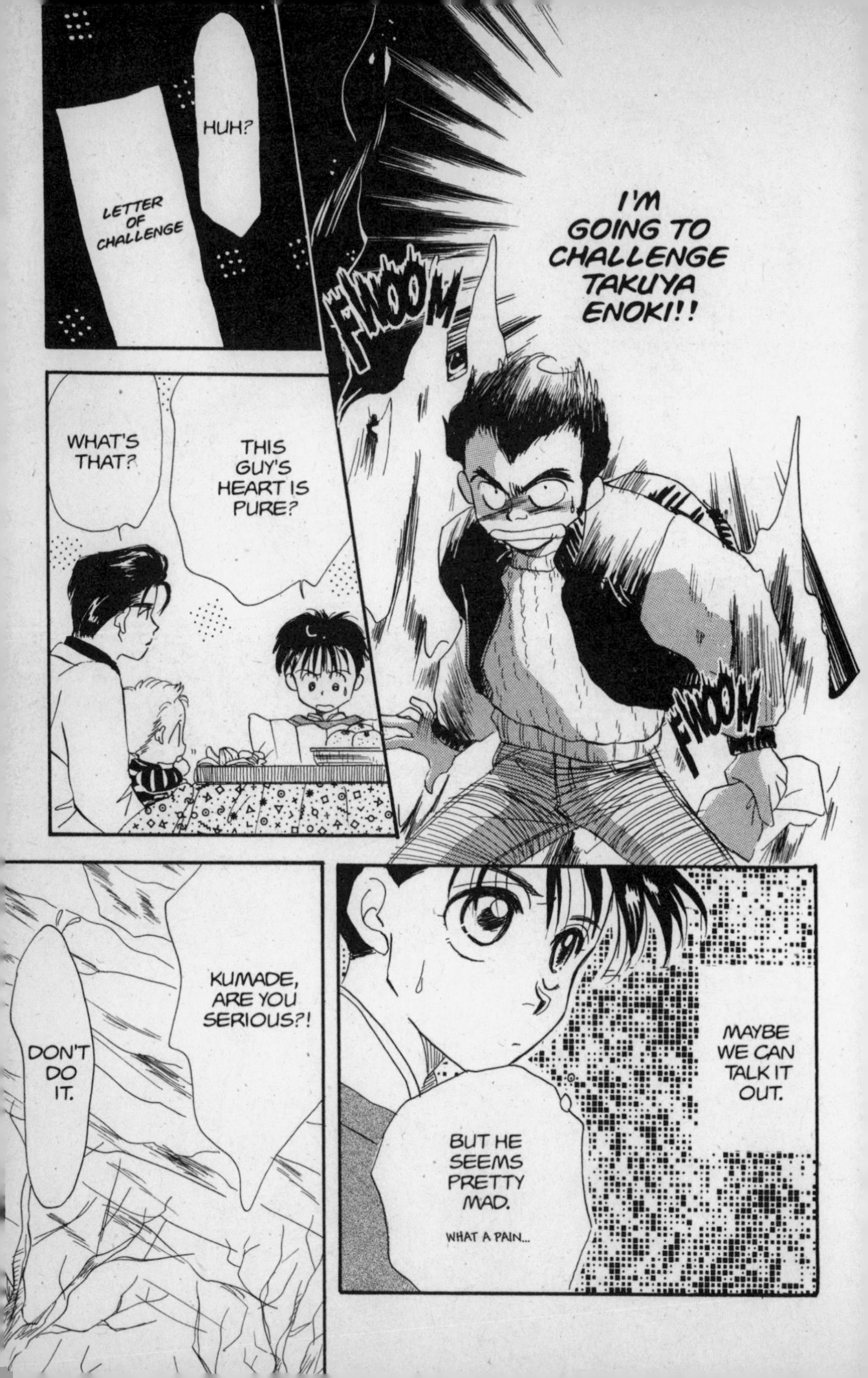
FWOOM
I'M GOING TO CHALLENGE TAKUYA ENOKI!!
FWOOM
HUH?
LETTER OF CHALLENGE
THIS GUY'S HEART IS PURE?
WHAT'S THAT?
MAYBE WE CAN TALK IT OUT.
BUT HE SEEMS PRETTY MAD.
WHAT A PAIN...
KUMADE, ARE YOU SERIOUS?!
DON'T DO IT.

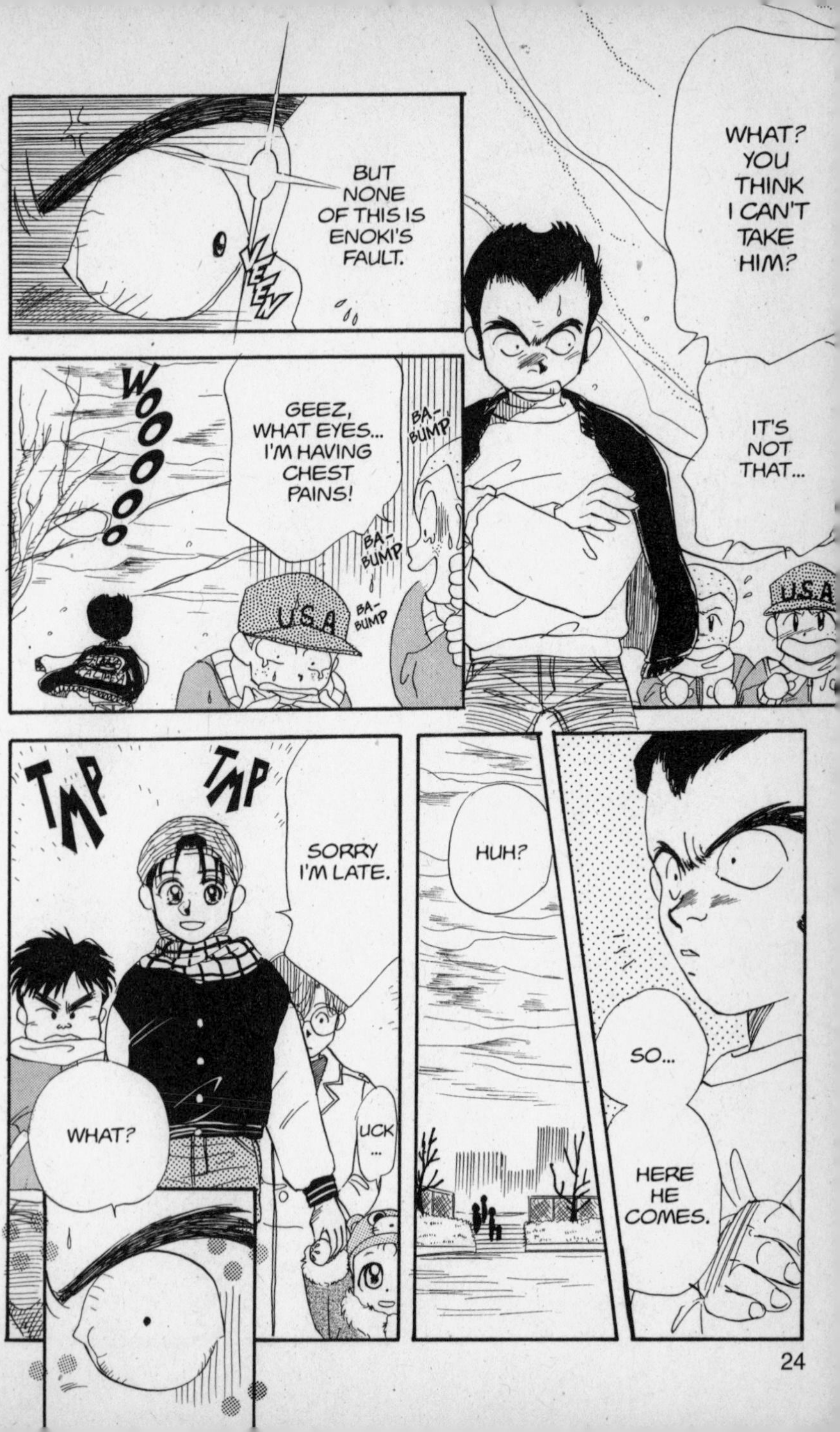
WHAT? YOU THINK I CAN'T TAKE HIM?
IT'S NOT THAT...
BUT NONE OF THIS IS ENOKI'S FAULT.
VEEN
BA-BUMP
GEEZ, WHAT EYES... I'M HAVING CHEST PAINS!
BA-BUMP
BA-BUMP
WOOOOOO
SO...
HERE HE COMES.
HUH?
TMP
TMP
SORRY I'M LATE.
UCK ...
WHAT?

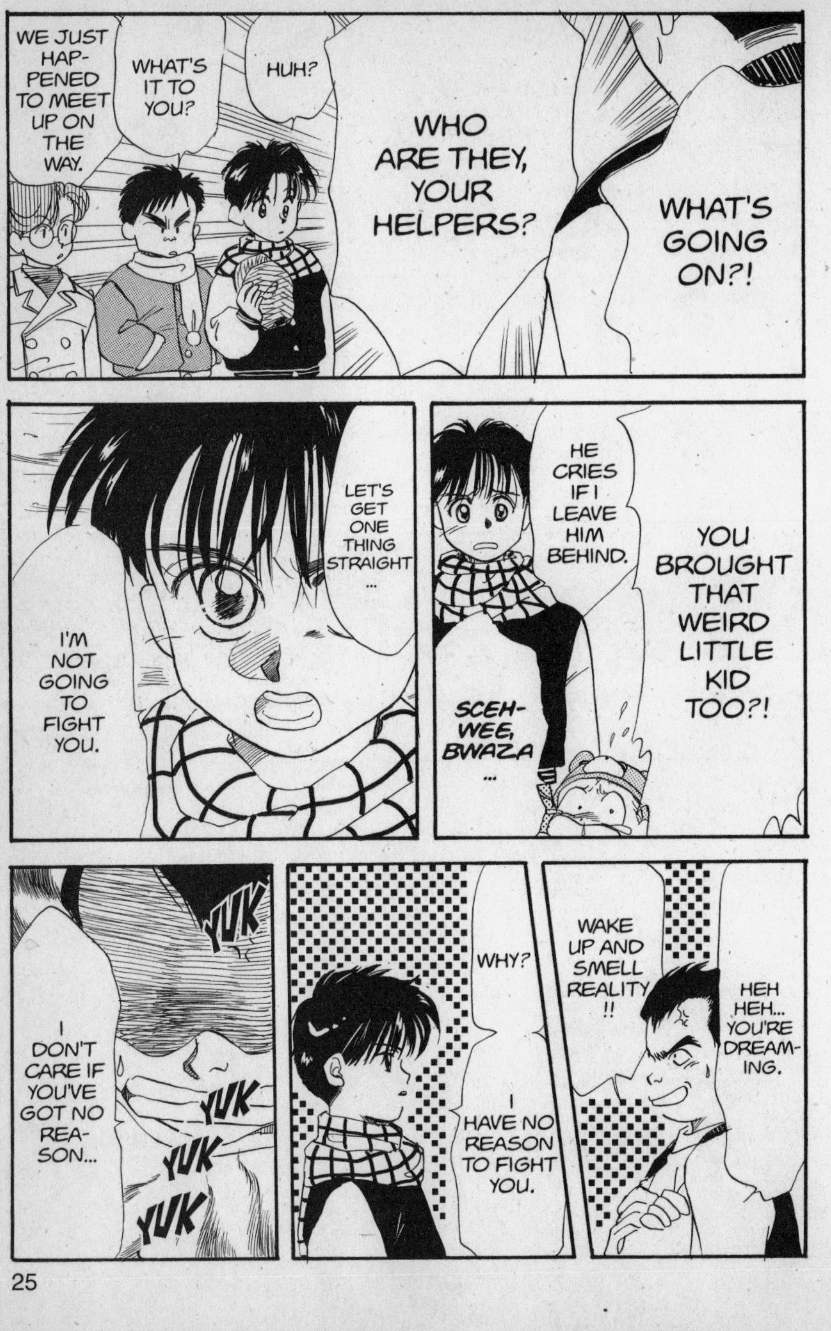
WHAT'S GOING ON?!
WHO ARE THEY, YOUR HELPERS?
HUH?
WHAT'S IT TO YOU?
WE JUST HAPPENED TO MEET UP ON THE WAY.
YOU BROUGHT THAT WEIRD LITTLE KID TOO?!
HE CRIES IF I LEAVE HIM BEHIND.
SCEH-WEE, BWAZA ...
LET'S GET ONE THING STRAIGHT ...
I'M NOT GOING TO FIGHT YOU.
HEH HEH... YOU'RE DREAMING.
WAKE UP AND SMELL REALITY !!
WHY?
I HAVE NO REASON TO FIGHT YOU.
YUK
YUK
YUK
YUK
I DON'T CARE IF YOU'VE GOT NO REASON...

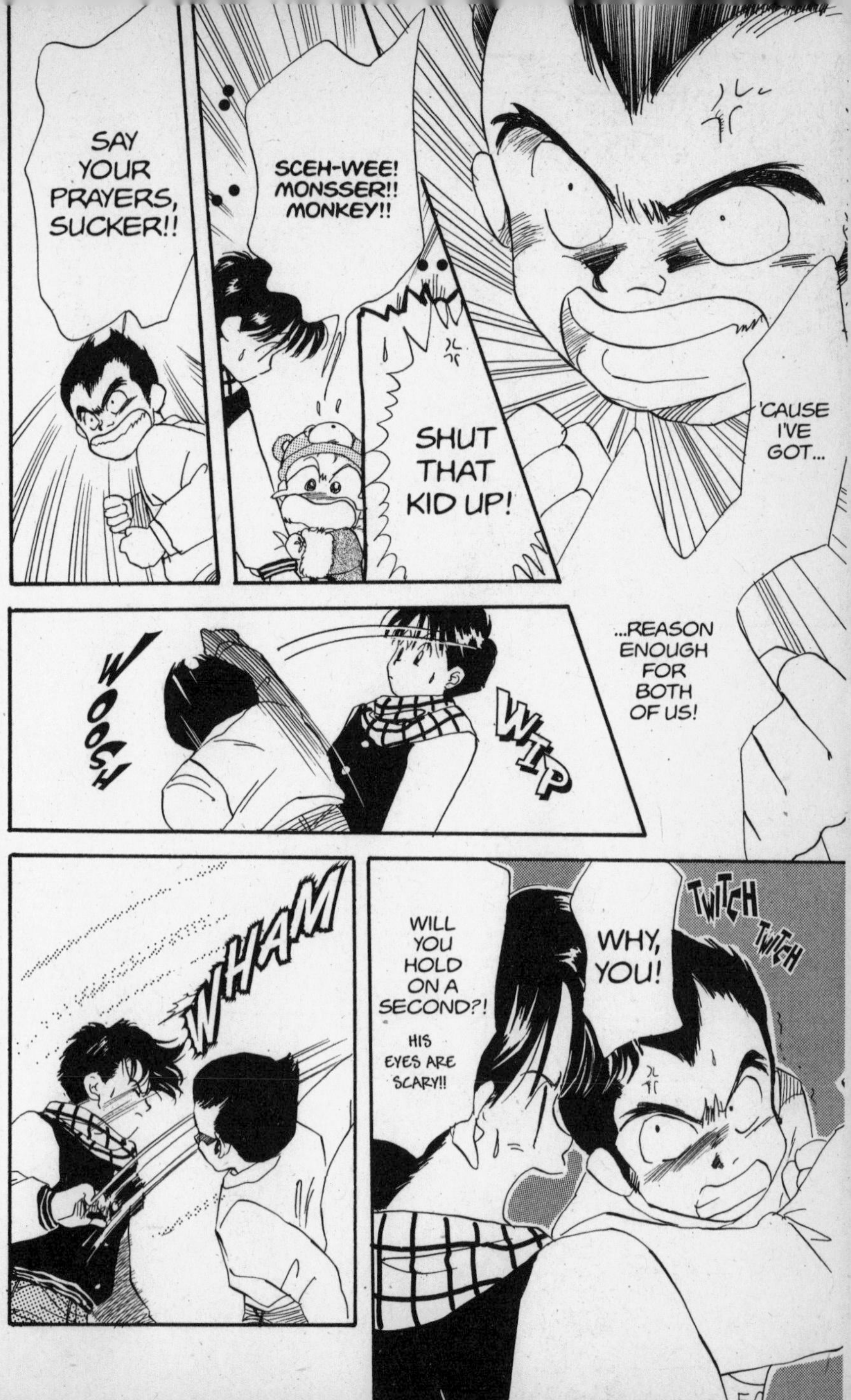
'CAUSE I'VE GOT...
...REASON ENOUGH FOR BOTH OF US!
SCEH-WEE! MONSSER!! MONKEY!!
SHUT THAT KID UP!
SAY YOUR PRAYERS, SUCKER!!
WIP
WOOOSH
TWITCH TWITCH
WHY, YOU!
WILL YOU HOLD ON A SECOND?!
HIS EYES ARE SCARY!!
WHAM

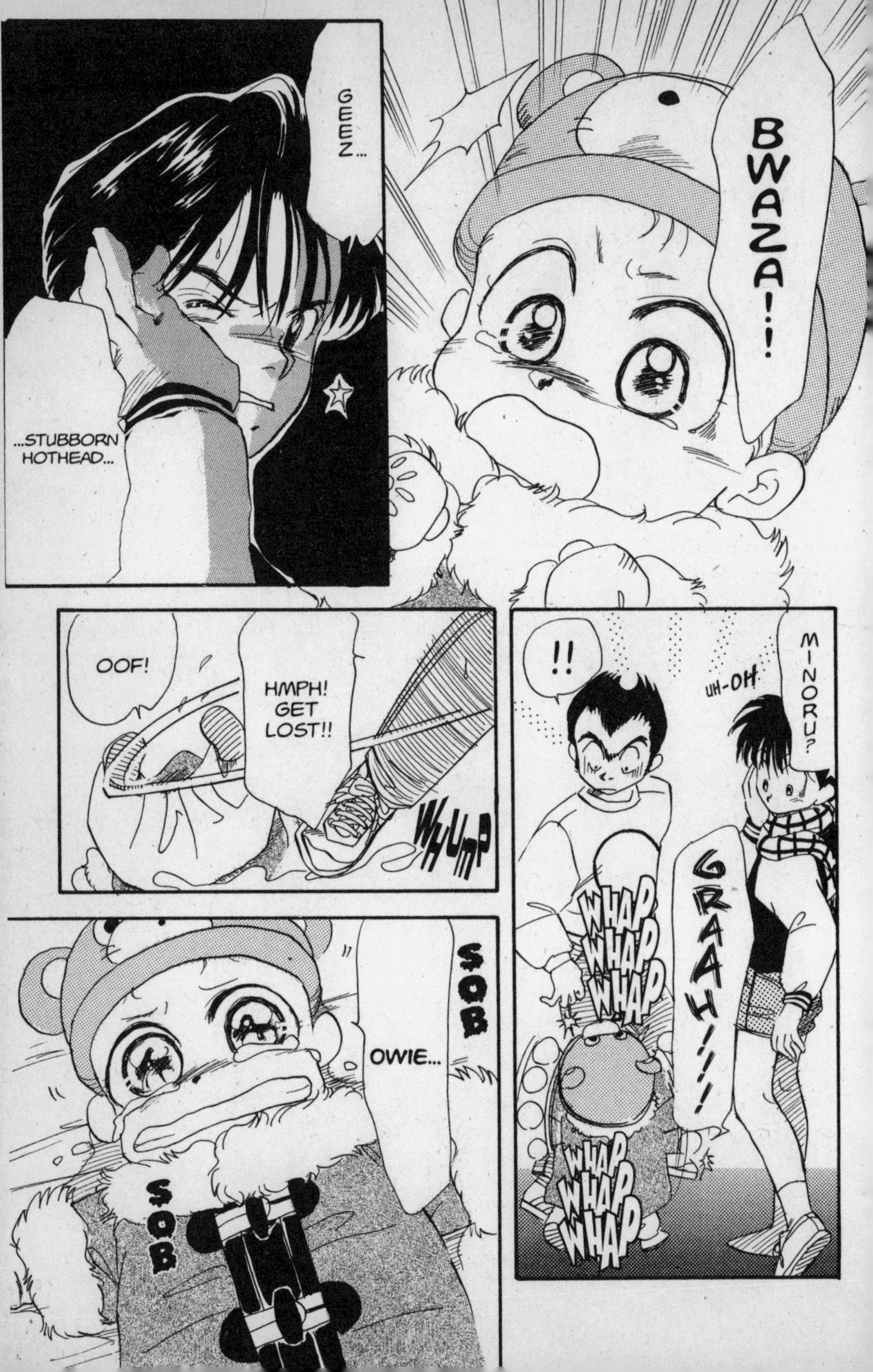
BWAZA!!
GEEZ...
...STUBBORN HOTHEAD...
MINORU?
UH-OH
!!
GRAAH!!!
WHAP WHAP WHAP
WHAP WHAP WHAP
HMPH! GET LOST!!
OOF!
WHUMP
SOB
OWIE...
SOB

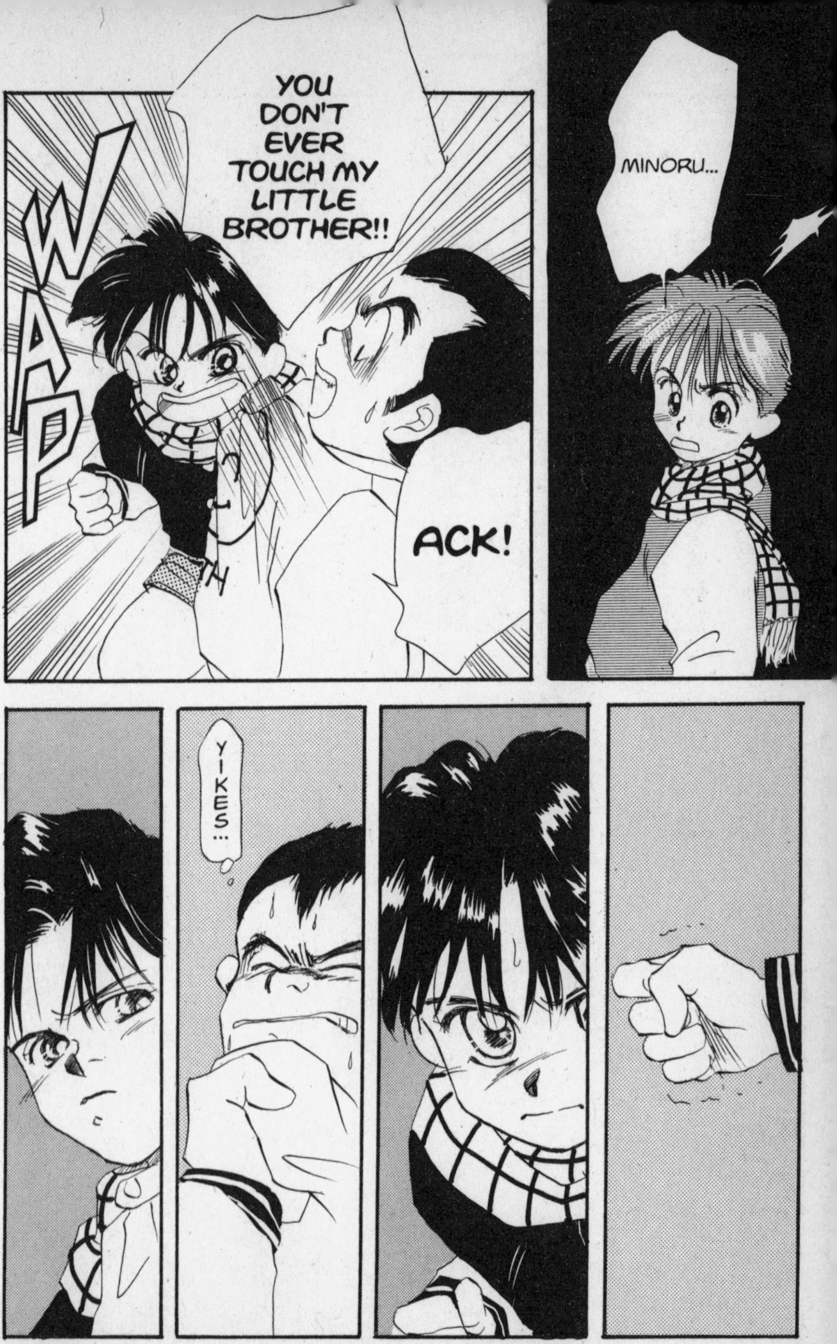
MINORU...
YOU DON'T EVER TOUCH MY LITTLE BROTHER!!
WAP
ACK!
YIKES...

? KOFF ?

SWUP

TH

LOOK...

I DIDN'T COME HERE TO FIGHT YOU.

I...

I'M SORRY.

...

OKAY...

ARE YOU OKAY, MINORU?

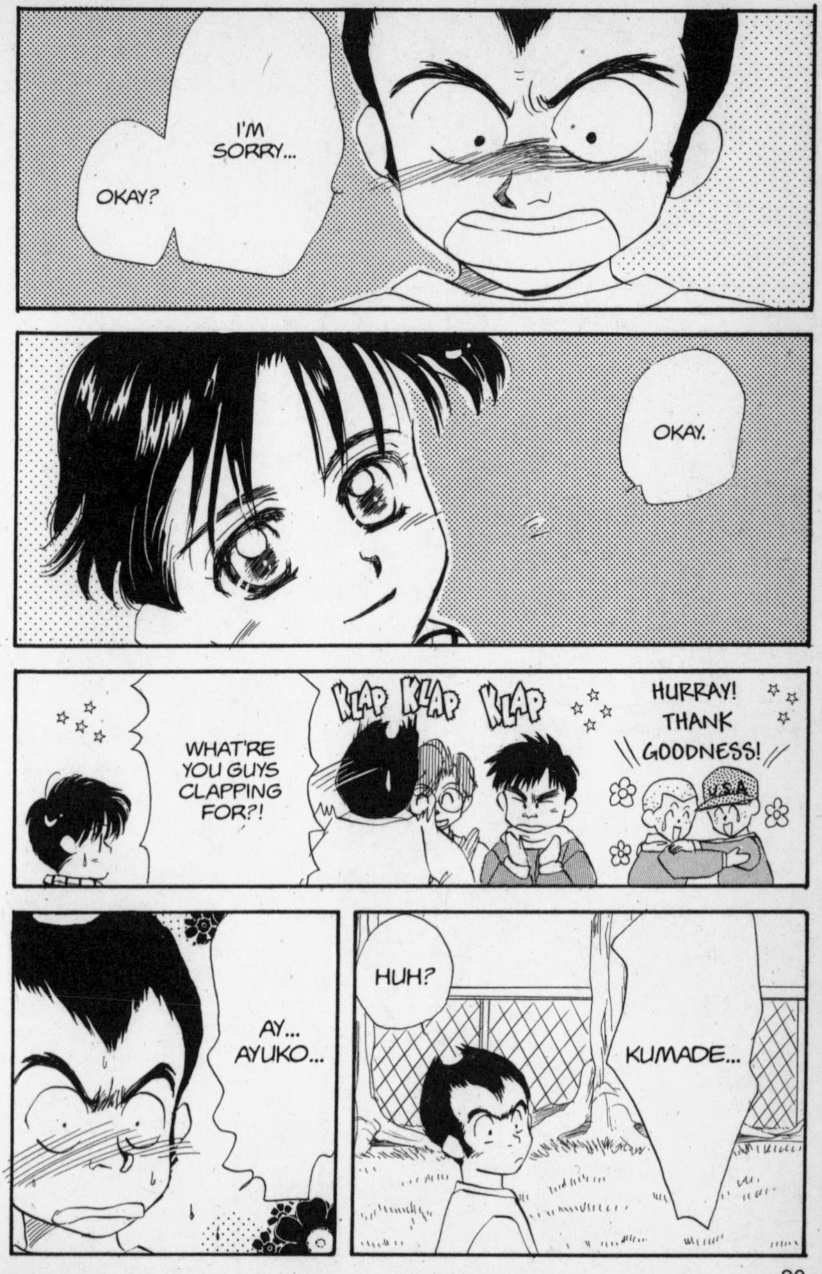
I'M SORRY...
OKAY?
OKAY.
HURRAY! THANK GOODNESS!
KLAP KLAP KLAP
WHAT'RE YOU GUYS CLAPPING FOR?!
KUMADE...
HUH?
AY... AYUKO...

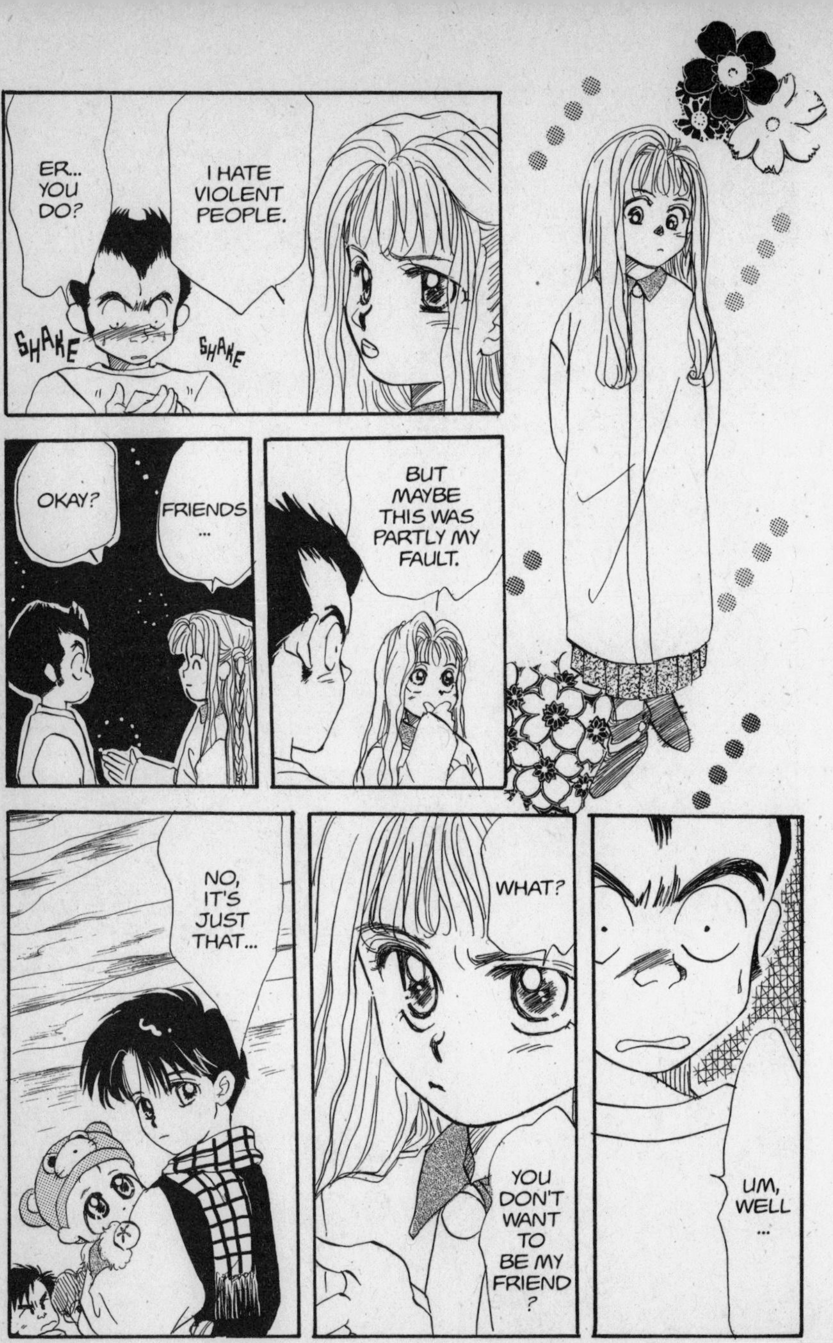
I HATE VIOLENT PEOPLE.
ER... YOU DO?
SHAKE
SHAKE
BUT MAYBE THIS WAS PARTLY MY FAULT.
FRIENDS...
OKAY?
UM, WELL...
WHAT?
YOU DON'T WANT TO BE MY FRIEND?
NO, IT'S JUST THAT...

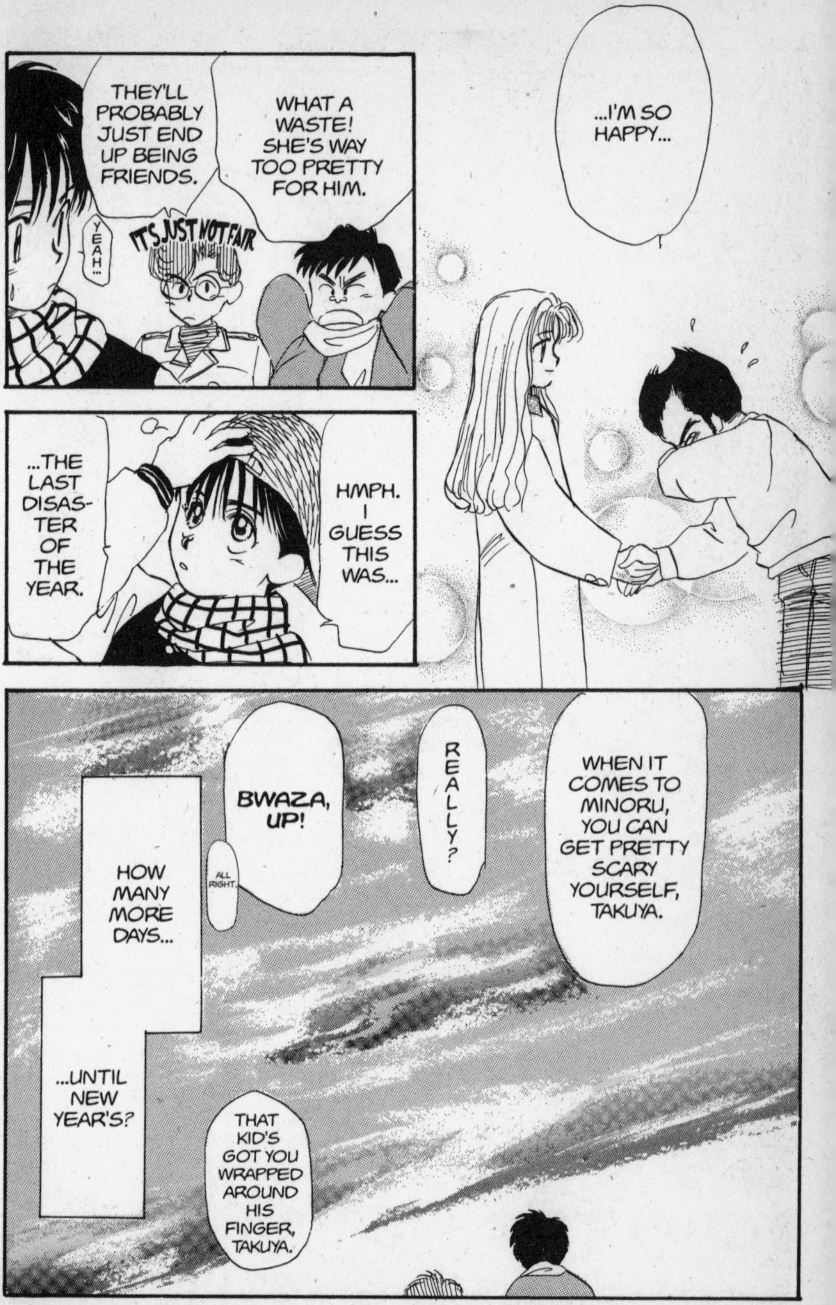
...I'M SO HAPPY...
WHAT A WASTE! SHE'S WAY TOO PRETTY FOR HIM.
THEY'LL PROBABLY JUST END UP BEING FRIENDS.
IT'S JUST NOT FAIR
YEAH...
HMPH. I GUESS THIS WAS...
...THE LAST DISASTER OF THE YEAR.
WHEN IT COMES TO MINORU, YOU CAN GET PRETTY SCARY YOURSELF, TAKUYA.
REALLY?
BWAZA, UP!
ALL RIGHT.
HOW MANY MORE DAYS...
THAT KID'S GOT YOU WRAPPED AROUND HIS FINGER, TAKUYA.
...UNTIL NEW YEAR'S?

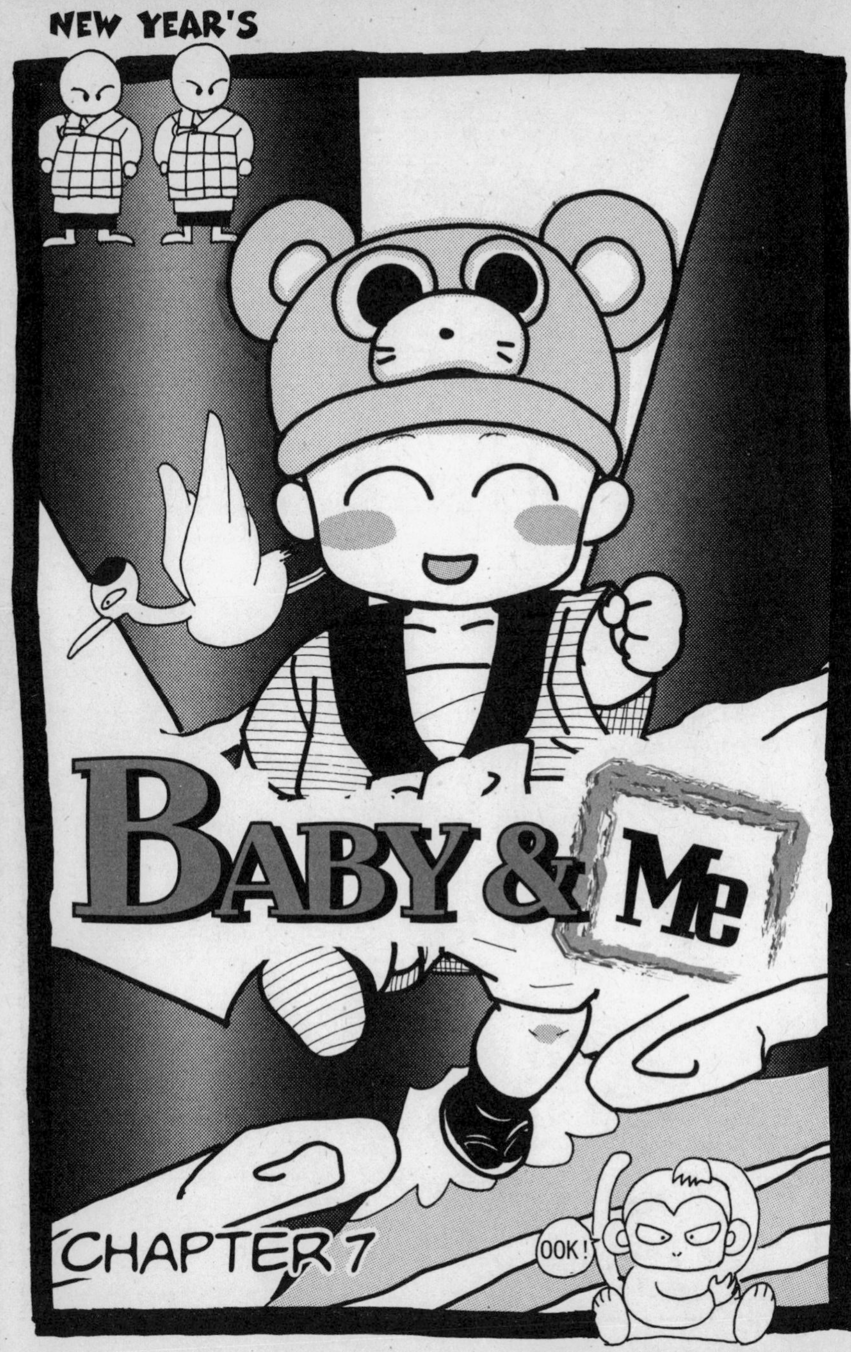
NEW YEAR'S
BABY & Me
CHAPTER 7
OOK!
1992 THE YEAR OF THE MONKEY

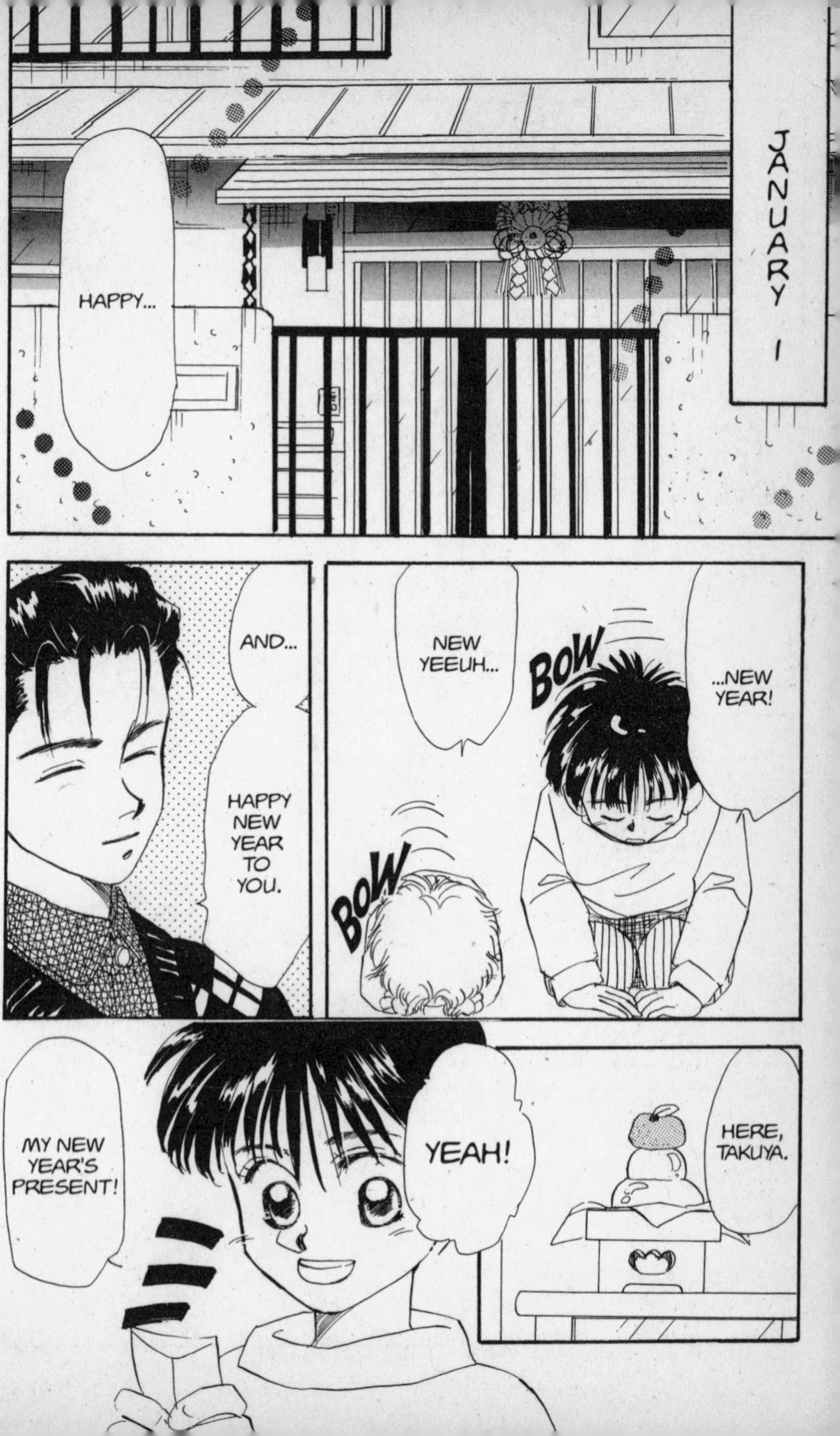
JANUARY 1
HAPPY...
...NEW YEAR!
BOW
NEW YEEUH...
BOW
AND...
HAPPY NEW YEAR TO YOU.
HERE, TAKUYA.
YEAH!
MY NEW YEAR'S PRESENT!

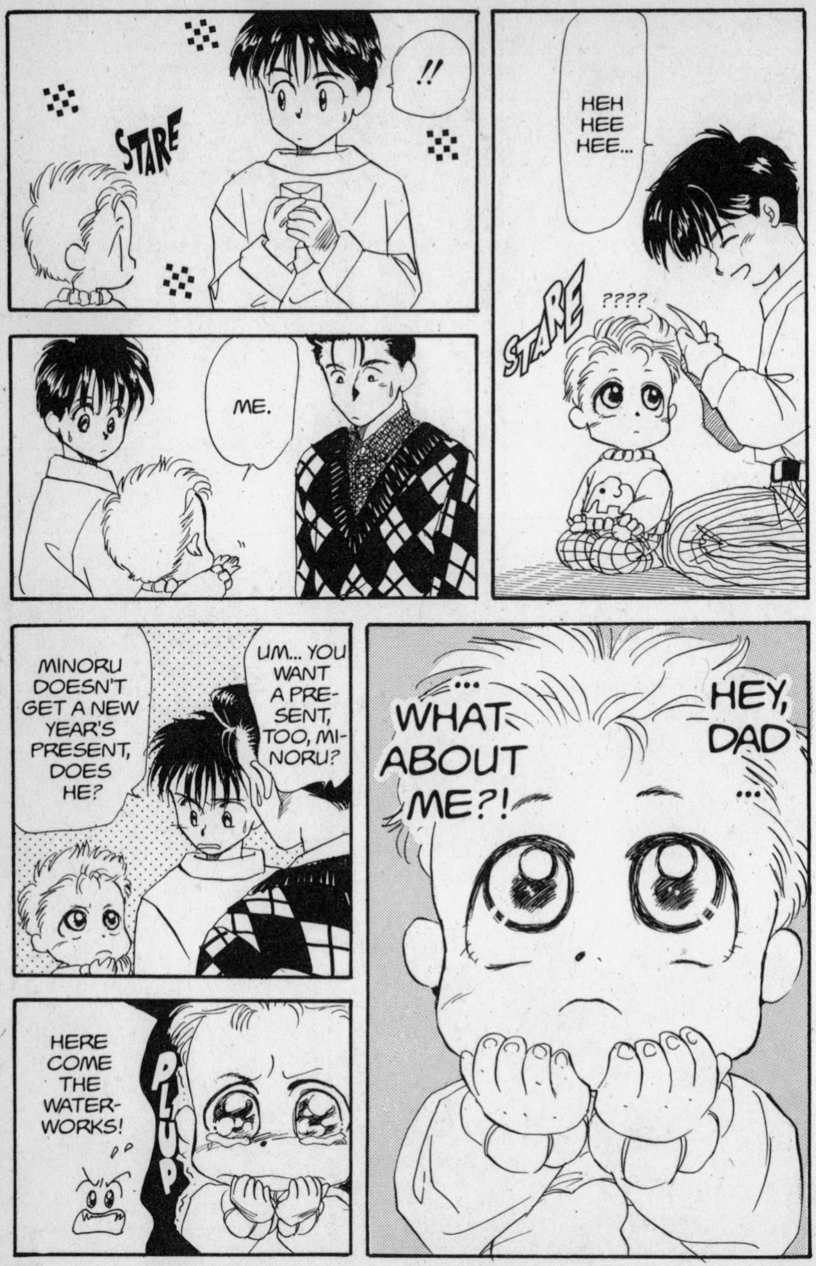
HEH HEE HEE...
????
STARE
!!
STARE
ME.
HEY, DAD...
...WHAT ABOUT ME?!
UM... YOU WANT A PRESENT, TOO, MINORU?
MINORU DOESN'T GET A NEW YEAR'S PRESENT, DOES HE?
PLUP
HERE COME THE WATERWORKS!

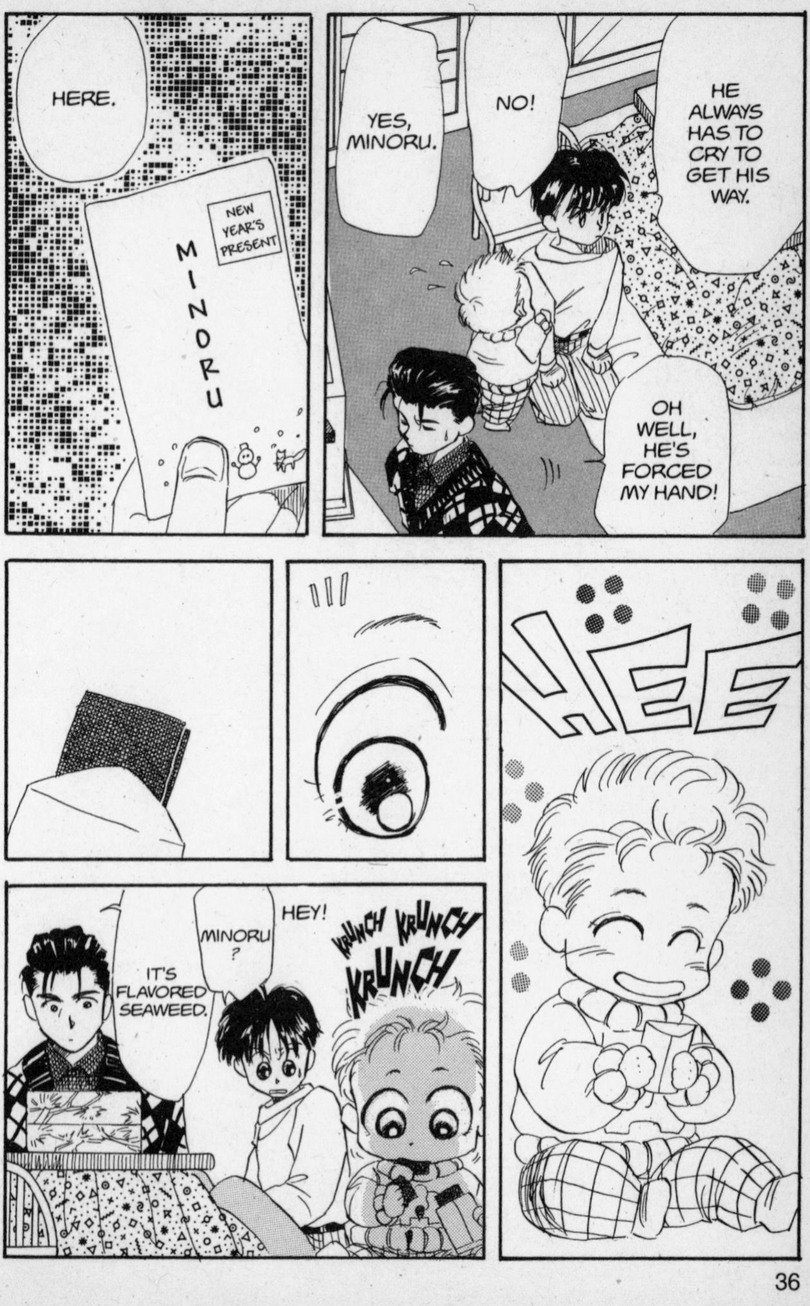
HE ALWAYS HAS TO CRY TO GET HIS WAY.
NO!
YES, MINORU.
OH WELL, HE'S FORCED MY HAND!
HERE.
NEW YEAR'S PRESENT
MINORU
HEE
KRUNCH KRUNCH
KRUNCH
HEY!
MINORU?
IT'S FLAVORED SEAWEED.

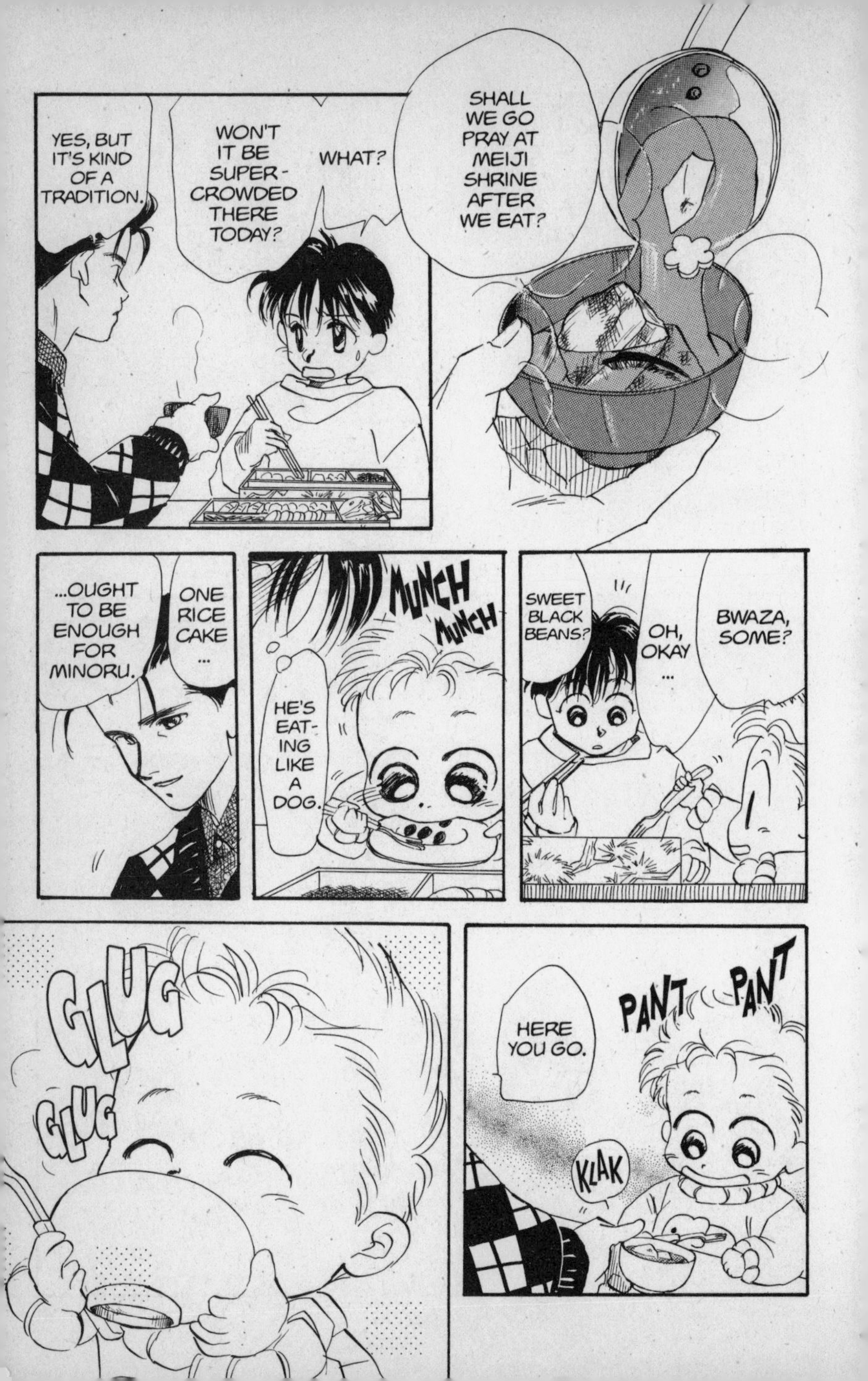
SHALL WE GO PRAY AT MEIJI SHRINE AFTER WE EAT?
WHAT?
WON'T IT BE SUPER-CROWDED THERE TODAY?
YES, BUT IT'S KIND OF A TRADITION.
BWAZA, SOME?
OH, OKAY ...
SWEET BLACK BEANS?
MUNCH
MUNCH
HE'S EATING LIKE A DOG.
ONE RICE CAKE ...
...OUGHT TO BE ENOUGH FOR MINORU.
PANT
PANT
HERE YOU GO.
KLAK
GLUG
GLUG

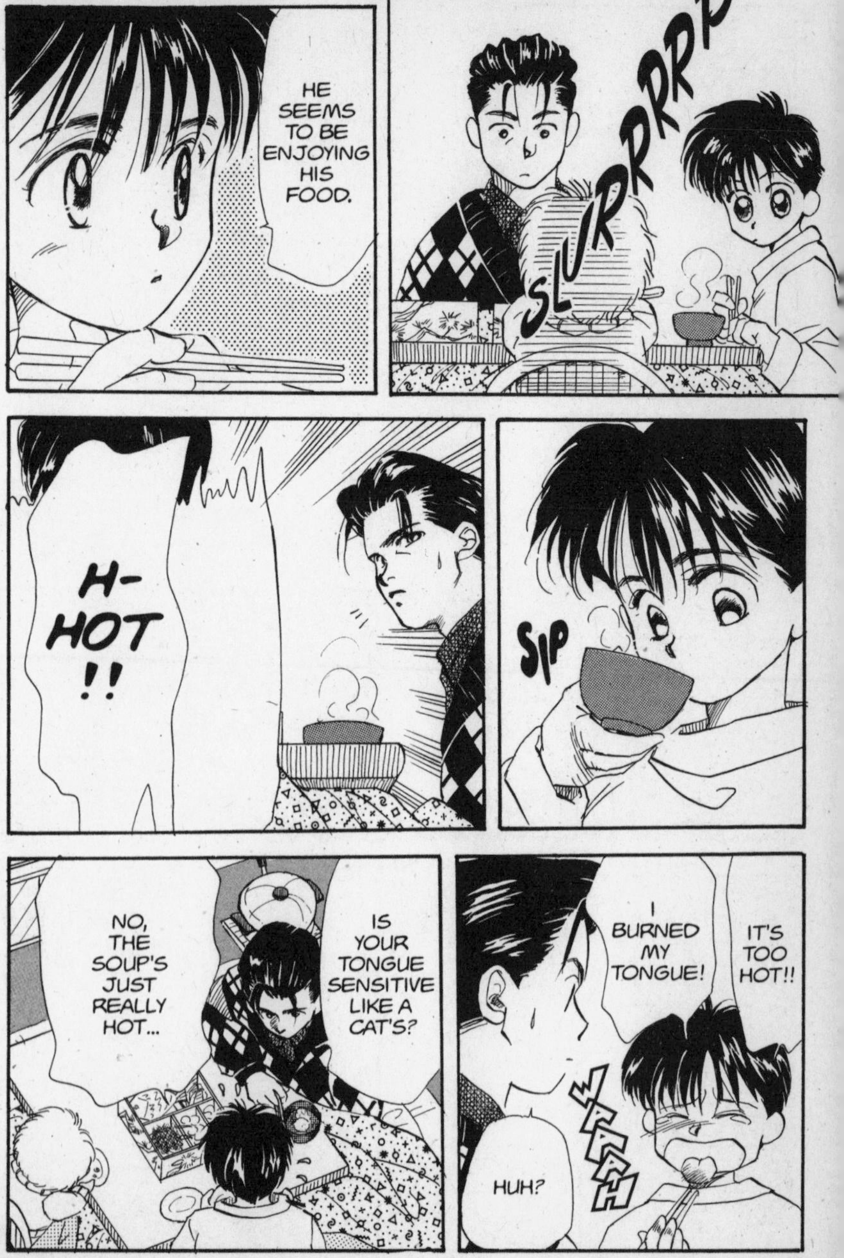
SLURRRRRP
HE SEEMS TO BE ENJOYING HIS FOOD.
SIP
H-HOT!!
IT'S TOO HOT!!
I BURNED MY TONGUE!
WAAAH
HUH?
IS YOUR TONGUE SENSITIVE LIKE A CAT'S?
NO, THE SOUP'S JUST REALLY HOT...

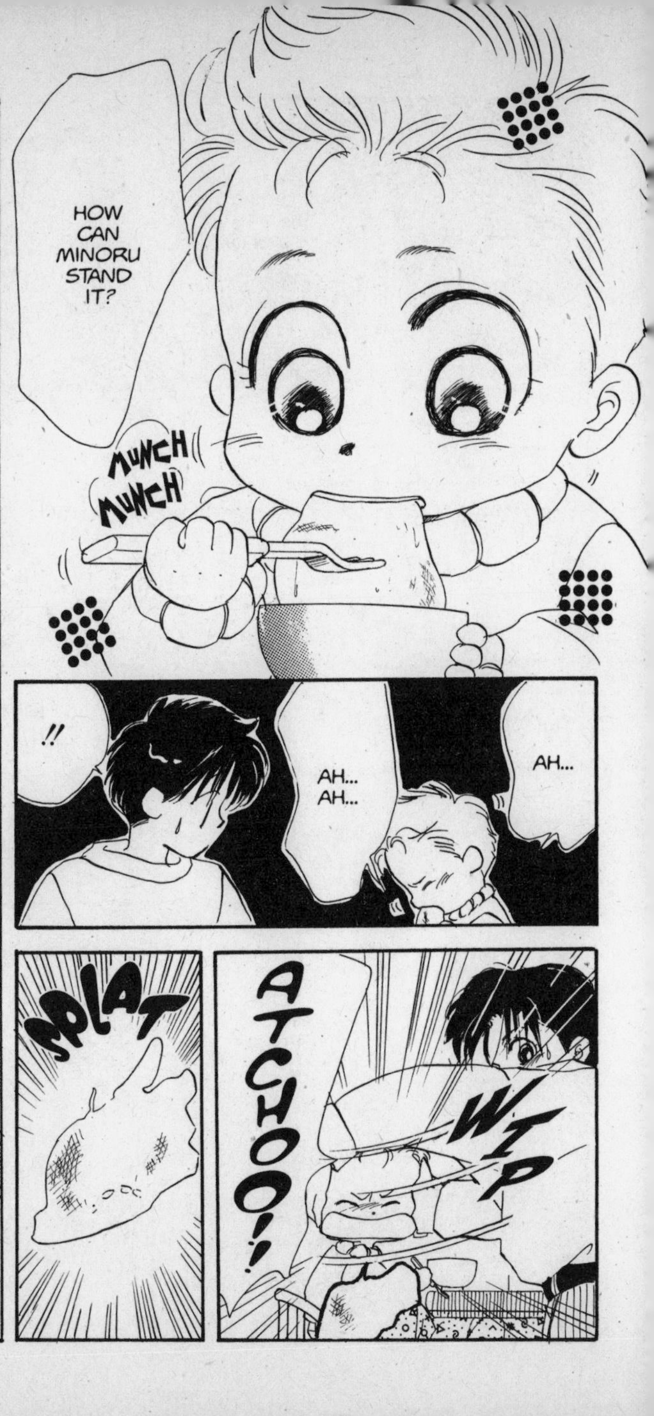
HOW CAN MINORU STAND IT?
MUNCH MUNCH
AH...
AH... AH...
!!
ATCHOO!!
WIP
SPLAT

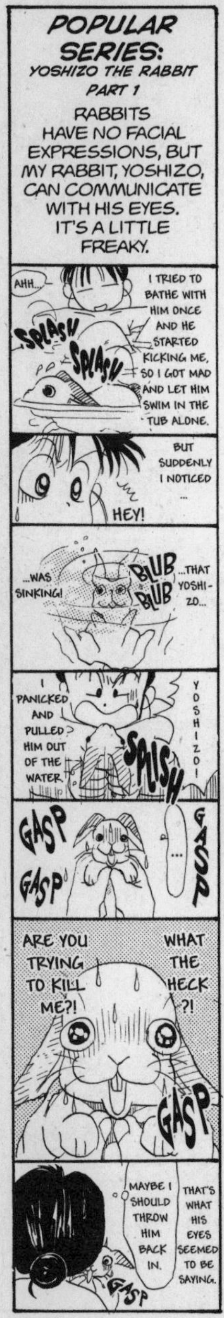
POPULAR SERIES:
YOSHIZO THE RABBIT
PART 1
RABBITS HAVE NO FACIAL EXPRESSIONS, BUT MY RABBIT, YOSHIZO, CAN COMMUNICATE WITH HIS EYES. IT'S A LITTLE FREAKY.
I TRIED TO BATHE WITH HIM ONCE AND HE STARTED KICKING ME, SO I GOT MAD AND LET HIM SWIM IN THE TUB ALONE.
AHH...
SPLASH
SPLASH
BUT SUDDENLY I NOTICED ...
HEY!
...THAT YOSHIZO...
BLUB BLUB
...WAS SINKING!
YOSHIZO!
I PANICKED AND PULLED HIM OUT OF THE WATER.
SPLISH
GASP
...
GASP GASP
WHAT THE HECK ?!
ARE YOU TRYING TO KILL ME?!
GASP
THAT'S WHAT HIS EYES SEEMED TO BE SAYING.
MAYBE I SHOULD THROW HIM BACK IN.
GASP

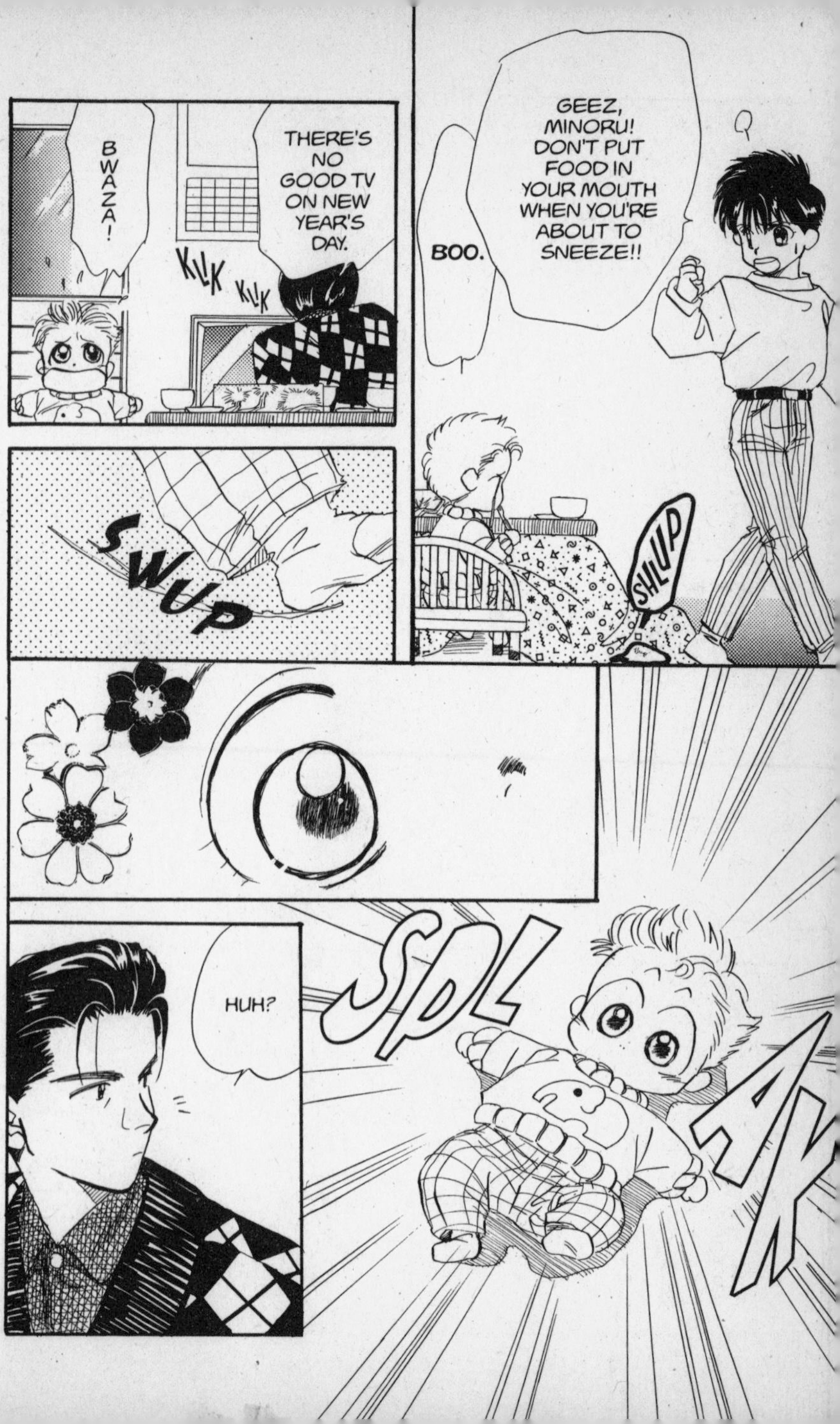
GEEZ, MINORU! DON'T PUT FOOD IN YOUR MOUTH WHEN YOU'RE ABOUT TO SNEEZE!!
BOO.
SHLUP
THERE'S NO GOOD TV ON NEW YEAR'S DAY.
BWAZA!
KLIK
KLIK
SWUP
SPL
AK
HUH?

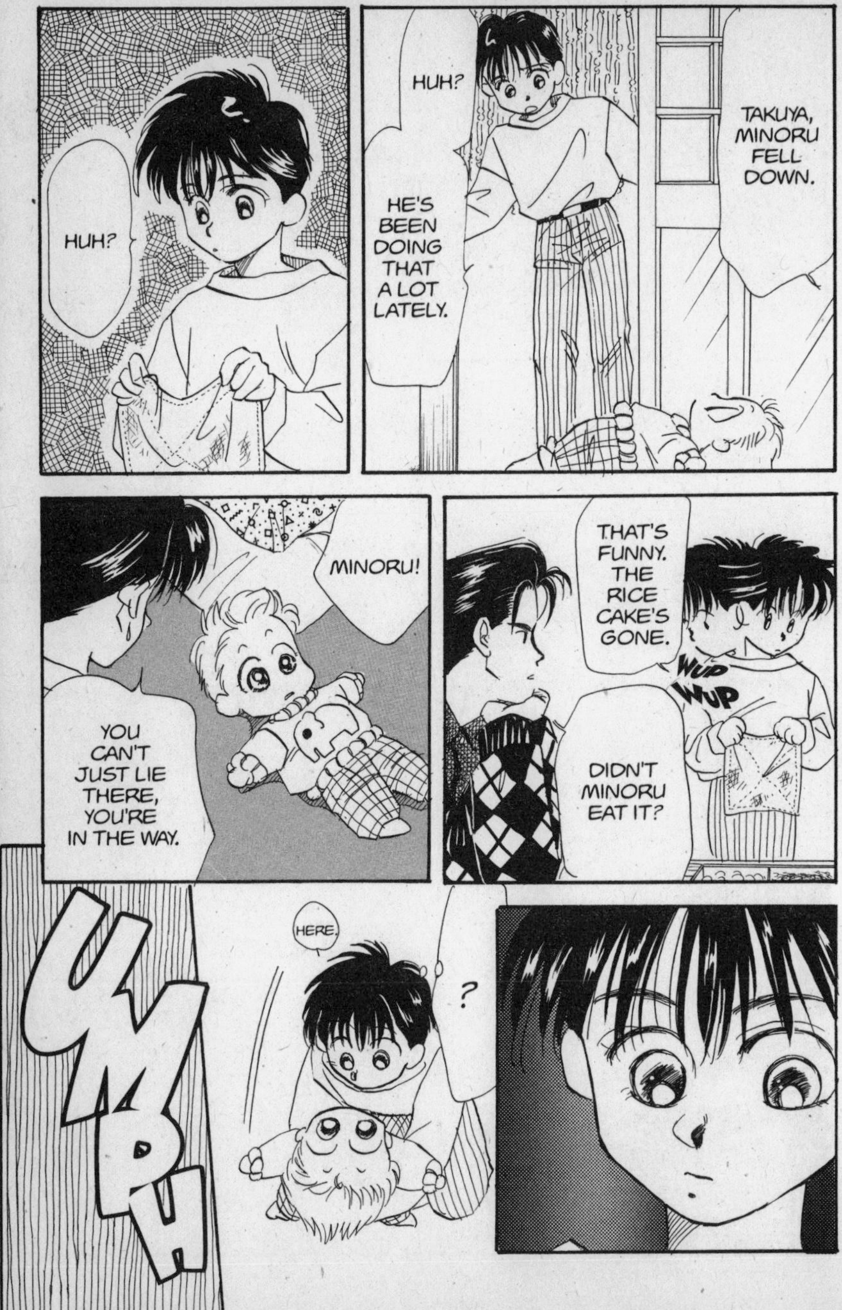
TAKUYA, MINORU FELL DOWN.
HUH?
HE'S BEEN DOING THAT A LOT LATELY.
HUH?
THAT'S FUNNY. THE RICE CAKE'S GONE.
WUP WUP
DIDN'T MINORU EAT IT?
MINORU!
YOU CAN'T JUST LIE THERE, YOU'RE IN THE WAY.
?
HERE.
UMPH

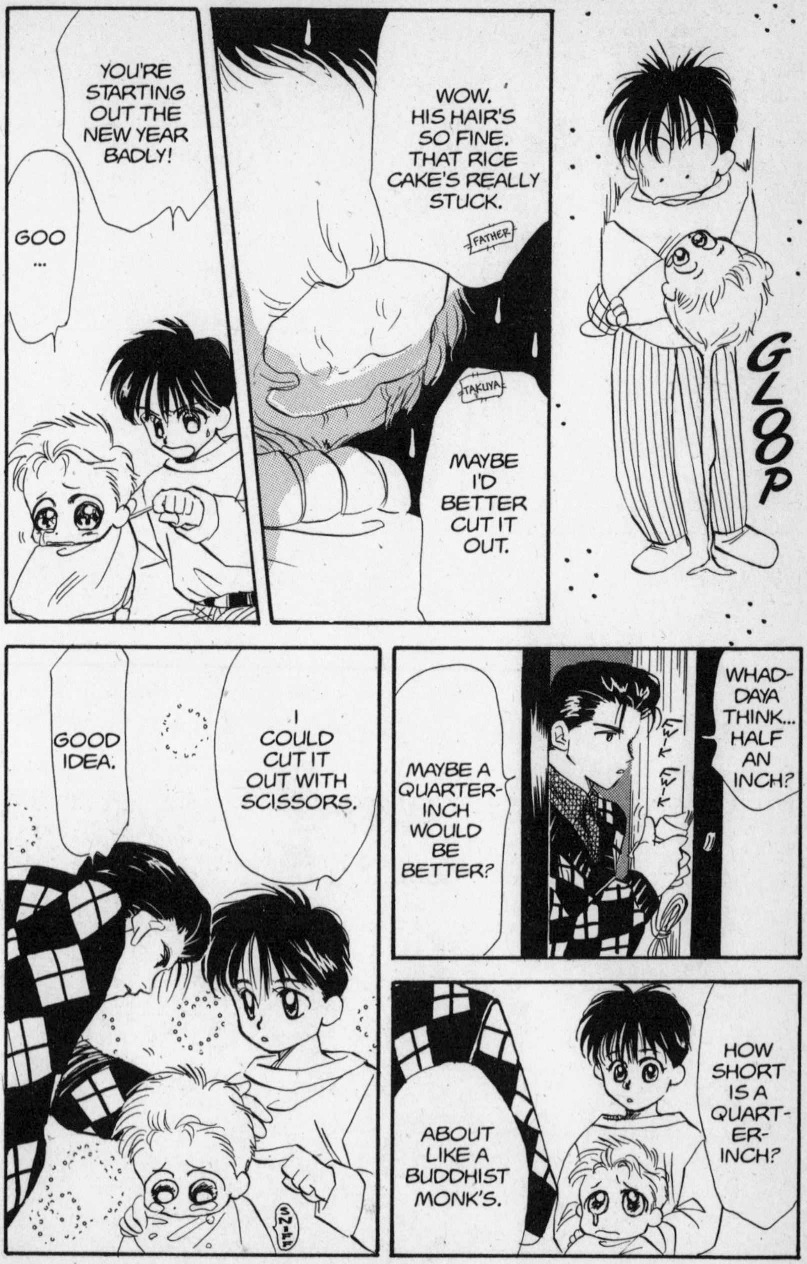
GLOOP
WOW. HIS HAIR'S SO FINE. THAT RICE CAKE'S REALLY STUCK.
FATHER
TAKUYA
MAYBE I'D BETTER CUT IT OUT.
YOU'RE STARTING OUT THE NEW YEAR BADLY!
GOO ...
WHADDAYA THINK... HALF AN INCH?
EWIK EWIK
MAYBE A QUARTER-INCH WOULD BE BETTER?
HOW SHORT IS A QUARTER-INCH?
ABOUT LIKE A BUDDHIST MONK'S.
I COULD CUT IT OUT WITH SCISSORS.
GOOD IDEA.
SNIFF

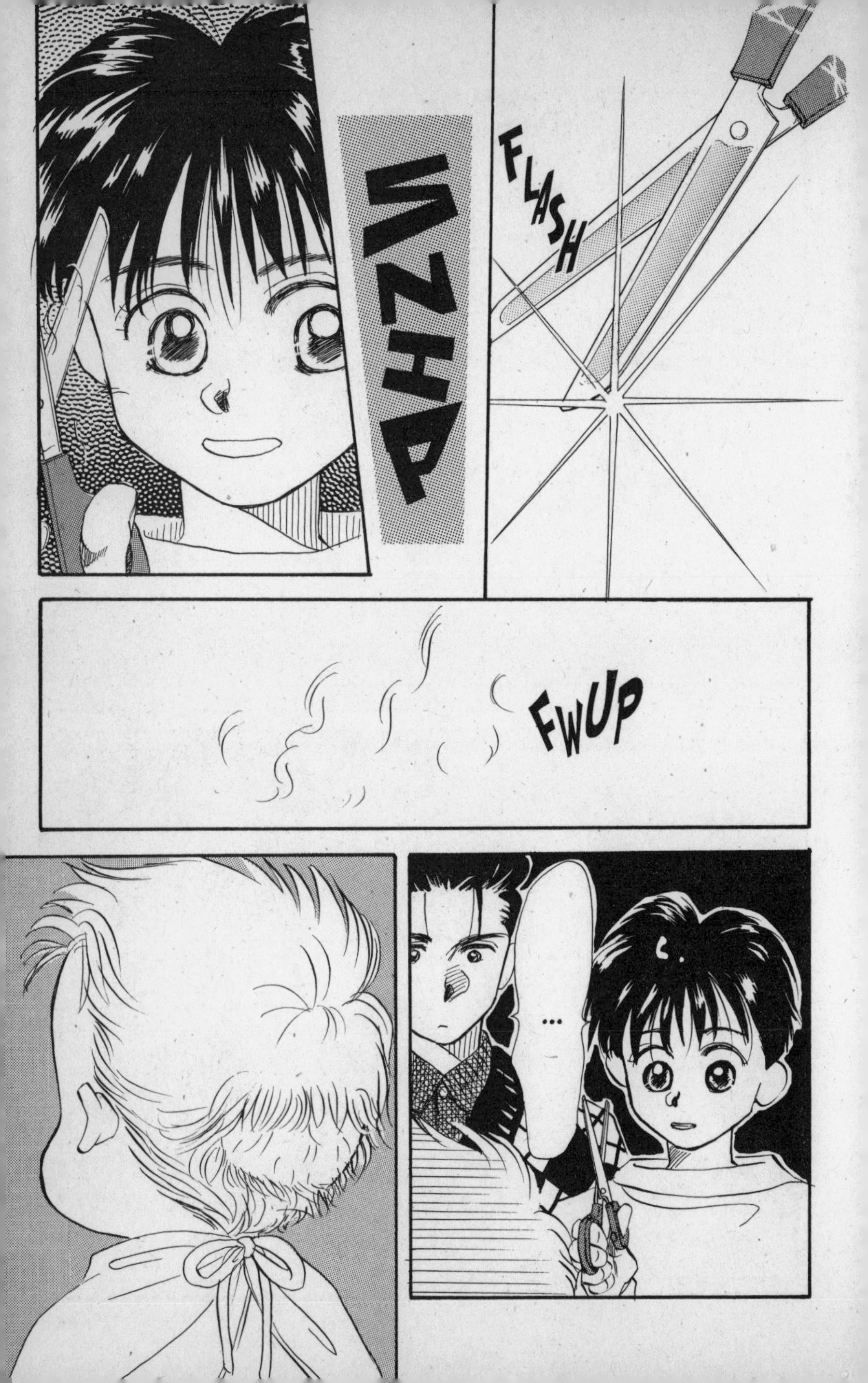
FLASH
SNZHP
FWUP
...

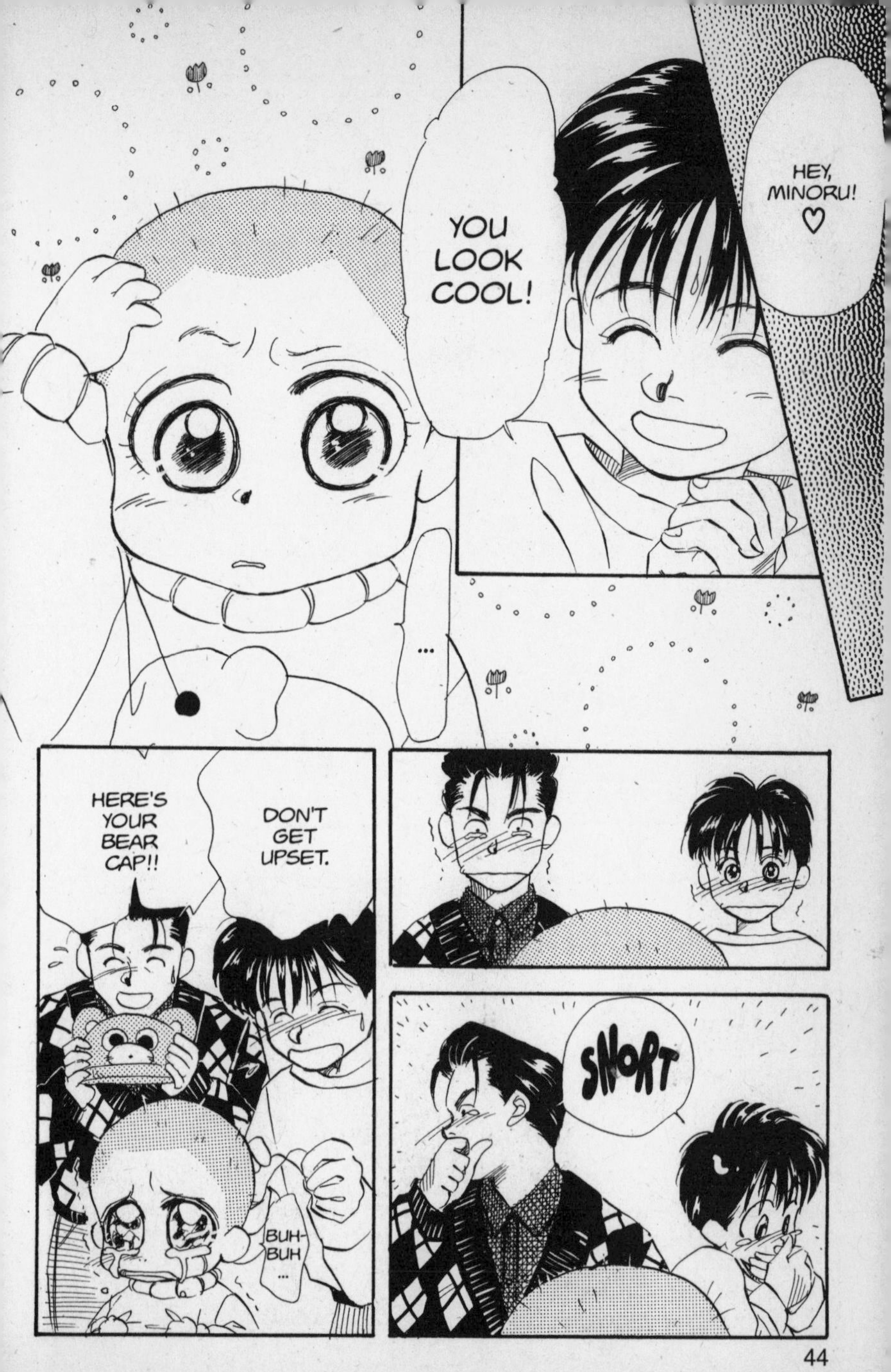
HEY, MINORU! ♡
YOU LOOK COOL!
...
SNORT
HERE'S YOUR BEAR CAP!!
DON'T GET UPSET.
BUH-BUH ...

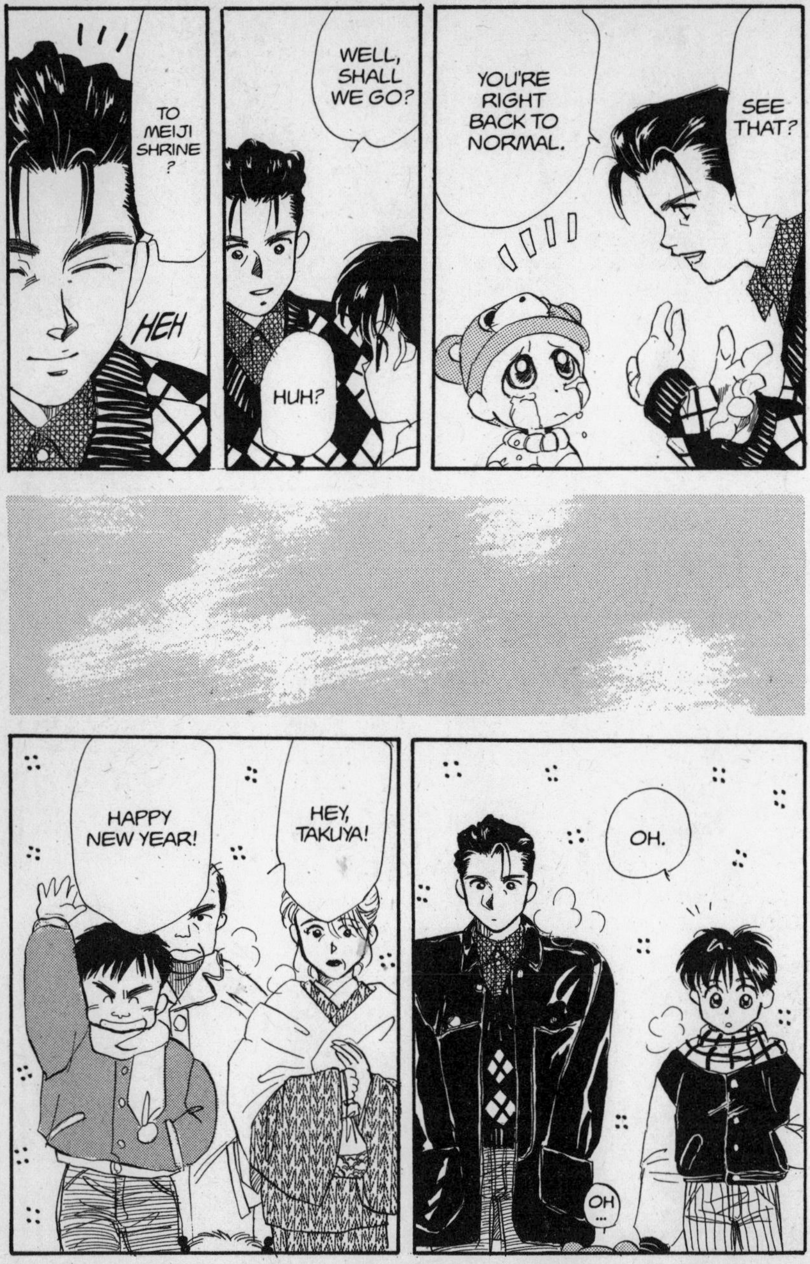
SEE THAT?
YOU'RE RIGHT BACK TO NORMAL.
WELL, SHALL WE GO?
HUH?
TO MEIJI SHRINE?
HEH
OH.
OH ...
HEY, TAKUYA!
HAPPY NEW YEAR!

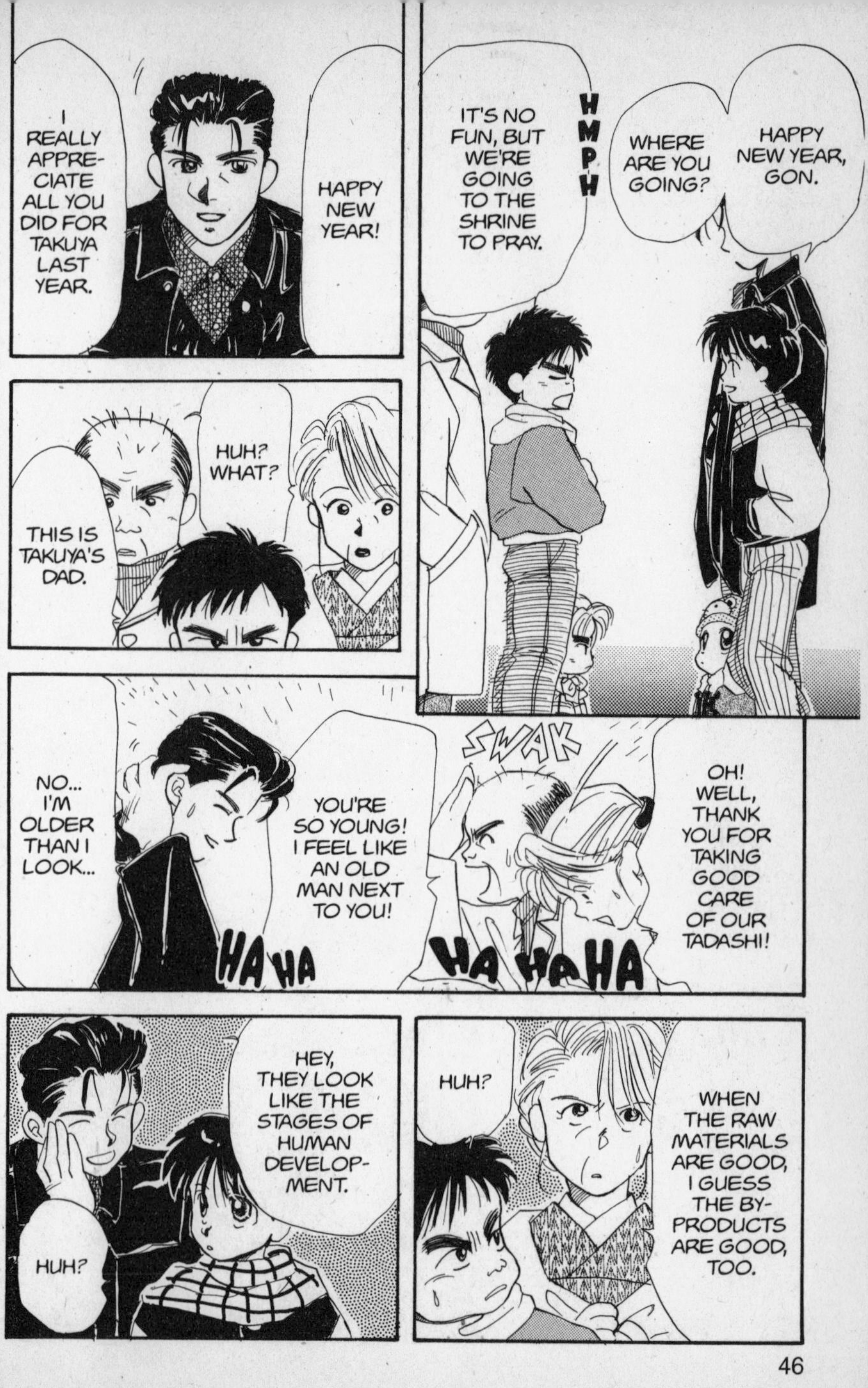
HAPPY NEW YEAR, GON.
WHERE ARE YOU GOING?
HMPH
IT'S NO FUN, BUT WE'RE GOING TO THE SHRINE TO PRAY.
HAPPY NEW YEAR!
I REALLY APPRECIATE ALL YOU DID FOR TAKUYA LAST YEAR.
HUH? WHAT?
THIS IS TAKUYA'S DAD.
OH! WELL, THANK YOU FOR TAKING GOOD CARE OF OUR TADASHI!
SWAK
HA HA HA HA
YOU'RE SO YOUNG! I FEEL LIKE AN OLD MAN NEXT TO YOU!
NO... I'M OLDER THAN I LOOK...
HA HA
WHEN THE RAW MATERIALS ARE GOOD, I GUESS THE BY-PRODUCTS ARE GOOD, TOO.
HUH?
HEY, THEY LOOK LIKE THE STAGES OF HUMAN DEVELOPMENT.
HUH?

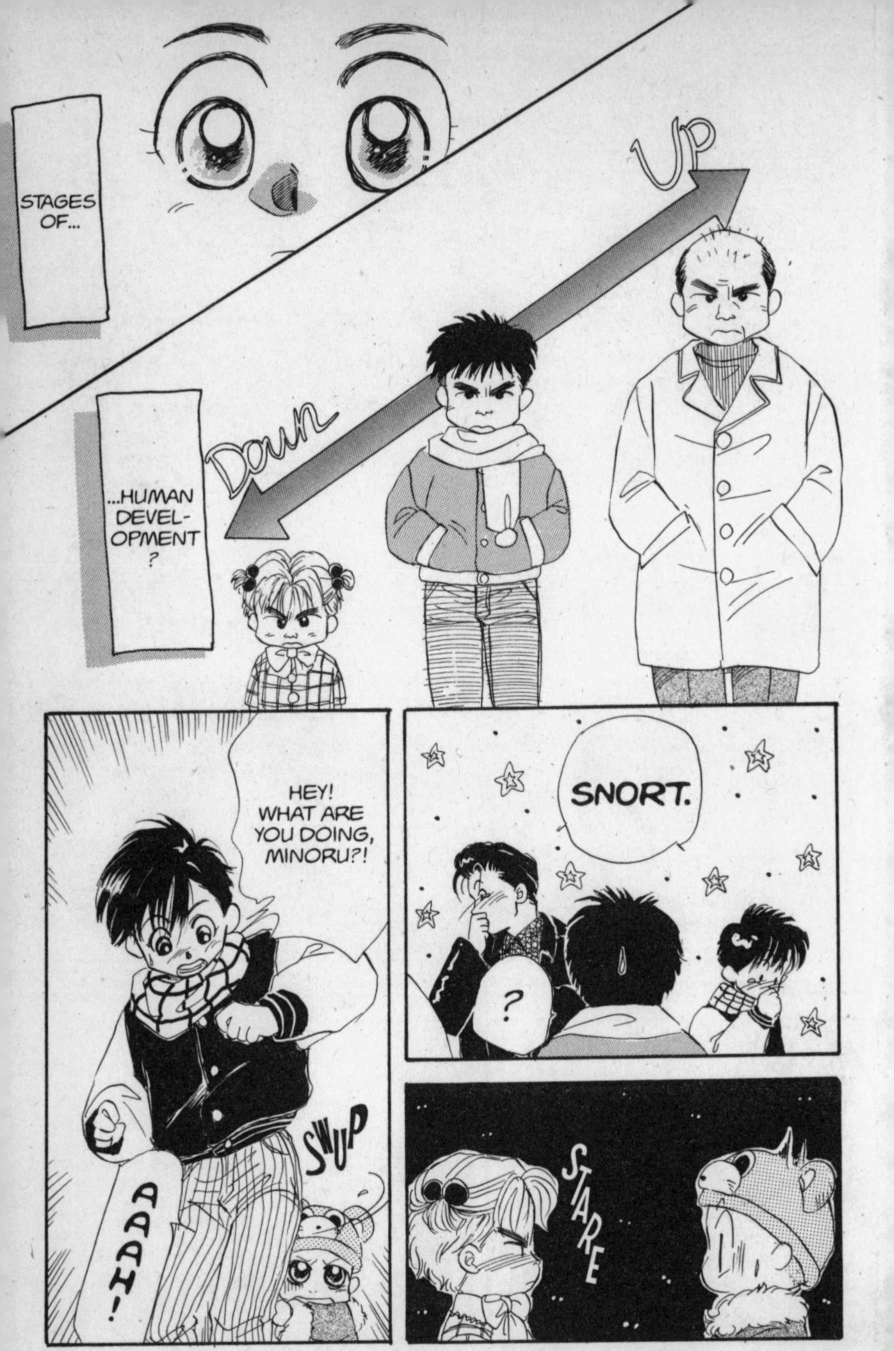
STAGES OF...
Up
Down
...HUMAN DEVEL-OPMENT?
SNORT.
?
STARE
HEY! WHAT ARE YOU DOING, MINORU?!
SWUP
AAAAH!

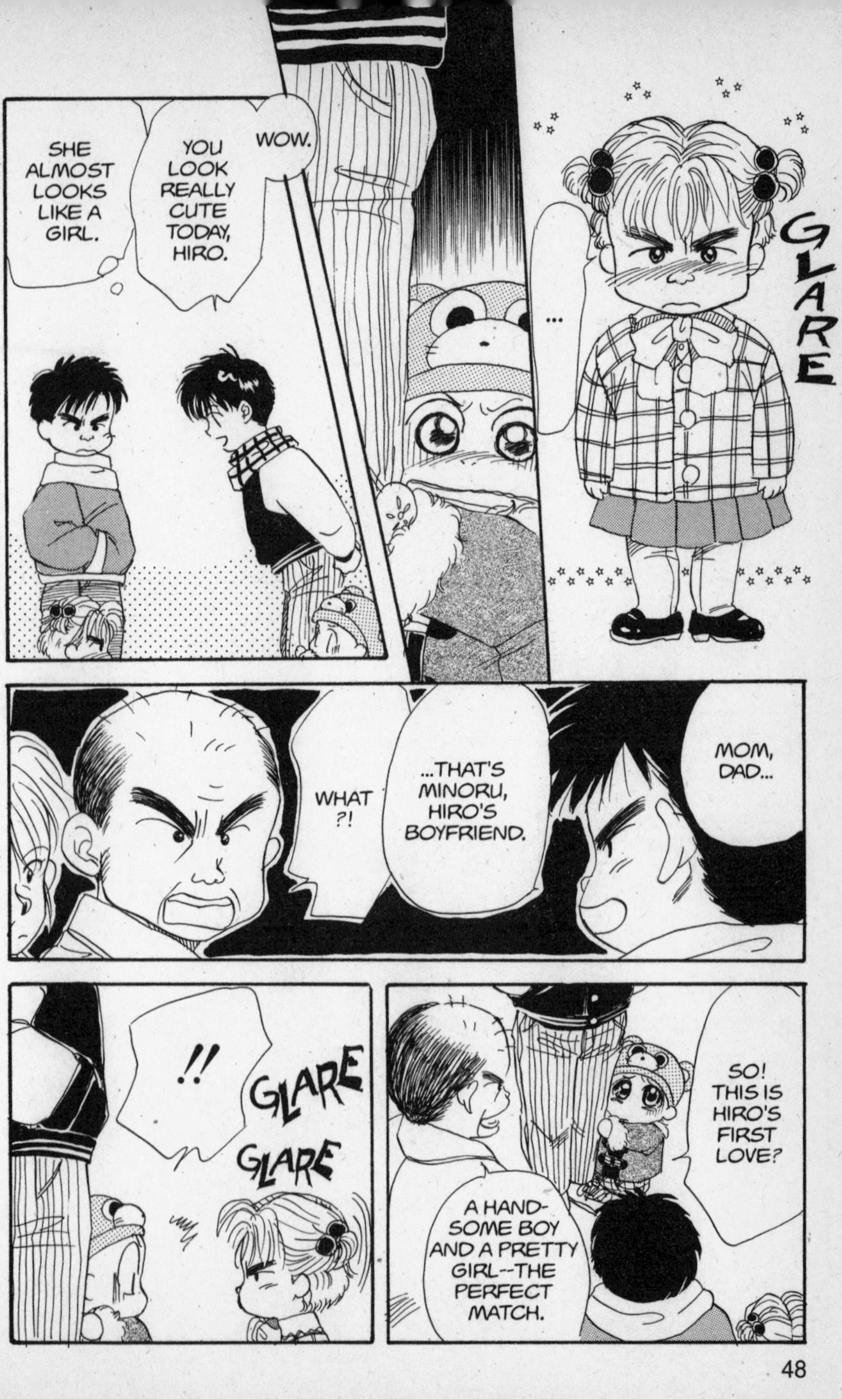
GLARE
...
WOW.
YOU LOOK REALLY CUTE TODAY, HIRO.
SHE ALMOST LOOKS LIKE A GIRL.
MOM, DAD...
...THAT'S MINORU, HIRO'S BOYFRIEND.
WHAT?!
SO! THIS IS HIRO'S FIRST LOVE?
A HAND-SOME BOY AND A PRETTY GIRL--THE PERFECT MATCH.
!!
GLARE
GLARE

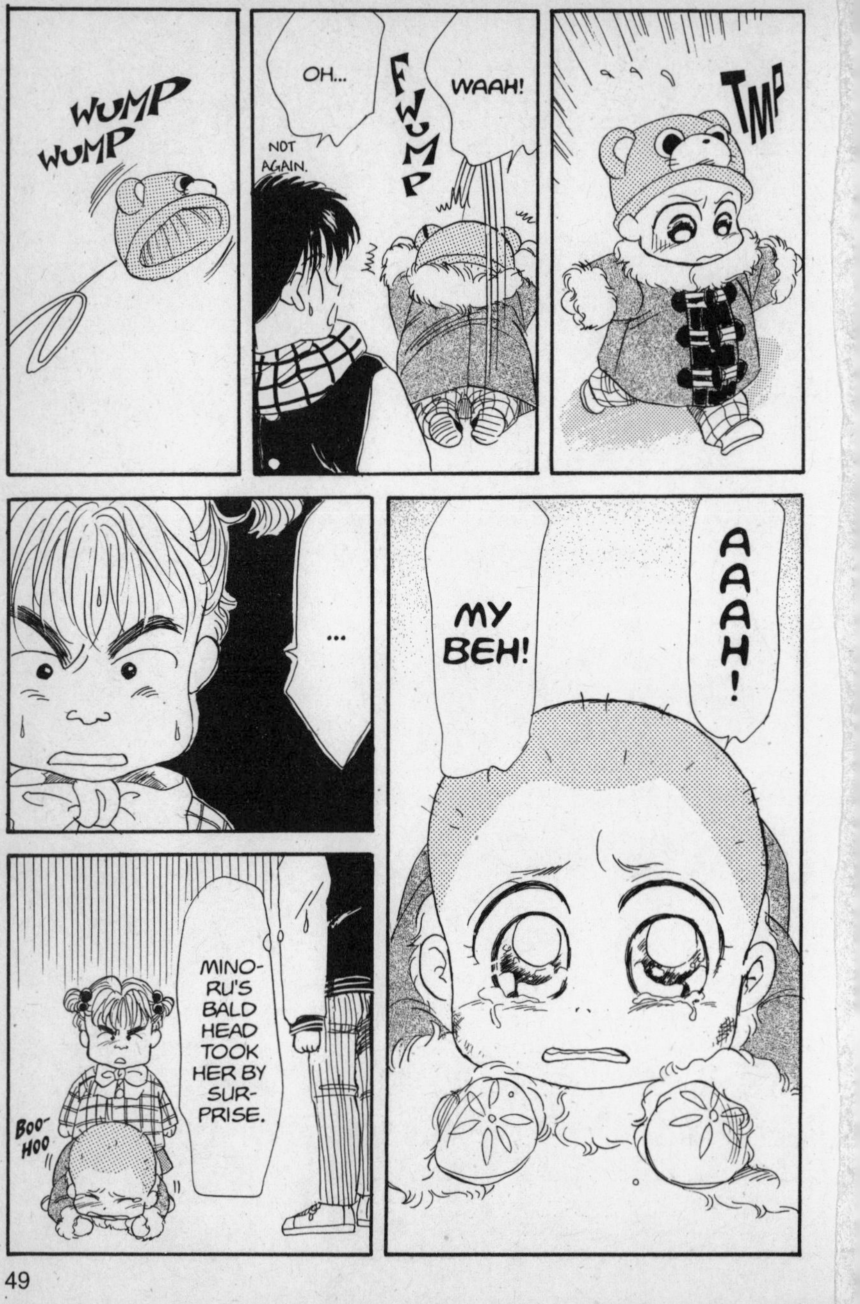
TMP
WAAH!
FWUMP
OH...
NOT AGAIN.
WUMP WUMP
AAAAH!
MY BEH!
...
MINO-RU'S BALD HEAD TOOK HER BY SUR-PRISE.
BOO-HOO

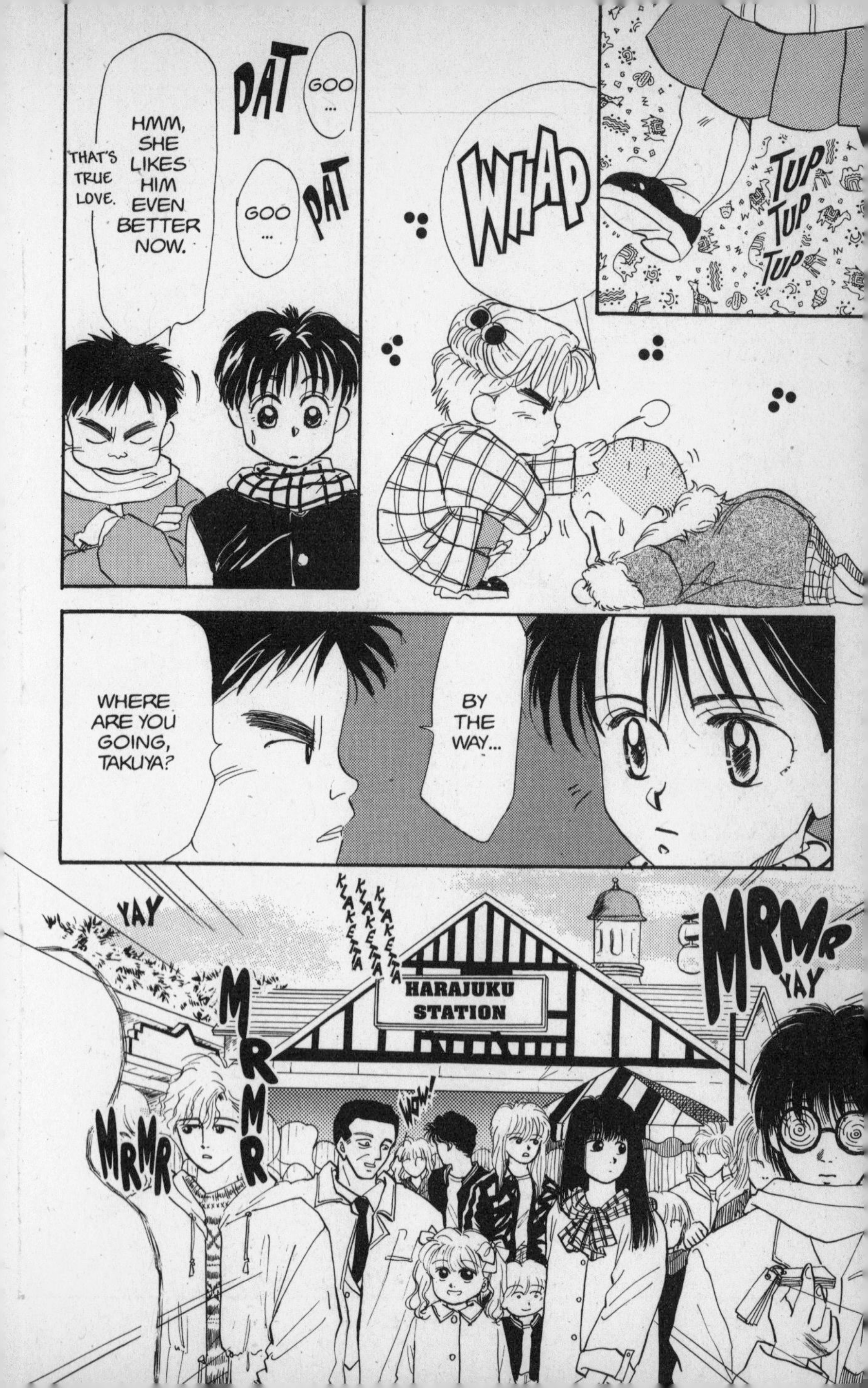
TUP
TUP
TUP
WHAP
GOO ...
PAT
PAT
GOO ...
HMM, SHE LIKES HIM EVEN BETTER NOW.
THAT'S TRUE LOVE.
BY THE WAY...
WHERE ARE YOU GOING, TAKUYA?
MRMR
YAY
KLAKETTA
KLAKETTA
KLAKETTA
HARAJUKU STATION
YAY
MRMR
WOW!
MRMR

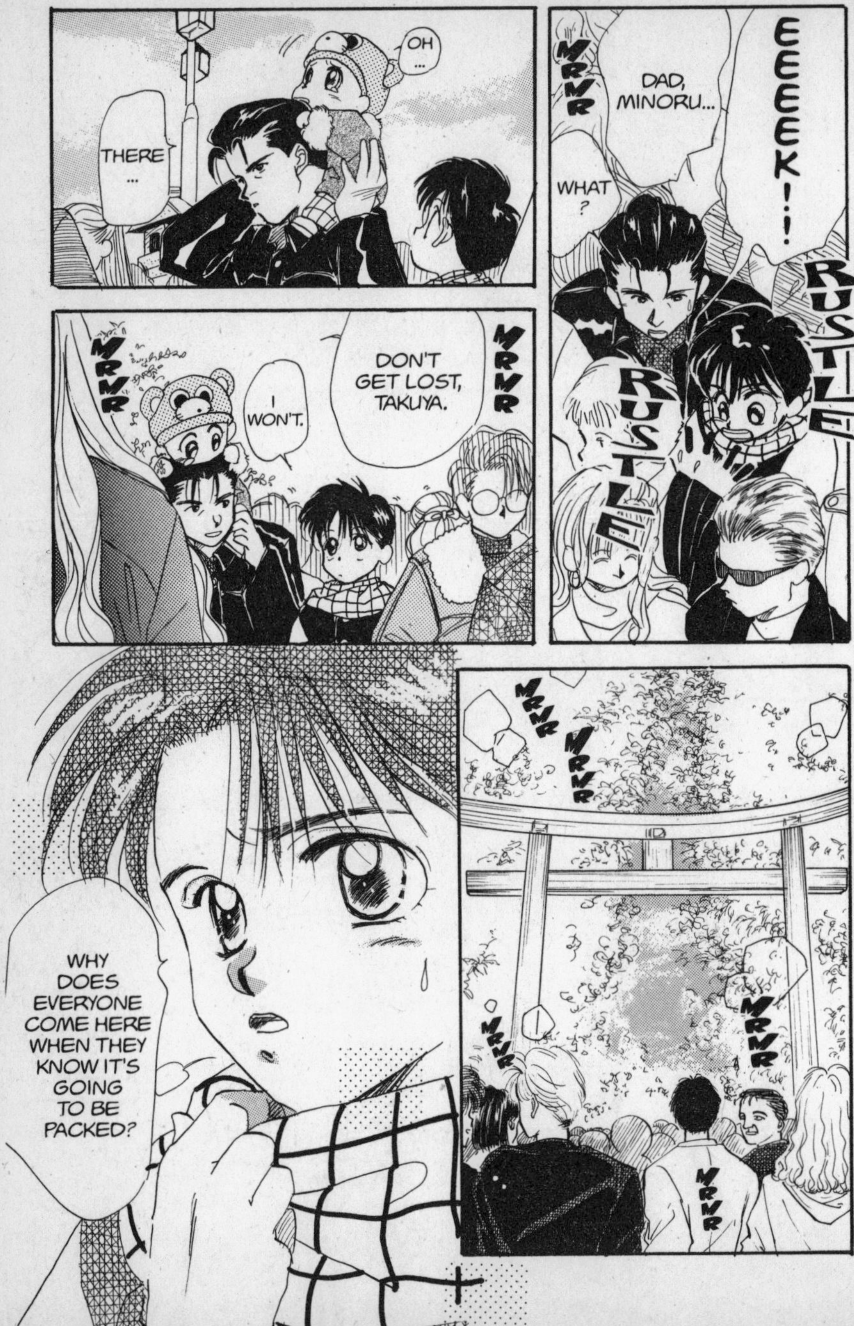
MRMR
EEEEEK!!
DAD, MINORU...
WHAT?
RUSTLE
RUSTLE
OH ...
THERE ...
MRMR
DON'T GET LOST, TAKUYA.
I WON'T.
MRMR
MRMR
MRMR
MRMR
MRMR
MRMR
WHY DOES EVERYONE COME HERE WHEN THEY KNOW IT'S GOING TO BE PACKED?

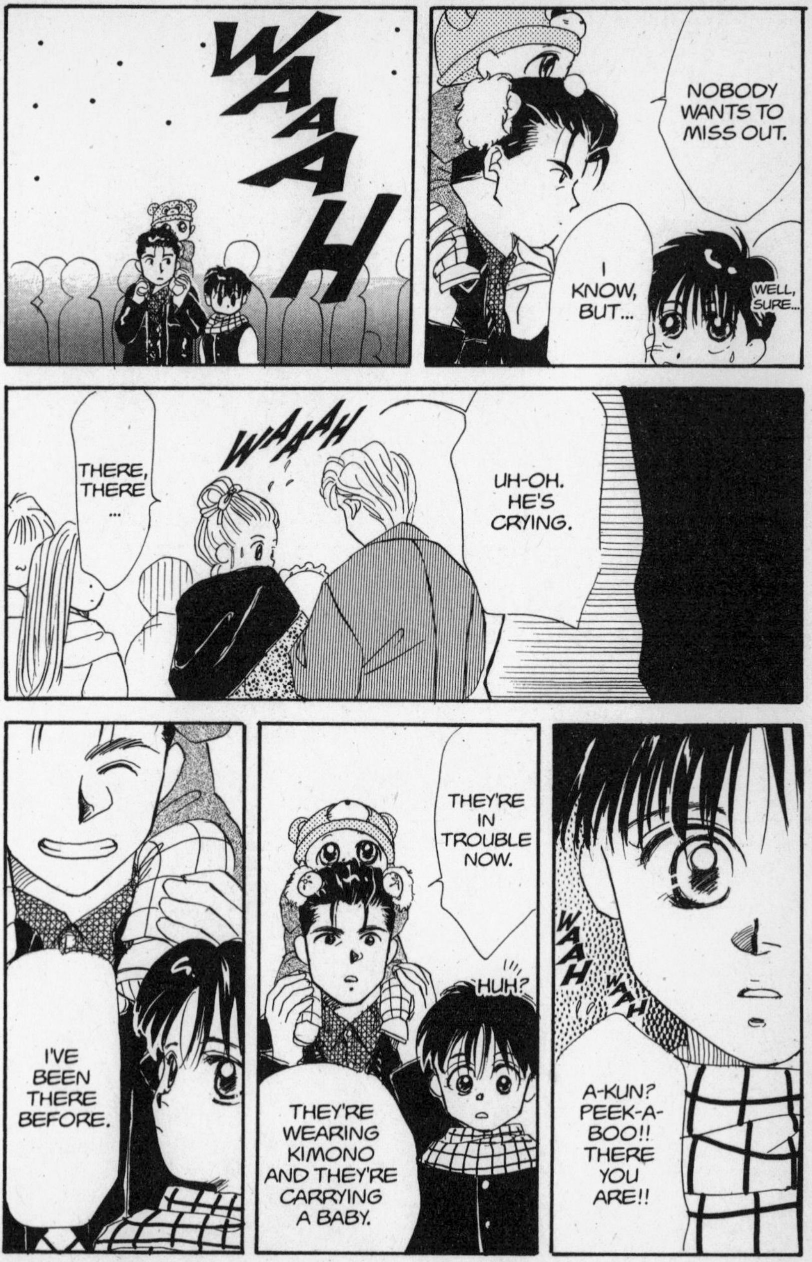
NOBODY WANTS TO MISS OUT.
WELL, SURE...
I KNOW, BUT...
WAAAH
UH-OH. HE'S CRYING.
WAAAH
THERE, THERE ...
WAAH WAAH
A-KUN? PEEK-A-BOO!! THERE YOU ARE!!
THEY'RE IN TROUBLE NOW.
HUH?
THEY'RE WEARING KIMONO AND THEY'RE CARRYING A BABY.
I'VE BEEN THERE BEFORE.

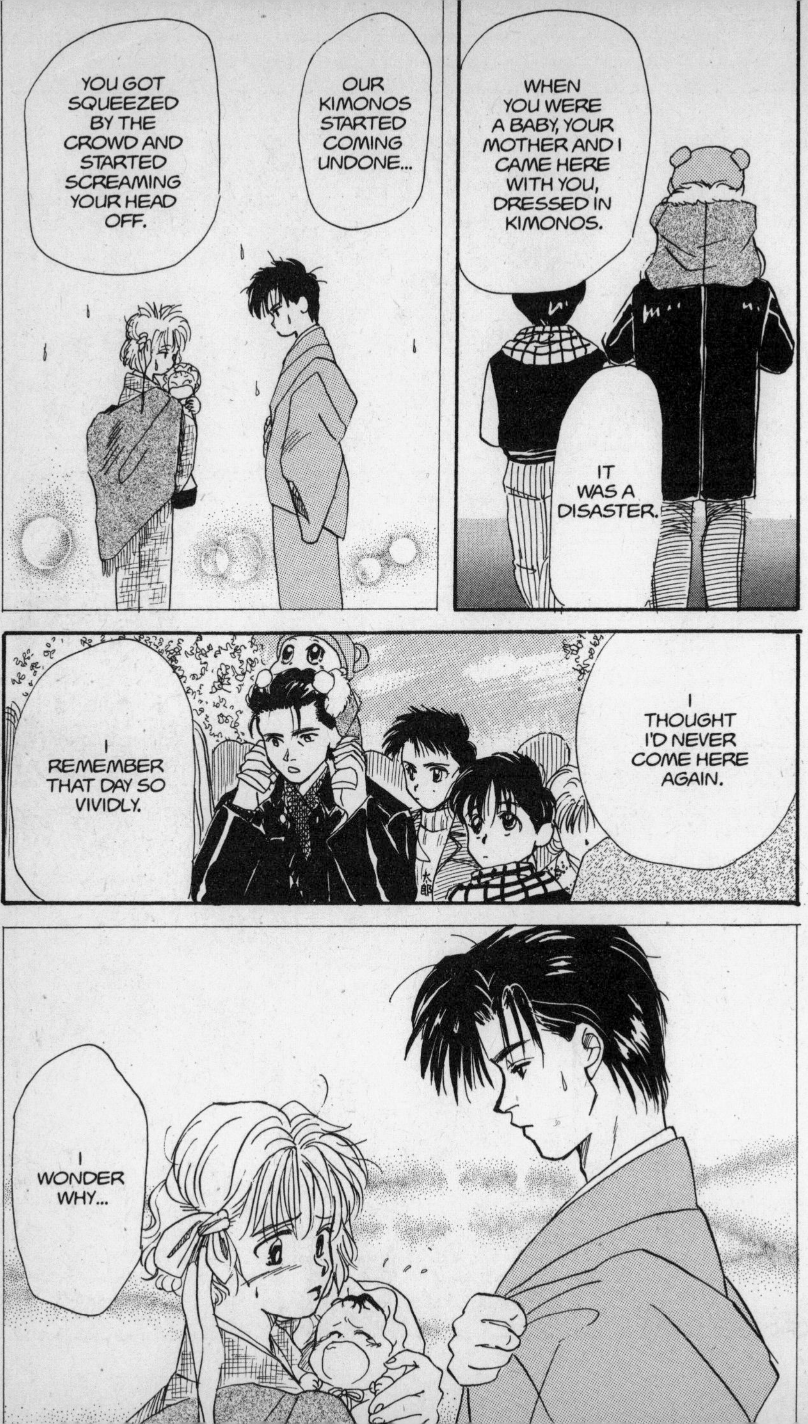
WHEN YOU WERE A BABY, YOUR MOTHER AND I CAME HERE WITH YOU, DRESSED IN KIMONOS.
IT WAS A DISASTER.
OUR KIMONOS STARTED COMING UNDONE...
YOU GOT SQUEEZED BY THE CROWD AND STARTED SCREAMING YOUR HEAD OFF.
I THOUGHT I'D NEVER COME HERE AGAIN.
I REMEMBER THAT DAY SO VIVIDLY.
I WONDER WHY...

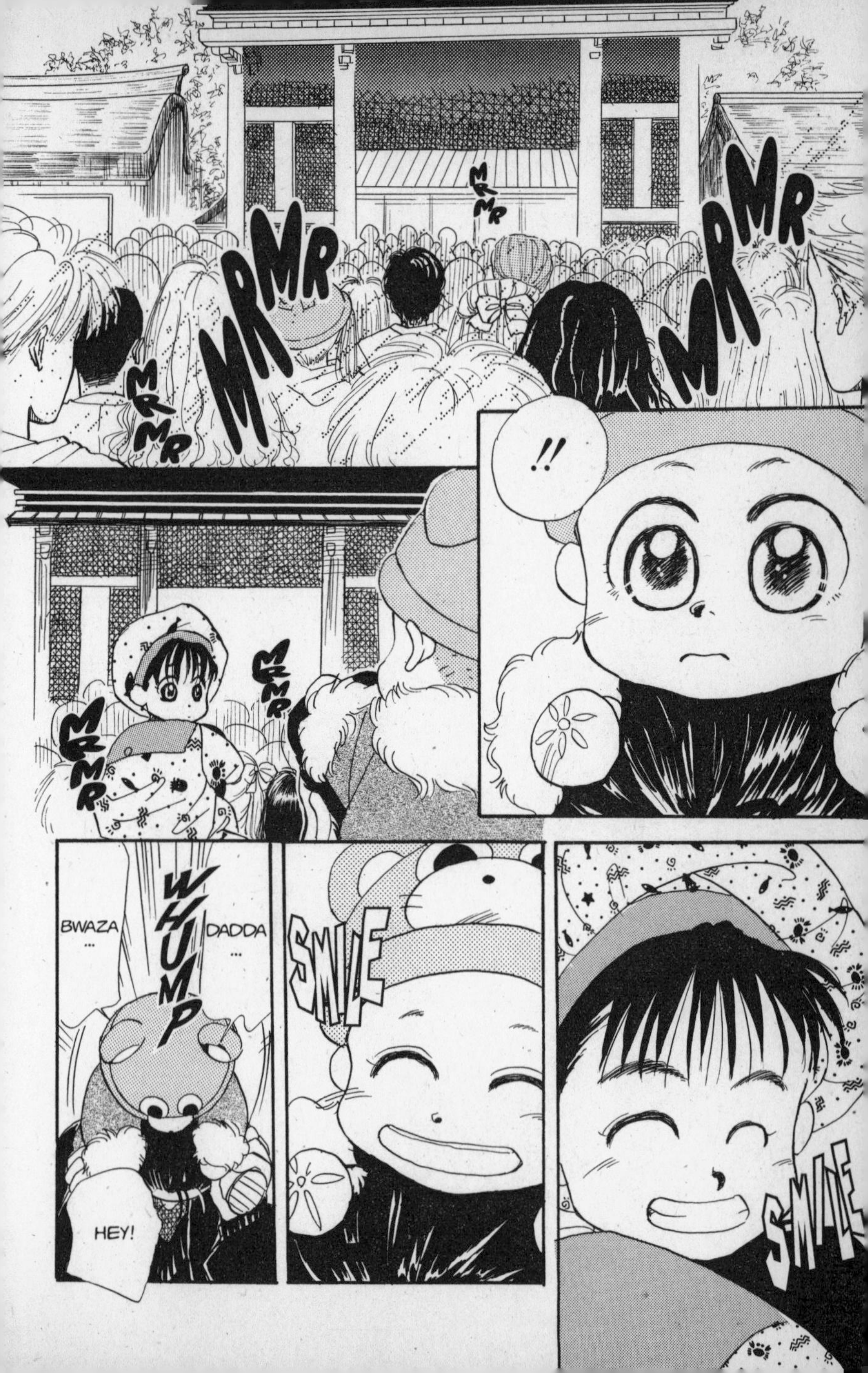
MRMR
MRMR
MRMR
MRMR
!!
MRMR
MRMR
SMILE
SMILE
DADDA ...
WHUMP
BWAZA ...
HEY!

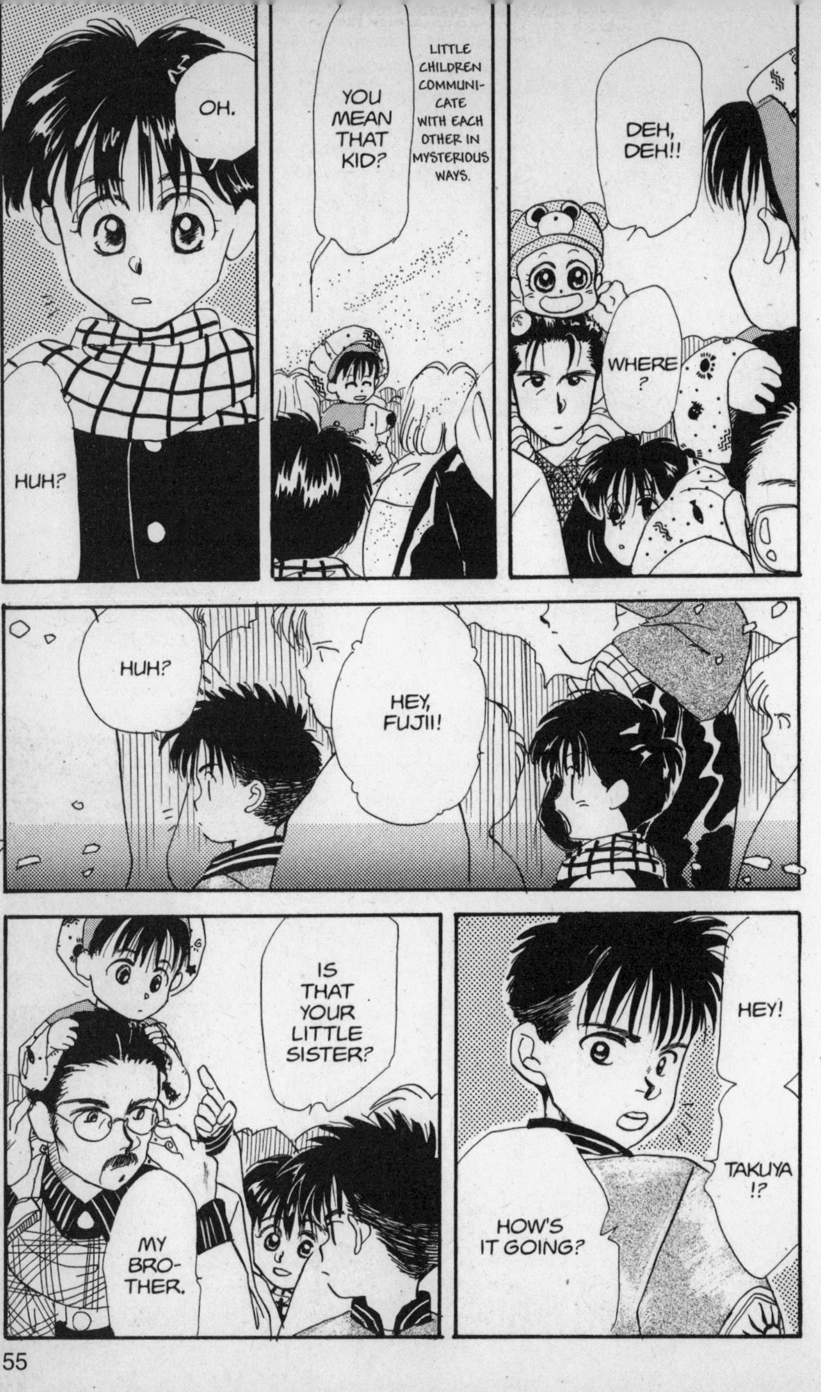
DEH, DEH!!
WHERE?
LITTLE CHILDREN COMMUNICATE WITH EACH OTHER IN MYSTERIOUS WAYS.
YOU MEAN THAT KID?
OH.
HUH?
HEY, FUJII!
HUH?
HEY!
TAKUYA!?
HOW'S IT GOING?
IS THAT YOUR LITTLE SISTER?
MY BROTHER.

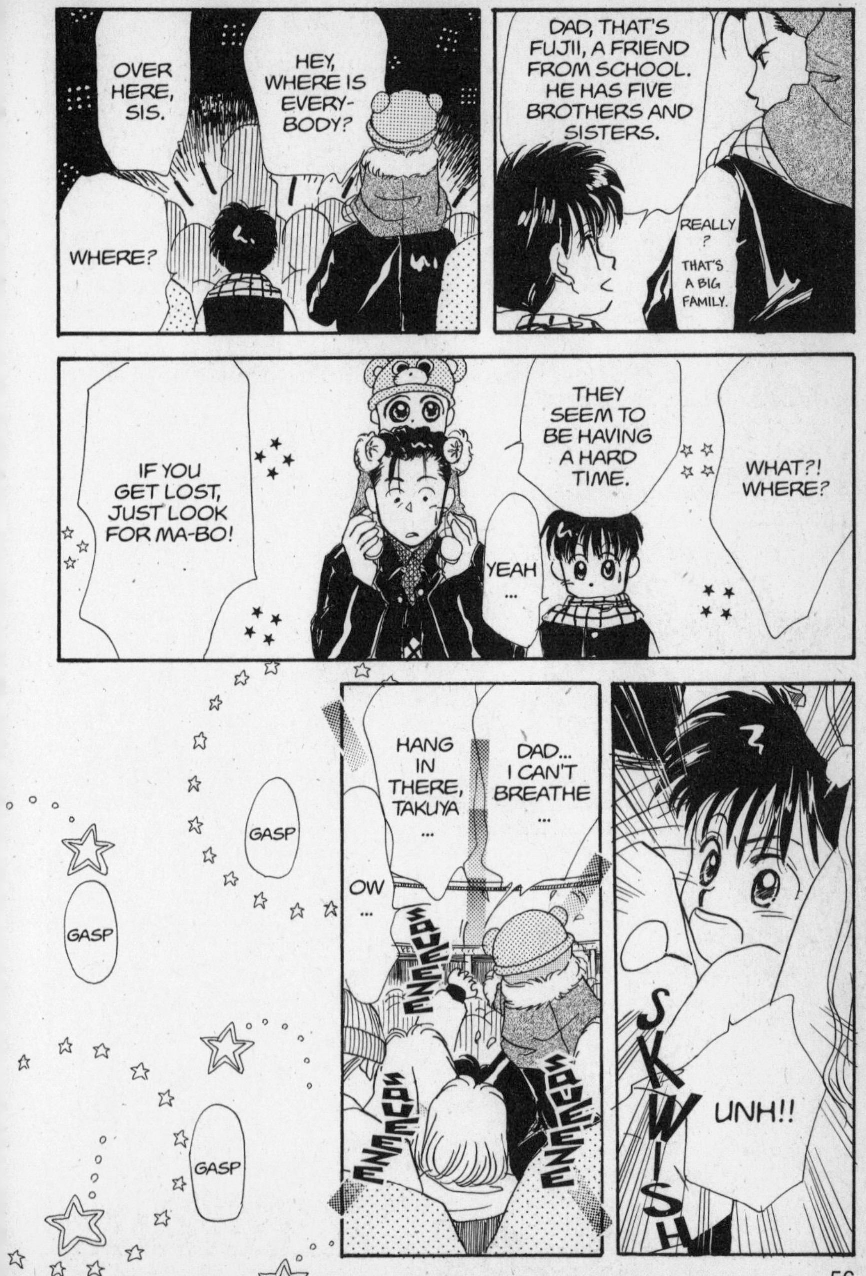
DAD, THAT'S FUJII, A FRIEND FROM SCHOOL. HE HAS FIVE BROTHERS AND SISTERS.
REALLY? THAT'S A BIG FAMILY.
HEY, WHERE IS EVERY-BODY?
OVER HERE, SIS.
WHERE?
WHAT?! WHERE?
THEY SEEM TO BE HAVING A HARD TIME.
YEAH...
IF YOU GET LOST, JUST LOOK FOR MA-BO!
SKWISH
UNH!!
DAD... I CAN'T BREATHE...
HANG IN THERE, TAKUYA...
SQUEEZE
OW...
SQUEEZE
SQUEEZE
GASP
GASP
GASP

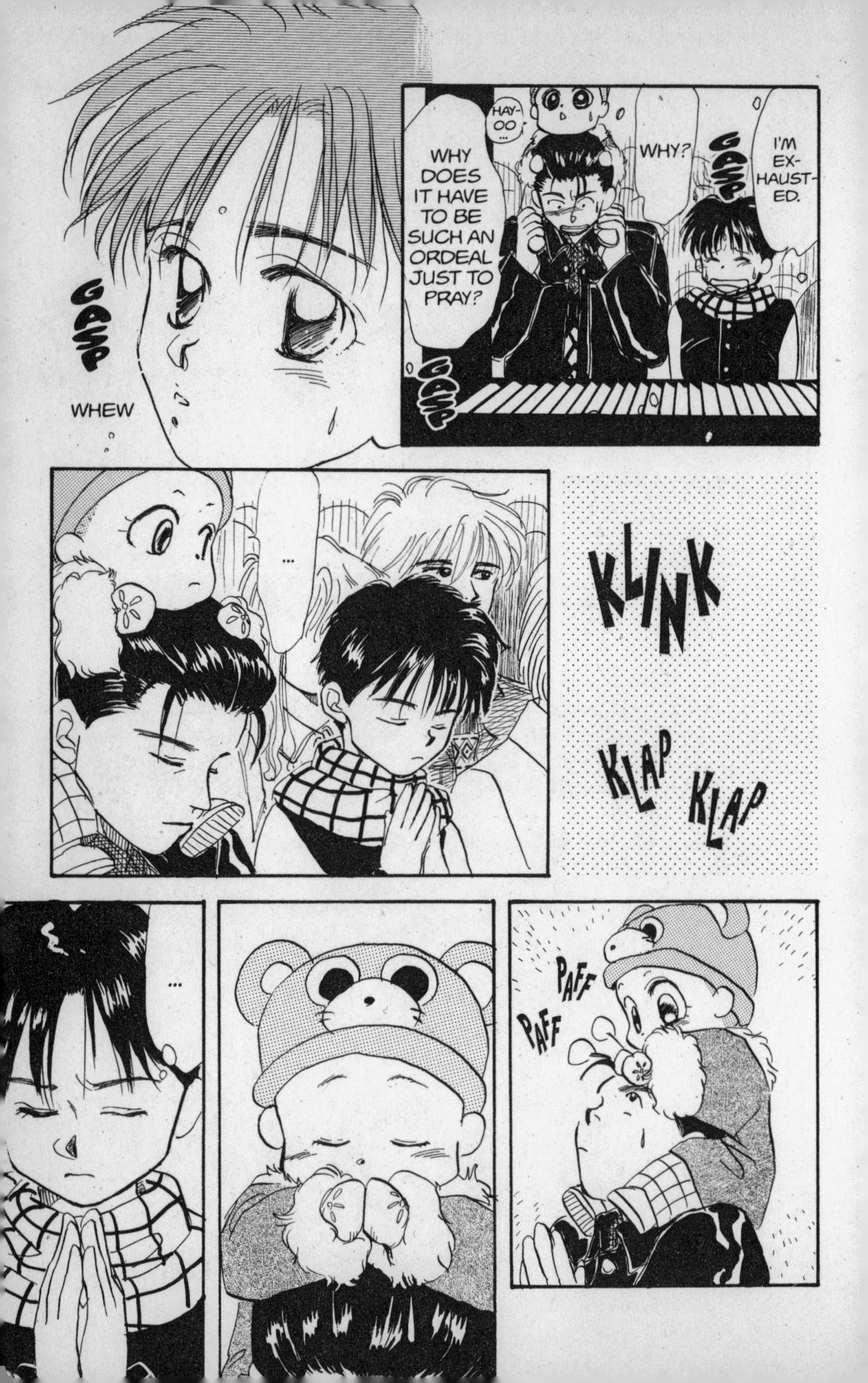
I'M EX-HAUST-ED.
GASP
WHY?
HAY-OO...
WHY DOES IT HAVE TO BE SUCH AN ORDEAL JUST TO PRAY?
GASP
GASP
WHEW
KLINK
KLAP KLAP
...
PAFF PAFF
...

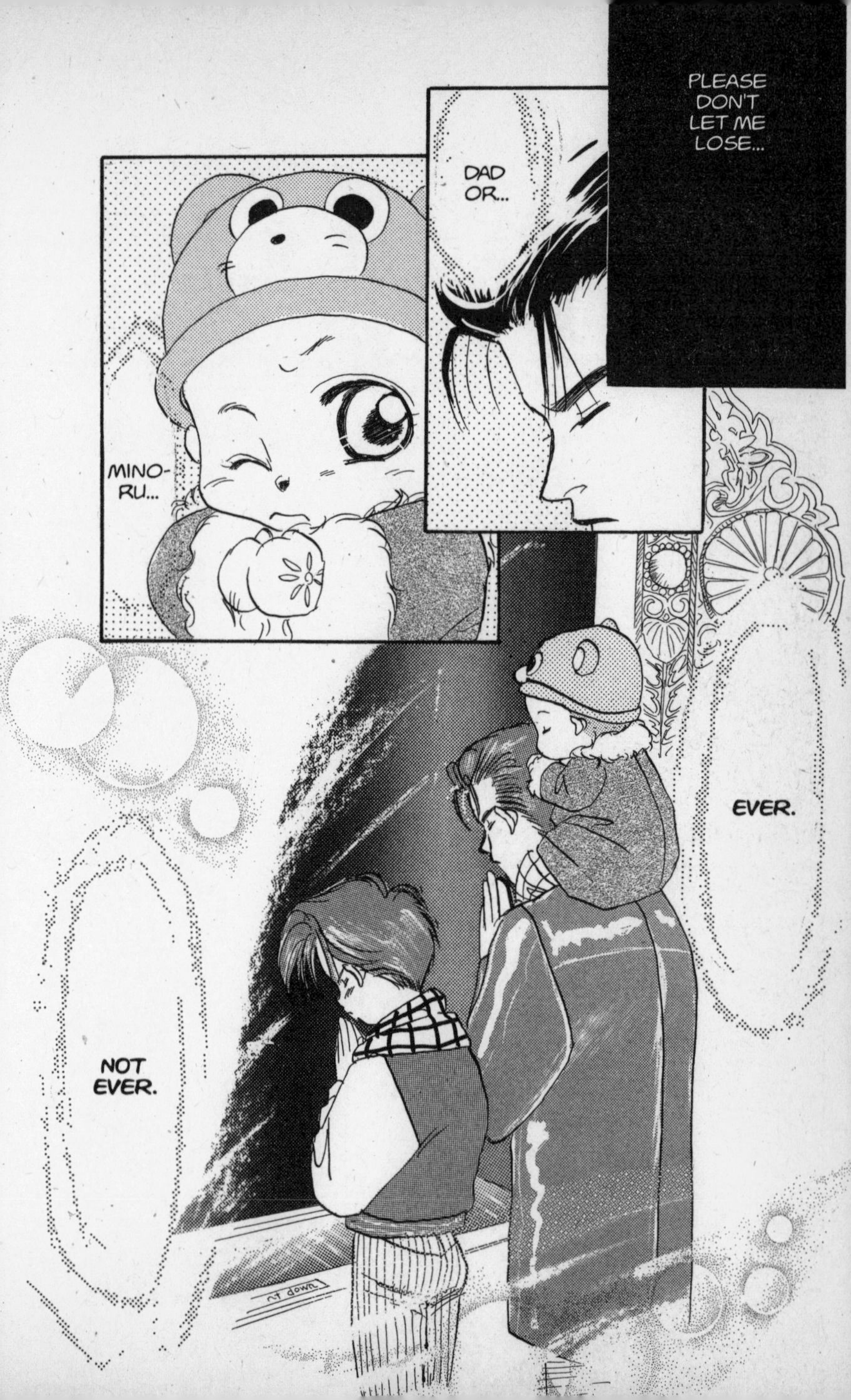
PLEASE DON'T LET ME LOSE...
DAD OR..
MINO-RU...
EVER.
NOT EVER.

HEY!

?

PRAY
PRAY

AND PLEASE LET MINORU'S HAIR GROW BACK QUICKLY.

ALL THINGS

I DON'T UNDERSTAND WHAT THIS MEANS.

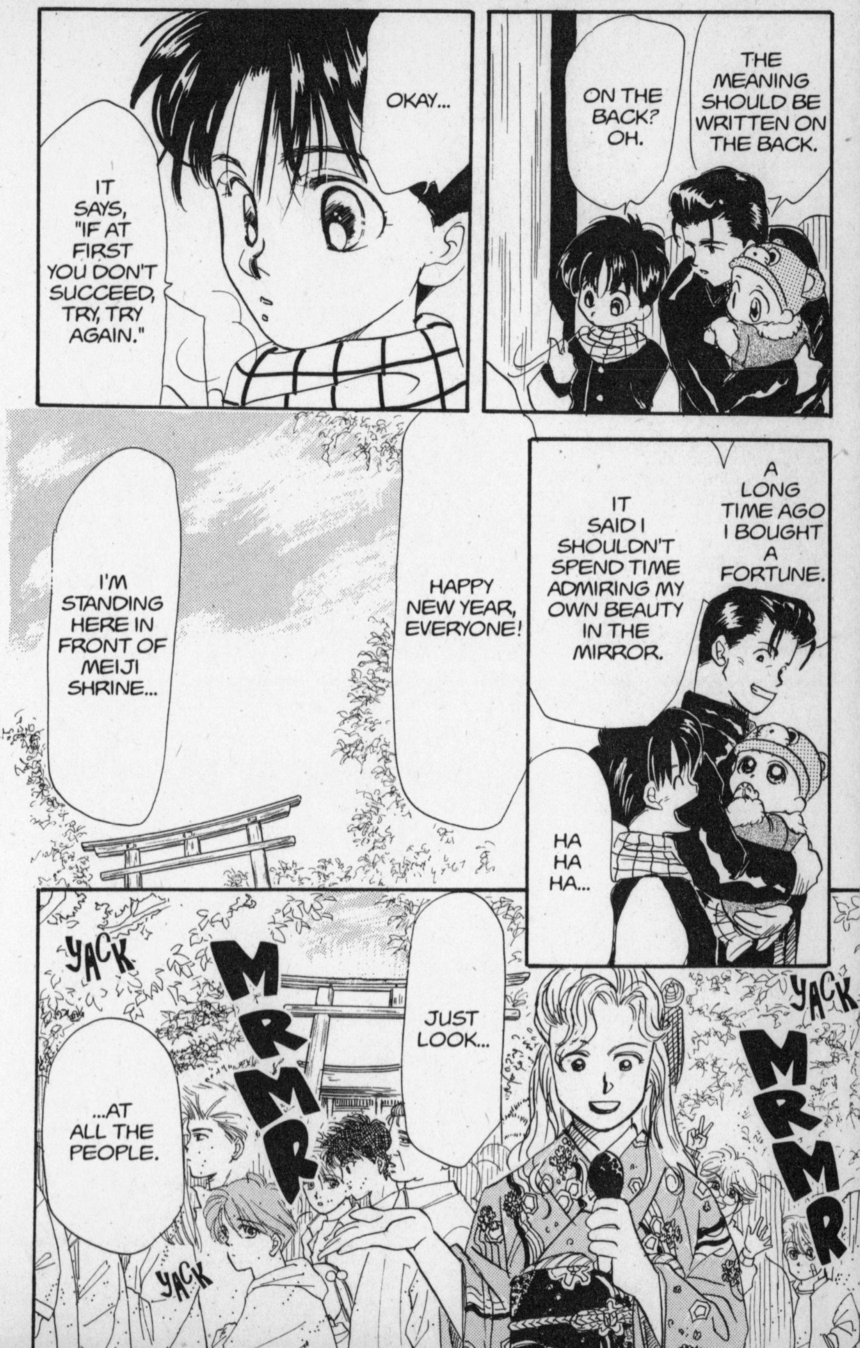
THE MEANING SHOULD BE WRITTEN ON THE BACK.
ON THE BACK? OH.
OKAY...
IT SAYS, "IF AT FIRST YOU DON'T SUCCEED, TRY, TRY AGAIN."
A LONG TIME AGO I BOUGHT A FORTUNE.
IT SAID I SHOULDN'T SPEND TIME ADMIRING MY OWN BEAUTY IN THE MIRROR.
HA HA HA...
HAPPY NEW YEAR, EVERYONE!
I'M STANDING HERE IN FRONT OF MEIJI SHRINE...
YACK
MRMR
JUST LOOK...
...AT ALL THE PEOPLE.
YACK
MRMR
YACK

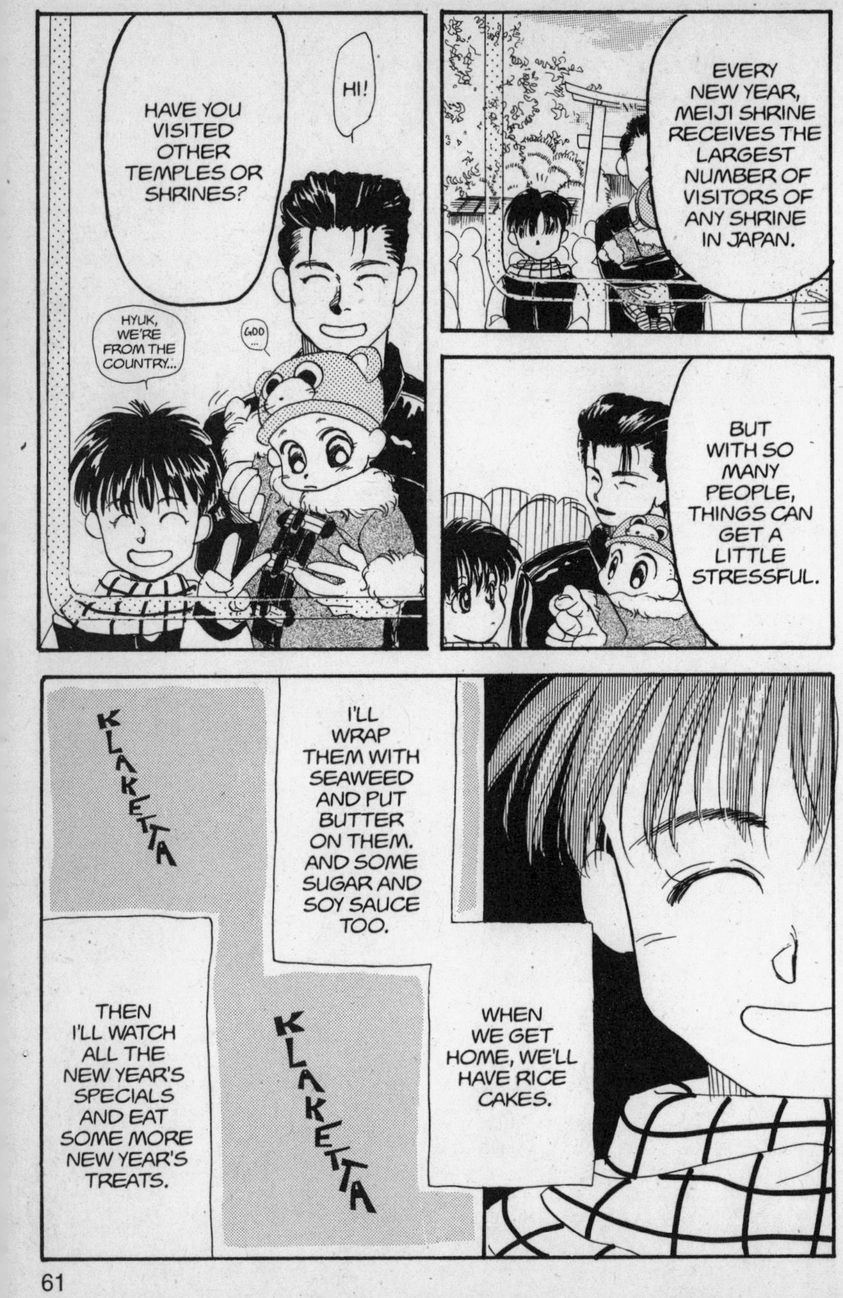
EVERY NEW YEAR, MEIJI SHRINE RECEIVES THE LARGEST NUMBER OF VISITORS OF ANY SHRINE IN JAPAN.
BUT WITH SO MANY PEOPLE, THINGS CAN GET A LITTLE STRESSFUL.
HI!
HAVE YOU VISITED OTHER TEMPLES OR SHRINES?
GDD ...
HYUK, WE'RE FROM THE COUNTRY...
WHEN WE GET HOME, WE'LL HAVE RICE CAKES.
I'LL WRAP THEM WITH SEAWEED AND PUT BUTTER ON THEM. AND SOME SUGAR AND SOY SAUCE TOO.
KLAKETTA
KLAKETTA
THEN I'LL WATCH ALL THE NEW YEAR'S SPECIALS AND EAT SOME MORE NEW YEAR'S TREATS.

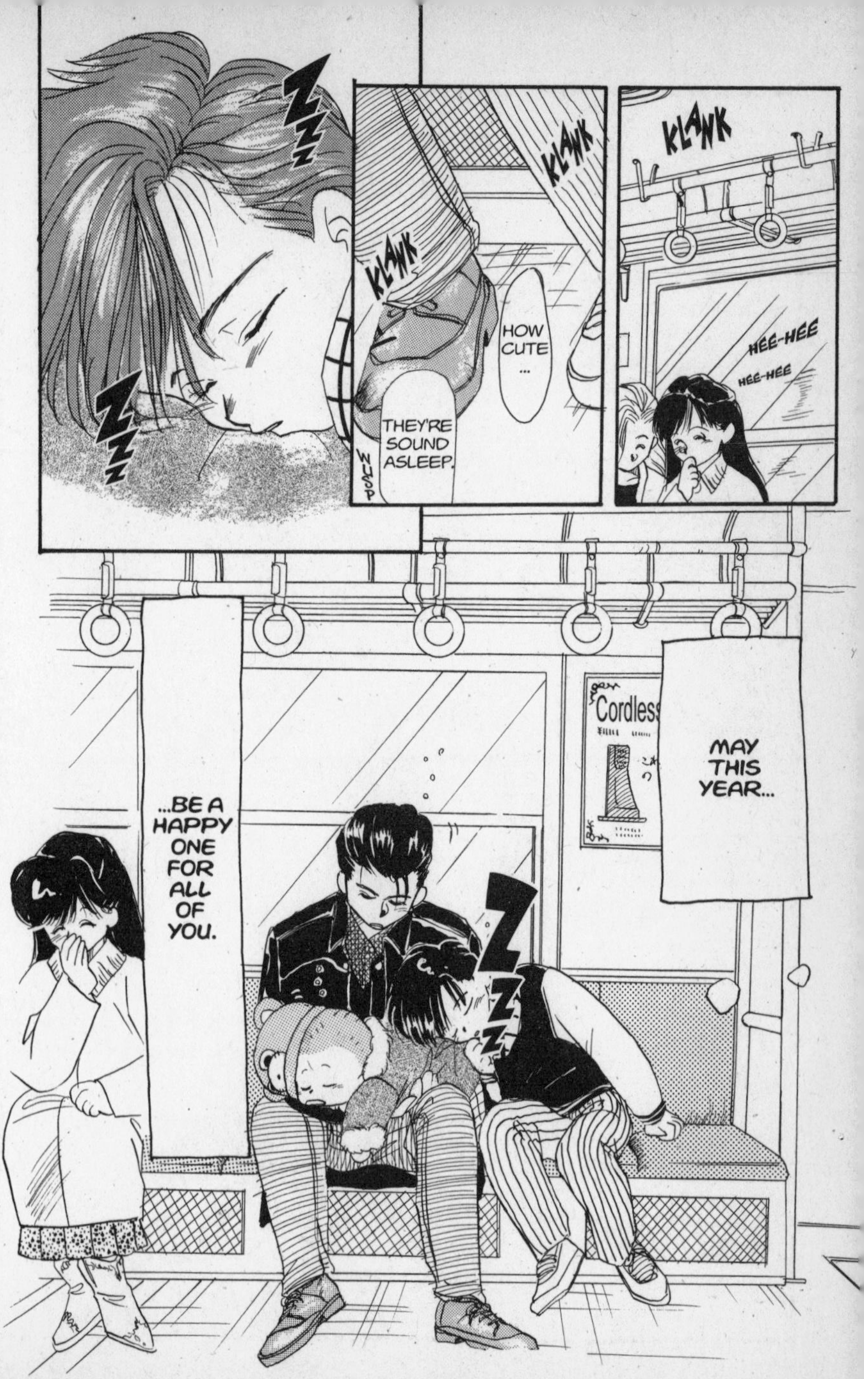
KLANK
HEE-HEE
HEE-HEE
KLANK
KLANK
HOW CUTE ...
THEY'RE SOUND ASLEEP.
WUSP
ZZZ
ZZZ
MAY THIS YEAR...
Cordless
...BE A HAPPY ONE FOR ALL OF YOU.
ZZZ

THE FUJII FAMILY

MY
PENMANSHIP
IS TERRIBLE.

AKIHIRO HAS FIVE BROTHERS AND SISTERS. I COME FROM A BIG FAMILY TOO--I HAVE FOUR SIBLINGS. EVER SINCE AKIHIRO CAME ON THE SCENE, I'VE GOTTEN A LOT OF LETTERS FROM PEOPLE WHO COME FROM BIG FAMILIES LIKE HIS. LIVING WITH THREE, FOUR, OR FIVE BROTHERS AND SISTERS ISN'T EASY. SOME PEOPLE EVEN FIND IT EMBARRASSING AND DON'T LIKE TO TALK ABOUT IT. OTHERS COMPLAIN THAT THEY HAVE TO DO TOO MUCH HOUSEWORK. BUT THEY ALL SAY THAT THEY LOVE THEIR FAMILIES DESPITE IT ALL.

THE FUJII FAMILY HAS BECOME JUST AS POPULAR AS THE ENOKI FAMILY. AKIHIRO AND TOMOYA ARE ESPECIALLY POPULAR. I ENJOY DRAWING THE FUJII FAMILY. TWO OF THEM THAT HAVEN'T APPEARED YET ARE ASAKO AND AKEMI, THE OLDER SISTERS. I HAVEN'T EVEN THOUGHT ABOUT WHAT SORT OF CHARACTERS THEY WILL BE.
SORRY.

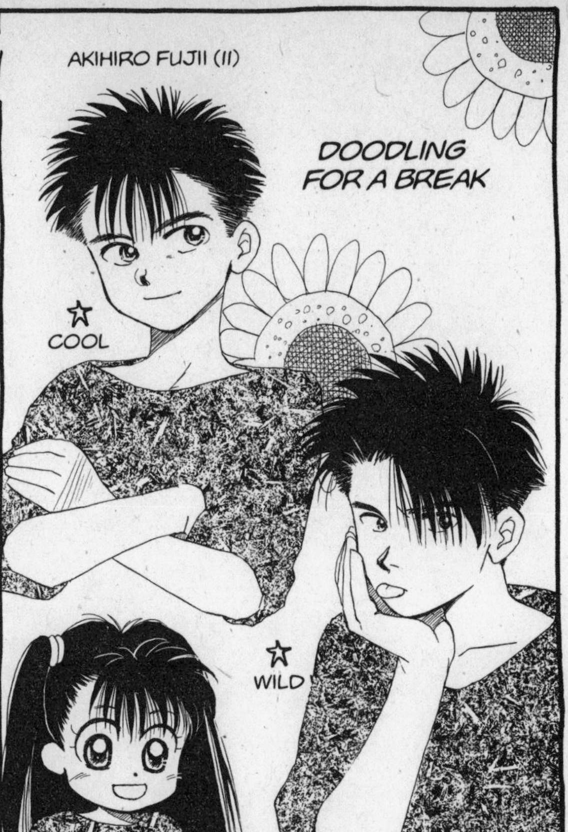
DOODLING FOR A BREAK
AKIHIRO FUJII (11)
☆ COOL
☆ WILD
TOMOYA FUJII (17)
☆ PRECOCIOUS
ICHIKA FUJII (4)
☆ TALKATIVE
MASAKI FUJII (3)

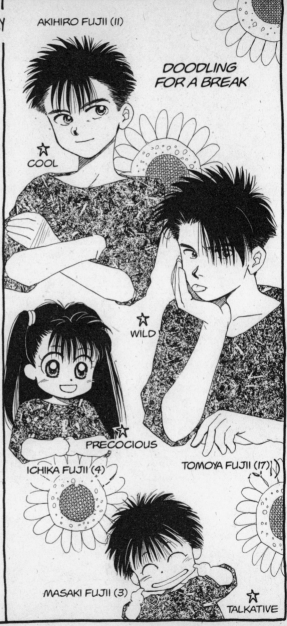

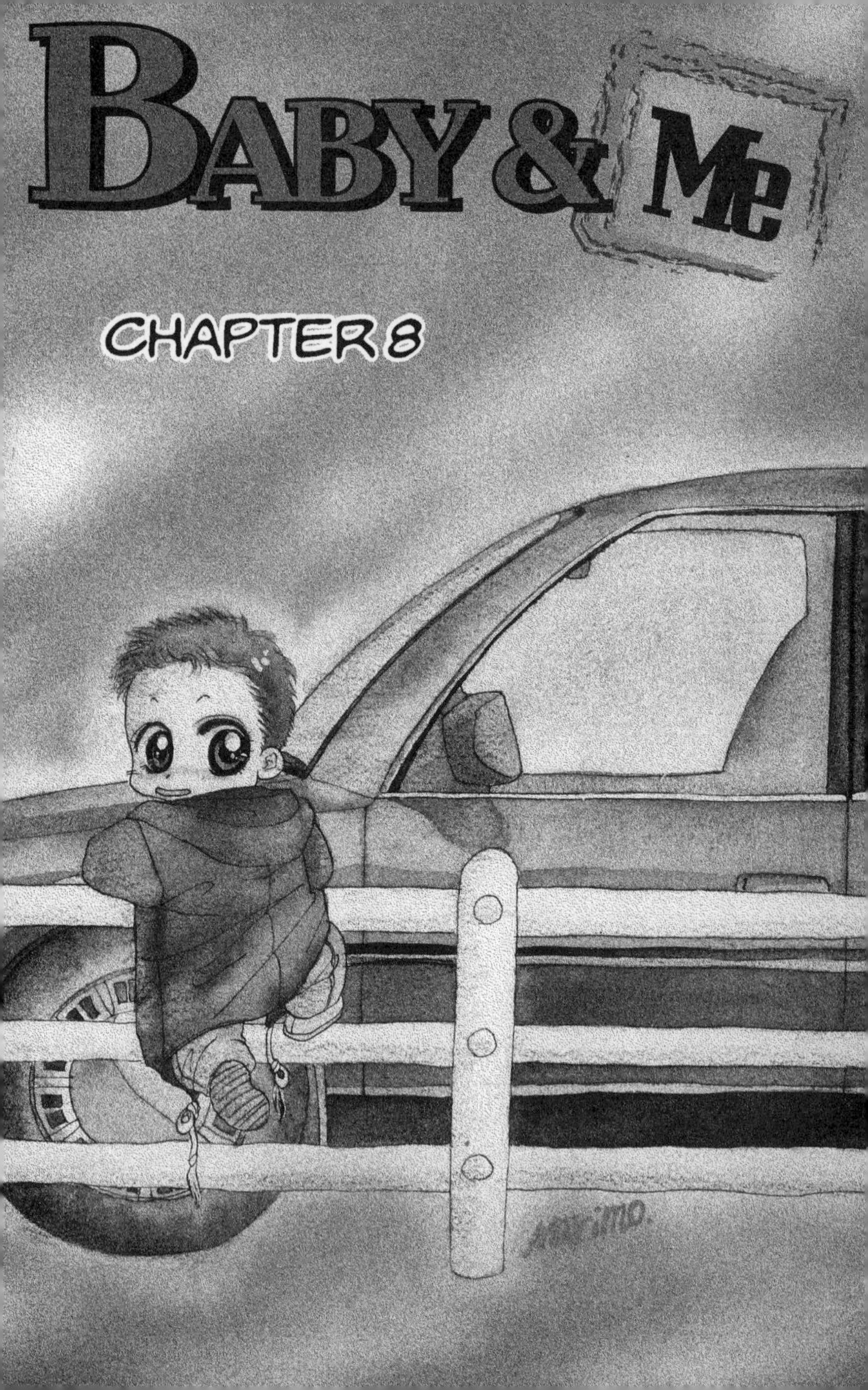
BABY & ME
CHAPTER 8

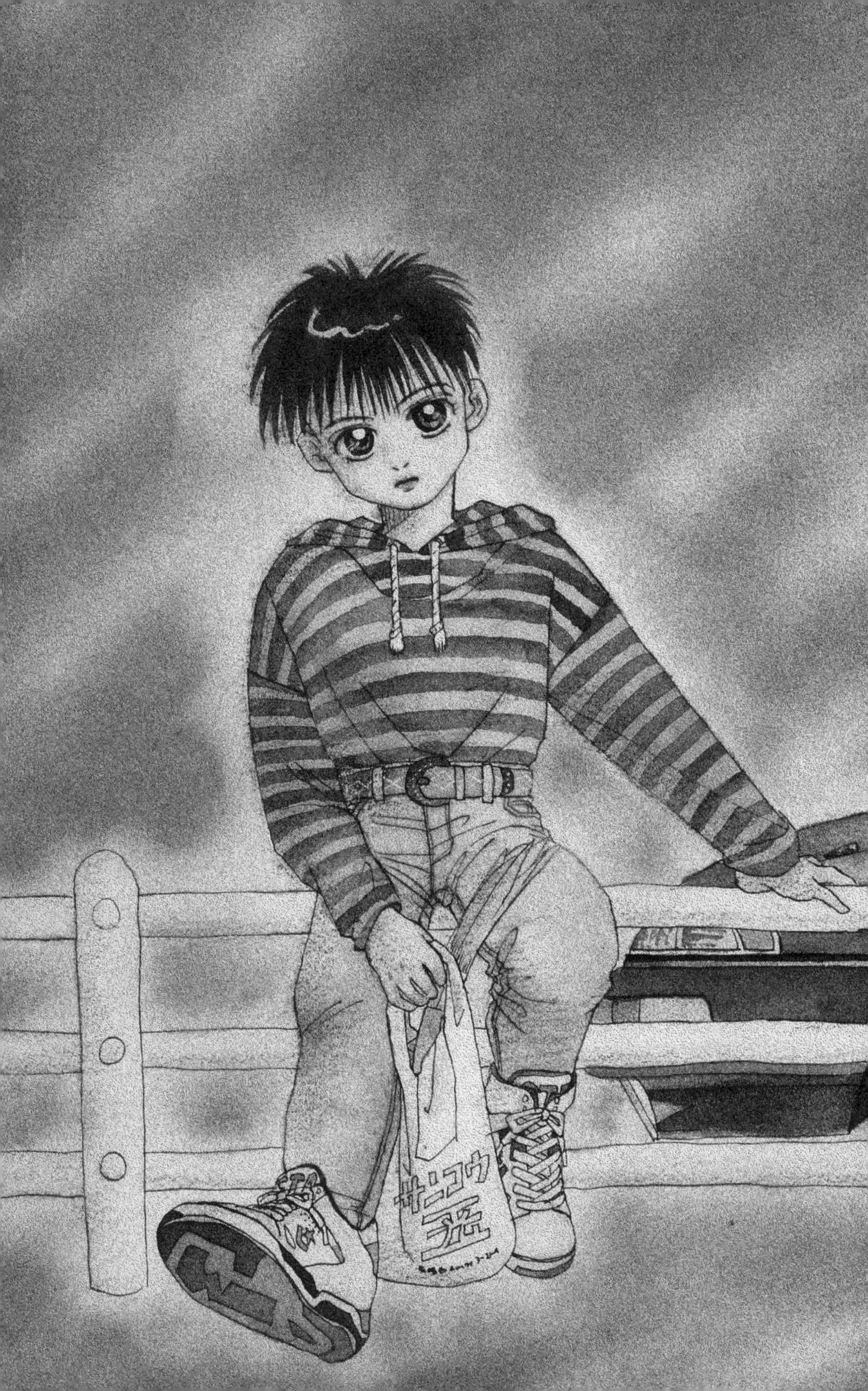
サンコウ

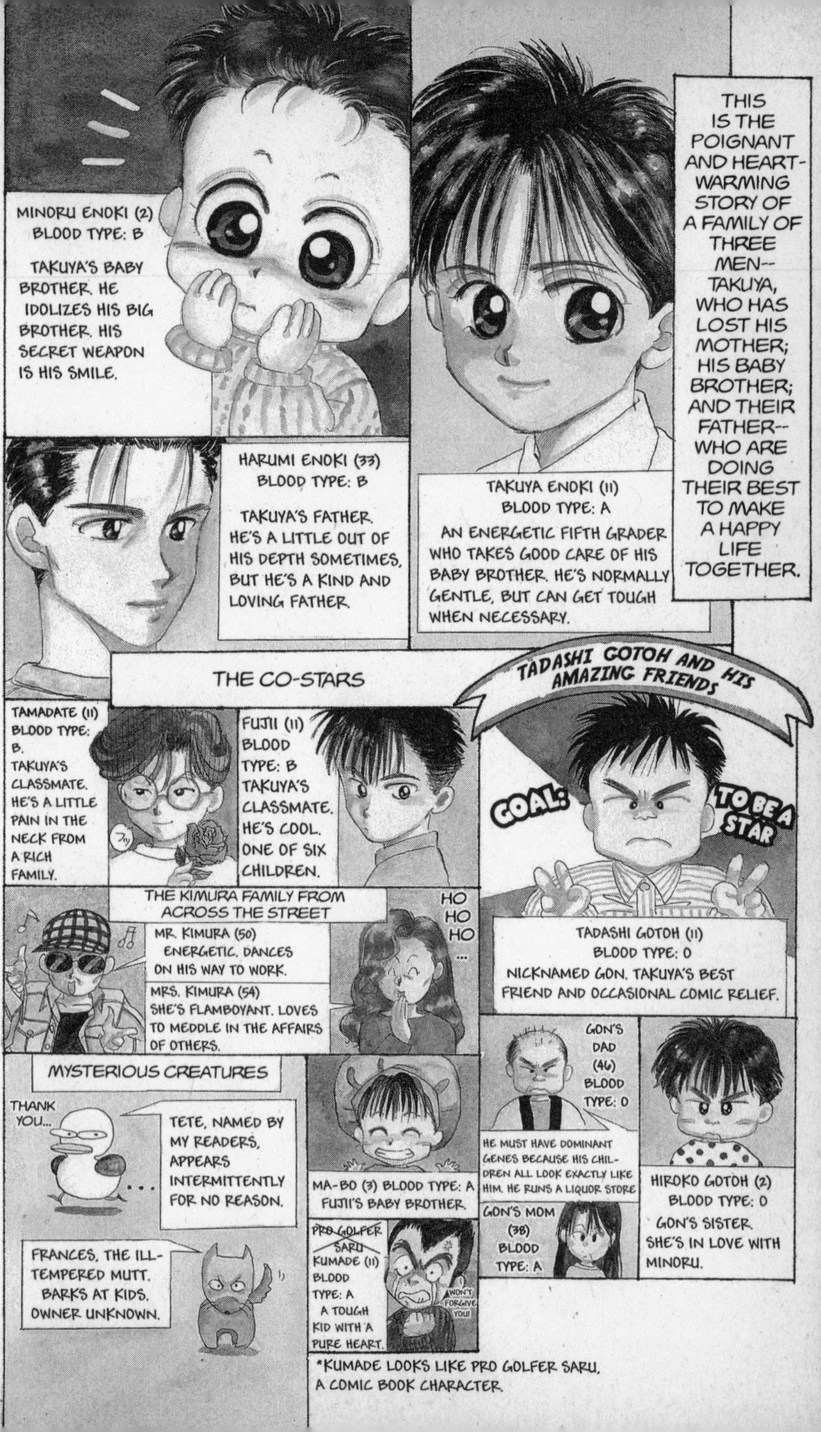
THIS IS THE POIGNANT AND HEART-WARMING STORY OF A FAMILY OF THREE MEN--TAKUYA, WHO HAS LOST HIS MOTHER; HIS BABY BROTHER; AND THEIR FATHER--WHO ARE DOING THEIR BEST TO MAKE A HAPPY LIFE TOGETHER.
TAKUYA ENOKI (11) BLOOD TYPE: A
AN ENERGETIC FIFTH GRADER WHO TAKES GOOD CARE OF HIS BABY BROTHER. HE'S NORMALLY GENTLE, BUT CAN GET TOUGH WHEN NECESSARY.
MINORU ENOKI (2) BLOOD TYPE: B
TAKUYA'S BABY BROTHER. HE IDOLIZES HIS BIG BROTHER. HIS SECRET WEAPON IS HIS SMILE.
HARUMI ENOKI (33) BLOOD TYPE: B
TAKUYA'S FATHER. HE'S A LITTLE OUT OF HIS DEPTH SOMETIMES, BUT HE'S A KIND AND LOVING FATHER.
TADASHI GOTOH AND HIS AMAZING FRIENDS
THE CO-STARS
GOAL: TO BE A STAR
TADASHI GOTOH (11) BLOOD TYPE: O
NICKNAMED GON. TAKUYA'S BEST FRIEND AND OCCASIONAL COMIC RELIEF.
FUJII (11) BLOOD TYPE: B TAKUYA'S CLASSMATE. HE'S COOL. ONE OF SIX CHILDREN.
TAMADATE (11) BLOOD TYPE: B. TAKUYA'S CLASSMATE. HE'S A LITTLE PAIN IN THE NECK FROM A RICH FAMILY.
THE KIMURA FAMILY FROM ACROSS THE STREET
HO HO HO ...
MR. KIMURA (50) ENERGETIC. DANCES ON HIS WAY TO WORK.
MRS. KIMURA (54) SHE'S FLAMBOYANT. LOVES TO MEDDLE IN THE AFFAIRS OF OTHERS.
HIROKO GOTOH (2) BLOOD TYPE: O
GON'S SISTER. SHE'S IN LOVE WITH MINORU.
GON'S DAD (46) BLOOD TYPE: O
HE MUST HAVE DOMINANT GENES BECAUSE HIS CHILDREN ALL LOOK EXACTLY LIKE HIM. HE RUNS A LIQUOR STORE
GON'S MOM (38) BLOOD TYPE: A
MA-BO (3) BLOOD TYPE: A FUJII'S BABY BROTHER.
PRO GOLFER SARU KUMADE (11) BLOOD TYPE: A A TOUGH KID WITH A PURE HEART.
WON'T FORGIVE YOU!
MYSTERIOUS CREATURES
THANK YOU...
TETE, NAMED BY MY READERS, APPEARS INTERMITTENTLY FOR NO REASON.
...
FRANCES, THE ILL-TEMPERED MUTT. BARKS AT KIDS. OWNER UNKNOWN.
*KUMADE LOOKS LIKE PRO GOLFER SARU, A COMIC BOOK CHARACTER.

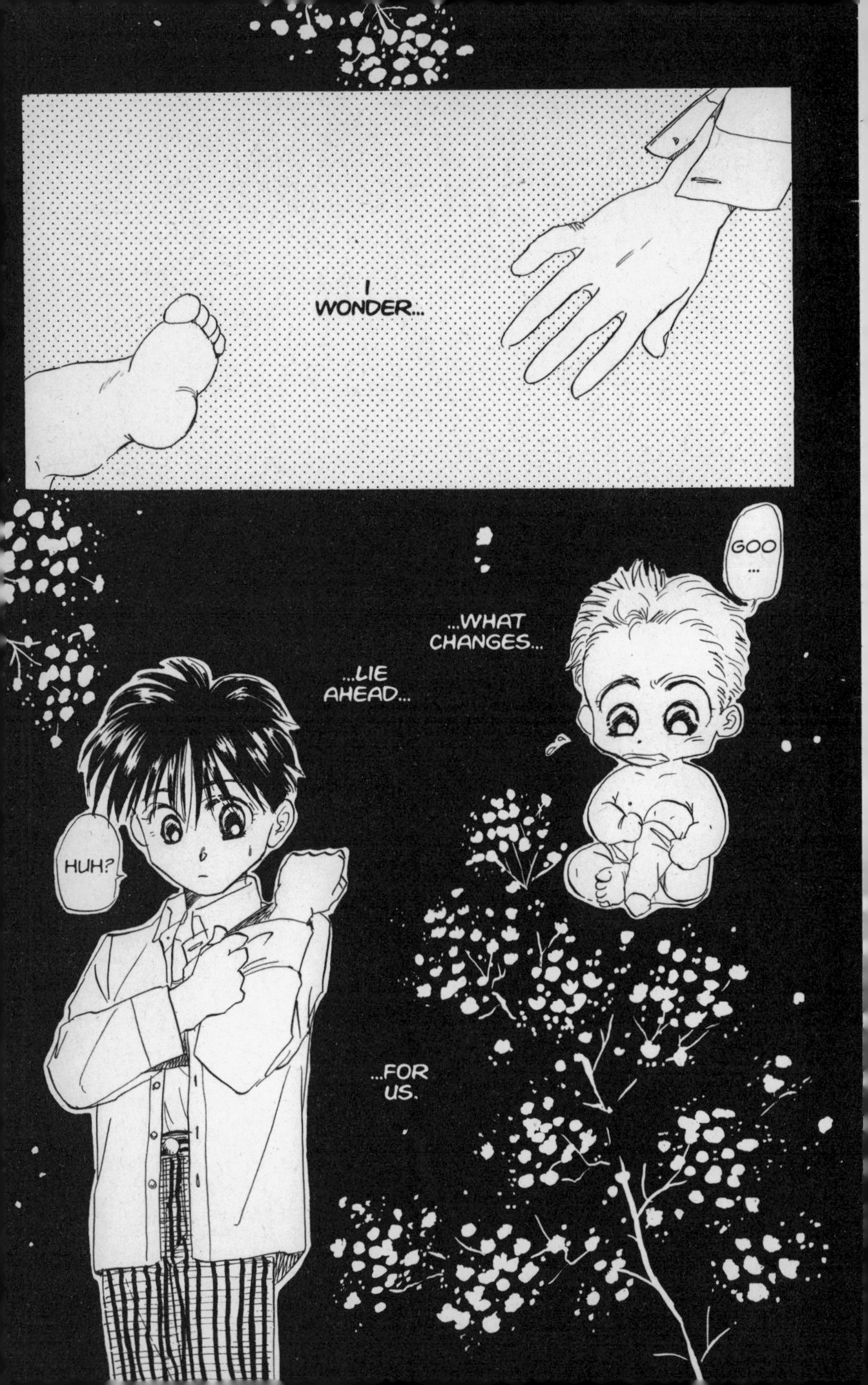
I WONDER...
GOO ...
...WHAT CHANGES...
...LIE AHEAD...
HUH?
...FOR US.

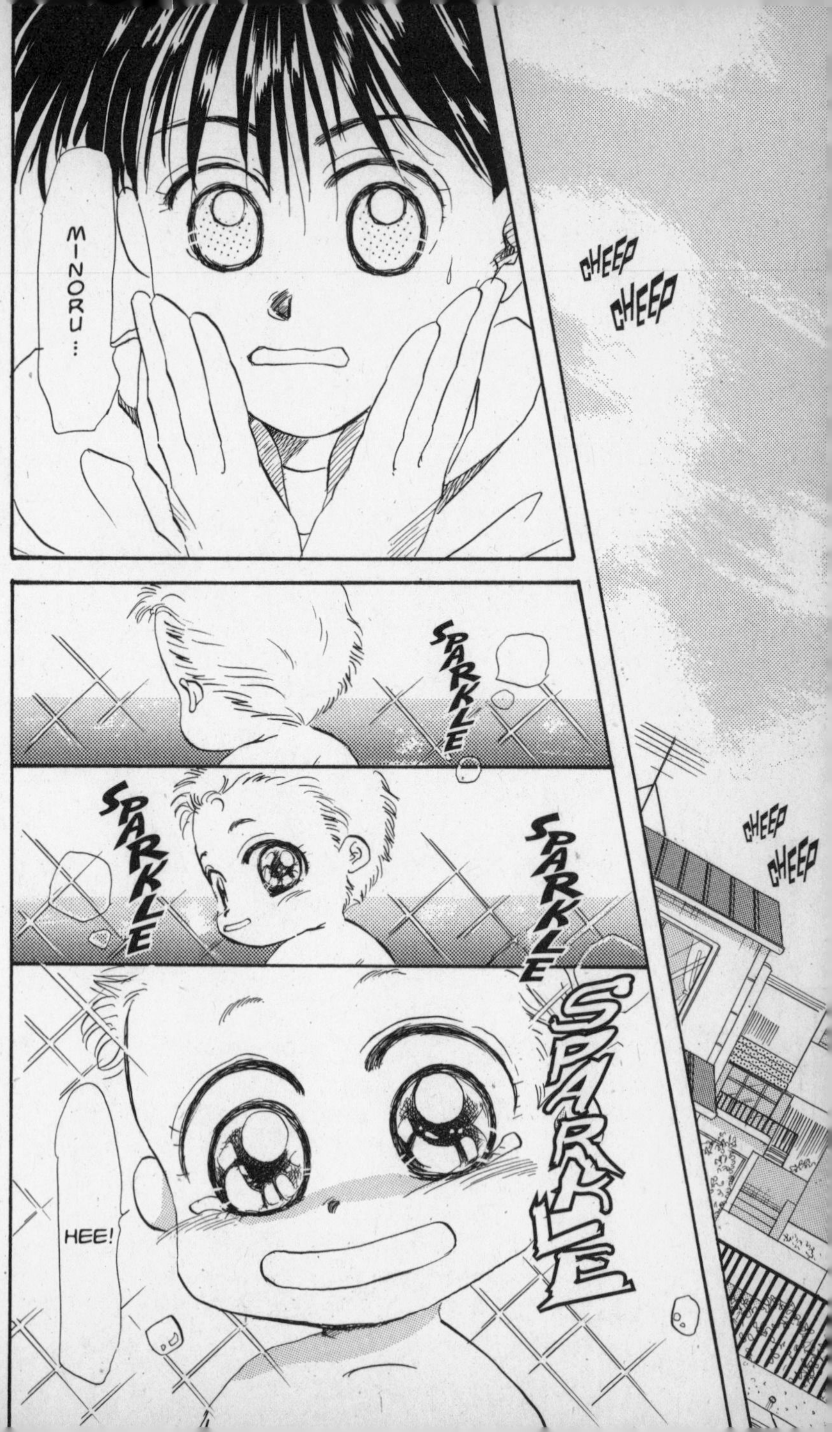
CHEEP CHEEP
MINORU...
SPARKLE
SPARKLE
SPARKLE
CHEEP CHEEP
SPARKLE
HEE!

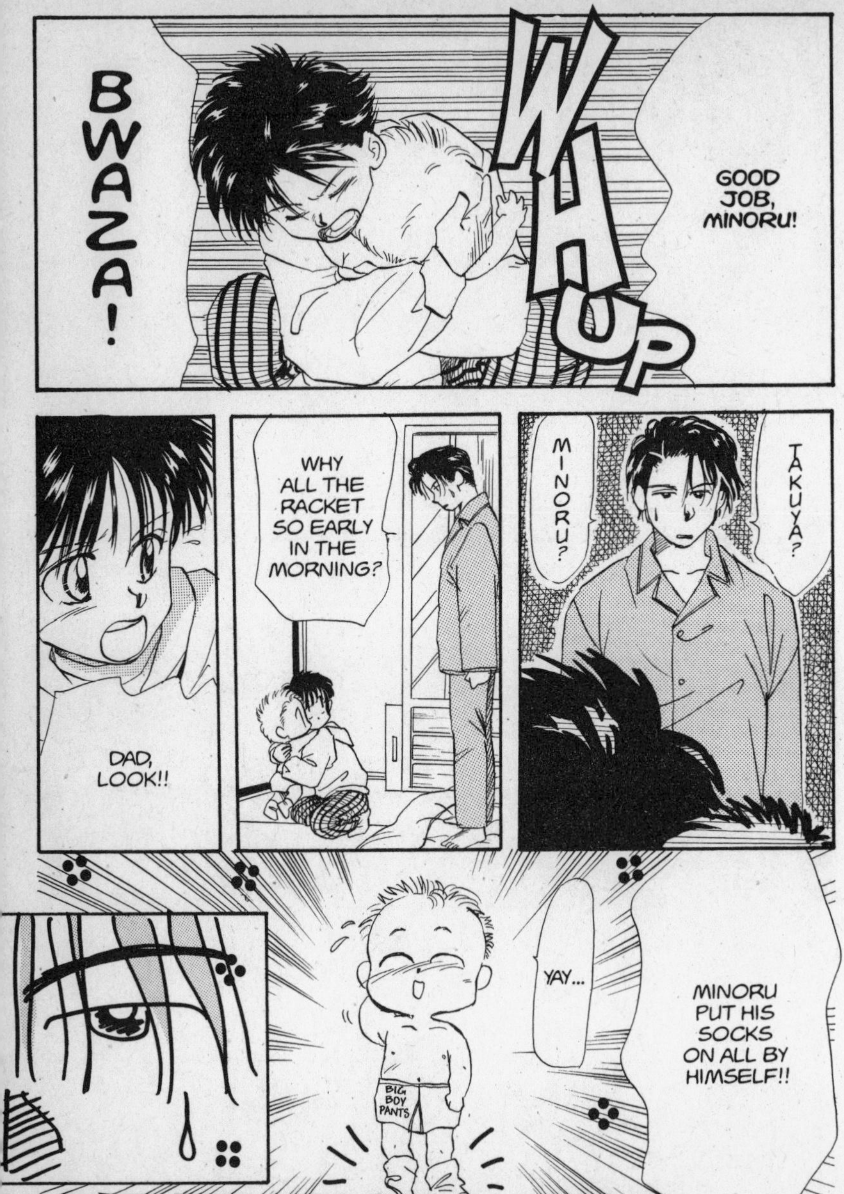
GOOD JOB, MINORU!
WAH UP
BWAZA!
TAKUYA?
MINORU?
WHY ALL THE RACKET SO EARLY IN THE MORNING?
DAD, LOOK!!
MINORU PUT HIS SOCKS ON ALL BY HIMSELF!!
YAY...
BIG BOY PANTS
DUNT DUNT-DA-DUM!

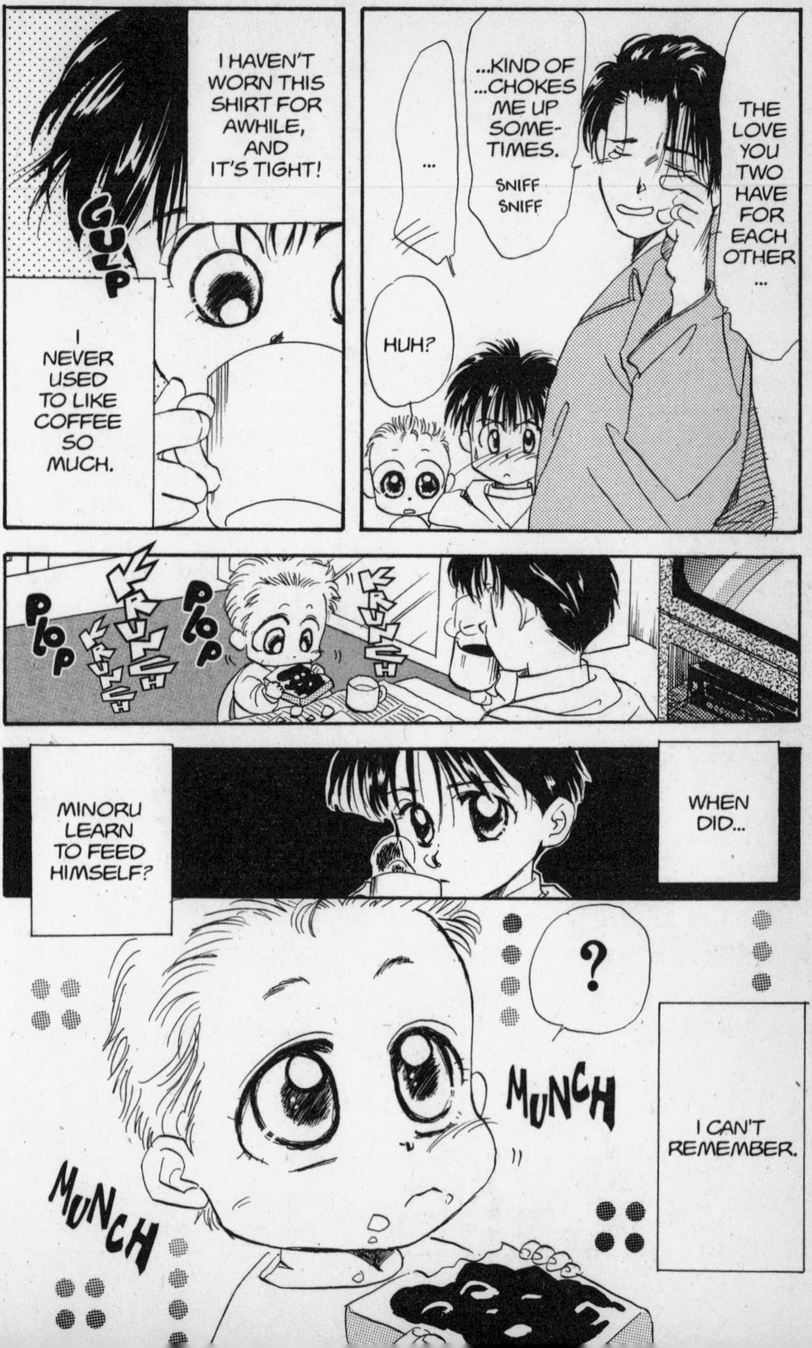
THE LOVE YOU TWO HAVE FOR EACH OTHER...
...KIND OF ...CHOKES ME UP SOME-TIMES.
SNIFF SNIFF
...
HUH?
I HAVEN'T WORN THIS SHIRT FOR AWHILE, AND IT'S TIGHT!
GULP
I NEVER USED TO LIKE COFFEE SO MUCH.
KRUNCH
PLOP
KRUNCH
KRUNCH
PLOP
WHEN DID...
MINORU LEARN TO FEED HIMSELF?
?
I CAN'T REMEMBER.
MUNCH
MUNCH

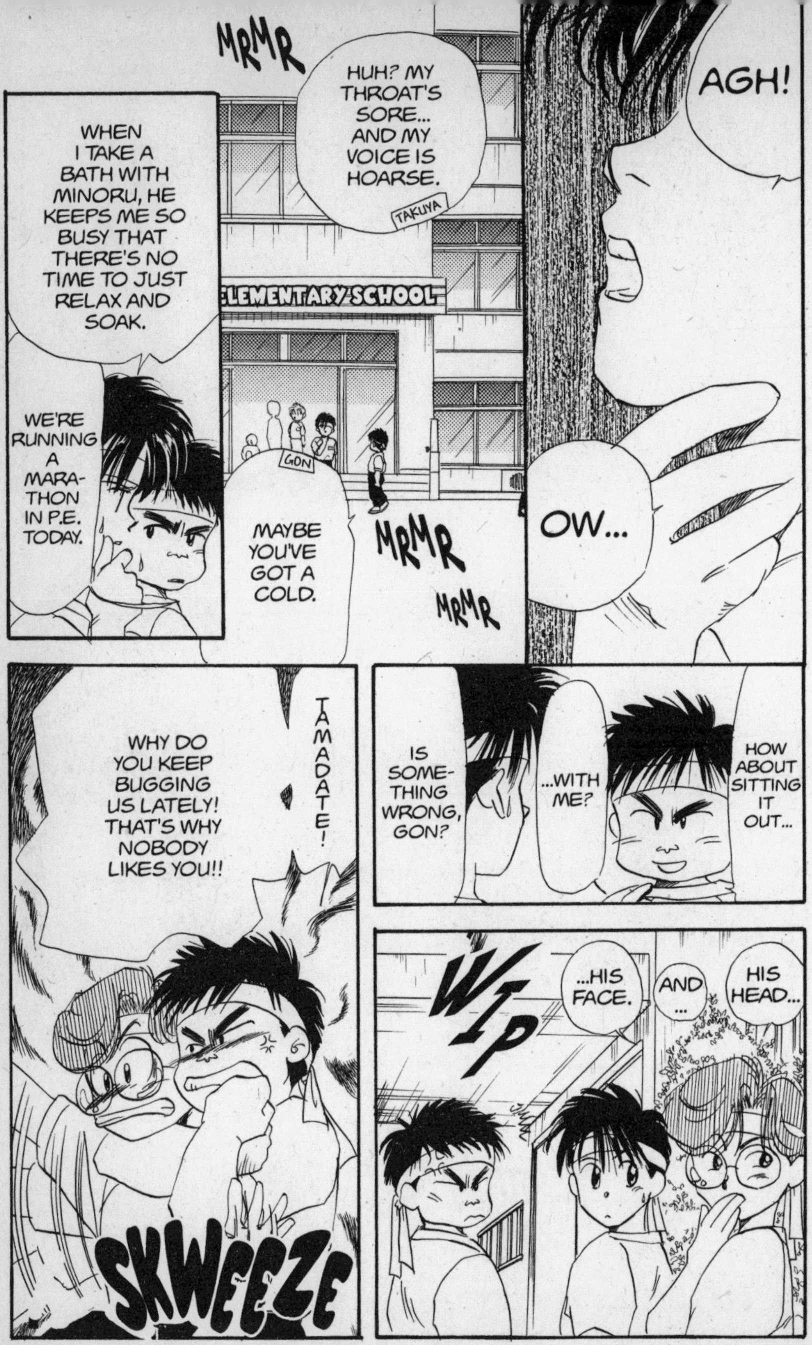
AGH!
OW...
MRMR
HUH? MY THROAT'S SORE... AND MY VOICE IS HOARSE.
TAKUYA
ELEMENTARY SCHOOL
GON
MAYBE YOU'VE GOT A COLD.
MRMR
MRMR
WHEN I TAKE A BATH WITH MINORU, HE KEEPS ME SO BUSY THAT THERE'S NO TIME TO JUST RELAX AND SOAK.
WE'RE RUNNING A MARATHON IN P.E. TODAY.
HOW ABOUT SITTING IT OUT...
...WITH ME?
IS SOMETHING WRONG, GON?
HIS HEAD...
AND...
...HIS FACE.
WIP
TAMADATE!
WHY DO YOU KEEP BUGGING US LATELY! THAT'S WHY NOBODY LIKES YOU!!
SKWEEZE

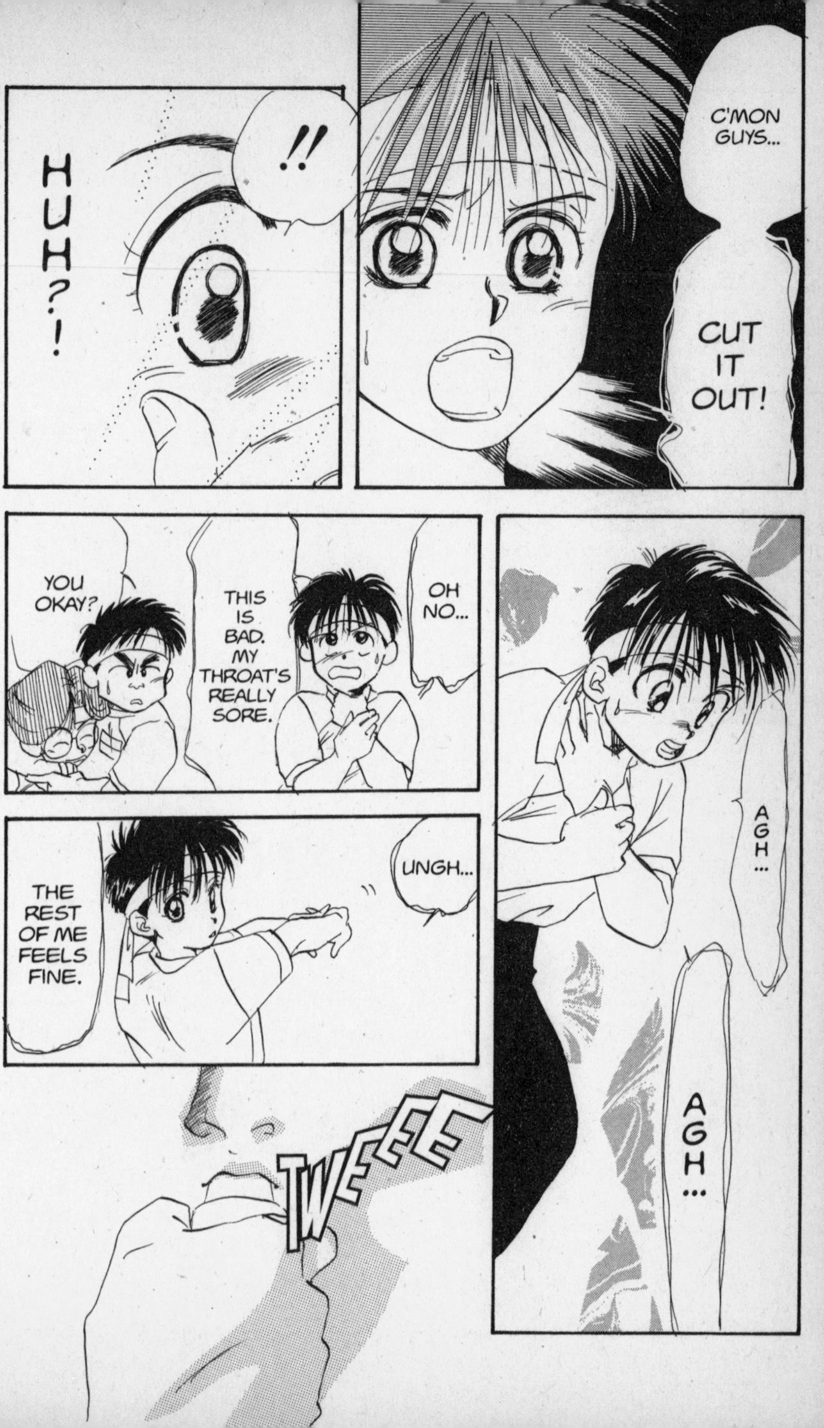
C'MON GUYS...
CUT IT OUT!
!!
HUH?!
AGH...
AGH...
OH NO...
THIS IS BAD. MY THROAT'S REALLY SORE.
YOU OKAY?
UNGH...
THE REST OF ME FEELS FINE.
TWEEEE

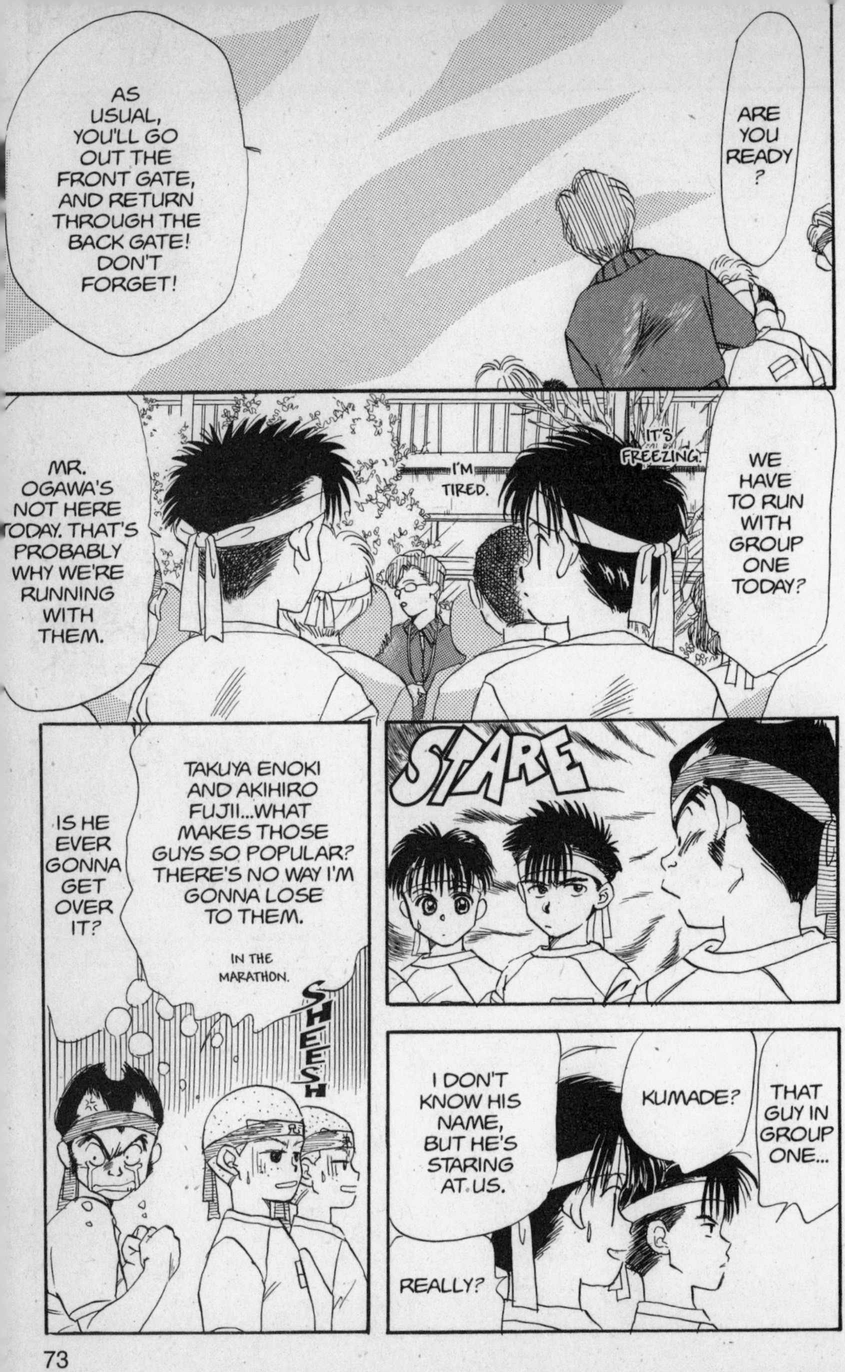
ARE YOU READY?
AS USUAL, YOU'LL GO OUT THE FRONT GATE, AND RETURN THROUGH THE BACK GATE! DON'T FORGET!
WE HAVE TO RUN WITH GROUP ONE TODAY?
IT'S FREEZING.
I'M TIRED.
MR. OGAWA'S NOT HERE TODAY. THAT'S PROBABLY WHY WE'RE RUNNING WITH THEM.
STARE
THAT GUY IN GROUP ONE...
KUMADE?
I DON'T KNOW HIS NAME, BUT HE'S STARING AT US.
REALLY?
TAKUYA ENOKI AND AKIHIRO FUJII...WHAT MAKES THOSE GUYS SO POPULAR? THERE'S NO WAY I'M GONNA LOSE TO THEM.
IN THE MARATHON.
IS HE EVER GONNA GET OVER IT?
SHEESH

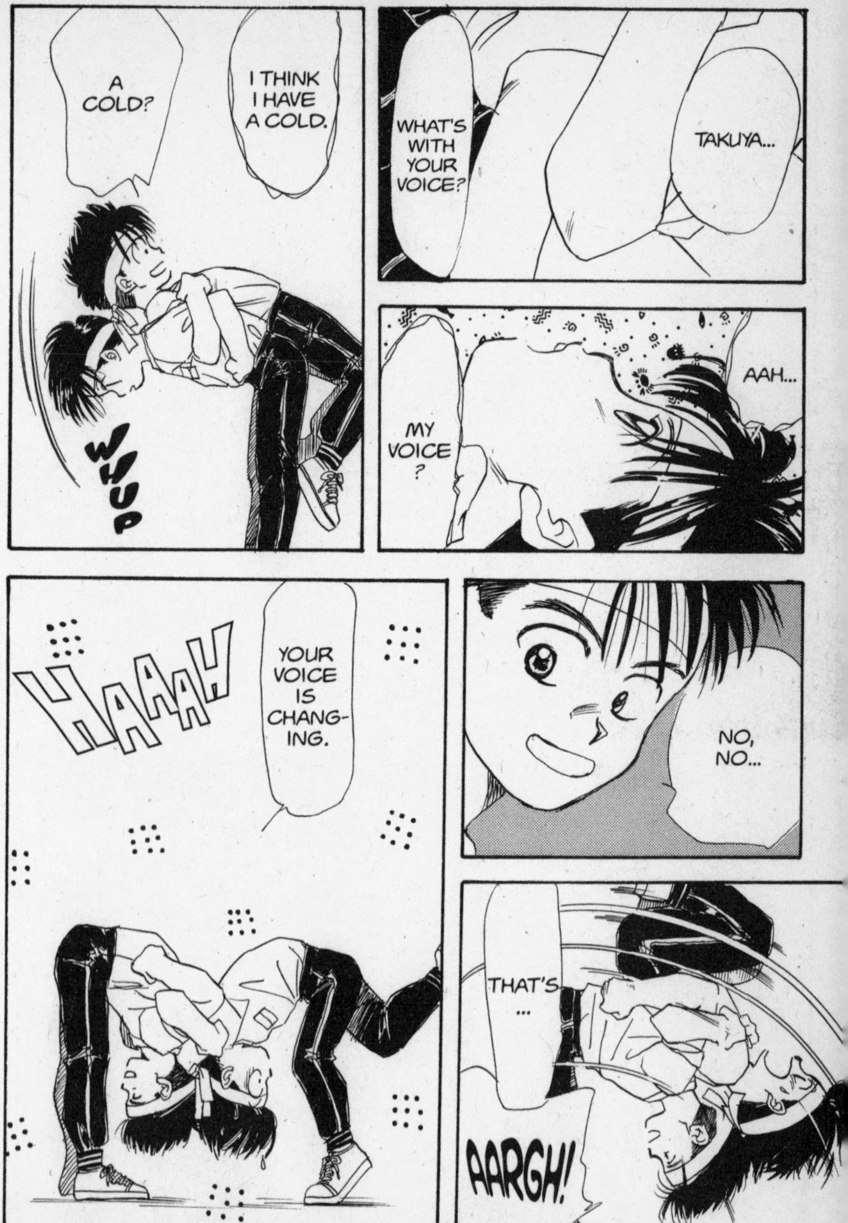
TAKUYA...
WHAT'S WITH YOUR VOICE?
AAH...
MY VOICE?
I THINK I HAVE A COLD.
A COLD?
WHUP
NO, NO...
THAT'S...
AARGH!
YOUR VOICE IS CHANG-ING.
HAAAAH

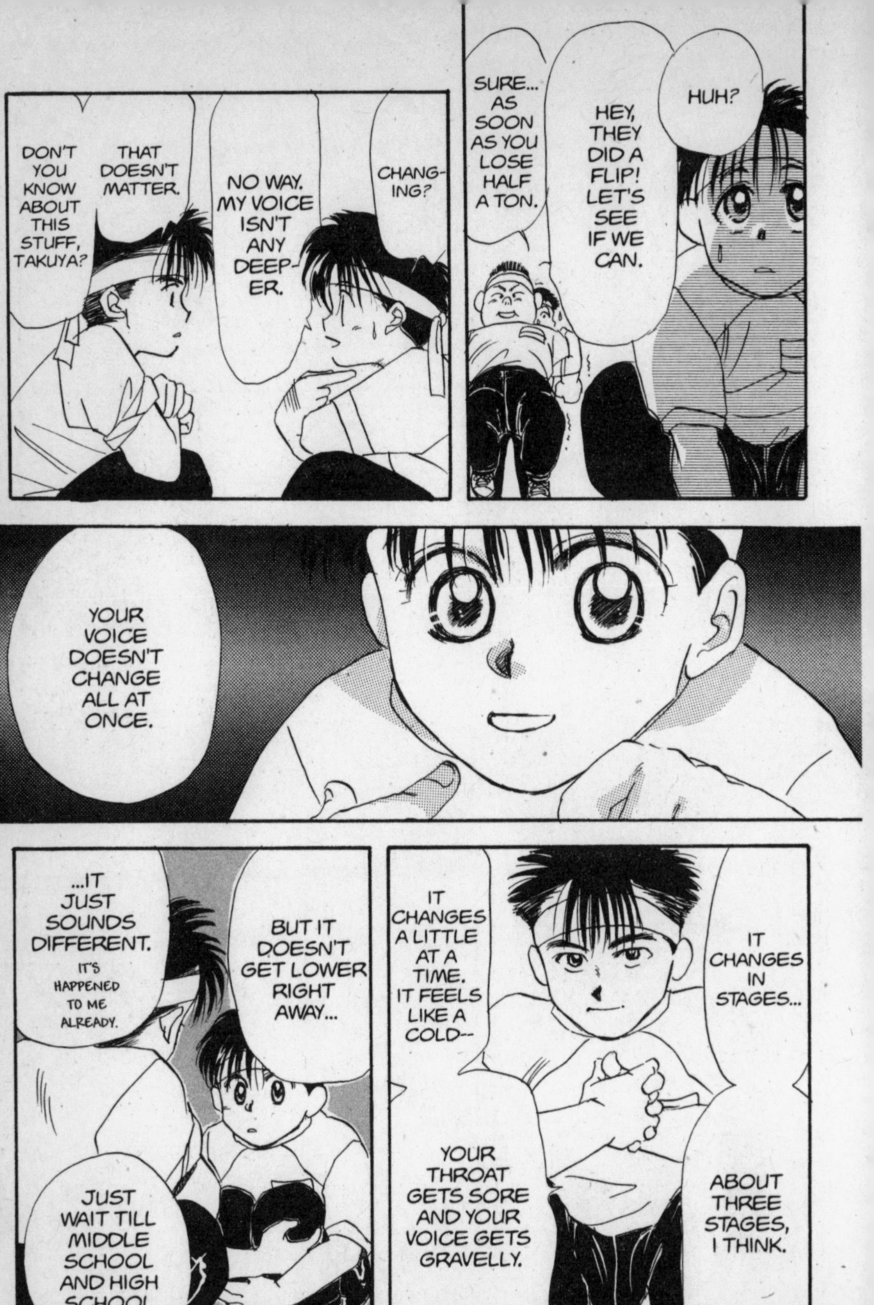
HUH?
HEY, THEY DID A FLIP! LET'S SEE IF WE CAN.
SURE... AS SOON AS YOU LOSE HALF A TON.
CHANGING?
NO WAY. MY VOICE ISN'T ANY DEEPER.
THAT DOESN'T MATTER.
DON'T YOU KNOW ABOUT THIS STUFF, TAKUYA?
YOUR VOICE DOESN'T CHANGE ALL AT ONCE.
IT CHANGES IN STAGES...
IT CHANGES A LITTLE AT A TIME. IT FEELS LIKE A COLD--
ABOUT THREE STAGES, I THINK.
YOUR THROAT GETS SORE AND YOUR VOICE GETS GRAVELLY.
BUT IT DOESN'T GET LOWER RIGHT AWAY...
...IT JUST SOUNDS DIFFERENT.
IT'S HAPPENED TO ME ALREADY.
JUST WAIT TILL MIDDLE SCHOOL AND HIGH SCHOOL.

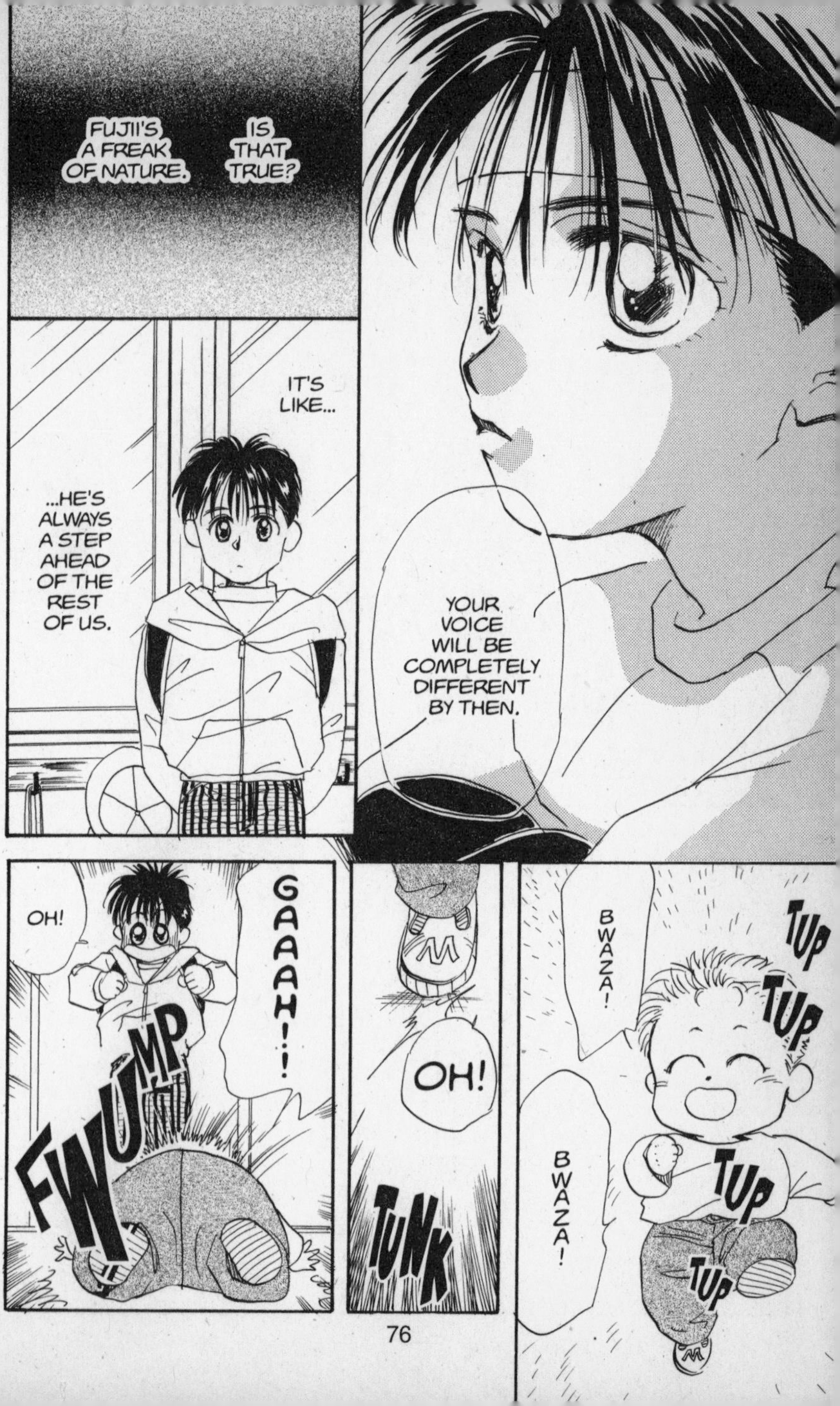
YOUR VOICE WILL BE COMPLETELY DIFFERENT BY THEN.
IS THAT TRUE?
FUJII'S A FREAK OF NATURE.
IT'S LIKE...
...HE'S ALWAYS A STEP AHEAD OF THE REST OF US.
TUP TUP
BWAZA!
BWAZA!
TUP TUP
OH!
TUNK
GAAAAH!!!
OH!
FWUMP

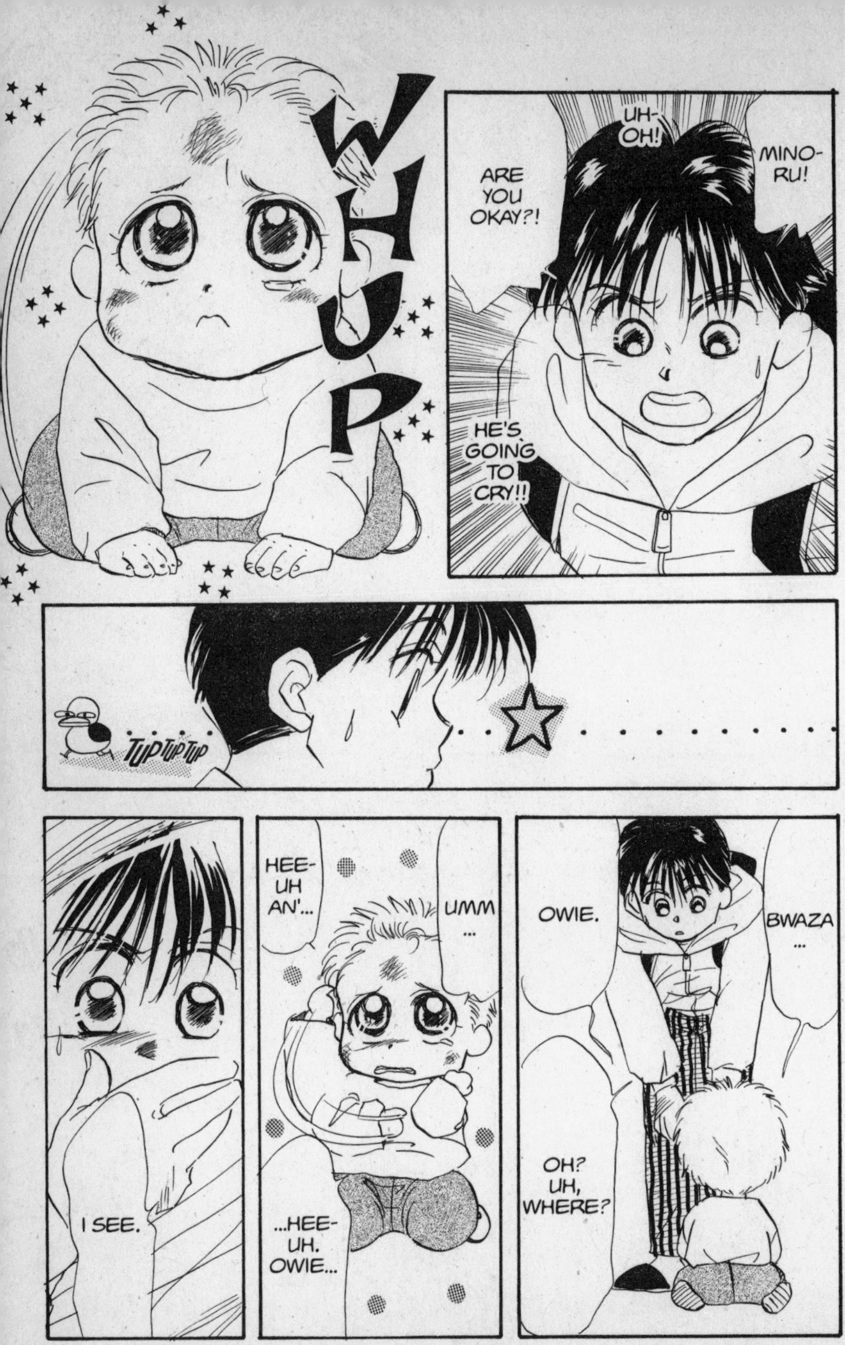
UH-OH!
MINO-RU!
ARE YOU OKAY?!
HE'S GOING TO CRY!!
WHUP
TUP TUP TUP
BWAZA ...
OWIE.
OH? UH, WHERE?
UMM ...
HEE-UH AN'...
...HEE-UH. OWIE...
I SEE.

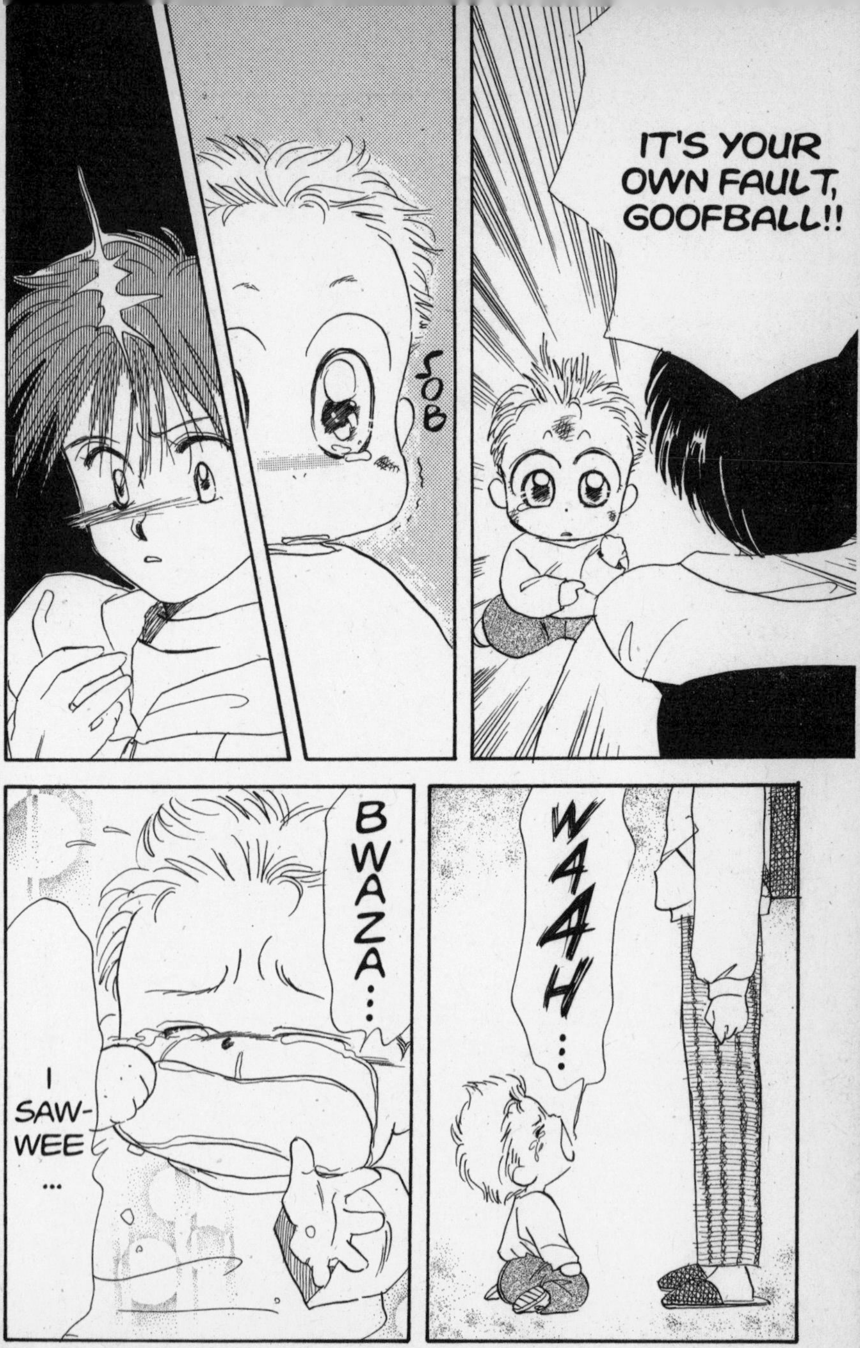
IT'S YOUR OWN FAULT, GOOFBALL!!
SOB
WAAH...
BWAZA...
I SAW-WEE...

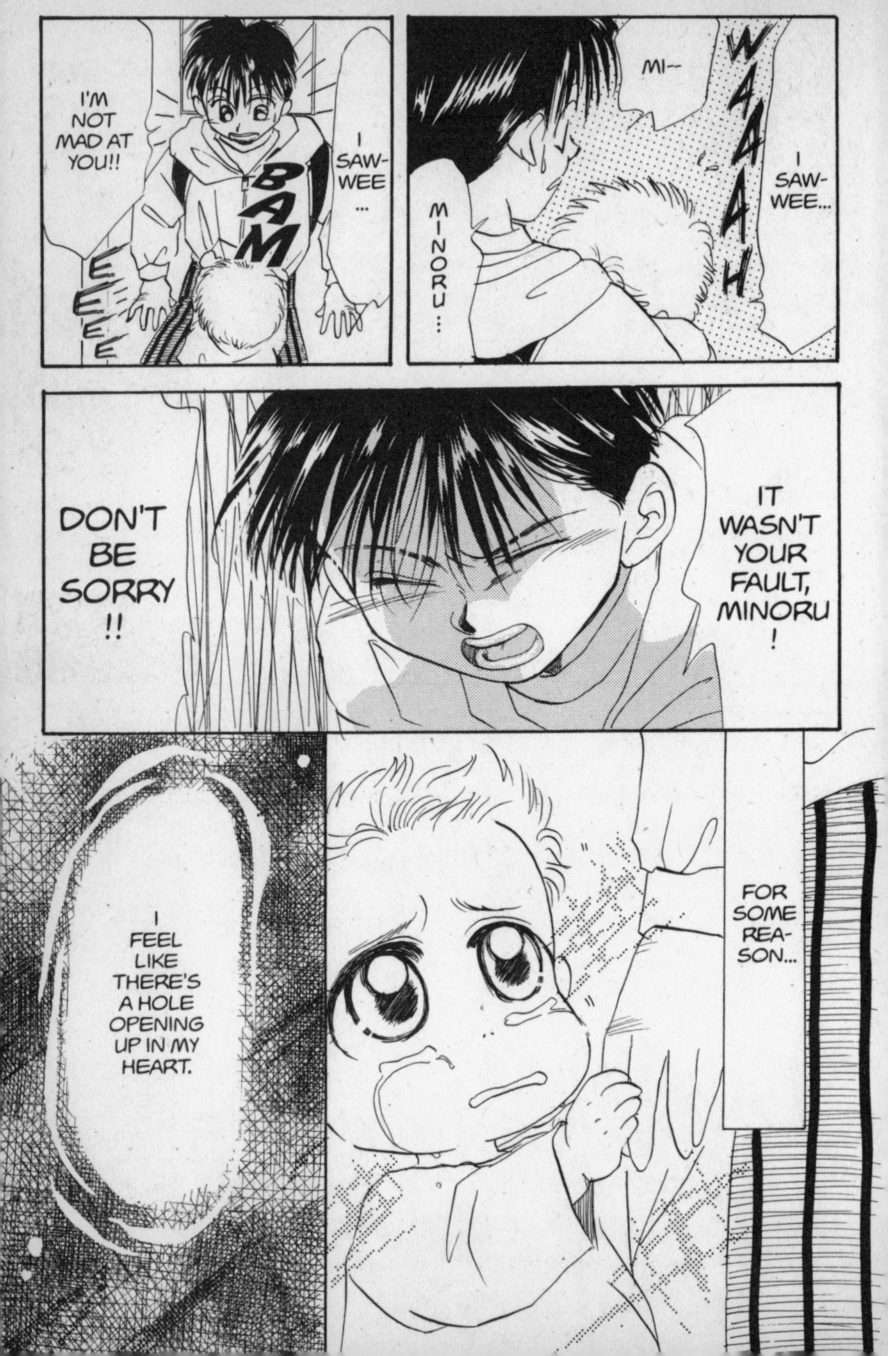
MI--
WAAAH
I SAW-WEE...
MINORU...
I SAW-WEE...
I'M NOT MAD AT YOU!!
BAM
EEEEE
IT WASN'T YOUR FAULT, MINORU!
DON'T BE SORRY!!
FOR SOME REA-SON...
I FEEL LIKE THERE'S A HOLE OPENING UP IN MY HEART.

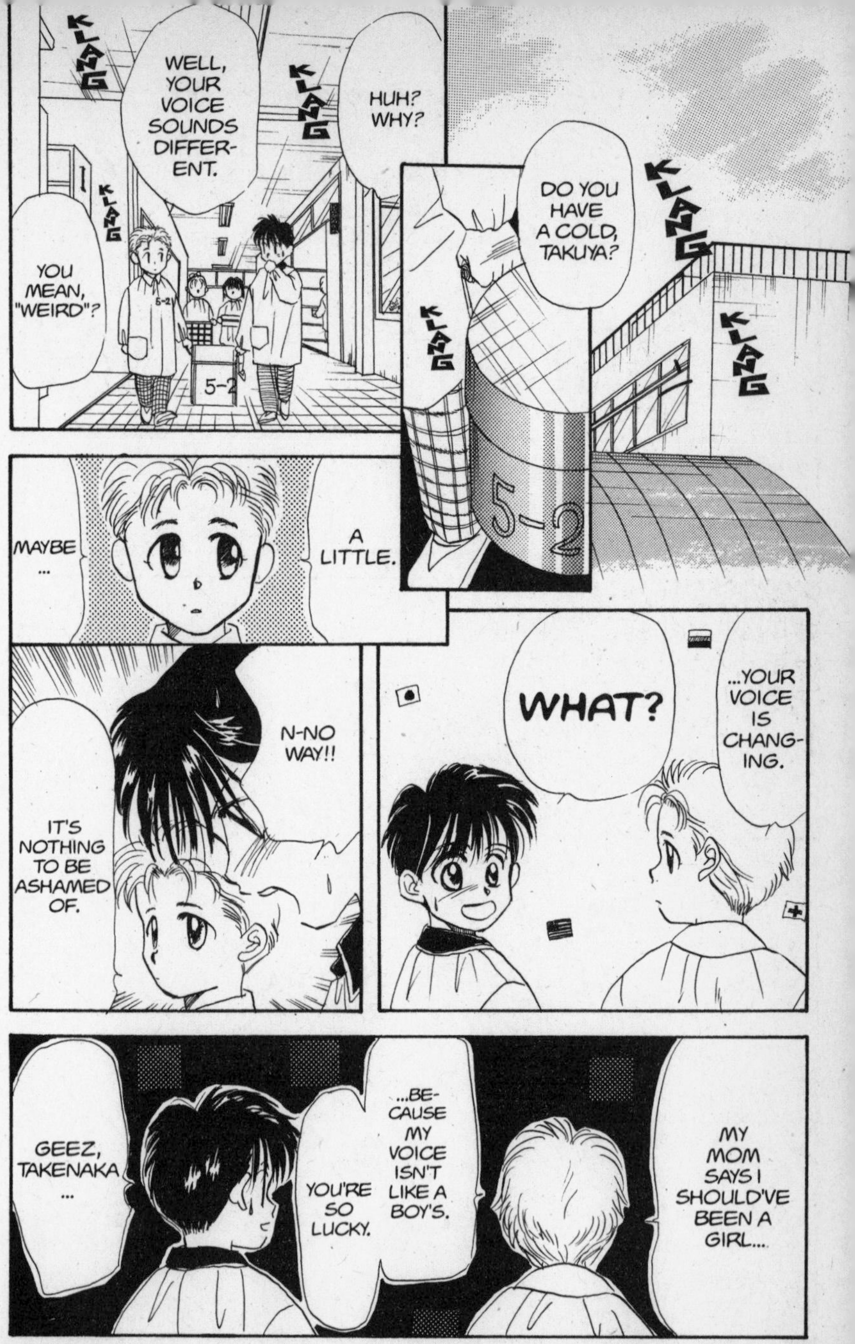
KLANG
KLANG
DO YOU HAVE A COLD, TAKUYA?
KLANG
KLANG
HUH? WHY?
KLANG
WELL, YOUR VOICE SOUNDS DIFFER-ENT.
KLANG
YOU MEAN, "WEIRD"?
MAYBE ...
A LITTLE.
...YOUR VOICE IS CHANG-ING.
WHAT?
N-NO WAY!!
IT'S NOTHING TO BE ASHAMED OF.
MY MOM SAYS I SHOULD'VE BEEN A GIRL...
...BE-CAUSE MY VOICE ISN'T LIKE A BOY'S.
YOU'RE SO LUCKY.
GEEZ, TAKENAKA ...

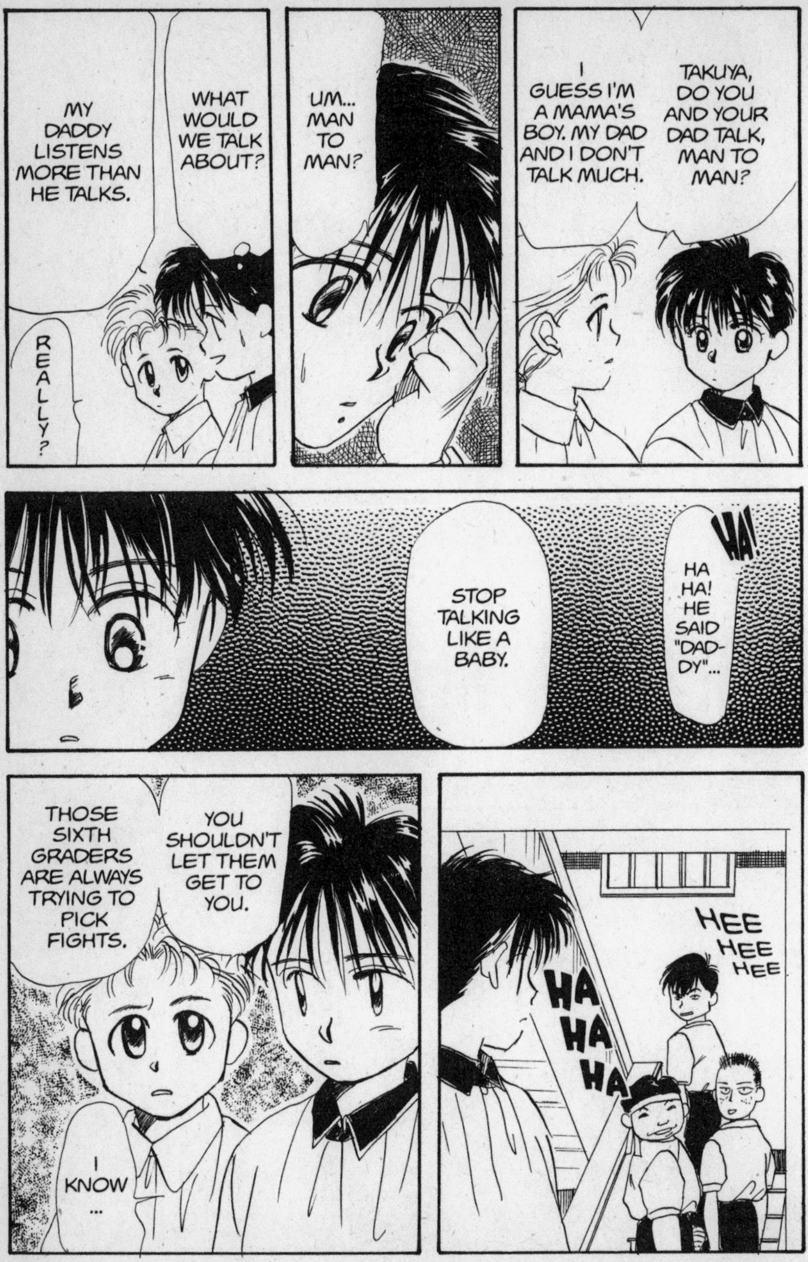
TAKUYA, DO YOU AND YOUR DAD TALK, MAN TO MAN?
I GUESS I'M A MAMA'S BOY. MY DAD AND I DON'T TALK MUCH.
UM... MAN TO MAN?
WHAT WOULD WE TALK ABOUT?
MY DADDY LISTENS MORE THAN HE TALKS.
REALLY?
HA!
HA HA! HE SAID "DAD-DY"...
STOP TALKING LIKE A BABY.
HEE HEE HEE
HA HA HA HA
YOU SHOULDN'T LET THEM GET TO YOU.
THOSE SIXTH GRADERS ARE ALWAYS TRYING TO PICK FIGHTS.
I KNOW ...

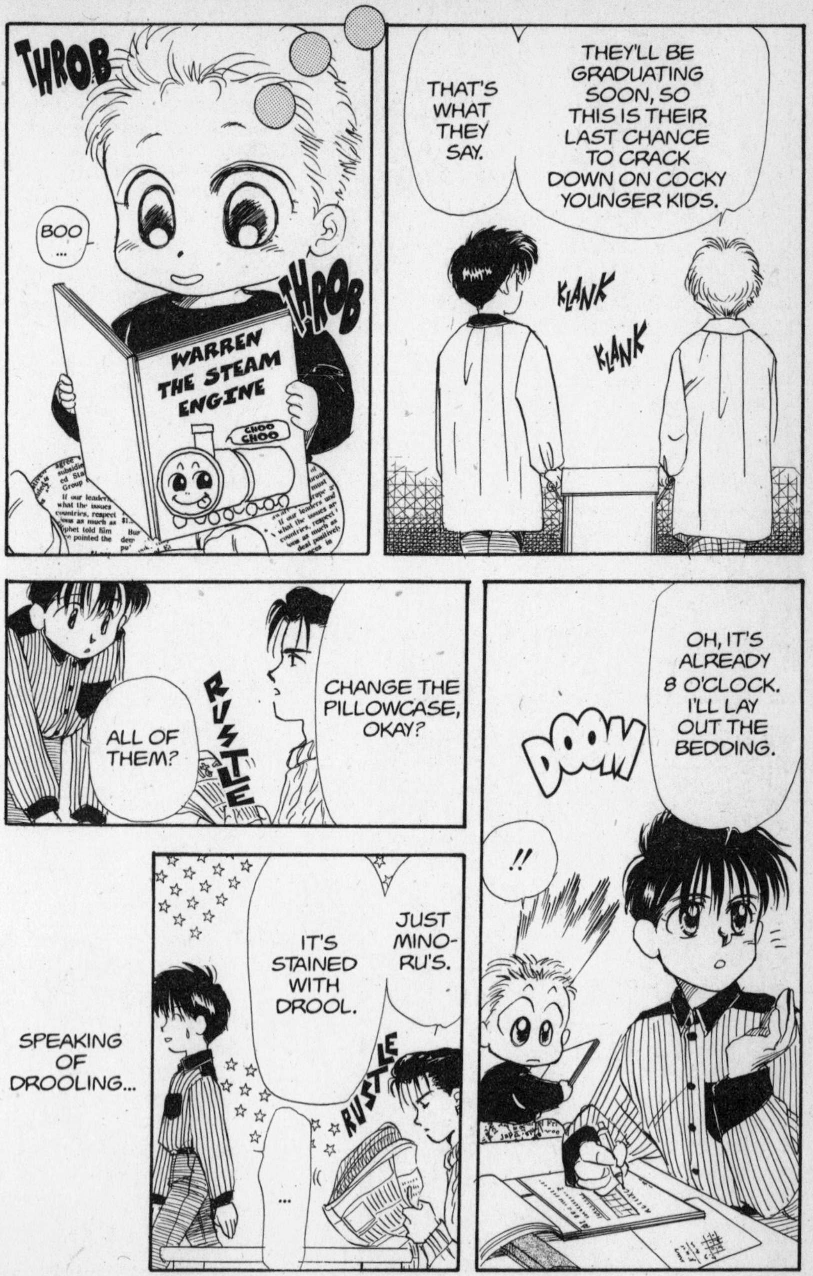

THEY'LL BE GRADUATING SOON, SO THIS IS THEIR LAST CHANCE TO CRACK DOWN ON COCKY YOUNGER KIDS.
THAT'S WHAT THEY SAY.
KLANK
KLANK
THROB
BOO ...
WARREN THE STEAM ENGINE
CHOO CHOO
THROB
OH, IT'S ALREADY 8 O'CLOCK. I'LL LAY OUT THE BEDDING.
DOOM
!!
CHANGE THE PILLOWCASE, OKAY?
RUSTLE
ALL OF THEM?
JUST MINO-RU'S.
IT'S STAINED WITH DROOL.
RUSTLE
...
SPEAKING OF DROOLING...

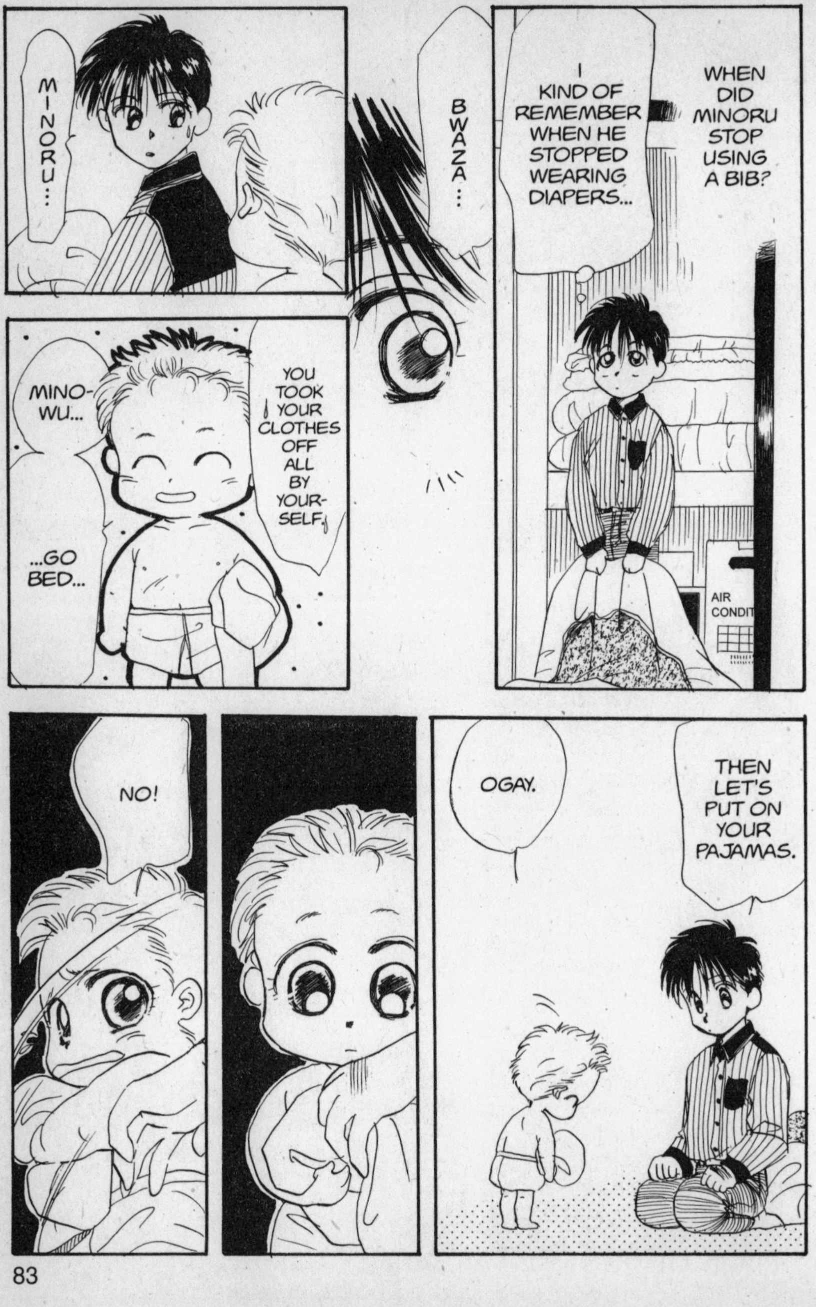

WHEN DID MINORU STOP USING A BIB?
I KIND OF REMEMBER WHEN HE STOPPED WEARING DIAPERS...
AIR CONDIT
BWAZA...
MINORU...
YOU TOOK YOUR CLOTHES OFF ALL BY YOURSELF.
MINO-WU...
...GO BED...
THEN LET'S PUT ON YOUR PAJAMAS.
OGAY.
NO!

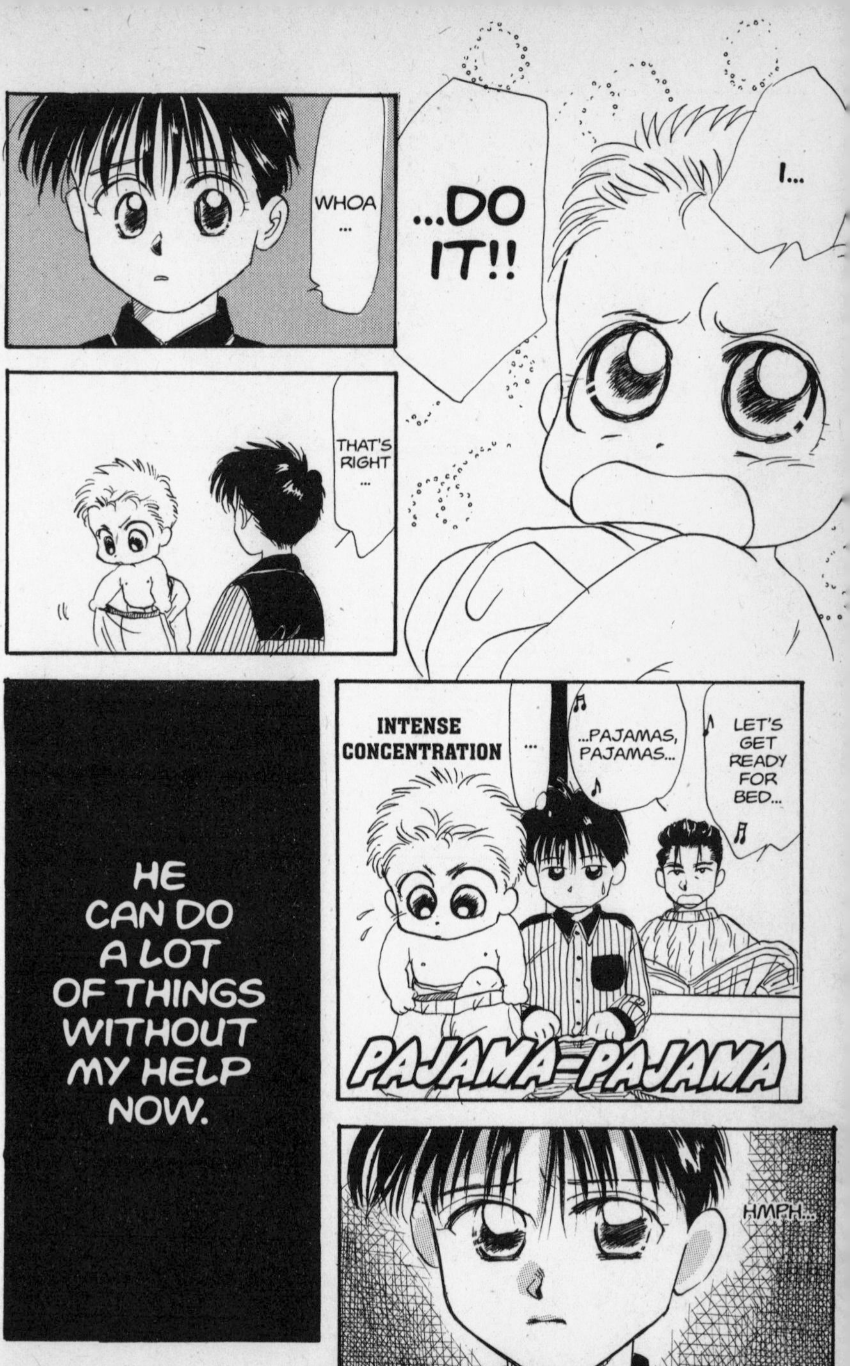
I...
...DO IT!!
WHOA ...
THAT'S RIGHT ...
LET'S GET READY FOR BED...
...PAJAMAS, PAJAMAS...
...
INTENSE CONCENTRATION
PAJAMA-PAJAMA
HMPH...
HE CAN DO A LOT OF THINGS WITHOUT MY HELP NOW.

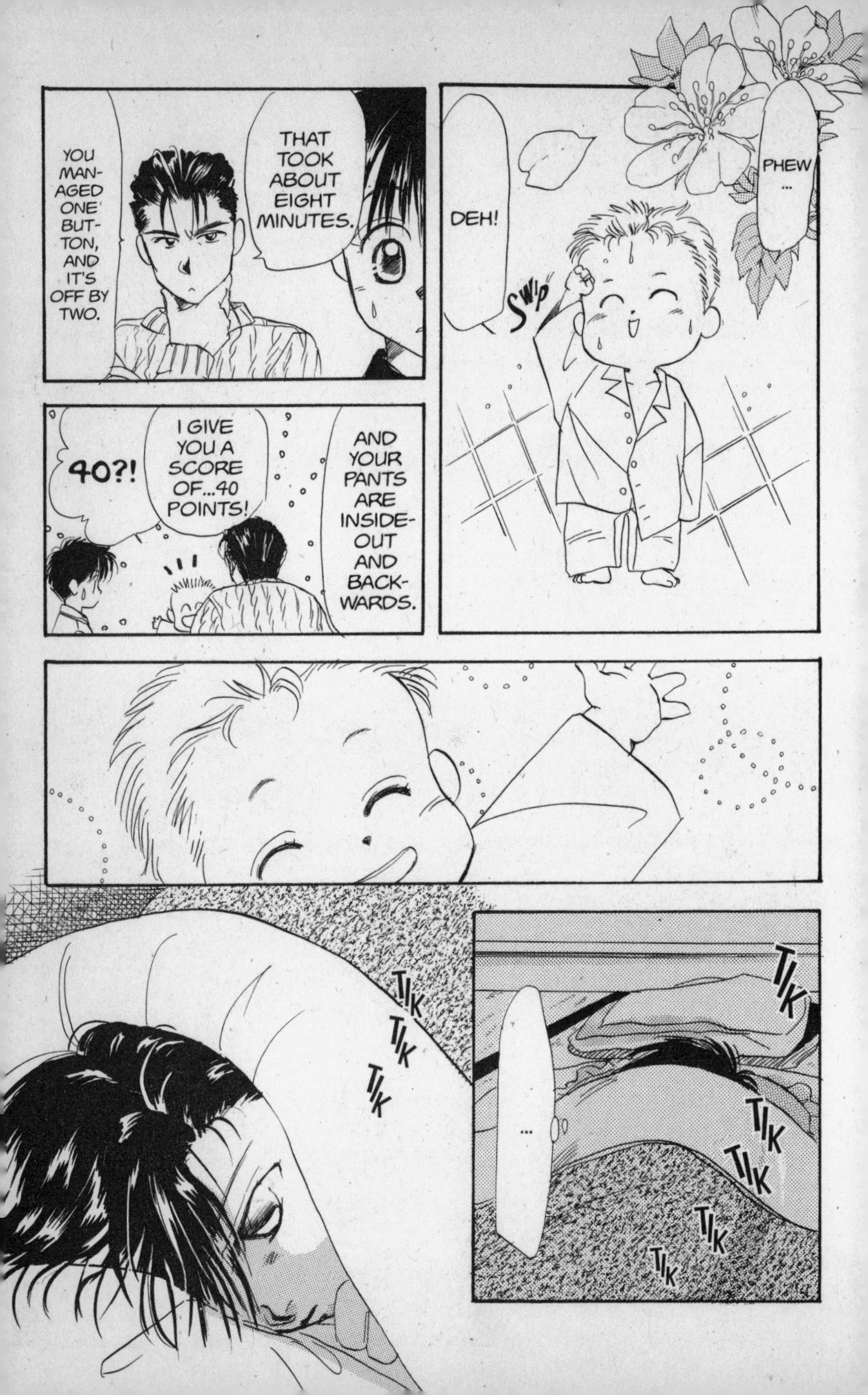
PHEW...
DEH!
SWIP
THAT TOOK ABOUT EIGHT MINUTES.
YOU MANAGED ONE BUTTON, AND IT'S OFF BY TWO.
AND YOUR PANTS ARE INSIDE-OUT AND BACKWARDS.
I GIVE YOU A SCORE OF...40 POINTS!
40?!
TIK TIK TIK TIK
...
TIK TIK TIK

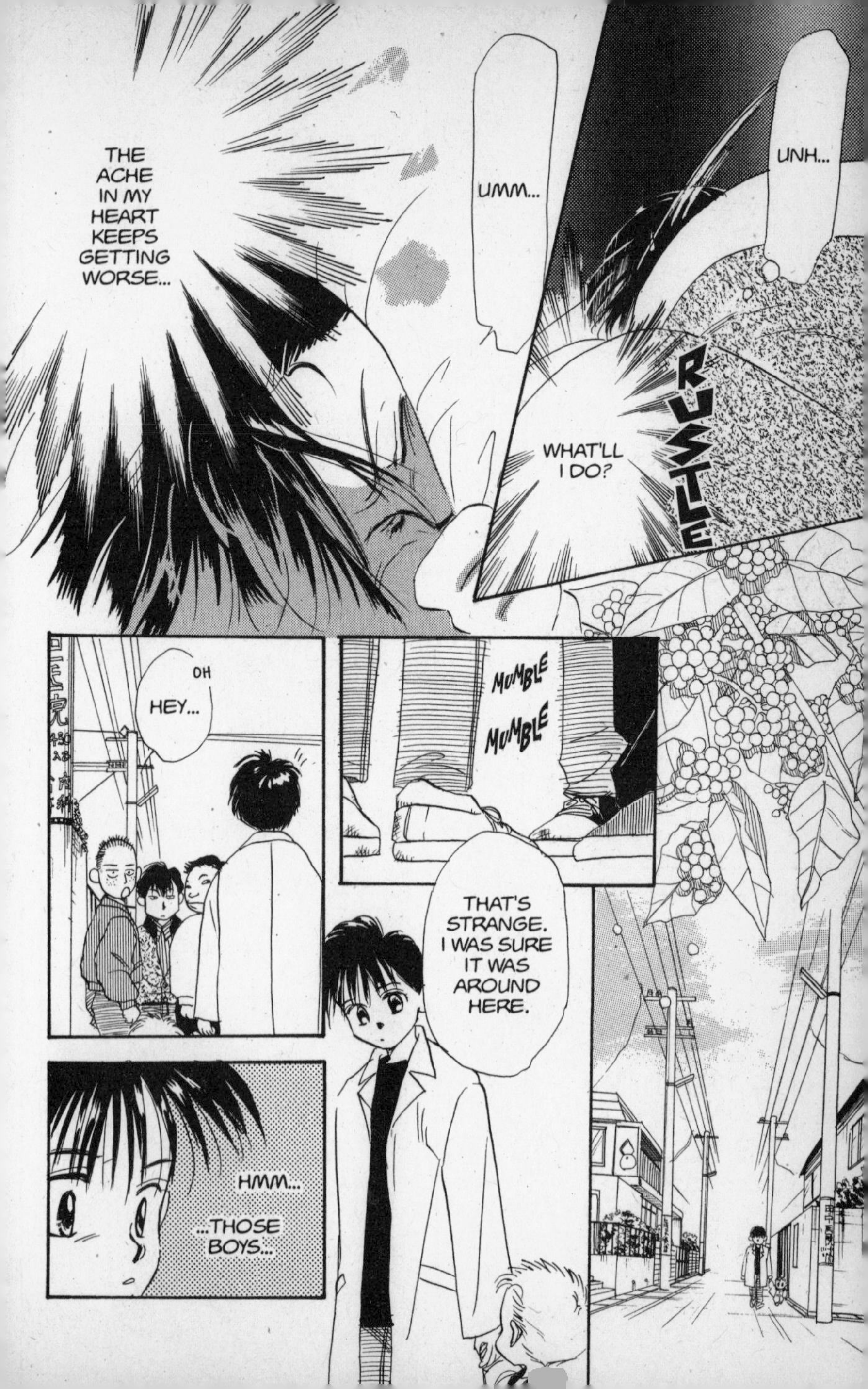
UNH...
RUSTLE
WHAT'LL I DO?
UMM...
THE ACHE IN MY HEART KEEPS GETTING WORSE...
MUMBLE
MUMBLE
OH
HEY...
THAT'S STRANGE. I WAS SURE IT WAS AROUND HERE.
HMM...
...THOSE BOYS...

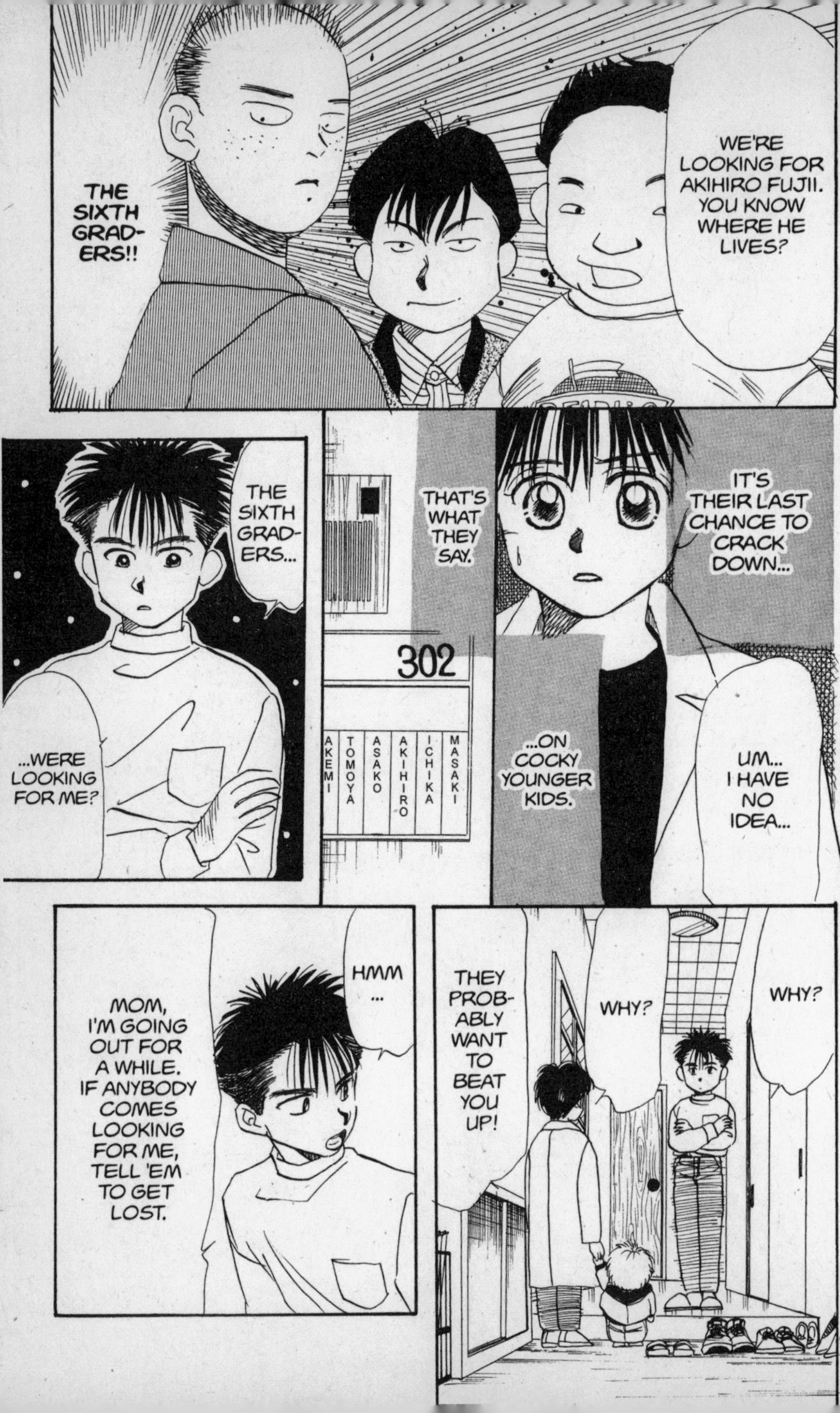
WE'RE LOOKING FOR AKIHIRO FUJII. YOU KNOW WHERE HE LIVES?
THE SIXTH GRAD-ERS!!
UM... I HAVE NO IDEA...
IT'S THEIR LAST CHANCE TO CRACK DOWN...
...ON COCKY YOUNGER KIDS.
THAT'S WHAT THEY SAY.
302
MASAKI
ICHIKA
AKIHIRO
ASAKO
TOMOYA
AKEMI
THE SIXTH GRAD-ERS...
...WERE LOOKING FOR ME?
WHY?
WHY?
THEY PROB-ABLY WANT TO BEAT YOU UP!
HMM ...
MOM, I'M GOING OUT FOR A WHILE. IF ANYBODY COMES LOOKING FOR ME, TELL 'EM TO GET LOST.

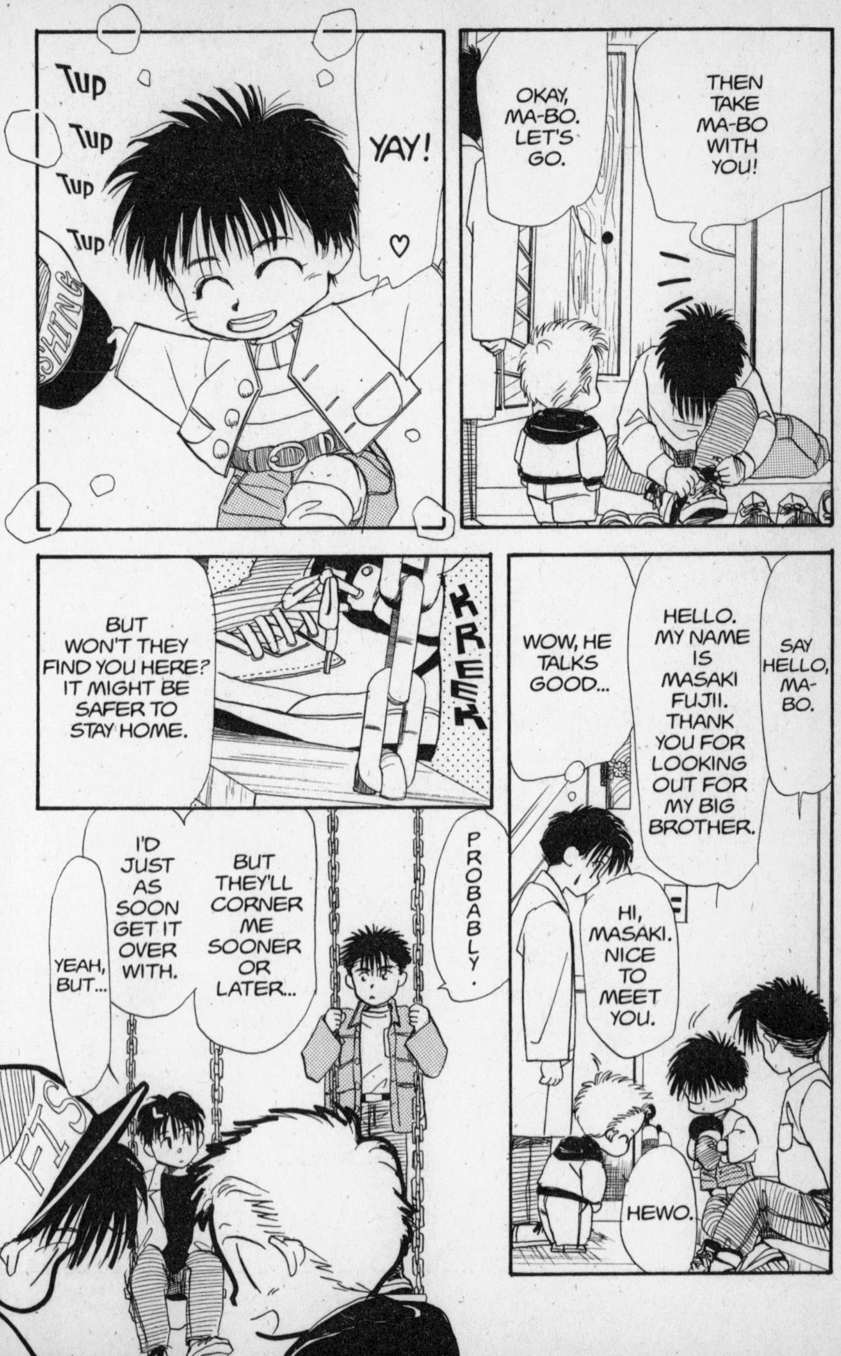
THEN TAKE MA-BO WITH YOU!
OKAY, MA-BO. LET'S GO.
YAY!
Tup
Tup
Tup
Tup
SAY HELLO, MA-BO.
HELLO. MY NAME IS MASAKI FUJII. THANK YOU FOR LOOKING OUT FOR MY BIG BROTHER.
WOW, HE TALKS GOOD...
HI, MASAKI. NICE TO MEET YOU.
HEWO.
KREEK
BUT WON'T THEY FIND YOU HERE? IT MIGHT BE SAFER TO STAY HOME.
PROBABLY.
BUT THEY'LL CORNER ME SOONER OR LATER...
I'D JUST AS SOON GET IT OVER WITH.
YEAH, BUT...

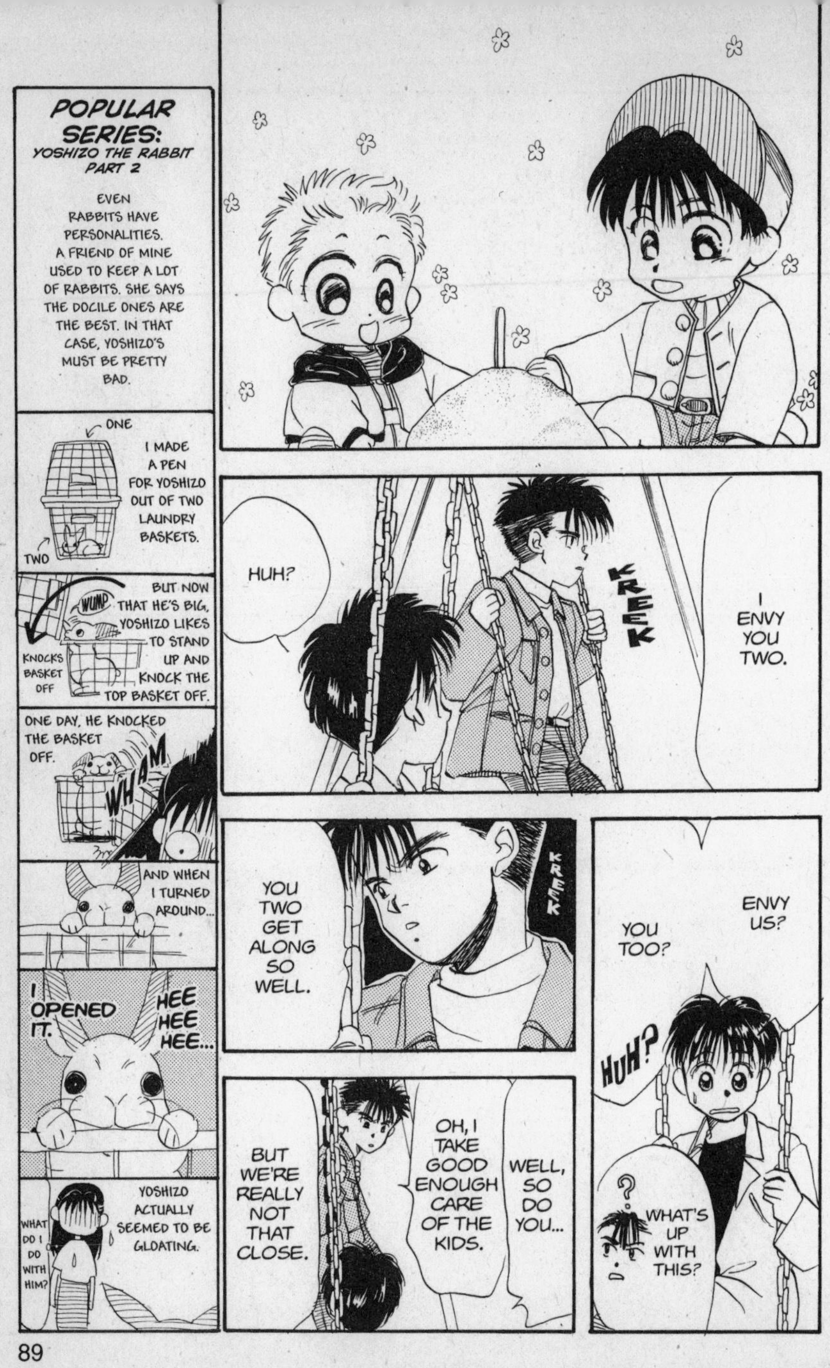
I ENVY YOU TWO.
KREEK
HUH?
ENVY US?
YOU TOO?
HUH?
WHAT'S UP WITH THIS?
?
KREEK
YOU TWO GET ALONG SO WELL.
WELL, SO DO YOU...
OH, I TAKE GOOD ENOUGH CARE OF THE KIDS.
BUT WE'RE REALLY NOT THAT CLOSE.
POPULAR SERIES:
YOSHIZO THE RABBIT PART 2
EVEN RABBITS HAVE PERSONALITIES. A FRIEND OF MINE USED TO KEEP A LOT OF RABBITS. SHE SAYS THE DOCILE ONES ARE THE BEST. IN THAT CASE, YOSHIZO'S MUST BE PRETTY BAD.
ONE
TWO
I MADE A PEN FOR YOSHIZO OUT OF TWO LAUNDRY BASKETS.
WUMP
BUT NOW THAT HE'S BIG, YOSHIZO LIKES TO STAND UP AND KNOCK THE TOP BASKET OFF.
KNOCKS BASKET OFF
ONE DAY, HE KNOCKED THE BASKET OFF.
WHAM
AND WHEN I TURNED AROUND...
HEE HEE HEE...
I OPENED IT.
YOSHIZO ACTUALLY SEEMED TO BE GLOATING.
WHAT DO I DO WITH HIM?

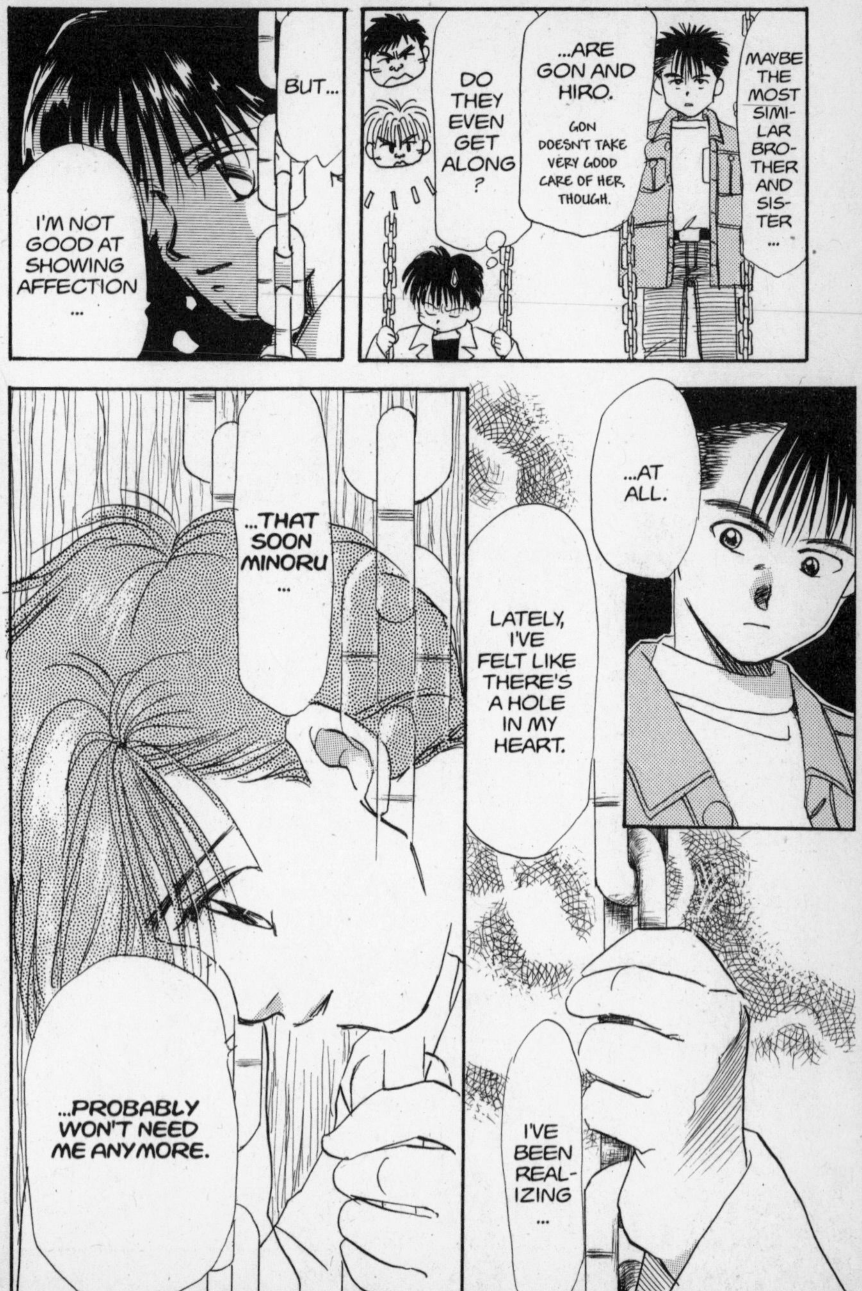
MAYBE THE MOST SIMILAR BROTHER AND SISTER...
...ARE GON AND HIRO.
GON DOESN'T TAKE VERY GOOD CARE OF HER, THOUGH.
DO THEY EVEN GET ALONG?
BUT...
I'M NOT GOOD AT SHOWING AFFECTION...
...AT ALL.
LATELY, I'VE FELT LIKE THERE'S A HOLE IN MY HEART.
I'VE BEEN REALIZING...
...THAT SOON MINORU...
...PROBABLY WON'T NEED ME ANYMORE.

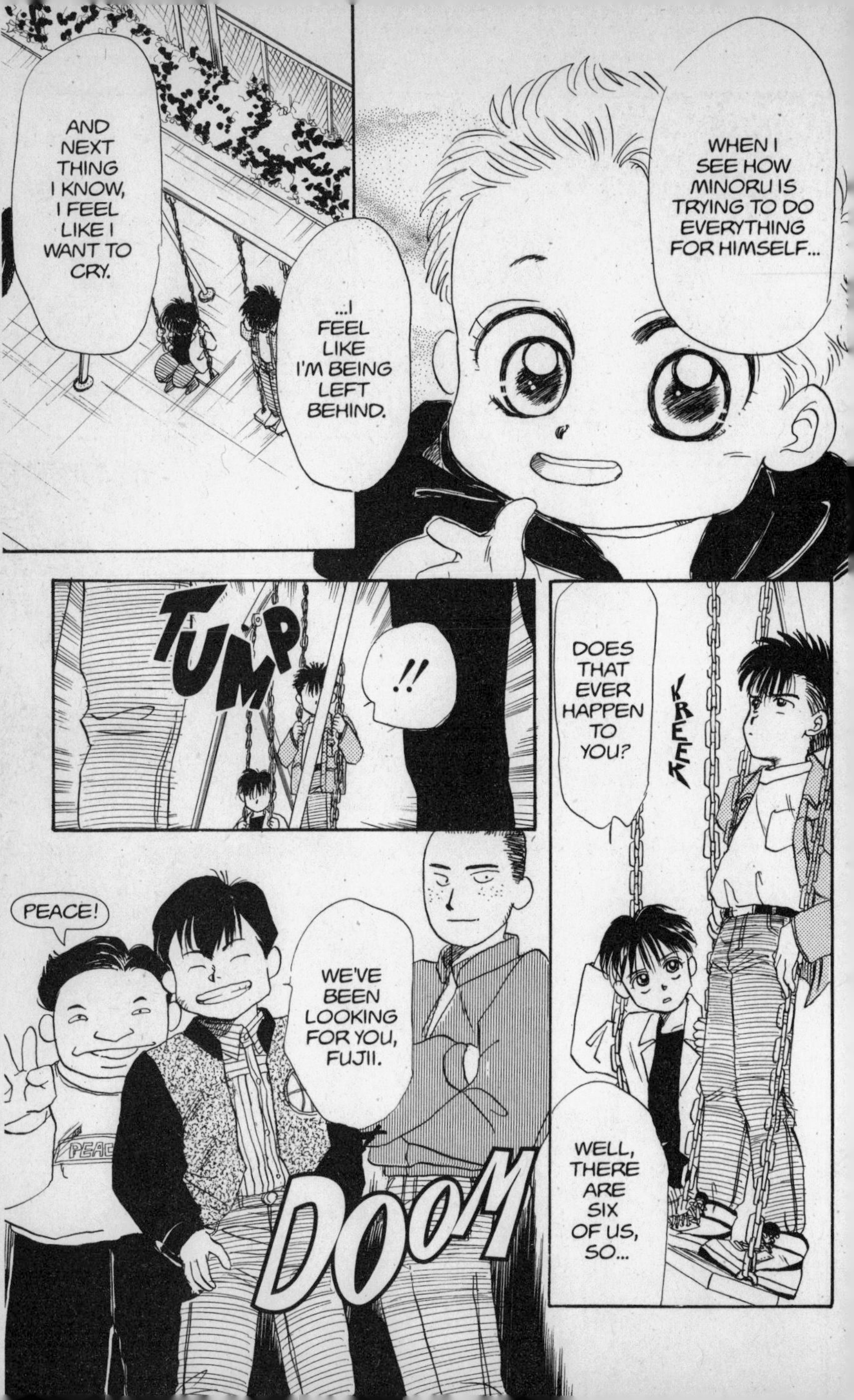
WHEN I SEE HOW MINORU IS TRYING TO DO EVERYTHING FOR HIMSELF...
...I FEEL LIKE I'M BEING LEFT BEHIND.
AND NEXT THING I KNOW, I FEEL LIKE I WANT TO CRY.
DOES THAT EVER HAPPEN TO YOU?
KREEK
WELL, THERE ARE SIX OF US, SO...
TUMP
!!
WE'VE BEEN LOOKING FOR YOU, FUJII.
DOOM
PEACE!
PEACE

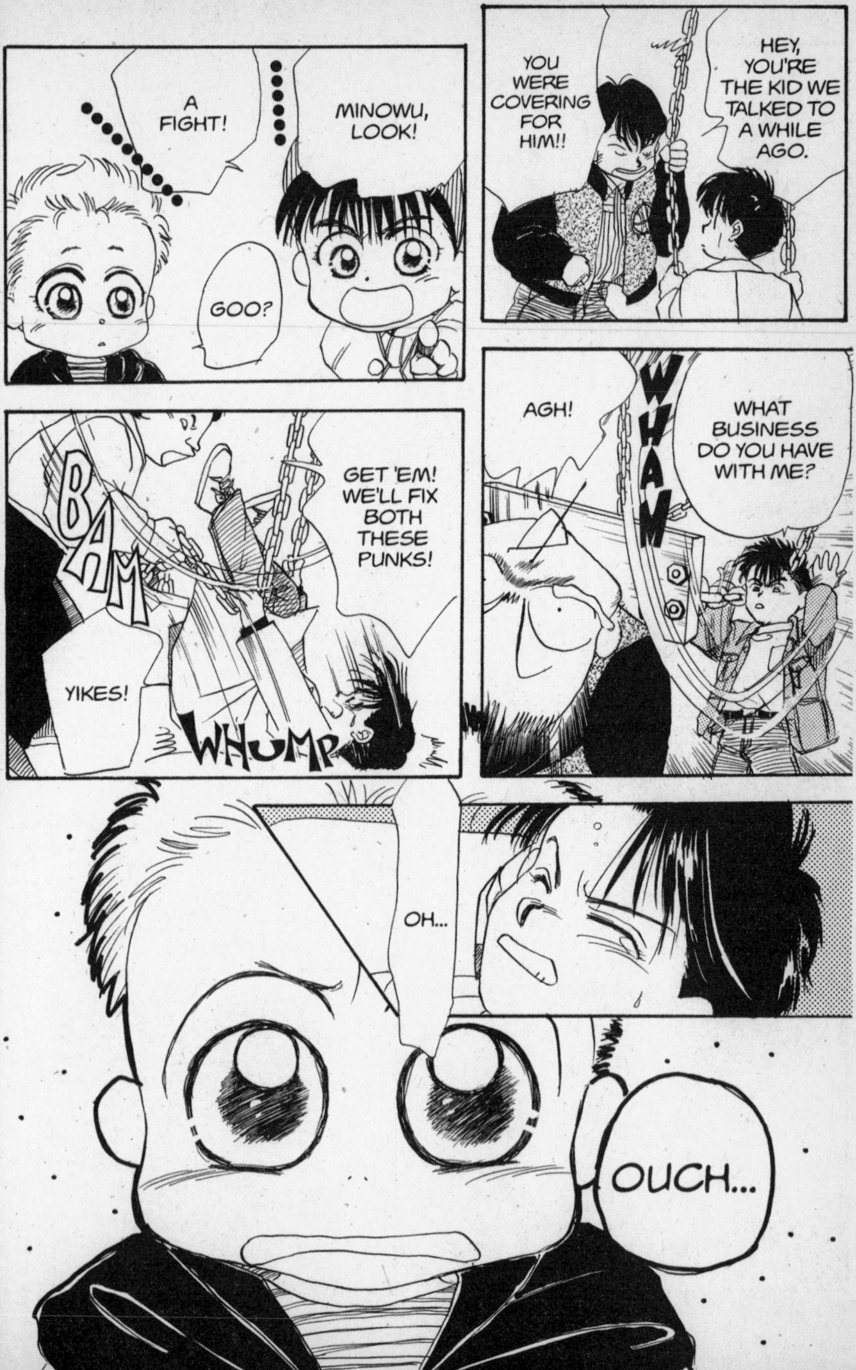
HEY, YOU'RE THE KID WE TALKED TO A WHILE AGO.
YOU WERE COVERING FOR HIM!!
MINOWU, LOOK!
A FIGHT!
GOO?
WHAT BUSINESS DO YOU HAVE WITH ME?
WHAM
AGH!
GET 'EM! WE'LL FIX BOTH THESE PUNKS!
BAM
YIKES!
WHUMP
OH...
OUCH...

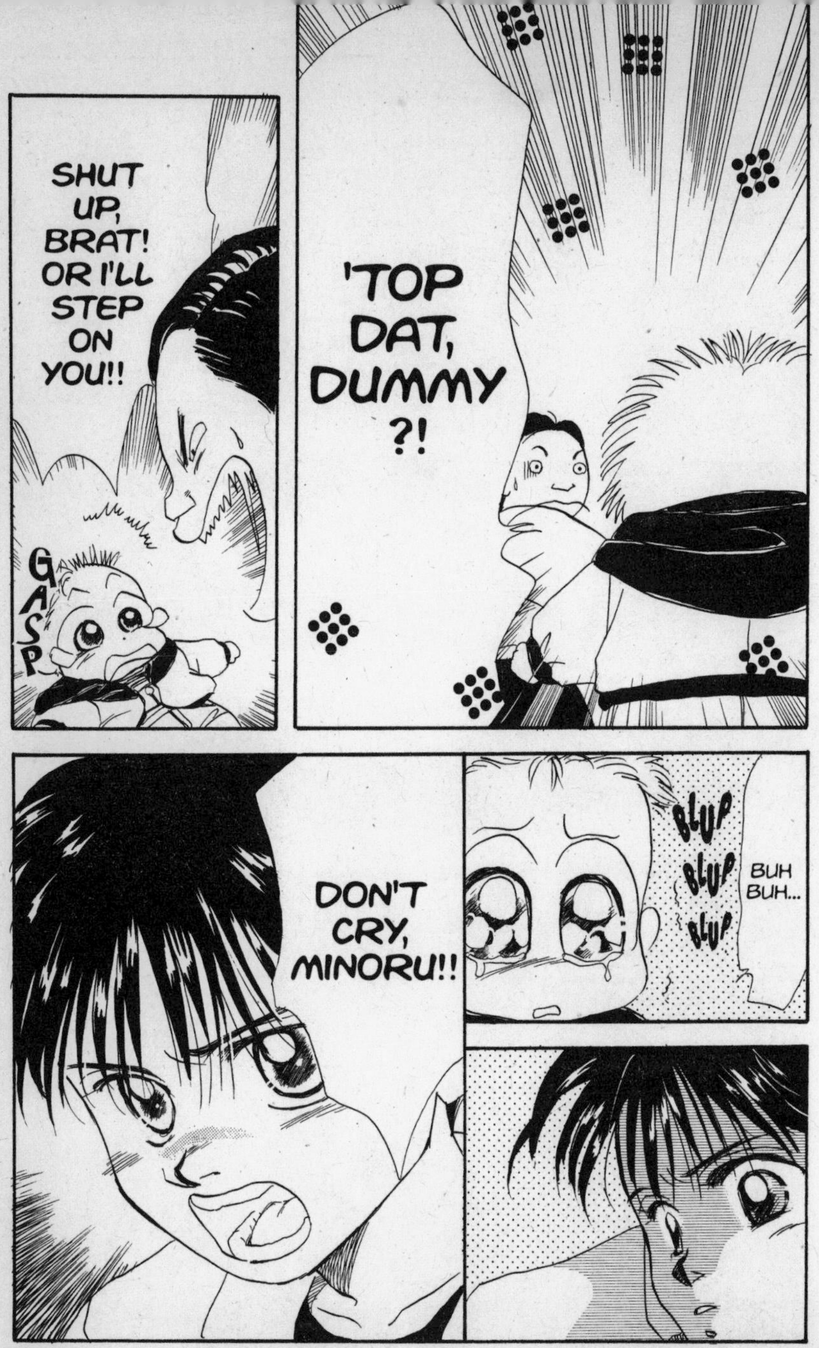
'TOP DAT, DUMMY ?!
SHUT UP, BRAT! OR I'LL STEP ON YOU!!
GASP
BUH BUH...
BLUP BLUP BLUP
DON'T CRY, MINORU!!

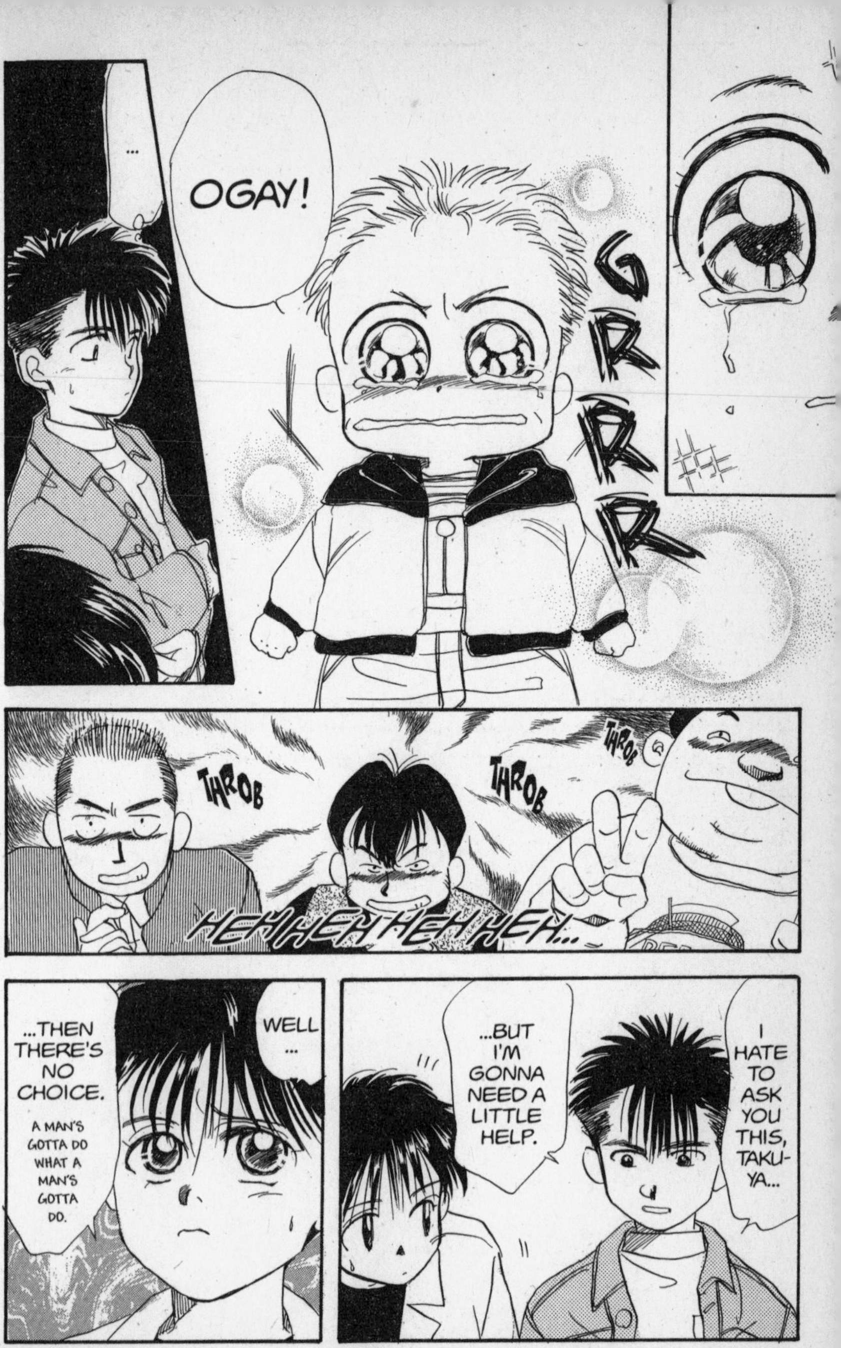
GRRRR
OGAY!
...
THROB
THROB
THROB
HEH HEH HEH HEH...
I HATE TO ASK YOU THIS, TAKUYA...
...BUT I'M GONNA NEED A LITTLE HELP.
WELL...
...THEN THERE'S NO CHOICE.
A MAN'S GOTTA DO WHAT A MAN'S GOTTA DO.

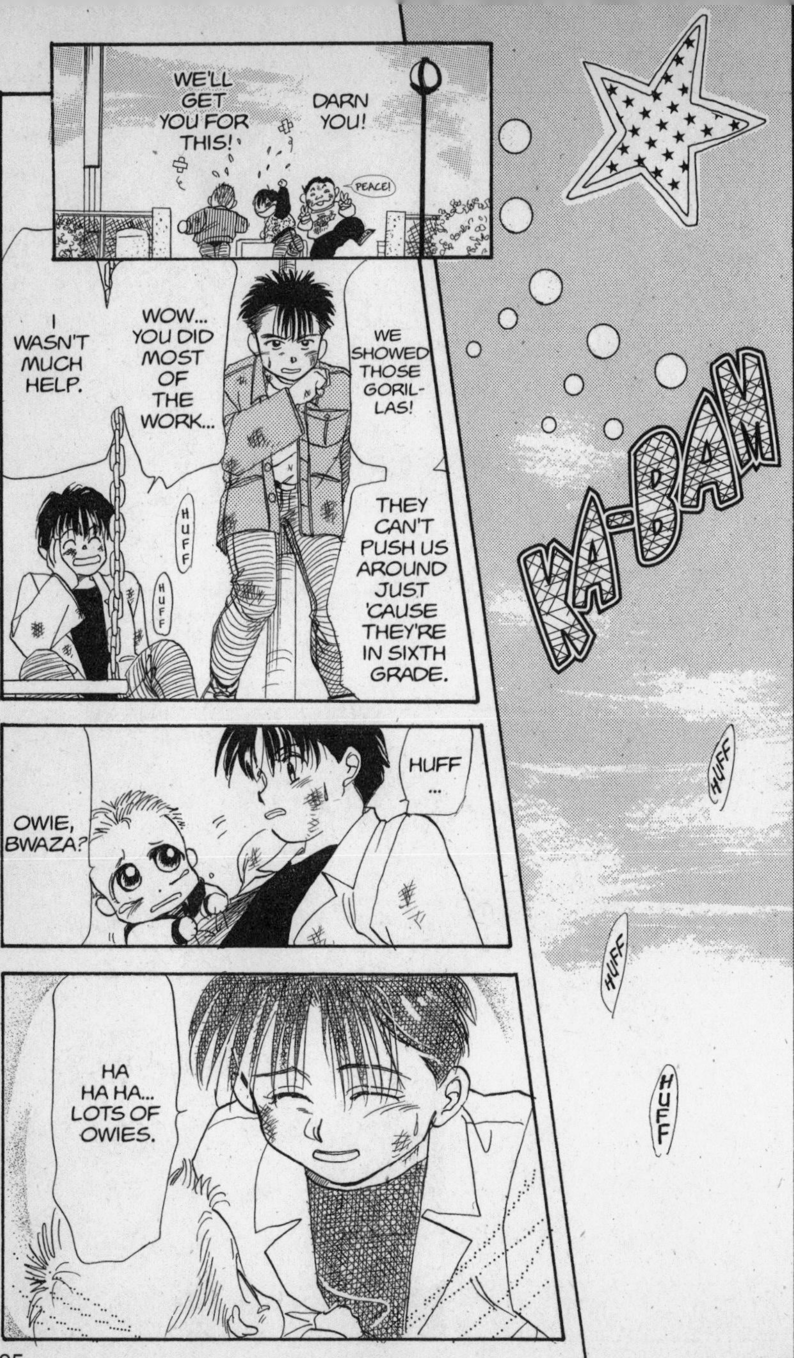
KA-BAM
HUFF
HUFF
HUFF
DARN YOU!
WE'LL GET YOU FOR THIS!
PEACE!
WE SHOWED THOSE GORIL-LAS!
THEY CAN'T PUSH US AROUND JUST 'CAUSE THEY'RE IN SIXTH GRADE.
HUFF
HUFF
WOW... YOU DID MOST OF THE WORK...
I WASN'T MUCH HELP.
HUFF ...
OWIE, BWAZA?
HA HA HA... LOTS OF OWIES.

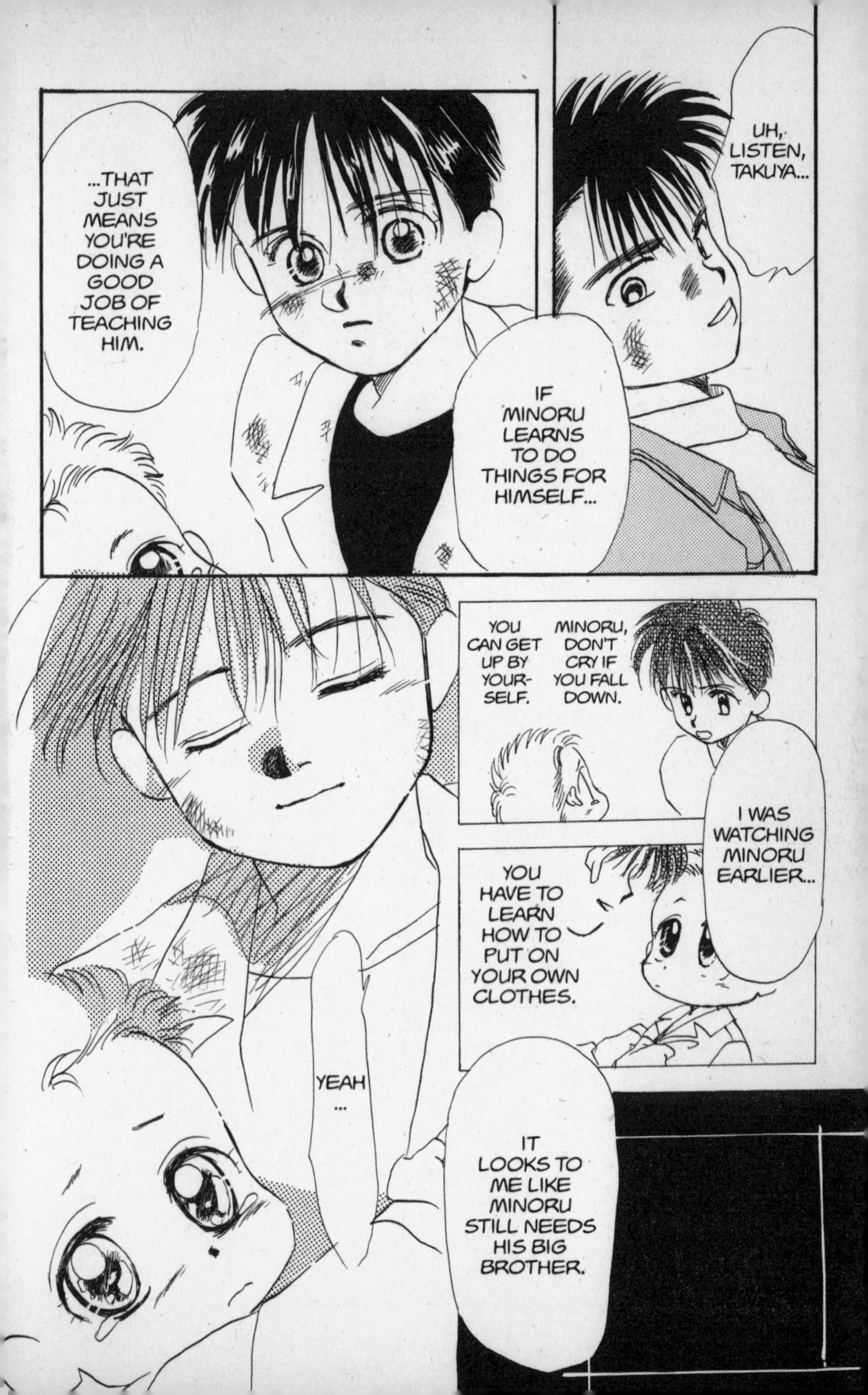
UH, LISTEN, TAKUYA...
IF MINORU LEARNS TO DO THINGS FOR HIMSELF...
...THAT JUST MEANS YOU'RE DOING A GOOD JOB OF TEACHING HIM.
I WAS WATCHING MINORU EARLIER...
MINORU, DON'T CRY IF YOU FALL DOWN.
YOU CAN GET UP BY YOUR-SELF.
YOU HAVE TO LEARN HOW TO PUT ON YOUR OWN CLOTHES.
IT LOOKS TO ME LIKE MINORU STILL NEEDS HIS BIG BROTHER.
YEAH ...

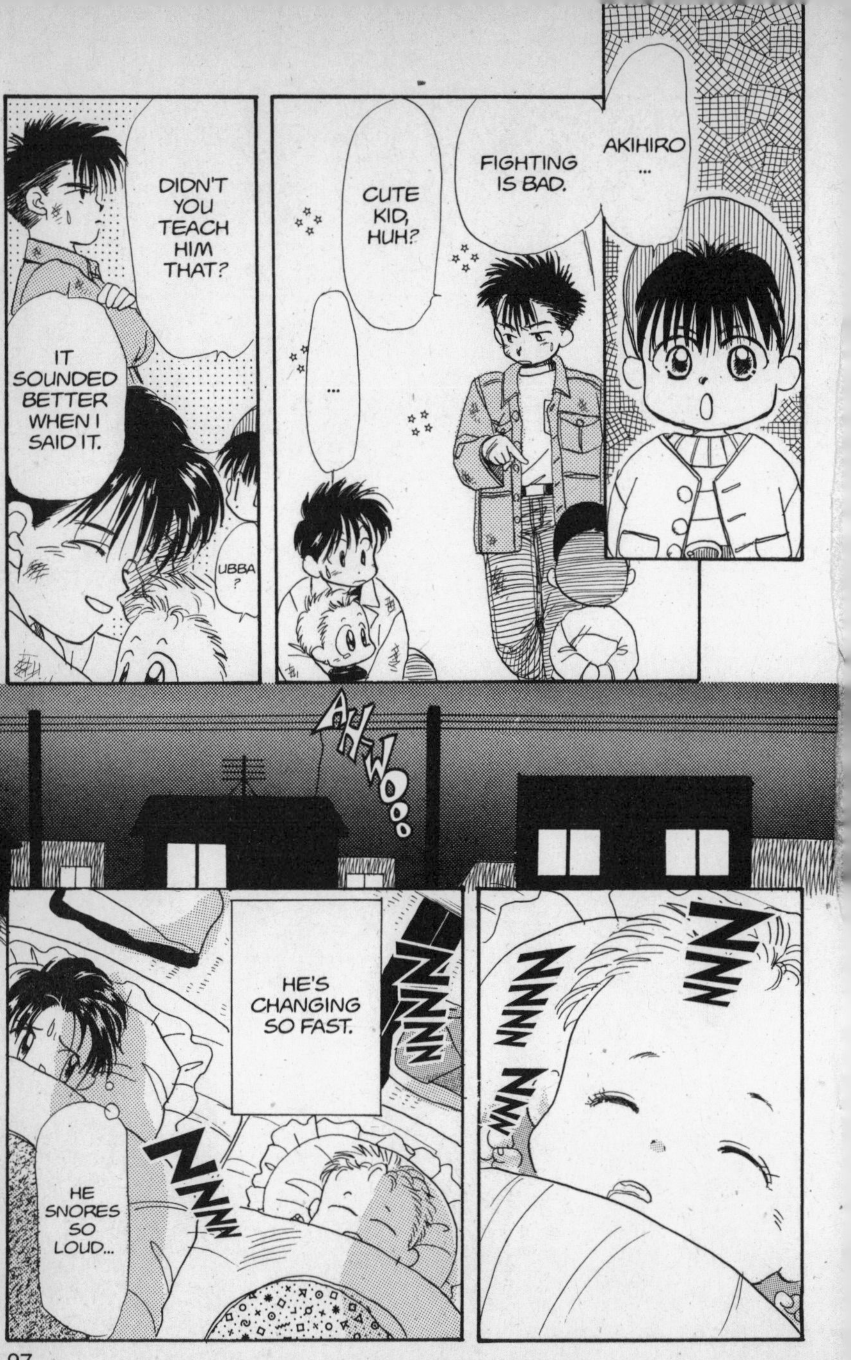
AKIHIRO ...
FIGHTING IS BAD.
CUTE KID, HUH?
...
DIDN'T YOU TEACH HIM THAT?
IT SOUNDED BETTER WHEN I SAID IT.
UBBA ?
AH-WOOO
NNN
NNNN
NNN
HE'S CHANGING SO FAST.
NNNN
HE SNORES SO LOUD...
NNNN

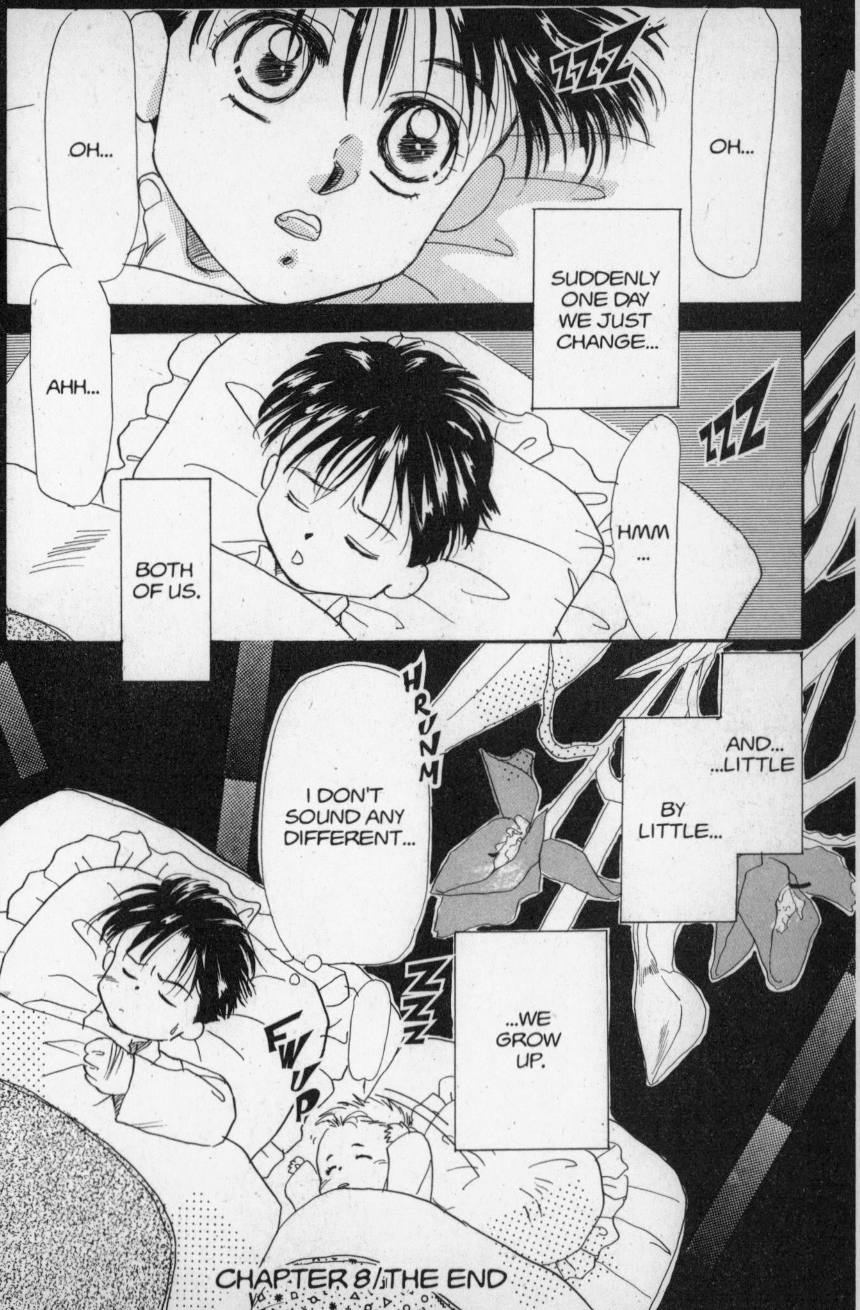
ZZZ
OH...
OH...
SUDDENLY ONE DAY WE JUST CHANGE...
ZZZ
HMM ...
AHH...
BOTH OF US.
AND... ...LITTLE BY LITTLE...
HRUNM
I DON'T SOUND ANY DIFFERENT...
...WE GROW UP.
ZZZ
FWUP
CHAPTER 8 / THE END

BABY & Me

CHAPTER 9

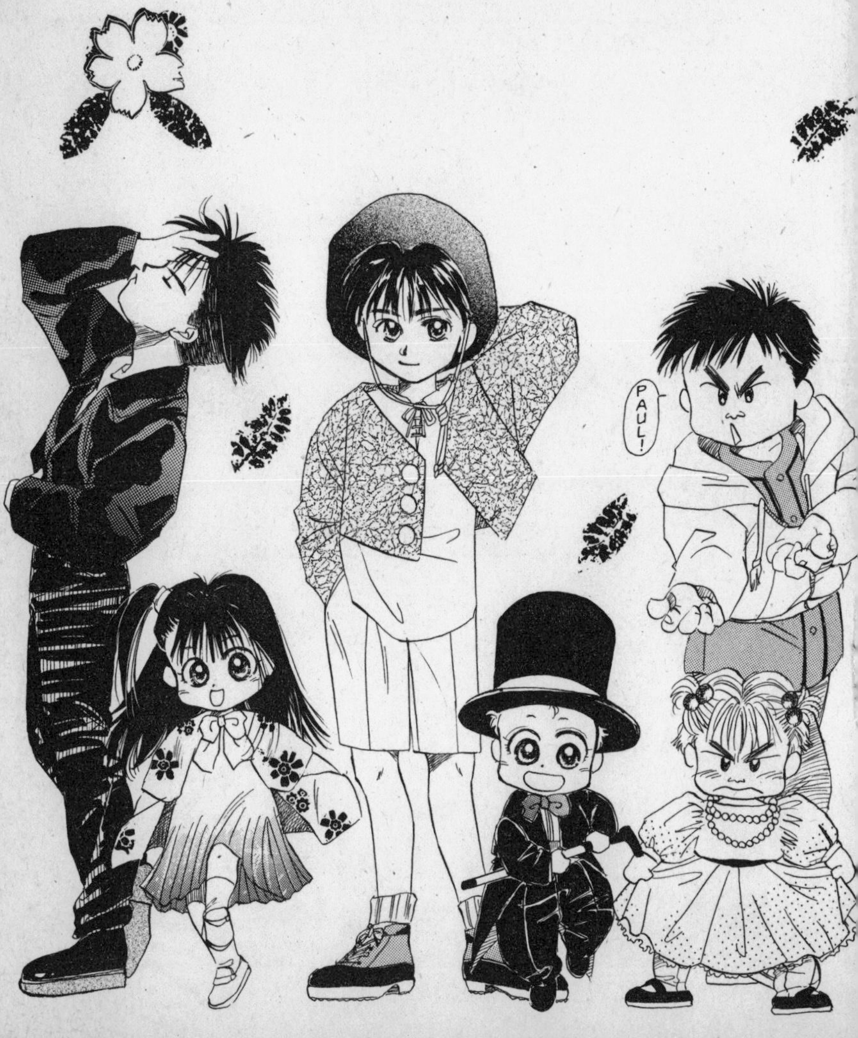
PAUL!

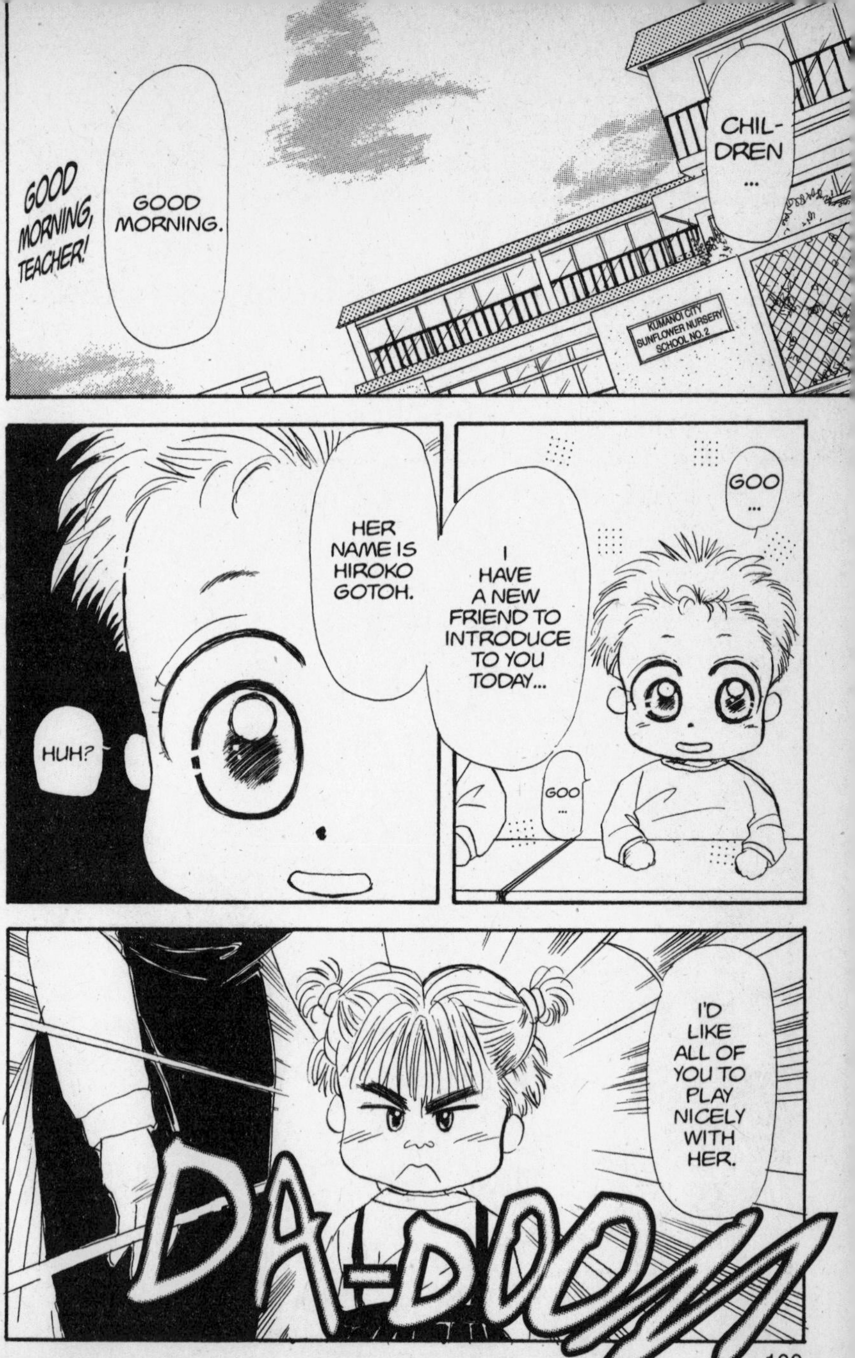
CHIL-DREN...
KUMANOI CITY SUNFLOWER NURSERY SCHOOL NO. 2
GOOD MORNING.
GOOD MORNING, TEACHER!
GOO...
I HAVE A NEW FRIEND TO INTRODUCE TO YOU TODAY...
GOO...
HER NAME IS HIROKO GOTOH.
HUH?
I'D LIKE ALL OF YOU TO PLAY NICELY WITH HER.
DA-DOOM

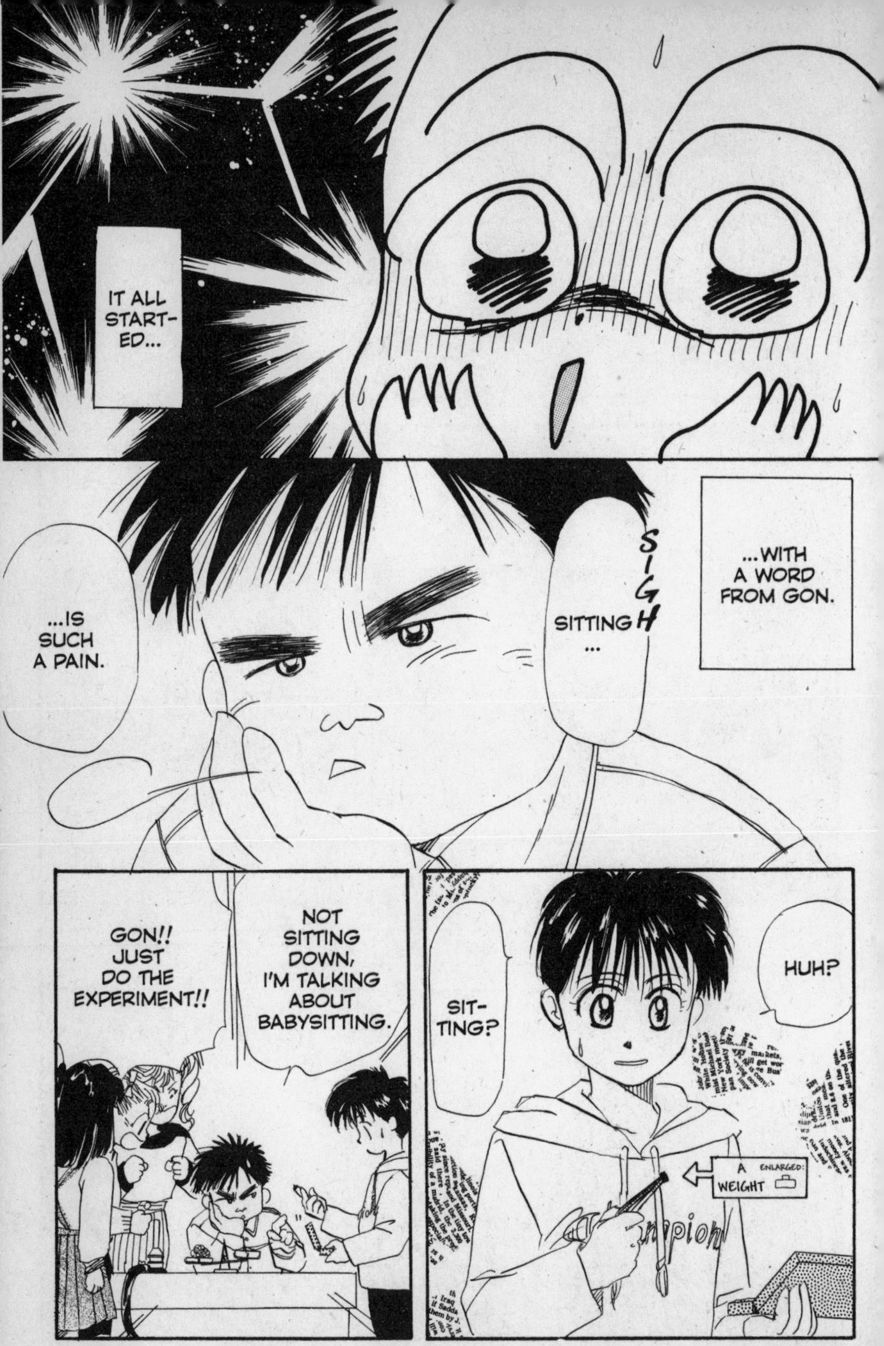
IT ALL START-ED...
...WITH A WORD FROM GON.
SITTING...
SIGH
...IS SUCH A PAIN.
HUH?
SIT-TING?
ENLARGED: A WEIGHT
NOT SITTING DOWN, I'M TALKING ABOUT BABYSITTING.
GON!! JUST DO THE EXPERIMENT!!

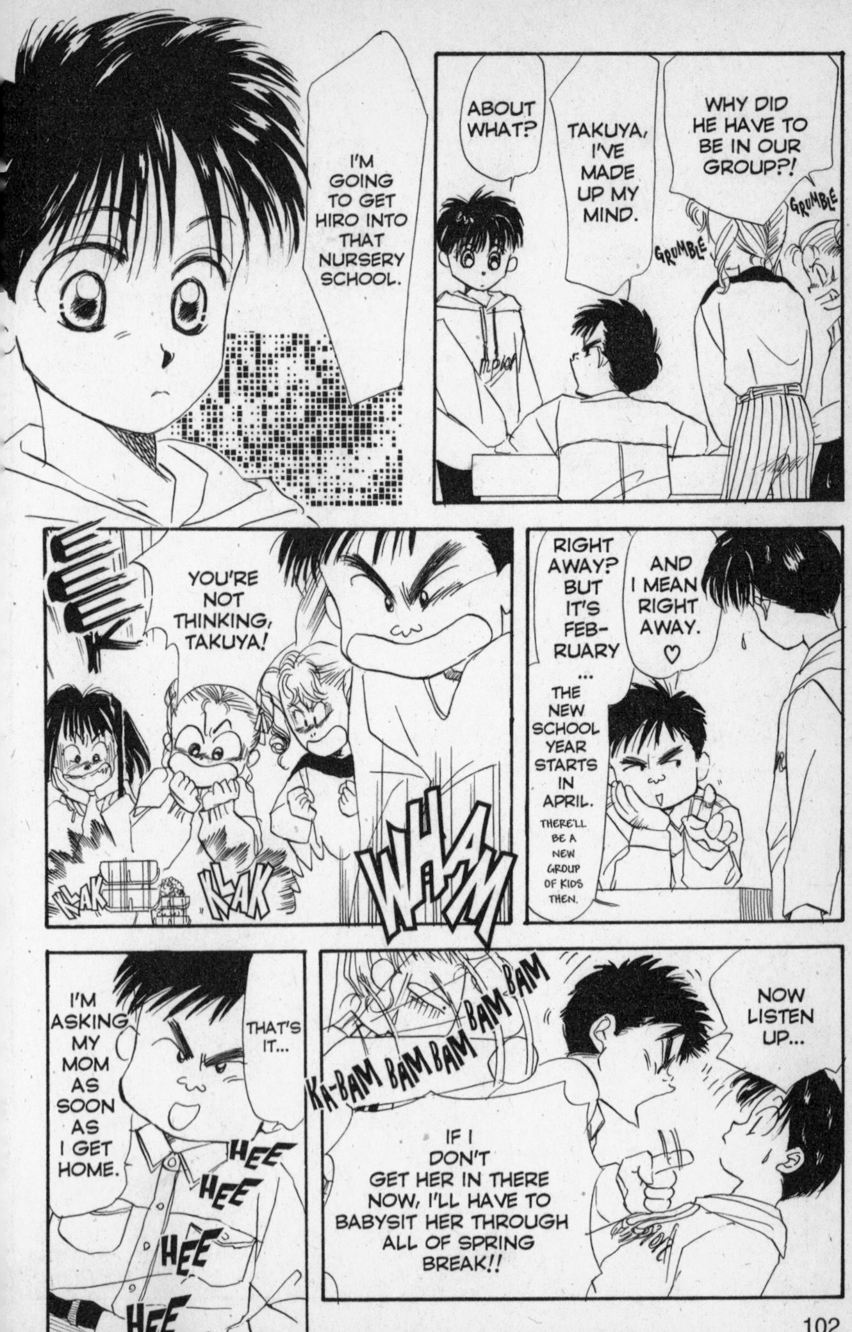
WHY DID HE HAVE TO BE IN OUR GROUP?!
GRUMBLE
GRUMBLE
TAKUYA, I'VE MADE UP MY MIND.
ABOUT WHAT?
I'M GOING TO GET HIRO INTO THAT NURSERY SCHOOL.
AND I MEAN RIGHT AWAY. ♡
RIGHT AWAY? BUT IT'S FEB- RUARY ... THE NEW SCHOOL YEAR STARTS IN APRIL.
THERE'LL BE A NEW GROUP OF KIDS THEN.
WHAM
YOU'RE NOT THINKING, TAKUYA!
EEEEK
KLAK
KLAK
NOW LISTEN UP...
IF I DON'T GET HER IN THERE NOW, I'LL HAVE TO BABYSIT HER THROUGH ALL OF SPRING BREAK!!
KA-BAM BAM BAM BAM BAM
THAT'S IT...
I'M ASKING MY MOM AS SOON AS I GET HOME.
HEE
HEE
HEE
HEE

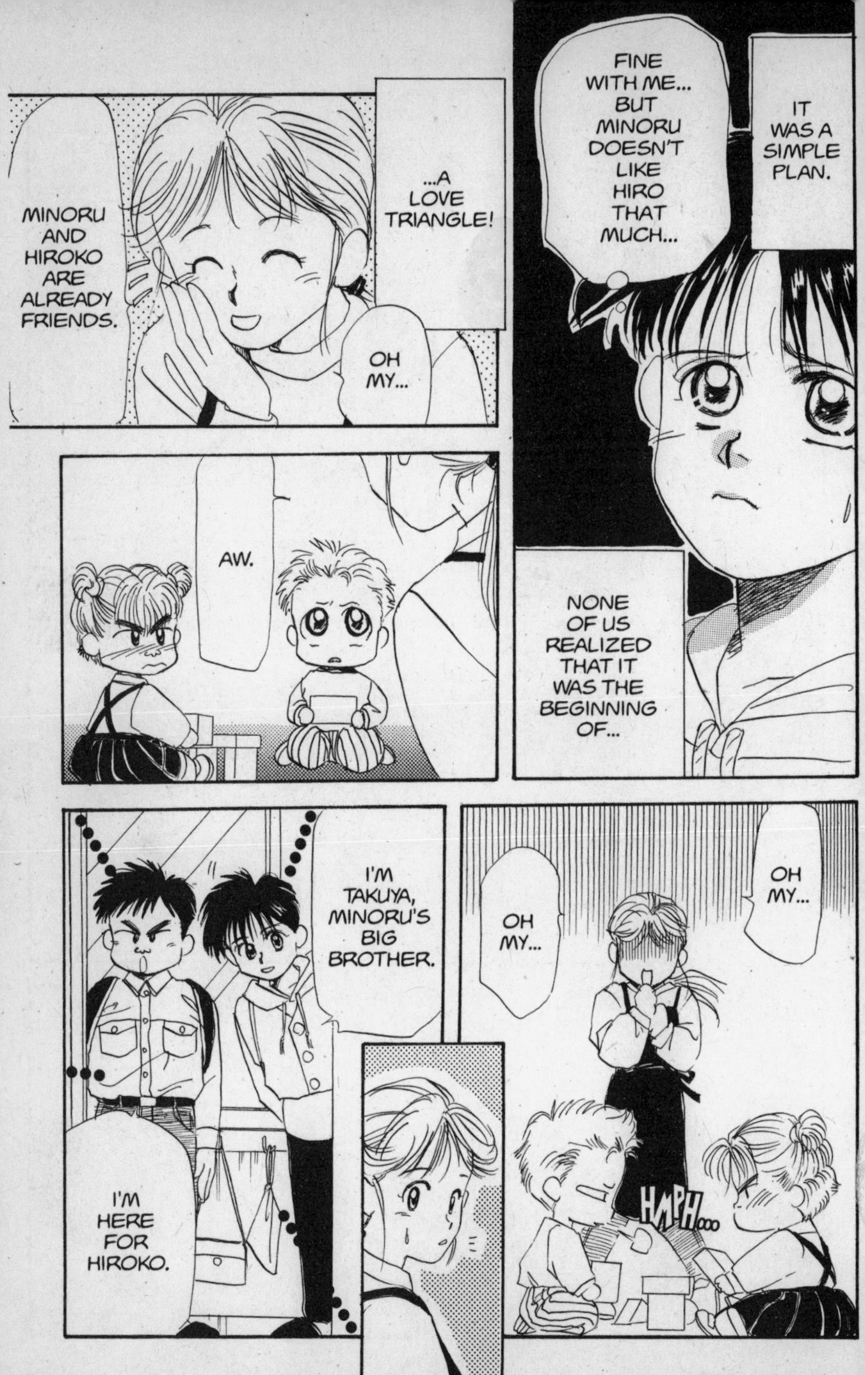
IT WAS A SIMPLE PLAN.
FINE WITH ME... BUT MINORU DOESN'T LIKE HIRO THAT MUCH...
NONE OF US REALIZED THAT IT WAS THE BEGINNING OF...
...A LOVE TRIANGLE!
OH MY...
MINORU AND HIROKO ARE ALREADY FRIENDS.
AW.
OH MY...
OH MY...
HMPH...
I'M TAKUYA, MINORU'S BIG BROTHER.
I'M HERE FOR HIROKO.

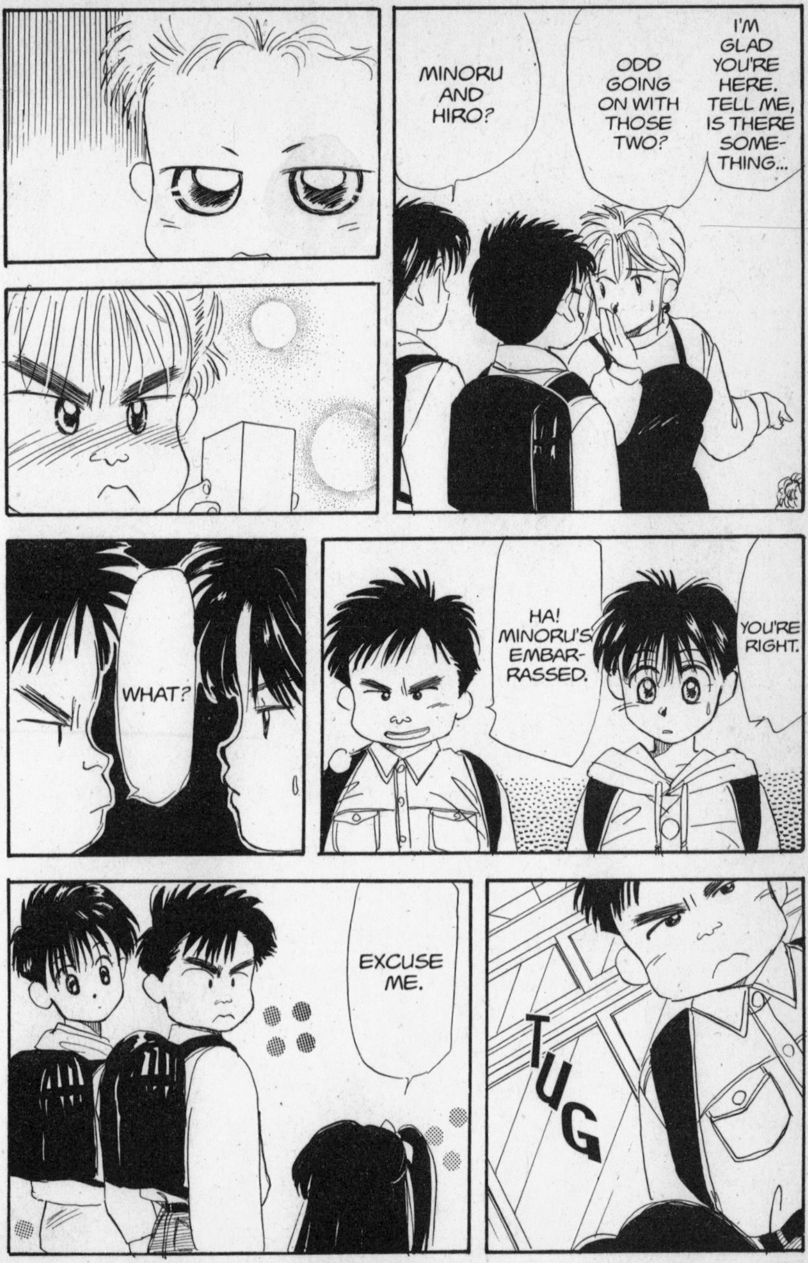
I'M GLAD YOU'RE HERE. TELL ME, IS THERE SOMETHING...
ODD GOING ON WITH THOSE TWO?
MINORU AND HIRO?
YOU'RE RIGHT.
HA! MINORU'S EMBARRASSED.
WHAT?
TUG
EXCUSE ME.

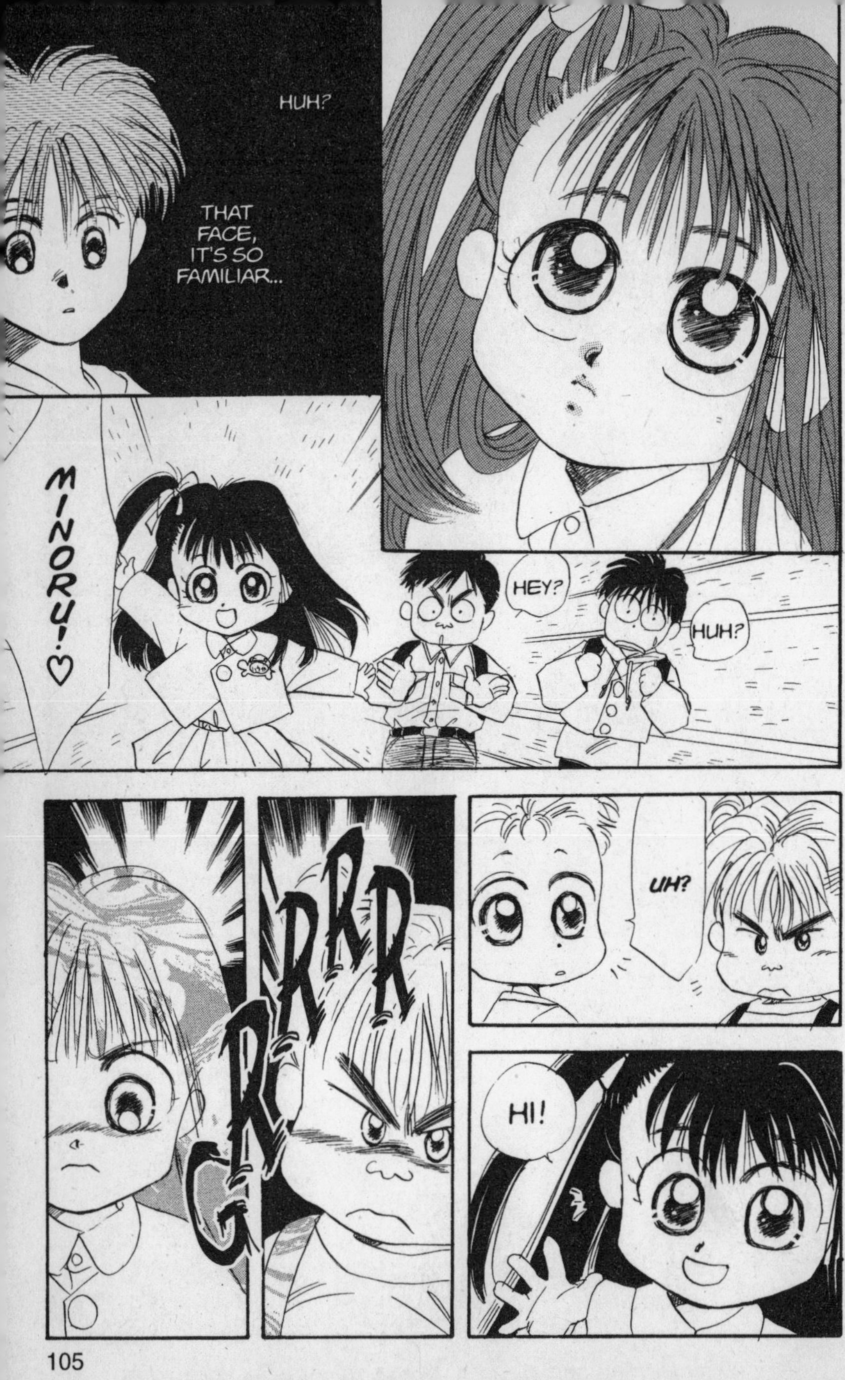
HUH?
THAT FACE, IT'S SO FAMILIAR...
MINORU!♡
HEY?
HUH?
UH?
HI!
GRRRR

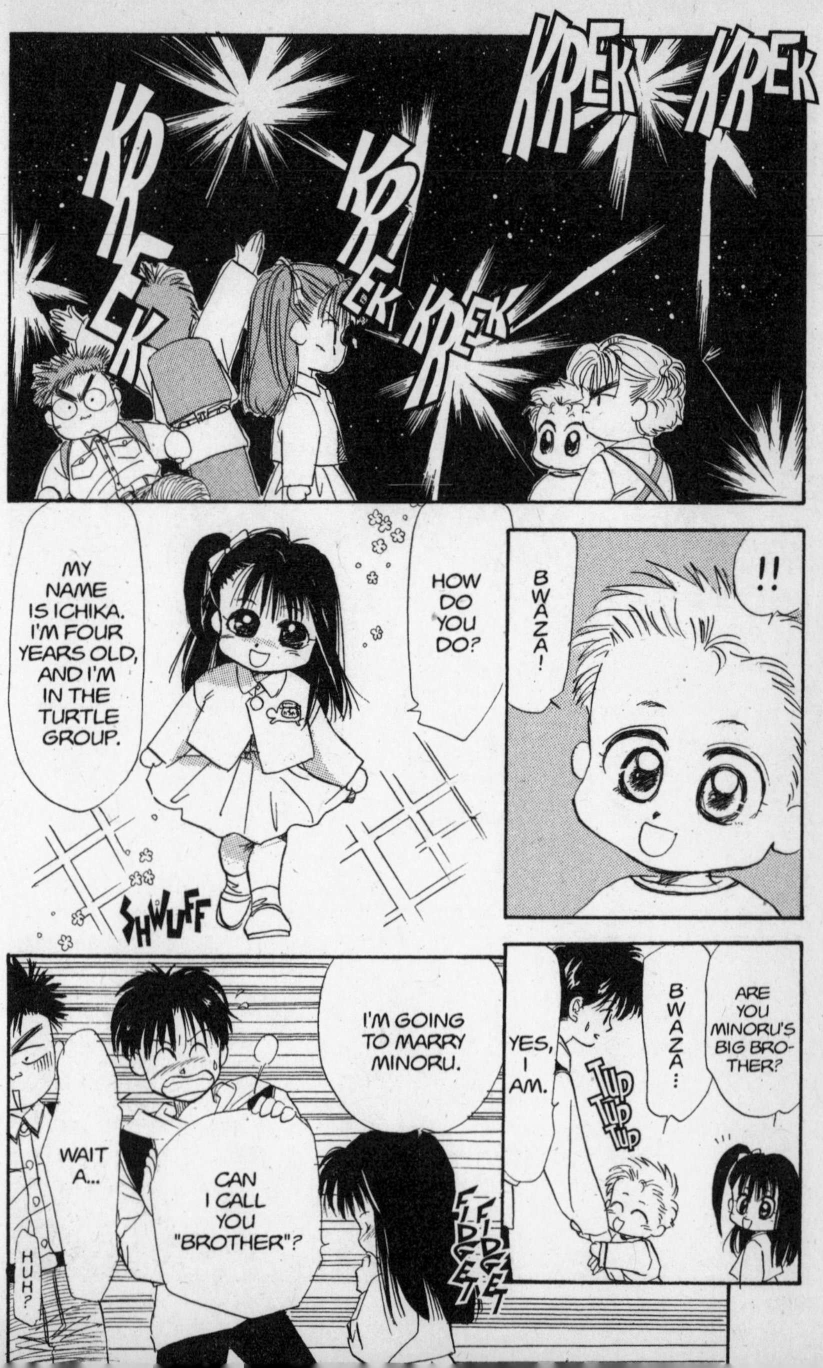
KREK KREK
KRIEK
KRIEK
KREK
KREK
!!
BWAZA!
HOW DO YOU DO?
MY NAME IS ICHIKA. I'M FOUR YEARS OLD, AND I'M IN THE TURTLE GROUP.
SHWUFF
ARE YOU MINORU'S BIG BRO-THER?
BWAZA...
YES, I AM.
TUP TUP TUP
I'M GOING TO MARRY MINORU.
CAN I CALL YOU "BROTHER"?
FIDGET FIDGET
WAIT A...
HUH?

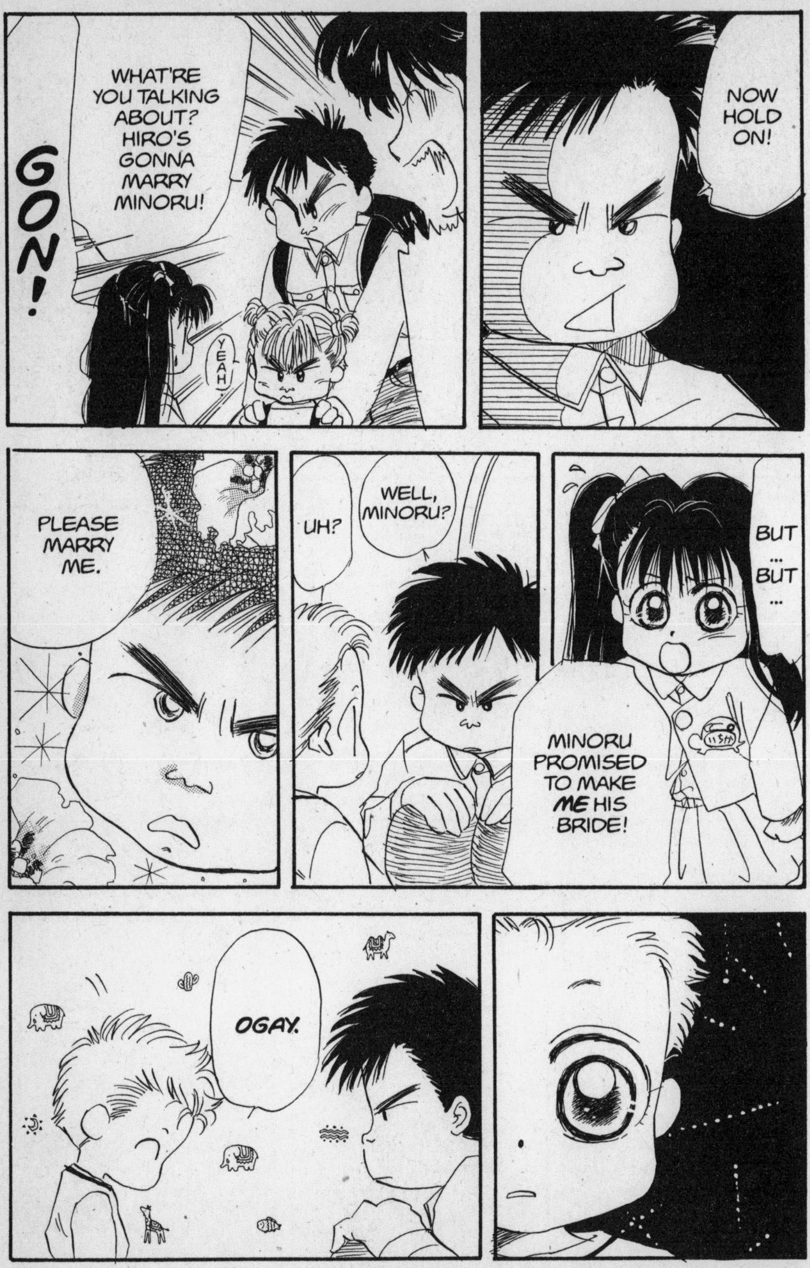
NOW HOLD ON!
WHAT'RE YOU TALKING ABOUT? HIRO'S GONNA MARRY MINORU!
GON!
YEAH
BUT ... BUT ...
MINORU PROMISED TO MAKE ME HIS BRIDE!
WELL, MINORU?
UH?
PLEASE MARRY ME.
OGAY.

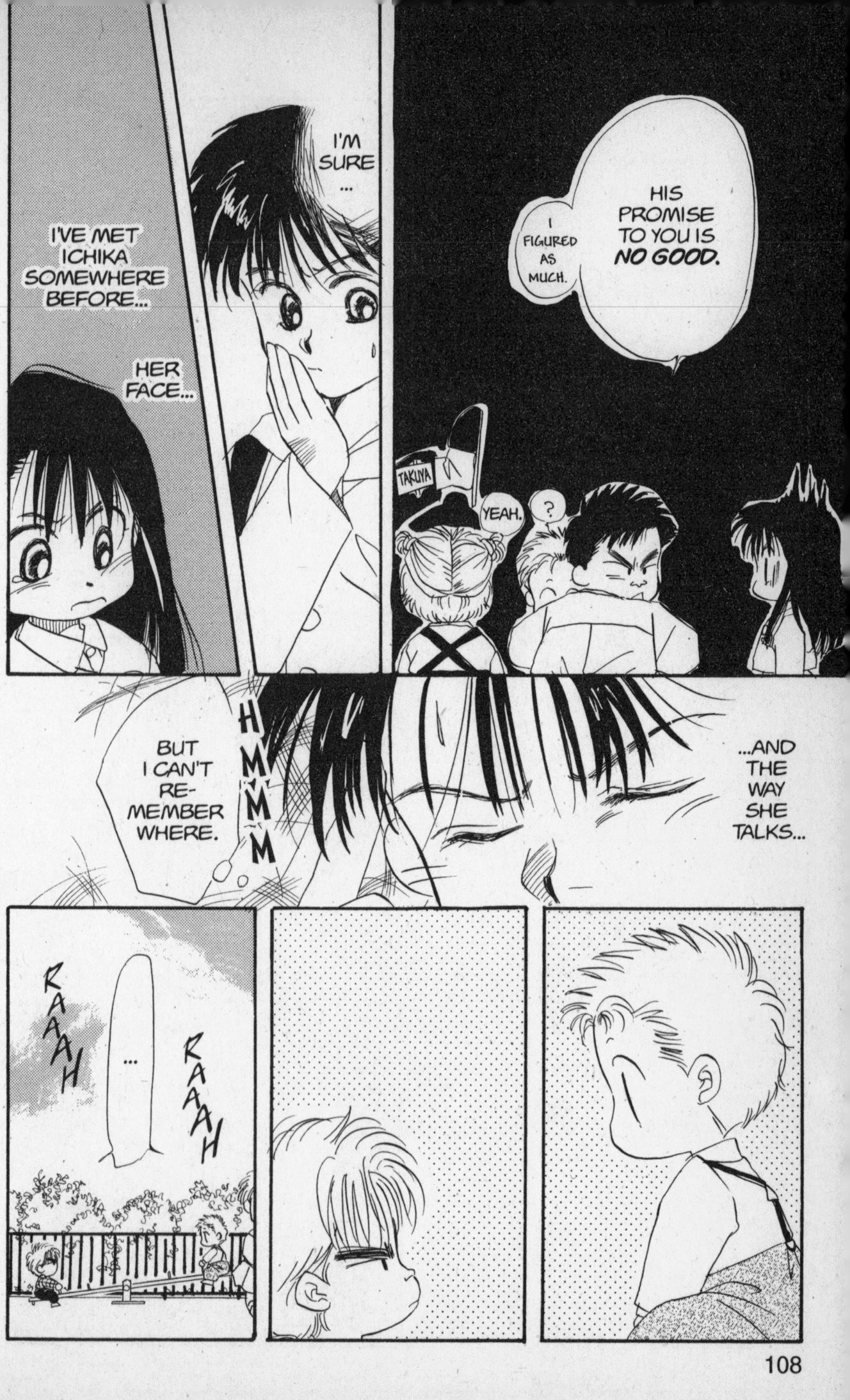
HIS PROMISE TO YOU IS **NO GOOD.**
I FIGURED AS MUCH.
TAKUYA
YEAH.
?
I'M SURE ...
I'VE MET ICHIKA SOMEWHERE BEFORE...
HER FACE...
...AND THE WAY SHE TALKS...
HMMMM
BUT I CAN'T RE-MEMBER WHERE.
RAAAH
...
RAAAH

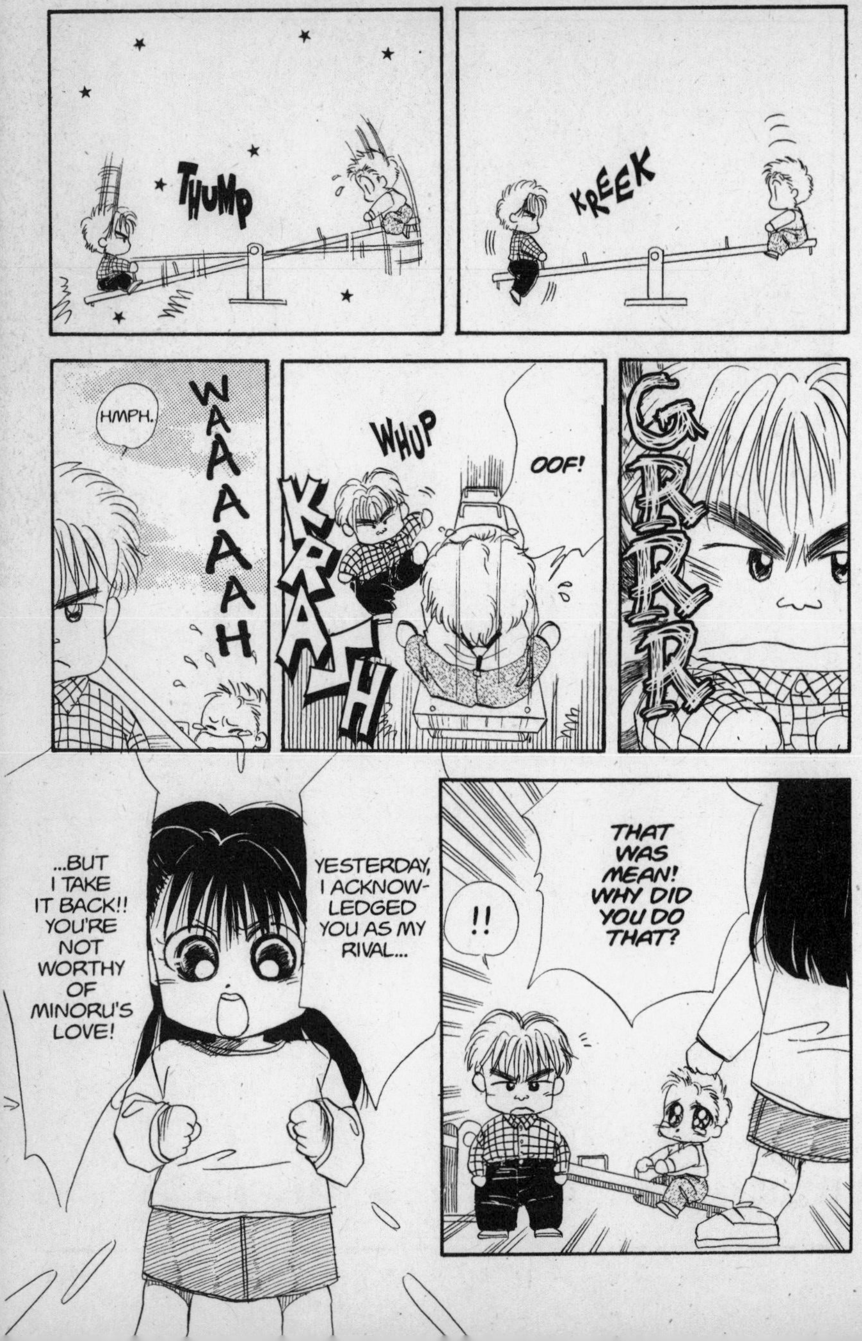
KREEK
THUMP
GRRRR
OOF!
WHUP
KRASH
WAAAAAH
HMPH.
THAT WAS MEAN! WHY DID YOU DO THAT?
!!
YESTERDAY, I ACKNOW-LEDGED YOU AS MY RIVAL...
...BUT I TAKE IT BACK!! YOU'RE NOT WORTHY OF MINORU'S LOVE!

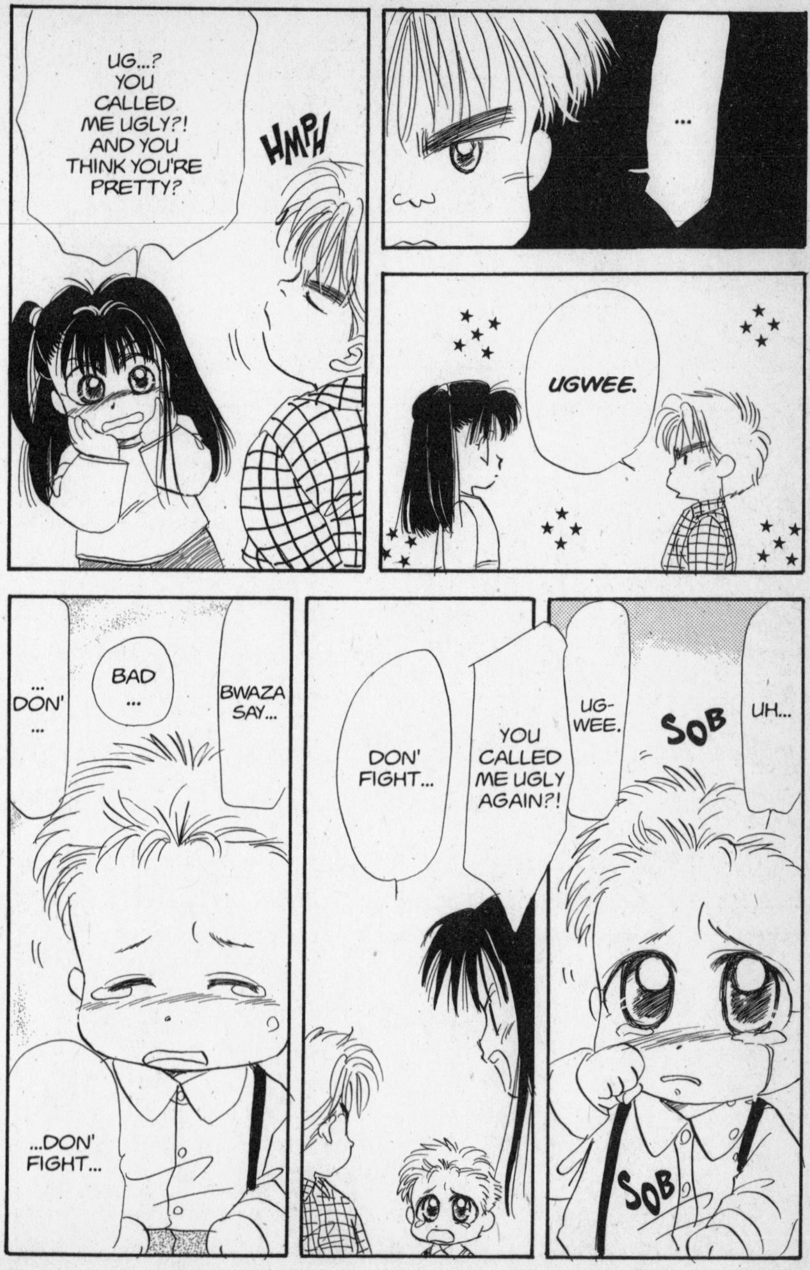
...
UGWEE.
UG...? YOU CALLED ME UGLY?! AND YOU THINK YOU'RE PRETTY?
HMPH
UH...
SOB
UG- WEE.
SOB
YOU CALLED ME UGLY AGAIN?!
DON' FIGHT...
BWAZA SAY...
BAD ...
... DON' ...
...DON' FIGHT...

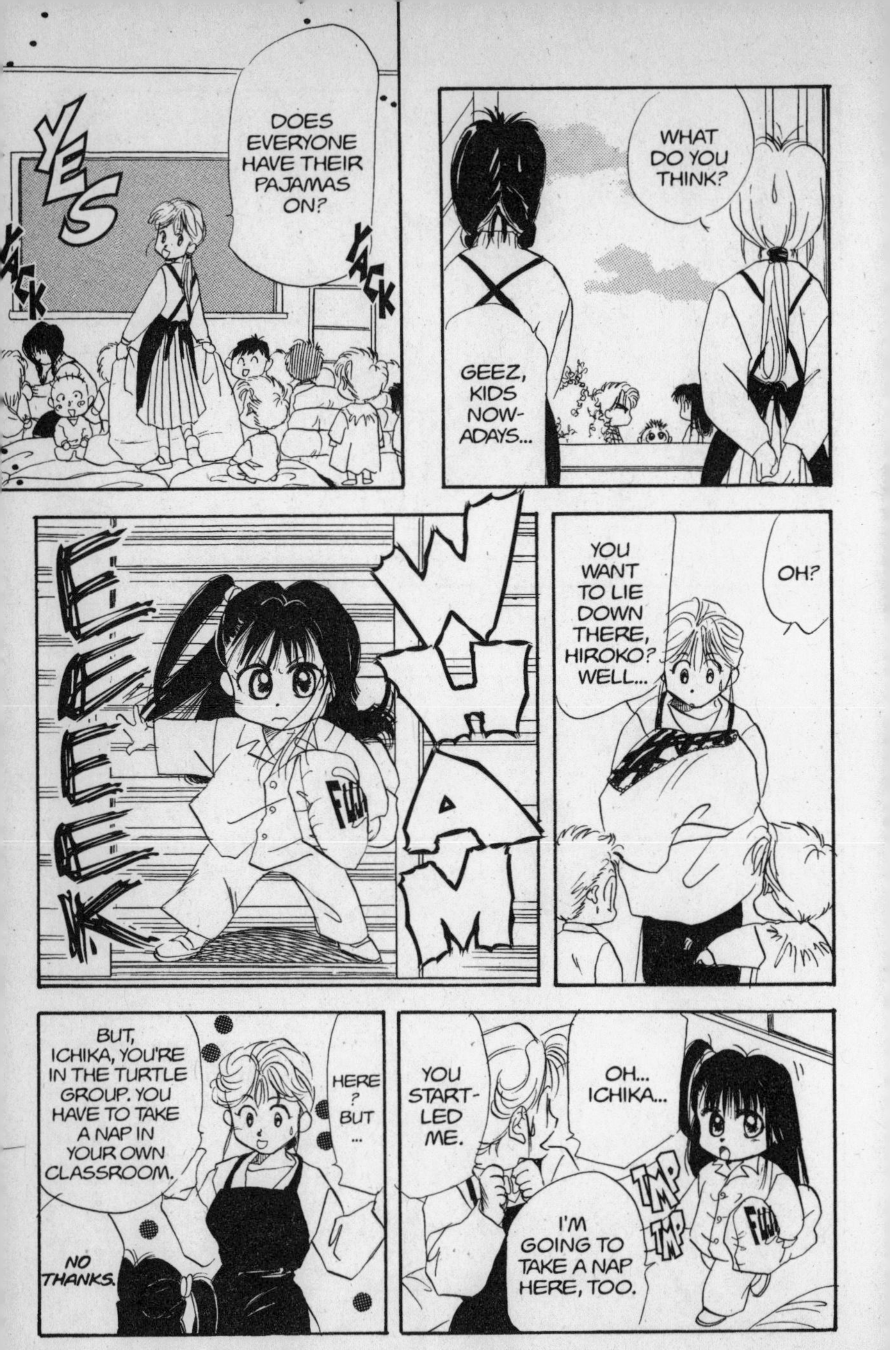
WHAT DO YOU THINK?
GEEZ, KIDS NOW-ADAYS...
DOES EVERYONE HAVE THEIR PAJAMAS ON?
YACK
YES
YACK
OH?
YOU WANT TO LIE DOWN THERE, HIROKO? WELL...
WHAM
EEEEEK
OH... ICHIKA...
YOU START-LED ME.
TMP TMP
I'M GOING TO TAKE A NAP HERE, TOO.
HERE? BUT...
BUT, ICHIKA, YOU'RE IN THE TURTLE GROUP. YOU HAVE TO TAKE A NAP IN YOUR OWN CLASSROOM.
NO THANKS.

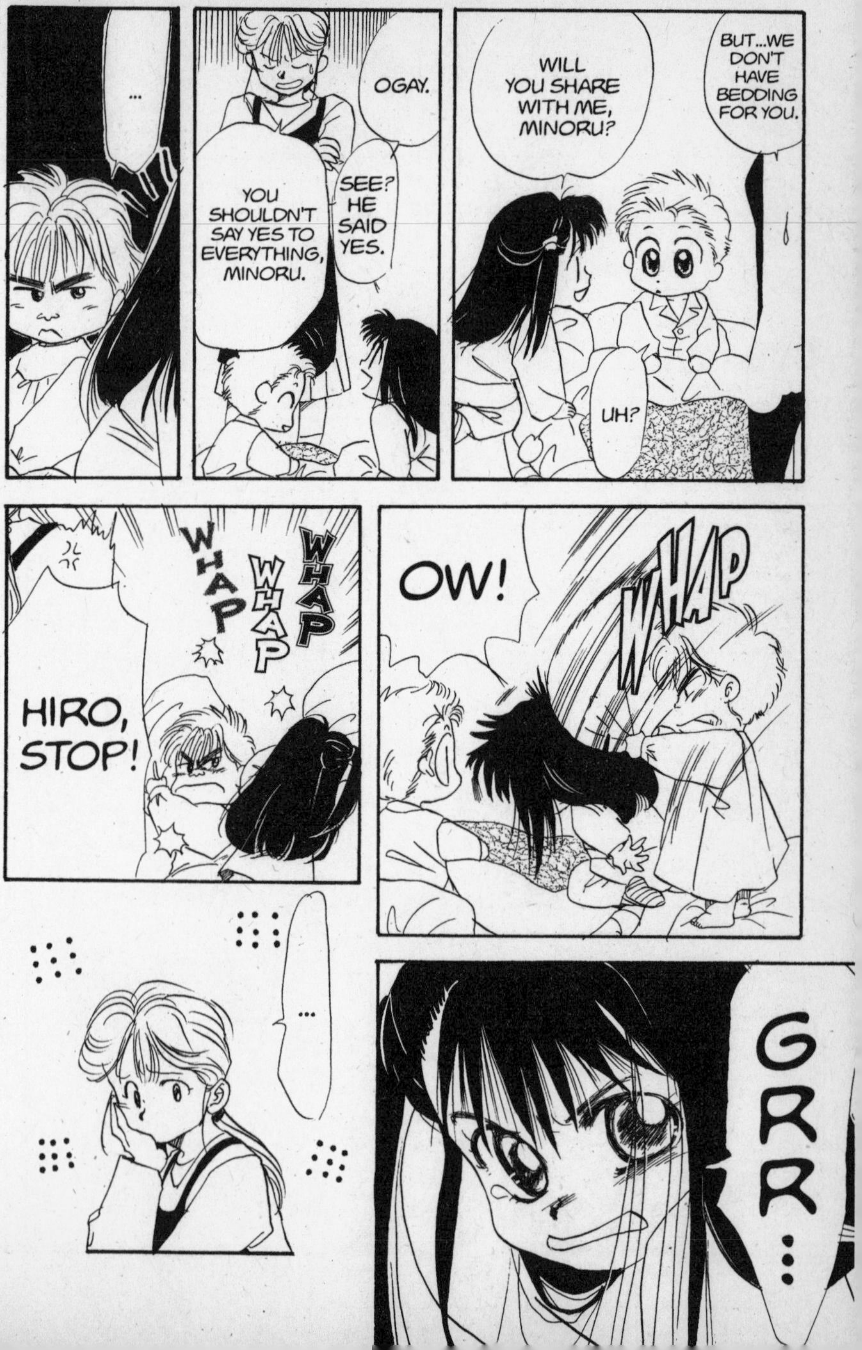
BUT...WE DON'T HAVE BEDDING FOR YOU.
WILL YOU SHARE WITH ME, MINORU?
UH?
OGAY.
SEE? HE SAID YES.
YOU SHOULDN'T SAY YES TO EVERYTHING, MINORU.
...
WHAP
OW!
WHAP
WHAP
WHAP
HIRO, STOP!
GRR...
...

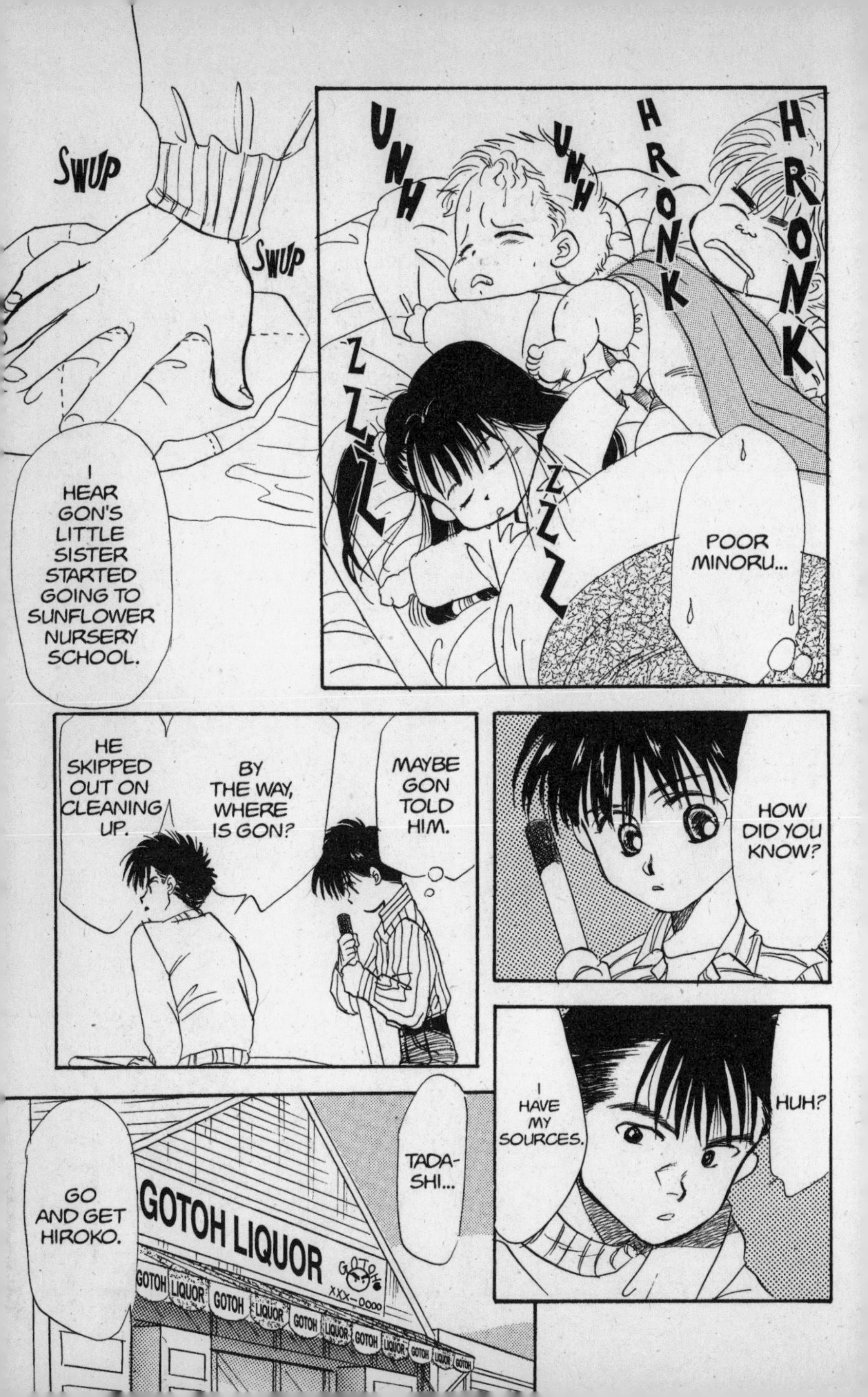
UNH
UNH
HRONK
HRONK
ZZZ
ZZZ
POOR MINORU...
SWUP
SWUP
I HEAR GON'S LITTLE SISTER STARTED GOING TO SUNFLOWER NURSERY SCHOOL.
HOW DID YOU KNOW?
MAYBE GON TOLD HIM.
BY THE WAY, WHERE IS GON?
HE SKIPPED OUT ON CLEANING UP.
HUH?
I HAVE MY SOURCES.
TADASHI...
GO AND GET HIROKO.
GOTOH LIQUOR
GOTOH
XXX-0000

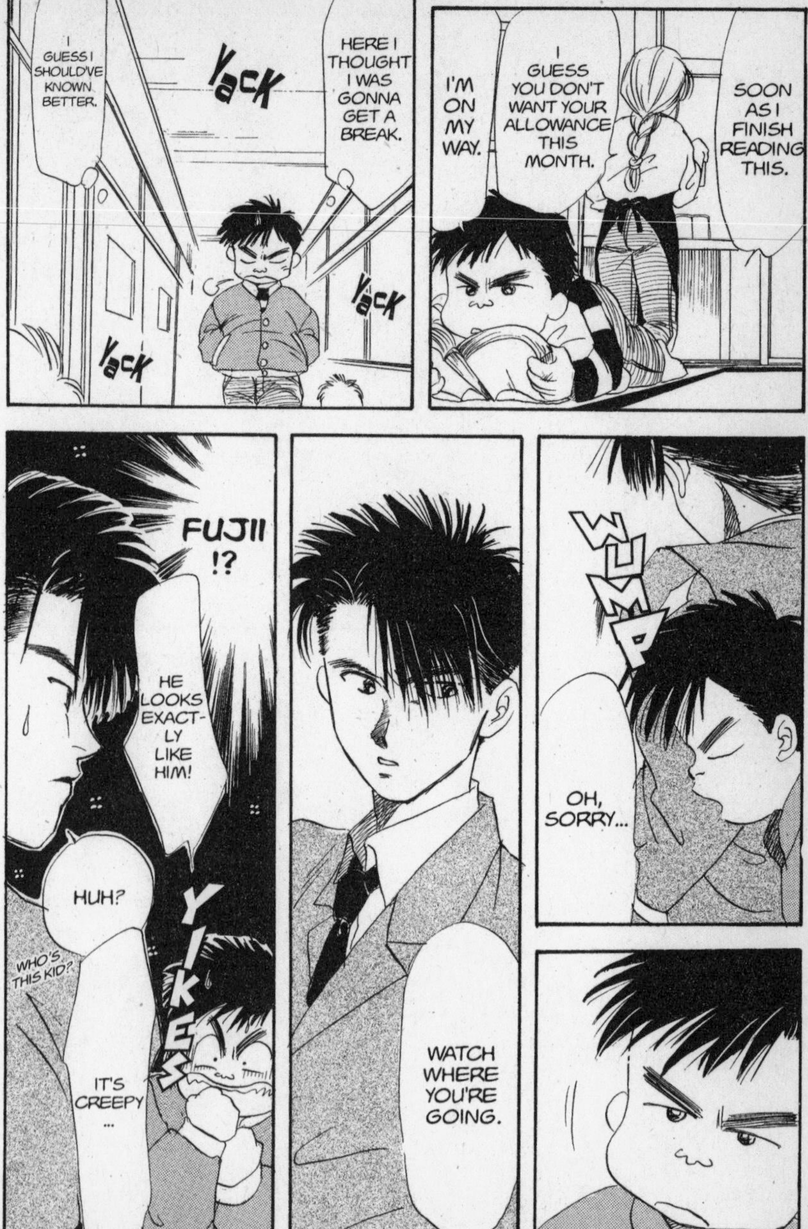
SOON AS I FINISH READING THIS.
I GUESS YOU DON'T WANT YOUR ALLOWANCE THIS MONTH.
I'M ON MY WAY.
HERE I THOUGHT I WAS GONNA GET A BREAK.
YACK
I GUESS I SHOULD'VE KNOWN BETTER.
YACK
YACK
WUMP
OH, SORRY...
WATCH WHERE YOU'RE GOING.
FUJII !?
HE LOOKS EXACTLY LIKE HIM!
HUH?
YIKES
WHO'S THIS KID?
IT'S CREEPY ...

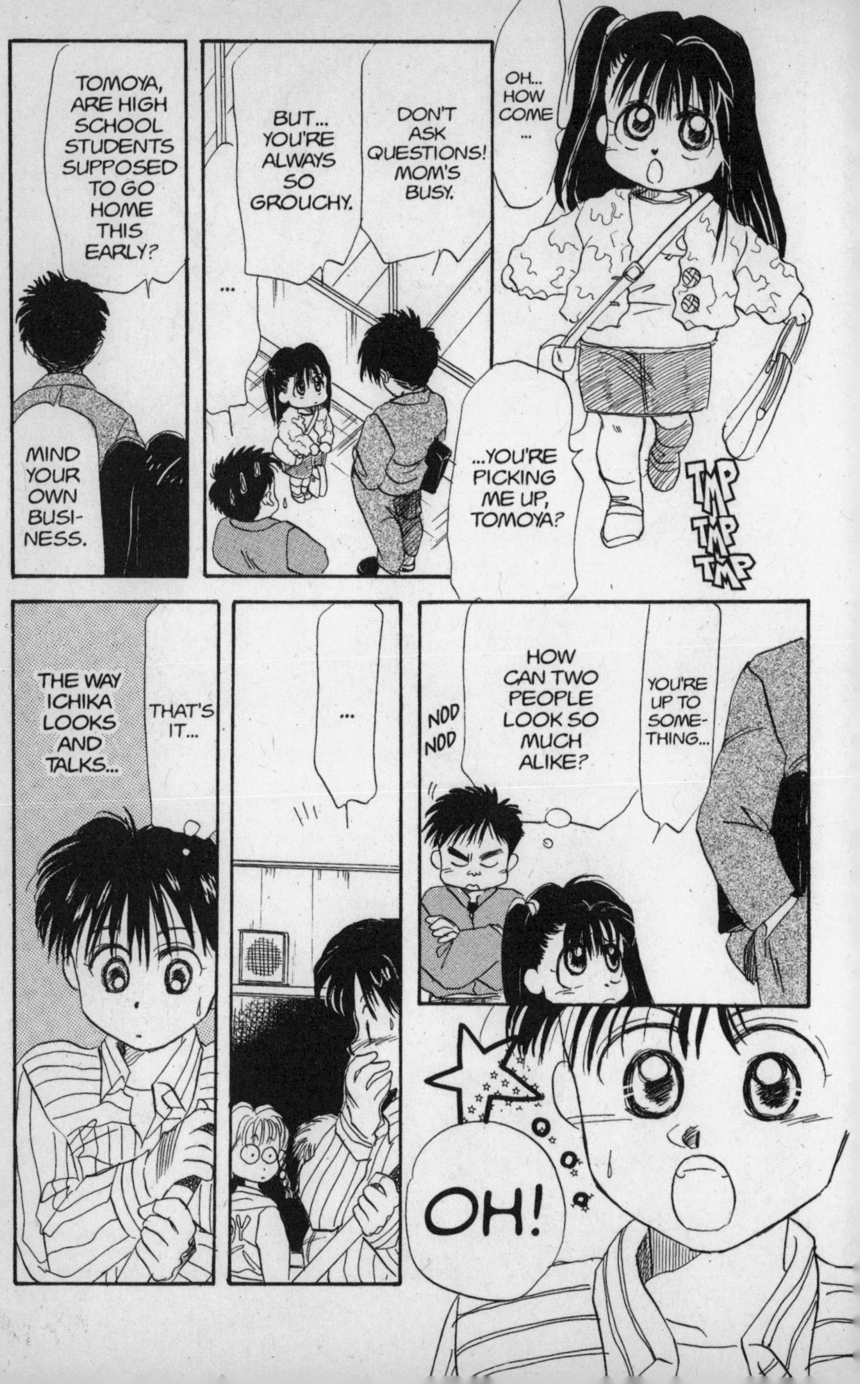
OH... HOW COME ...
...YOU'RE PICKING ME UP, TOMOYA?
TMP TMP TMP
DON'T ASK QUESTIONS! MOM'S BUSY.
BUT... YOU'RE ALWAYS SO GROUCHY.
...
TOMOYA, ARE HIGH SCHOOL STUDENTS SUPPOSED TO GO HOME THIS EARLY?
MIND YOUR OWN BUSI-NESS.
YOU'RE UP TO SOME-THING...
HOW CAN TWO PEOPLE LOOK SO MUCH ALIKE?
NOD NOD
OH!
...
THAT'S IT...
THE WAY ICHIKA LOOKS AND TALKS...

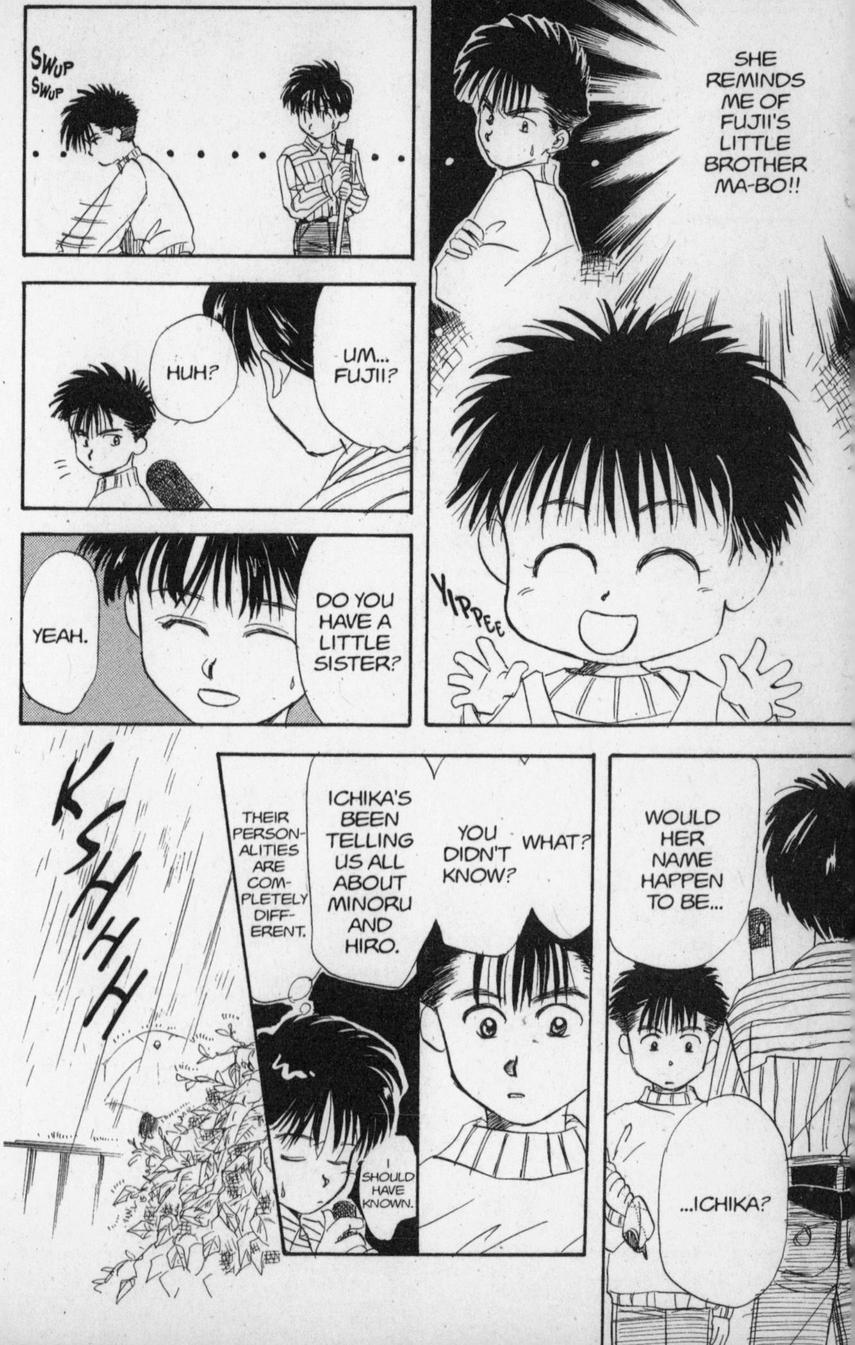
SHE REMINDS ME OF FUJII'S LITTLE BROTHER MA-BO!!
YIPPEE
SWUP SWUP
UM... FUJII?
HUH?
DO YOU HAVE A LITTLE SISTER?
YEAH.
WOULD HER NAME HAPPEN TO BE...
...ICHIKA?
WHAT?
YOU DIDN'T KNOW?
ICHIKA'S BEEN TELLING US ALL ABOUT MINORU AND HIRO.
THEIR PERSON-ALITIES ARE COM-PLETELY DIFF-ERENT.
I SHOULD HAVE KNOWN.
KSHHH

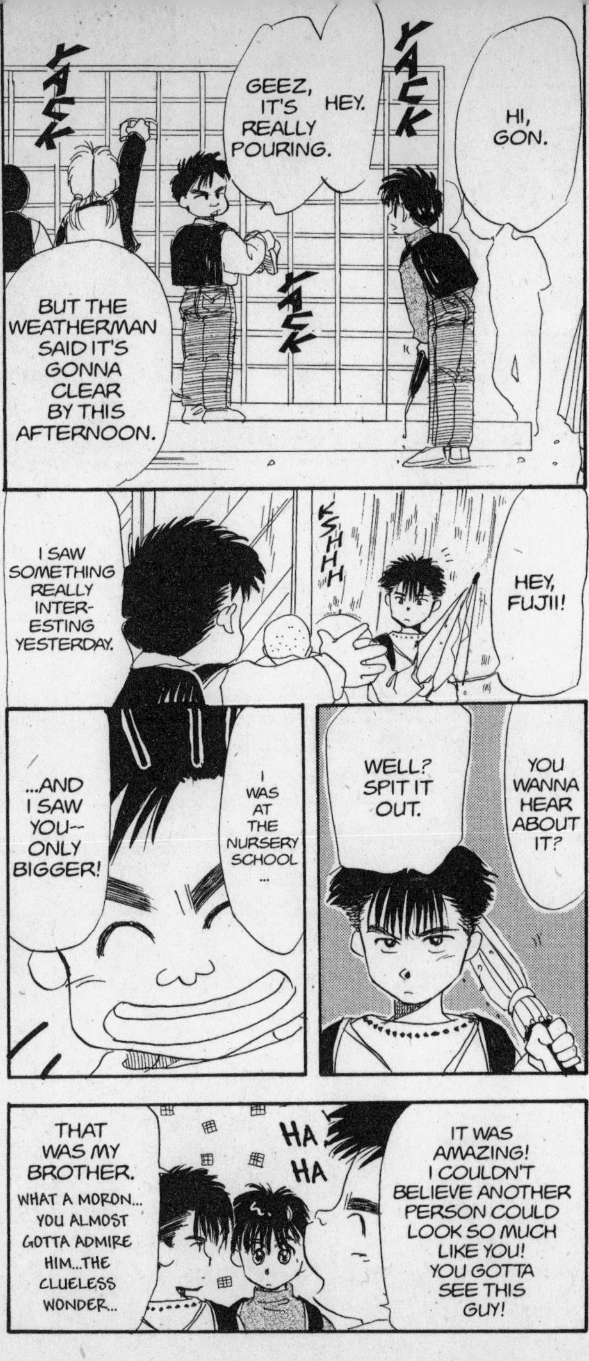
HI, GON.
YACK
HEY.
GEEZ, IT'S REALLY POURING.
YACK
BUT THE WEATHERMAN SAID IT'S GONNA CLEAR BY THIS AFTERNOON.
YACK
HEY, FUJII!
KSHHH
I SAW SOMETHING REALLY INTER-ESTING YESTERDAY.
YOU WANNA HEAR ABOUT IT?
WELL? SPIT IT OUT.
I WAS AT THE NURSERY SCHOOL ...
...AND I SAW YOU-- ONLY BIGGER!
IT WAS AMAZING! I COULDN'T BELIEVE ANOTHER PERSON COULD LOOK SO MUCH LIKE YOU! YOU GOTTA SEE THIS GUY!
HA HA
THAT WAS MY BROTHER.
WHAT A MORON... YOU ALMOST GOTTA ADMIRE HIM...THE CLUELESS WONDER...

POPULAR SERIES:

YOSHIZO THE RABBIT PART 3

I THINK I WROTE IN VOLUME I THAT YOSHIZO HAD GROWN TO TWICE HIS ORIGINAL SIZE. WELL, NOW HE'S FOUR TIMES THAT BIG. LATELY, I'VE BEGUN TO DOUBT THAT HE'S A "MINI"-RABBIT AT ALL.

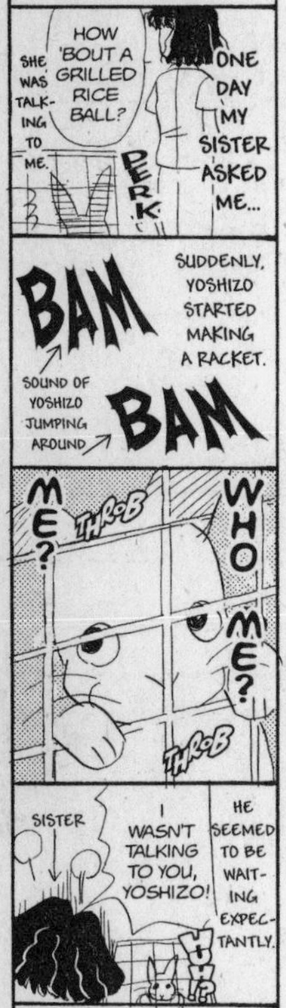
ONE DAY MY SISTER ASKED ME...
HOW 'BOUT A GRILLED RICE BALL?
SHE WAS TALK-ING TO ME.
PERK
SUDDENLY, YOSHIZO STARTED MAKING A RACKET.
BAM
SOUND OF YOSHIZO JUMPING AROUND
BAM
WHO ME?
THROB
ME?
THROB
HE SEEMED TO BE WAIT-ING EXPECT-ANTLY.
I WASN'T TALKING TO YOU, YOSHIZO!
SISTER

I RECEIVED SOME PHOTOSFROM PEOPLE WITH RABBITS.THEIR RABBITS ALL LOOKED VERY WELL BEHAVED. SOMEONE SENT ME SOME COOKIES ESPECIALLY FOR RABBITS CALLED "BRUNCH."MY LITTLE BROTHER ATE ONE, AND HE SAID IT TASTED PRETTY GOOD.

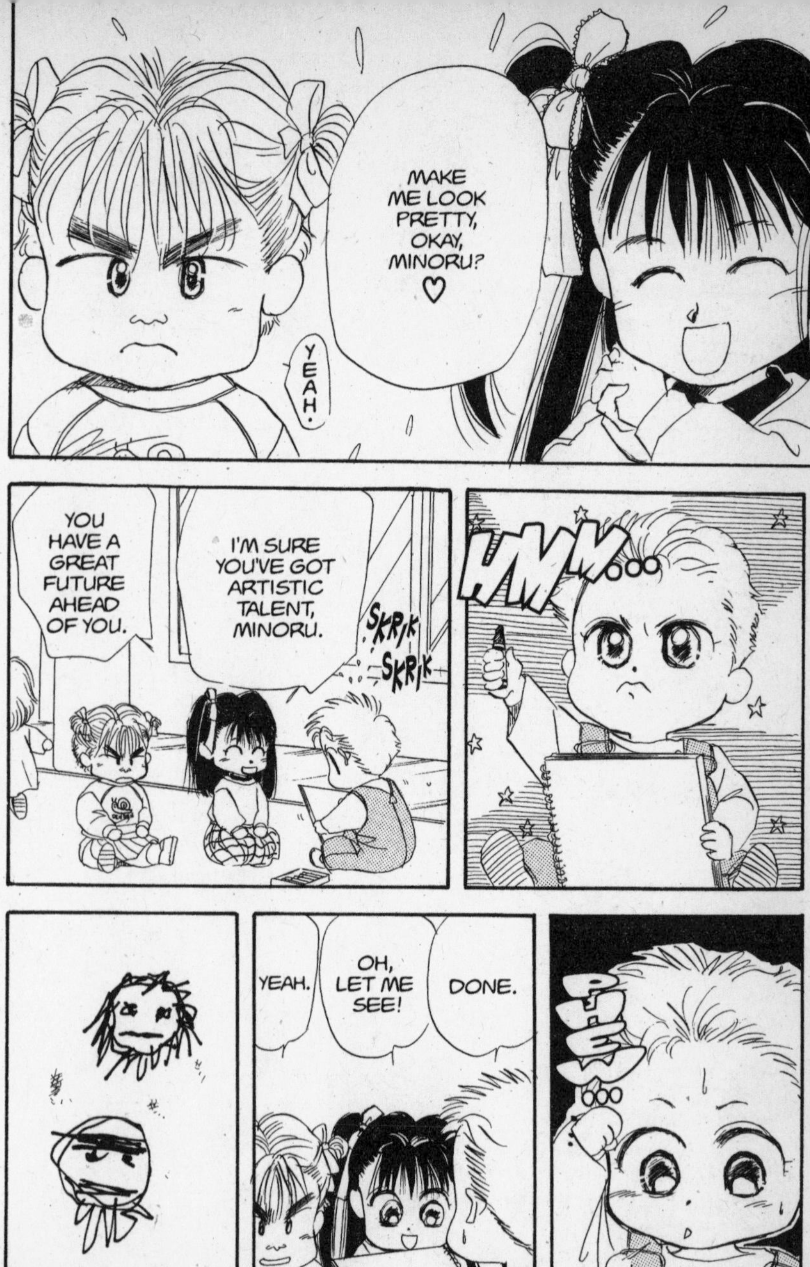
MAKE ME LOOK PRETTY, OKAY, MINORU? ♡
YEAH.
HMM...
SKRIK SKRIK
I'M SURE YOU'VE GOT ARTISTIC TALENT, MINORU.
YOU HAVE A GREAT FUTURE AHEAD OF YOU.
PHEW...
DONE.
OH, LET ME SEE!
YEAH.

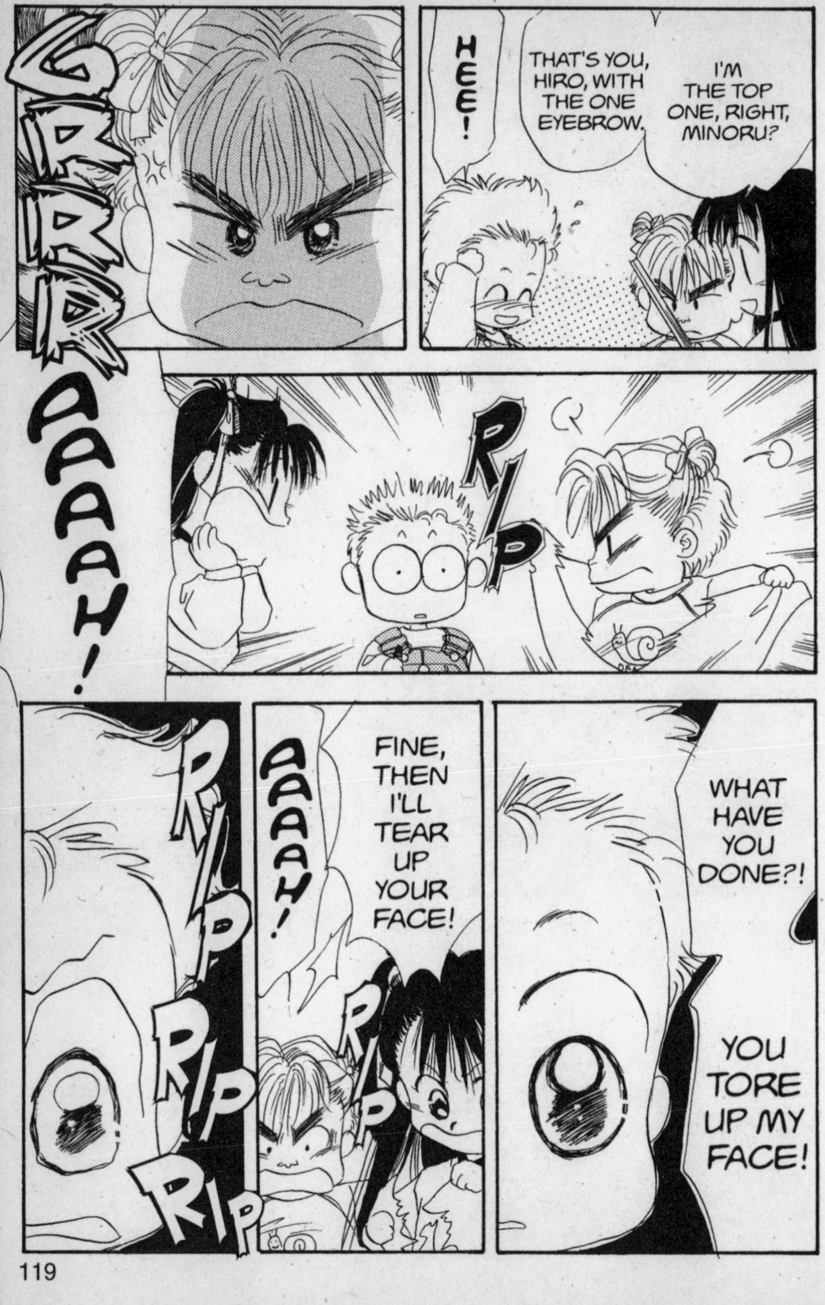
I'M THE TOP ONE, RIGHT, MINORU?
THAT'S YOU, HIRO, WITH THE ONE EYEBROW.
HEE!
GRRRAAAAH!
RIP
WHAT HAVE YOU DONE?!
YOU TORE UP MY FACE!
FINE, THEN I'LL TEAR UP YOUR FACE!
AAAAH!
RIP
RIP
RIP
RIP

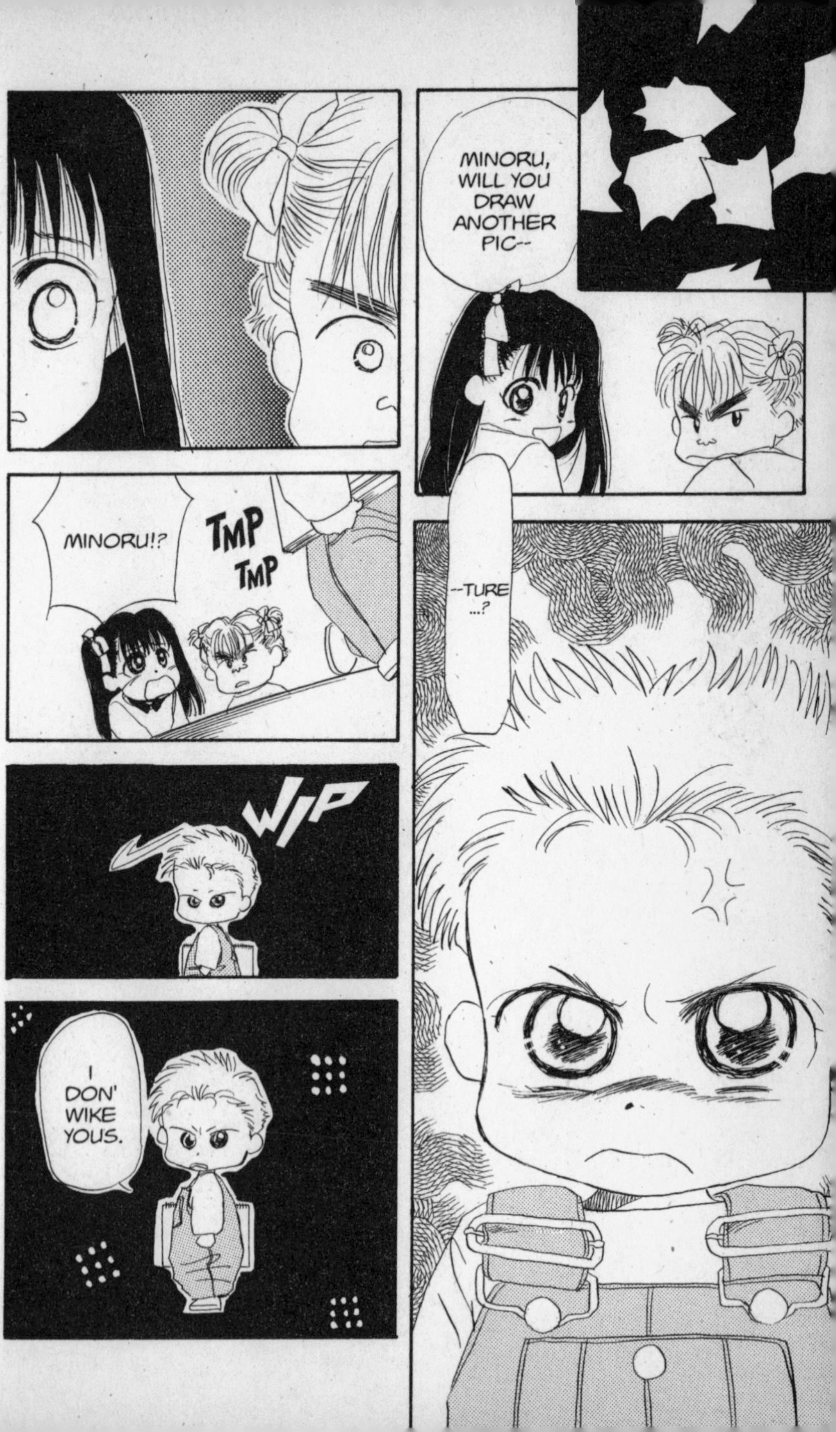
MINORU, WILL YOU DRAW ANOTHER PIC--
--TURE ...?
MINORU!?
TMP
TMP
WIP
I DON' WIKE YOUS.

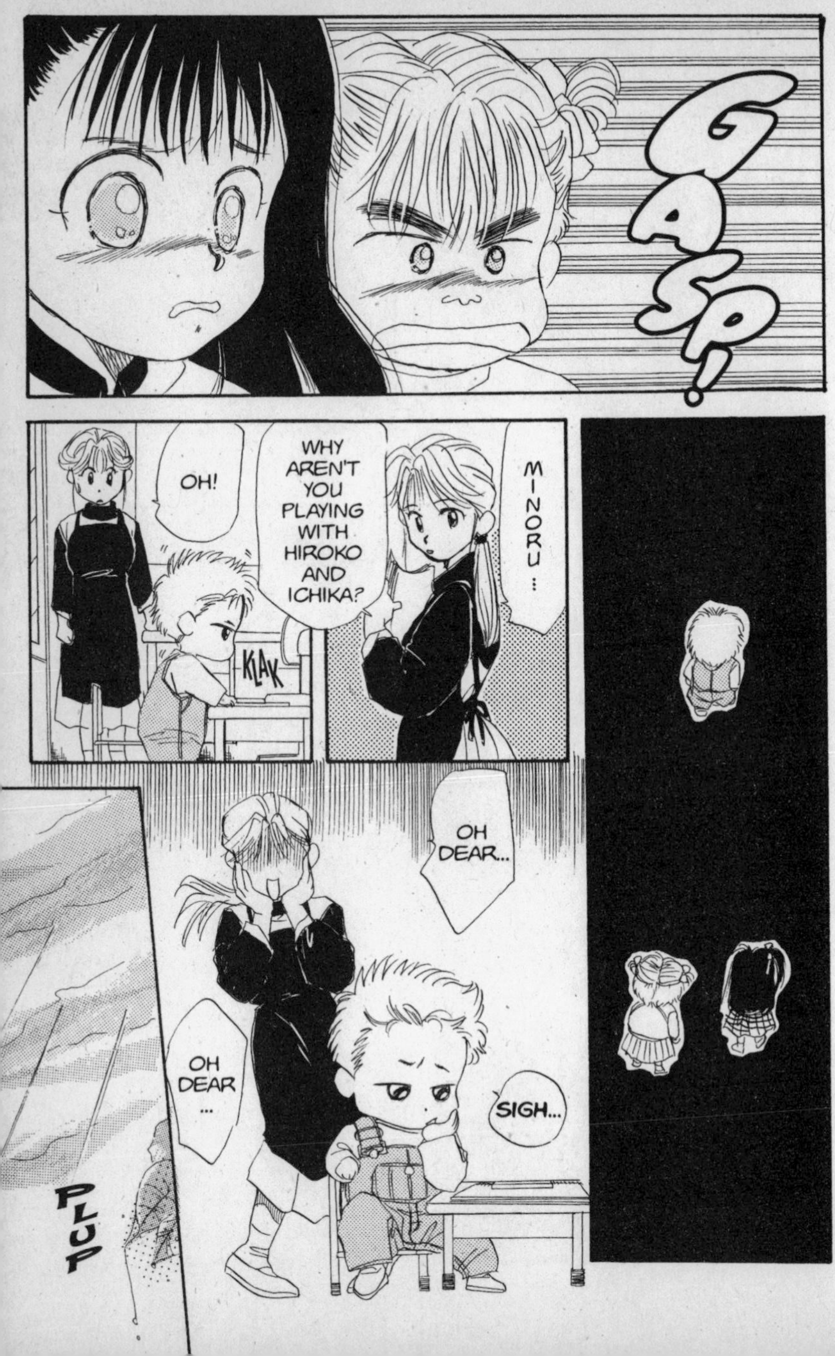
GASP!
MINORU...
WHY AREN'T YOU PLAYING WITH HIROKO AND ICHIKA?
OH!
KLAK
OH DEAR...
SIGH...
OH DEAR...
PLUP

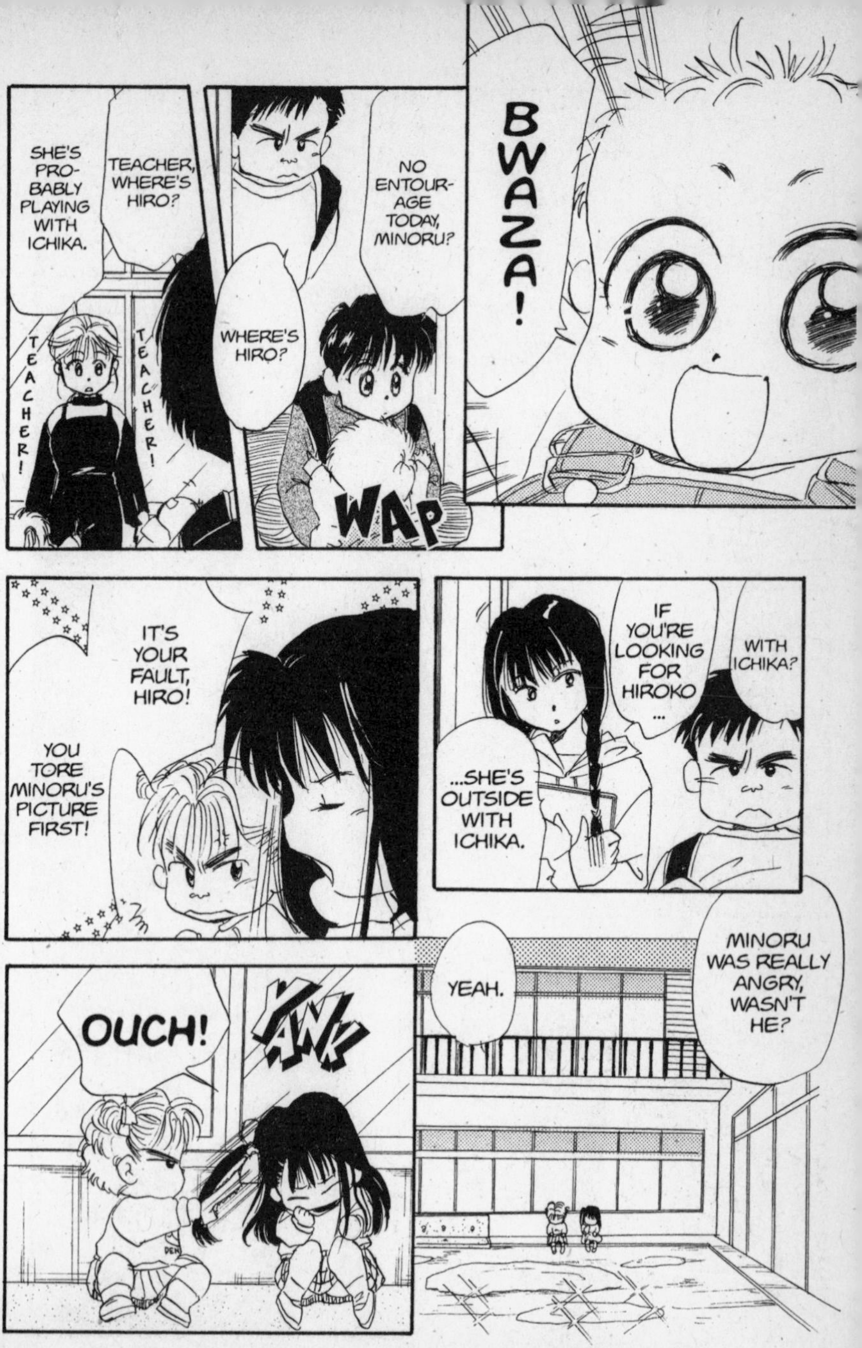
BWAZA!
NO ENTOURAGE TODAY, MINORU?
WHERE'S HIRO?
WAP
TEACHER, WHERE'S HIRO?
SHE'S PROBABLY PLAYING WITH ICHIKA.
TEACHER!
TEACHER!
IF YOU'RE LOOKING FOR HIROKO...
...SHE'S OUTSIDE WITH ICHIKA.
WITH ICHIKA?
IT'S YOUR FAULT, HIRO!
YOU TORE MINORU'S PICTURE FIRST!
MINORU WAS REALLY ANGRY, WASN'T HE?
YEAH.
YANK
OUCH!

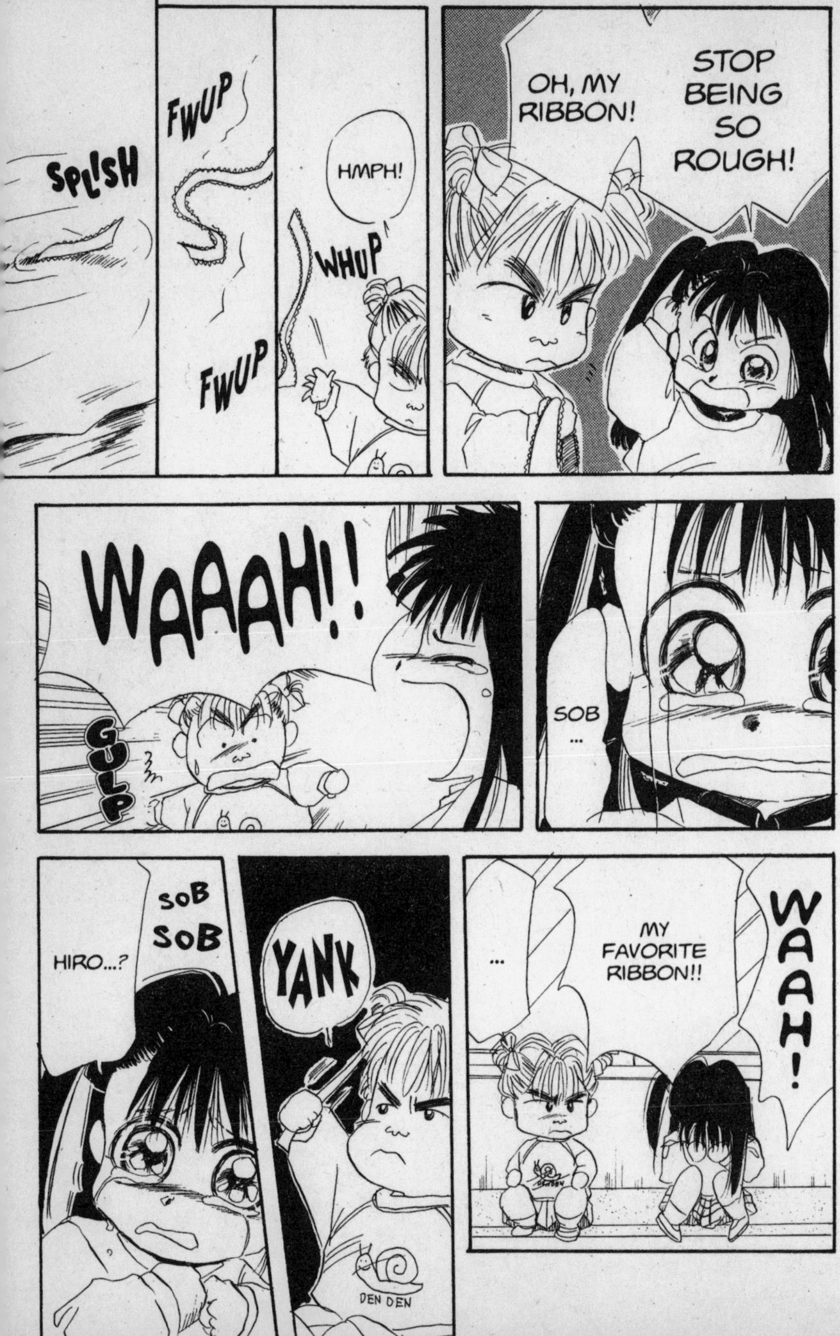
STOP BEING SO ROUGH!
OH, MY RIBBON!
HMPH!
WHUP
FWUP
FWUP
SPL!SH
SOB ...
WAAAH!!
GULP
WAAAH!
MY FAVORITE RIBBON!!
...
YANK
DEN DEN
SOB SOB
HIRO...?

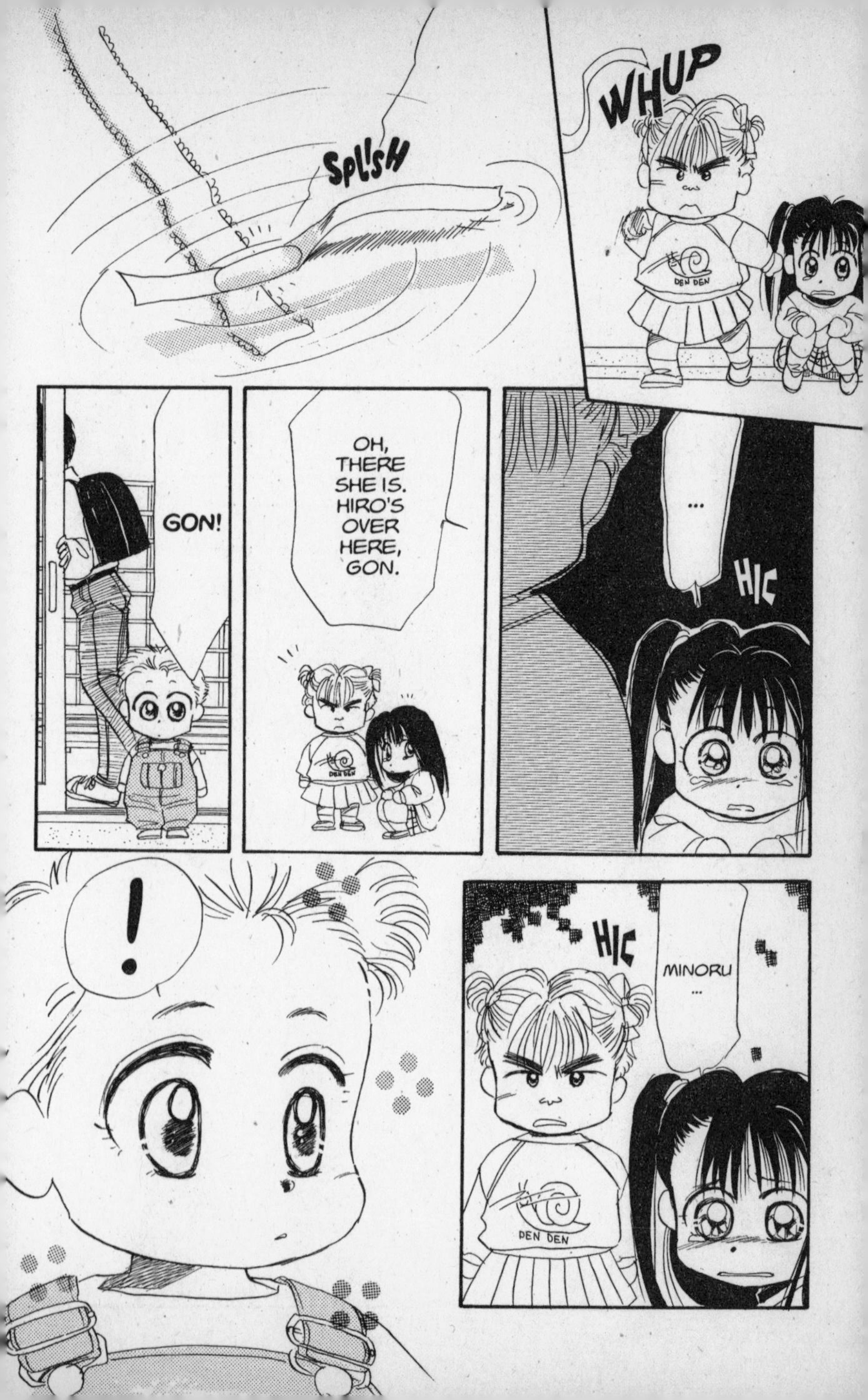
WHUP
SPL!SH
...
HIC
OH, THERE SHE IS. HIRO'S OVER HERE, GON.
GON!
HIC
MINORU ...
!

MINORU?

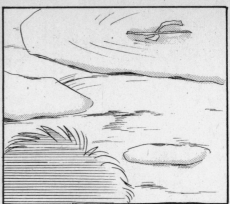

SPLASH

SPLASH

SPLASH SPLASH

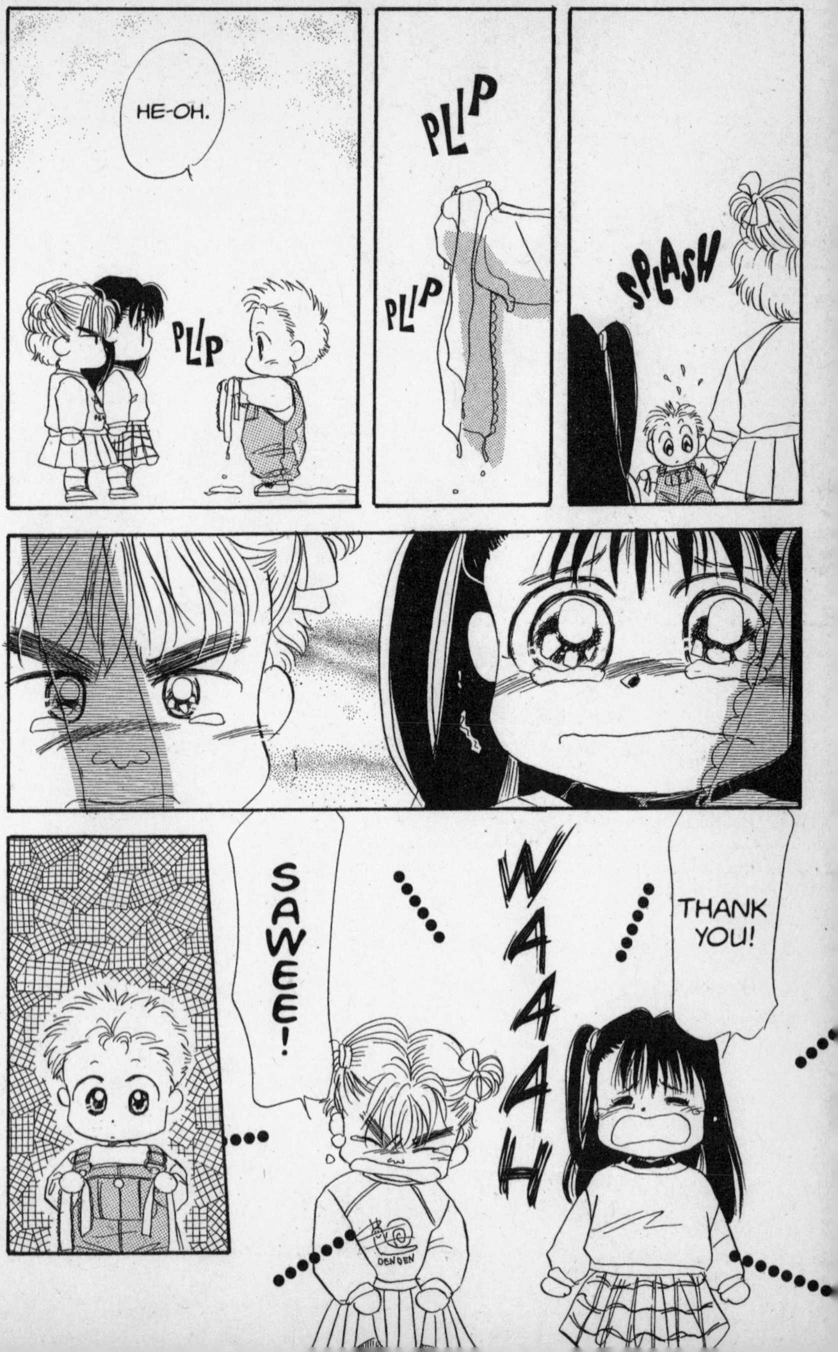
SPLASH
PLIP
PLIP
HE-OH.
PLIP
THANK YOU!
...
WAAAAH
...
SAWEE!
...

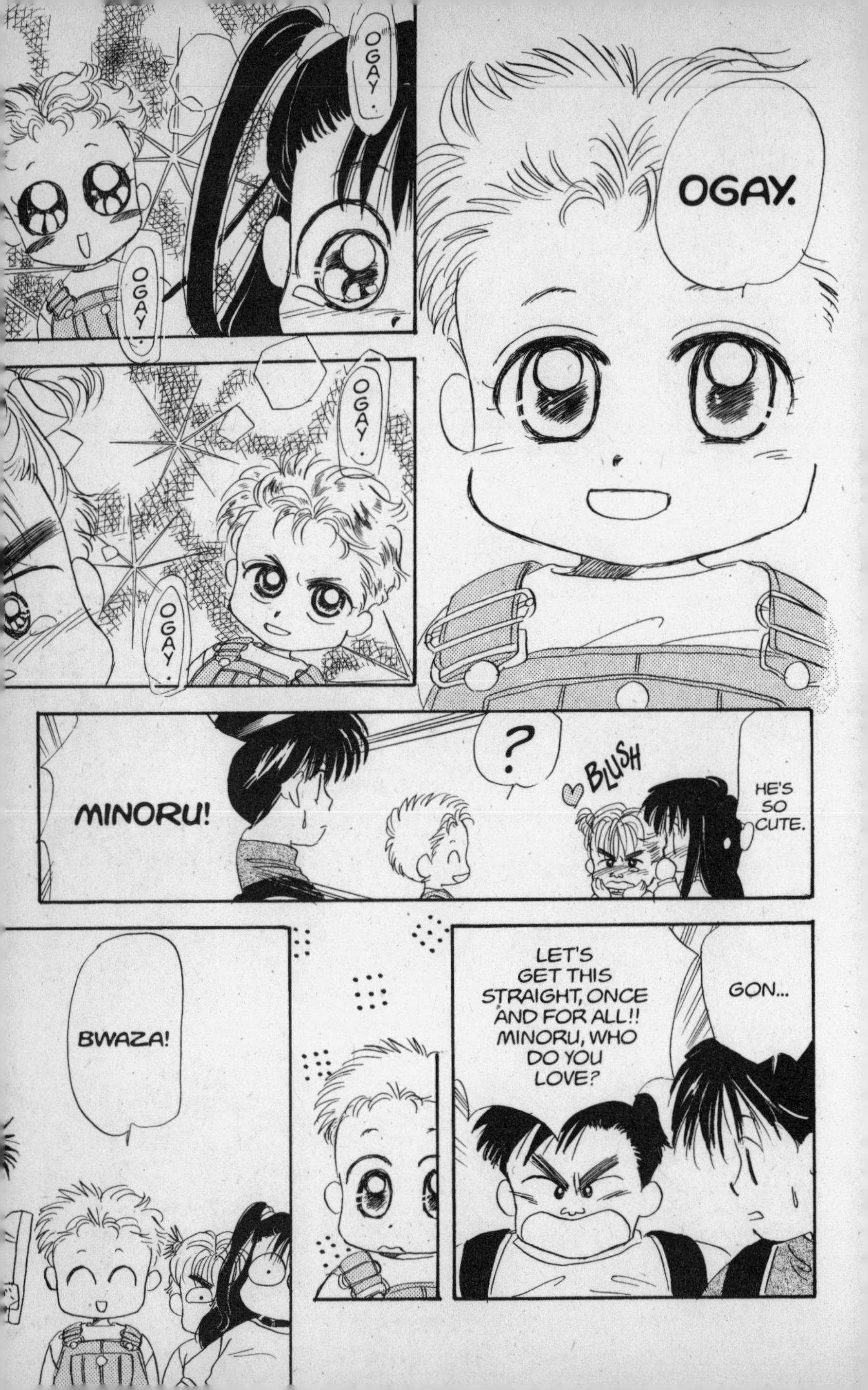
OGAY.
OGAY.
OGAY.
OGAY.
OGAY.
HE'S SO CUTE.
BLUSH
?
MINORU!
GON...
LET'S GET THIS STRAIGHT, ONCE AND FOR ALL!! MINORU, WHO DO YOU LOVE?
BWAZA!

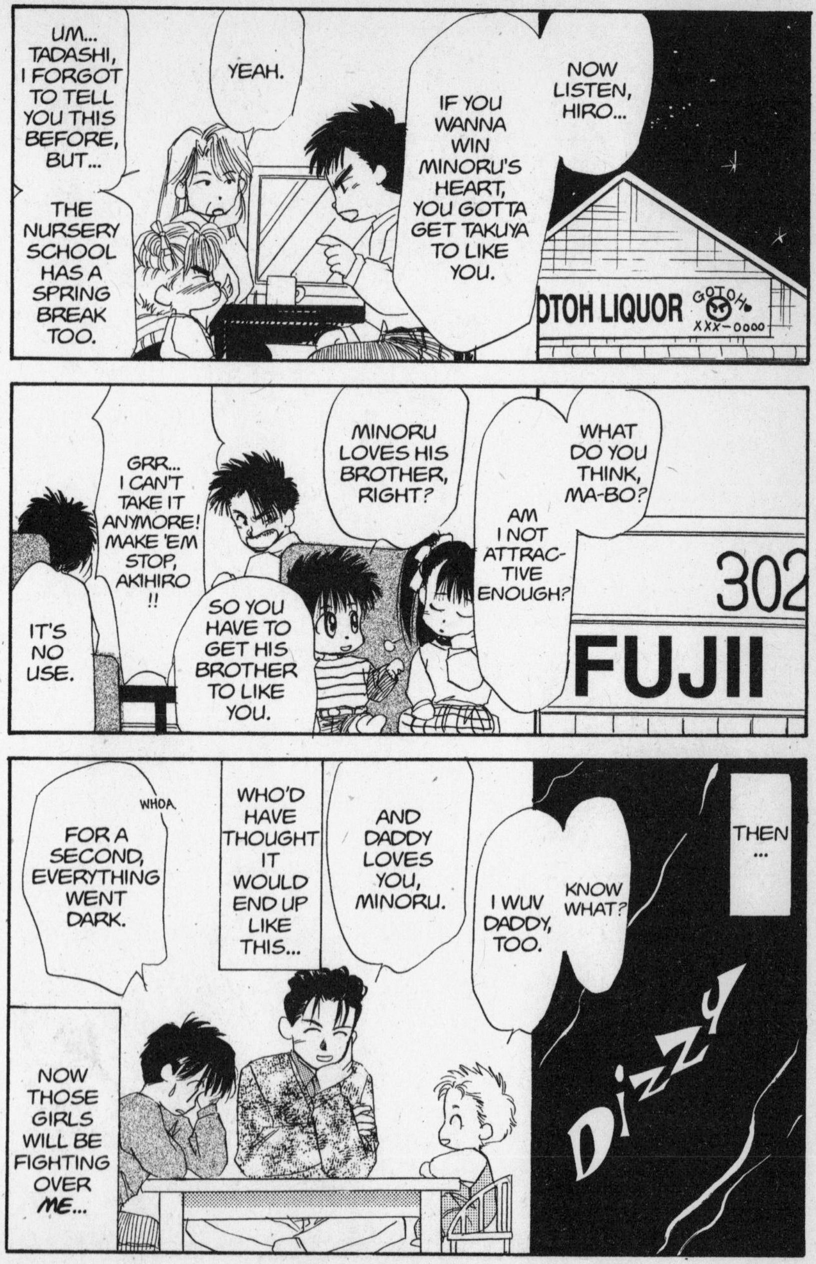
NOW LISTEN, HIRO...
IF YOU WANNA WIN MINORU'S HEART, YOU GOTTA GET TAKUYA TO LIKE YOU.
OTOH LIQUOR
GOTOH
XXX-0000
YEAH.
UM... TADASHI, I FORGOT TO TELL YOU THIS BEFORE, BUT...
THE NURSERY SCHOOL HAS A SPRING BREAK TOO.
302
FUJII
WHAT DO YOU THINK, MA-BO?
AM I NOT ATTRACTIVE ENOUGH?
MINORU LOVES HIS BROTHER, RIGHT?
SO YOU HAVE TO GET HIS BROTHER TO LIKE YOU.
GRR... I CAN'T TAKE IT ANYMORE! MAKE 'EM STOP, AKIHIRO !!
IT'S NO USE.
THEN...
KNOW WHAT?
I WUV DADDY, TOO.
Dizzy
AND DADDY LOVES YOU, MINORU.
WHO'D HAVE THOUGHT IT WOULD END UP LIKE THIS...
WHOA
FOR A SECOND, EVERYTHING WENT DARK.
NOW THOSE GIRLS WILL BE FIGHTING OVER ME...

CHAPTER 9/THE END

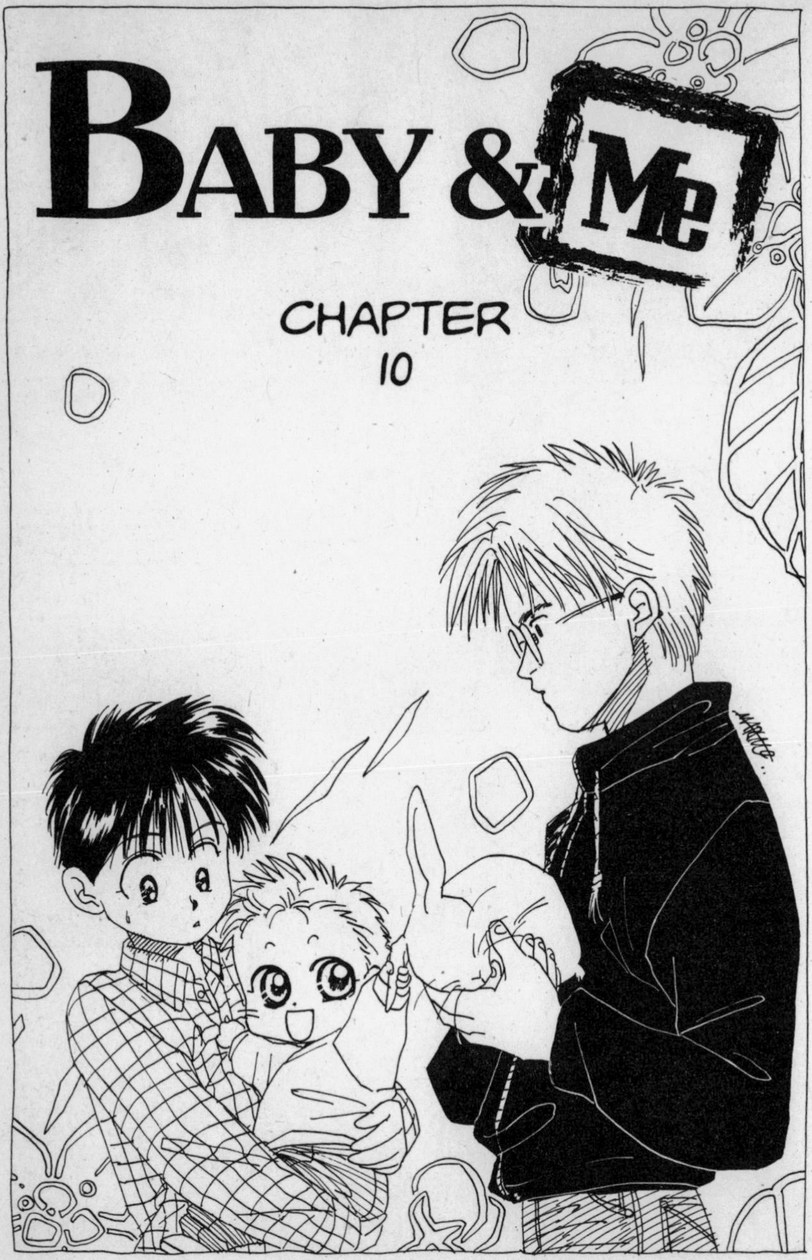
BABY & Me
CHAPTER
10

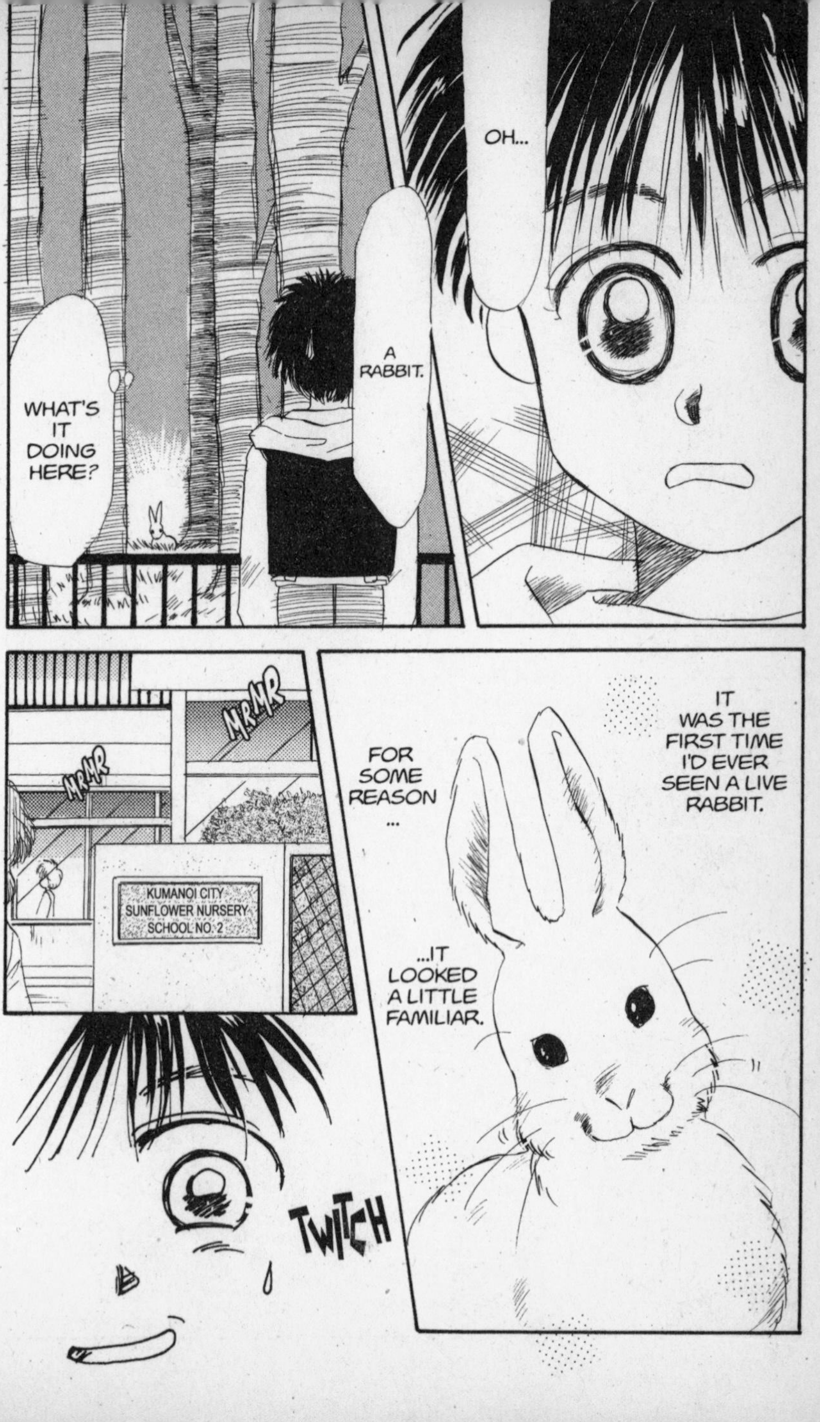
OH...
A RABBIT.
WHAT'S IT DOING HERE?
IT WAS THE FIRST TIME I'D EVER SEEN A LIVE RABBIT.
FOR SOME REASON ...
...IT LOOKED A LITTLE FAMILIAR.
MRMR
MRMR
KUMANOI CITY SUNFLOWER NURSERY SCHOOL NO. 2
TWITCH

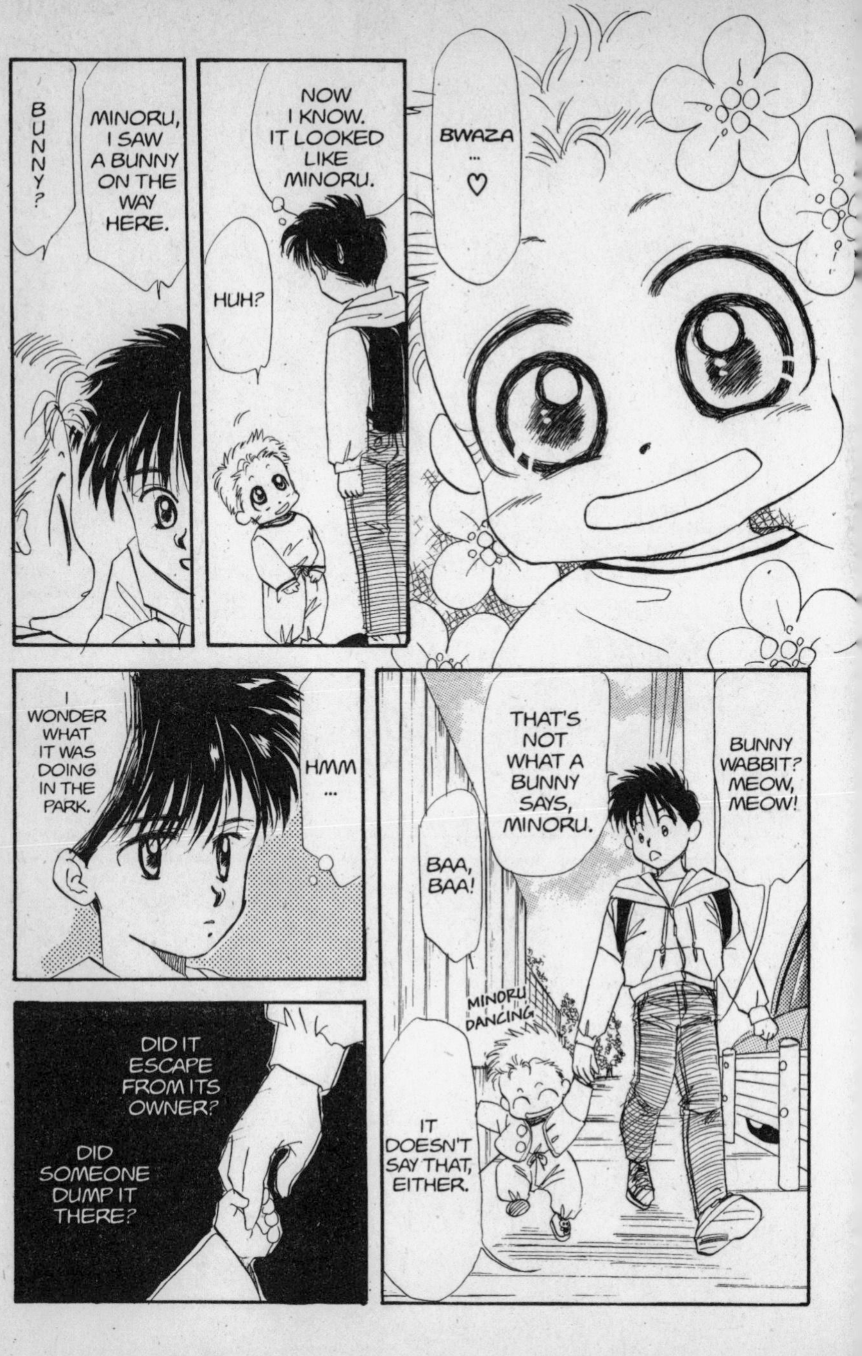
BWAZA ... ♡
NOW I KNOW. IT LOOKED LIKE MINORU.
HUH?
MINORU, I SAW A BUNNY ON THE WAY HERE.
BUNNY?
BUNNY WABBIT? MEOW, MEOW!
THAT'S NOT WHAT A BUNNY SAYS, MINORU.
BAA, BAA!
MINORU DANCING
IT DOESN'T SAY THAT, EITHER.
HMM ...
I WONDER WHAT IT WAS DOING IN THE PARK.
DID IT ESCAPE FROM ITS OWNER?
DID SOMEONE DUMP IT THERE?

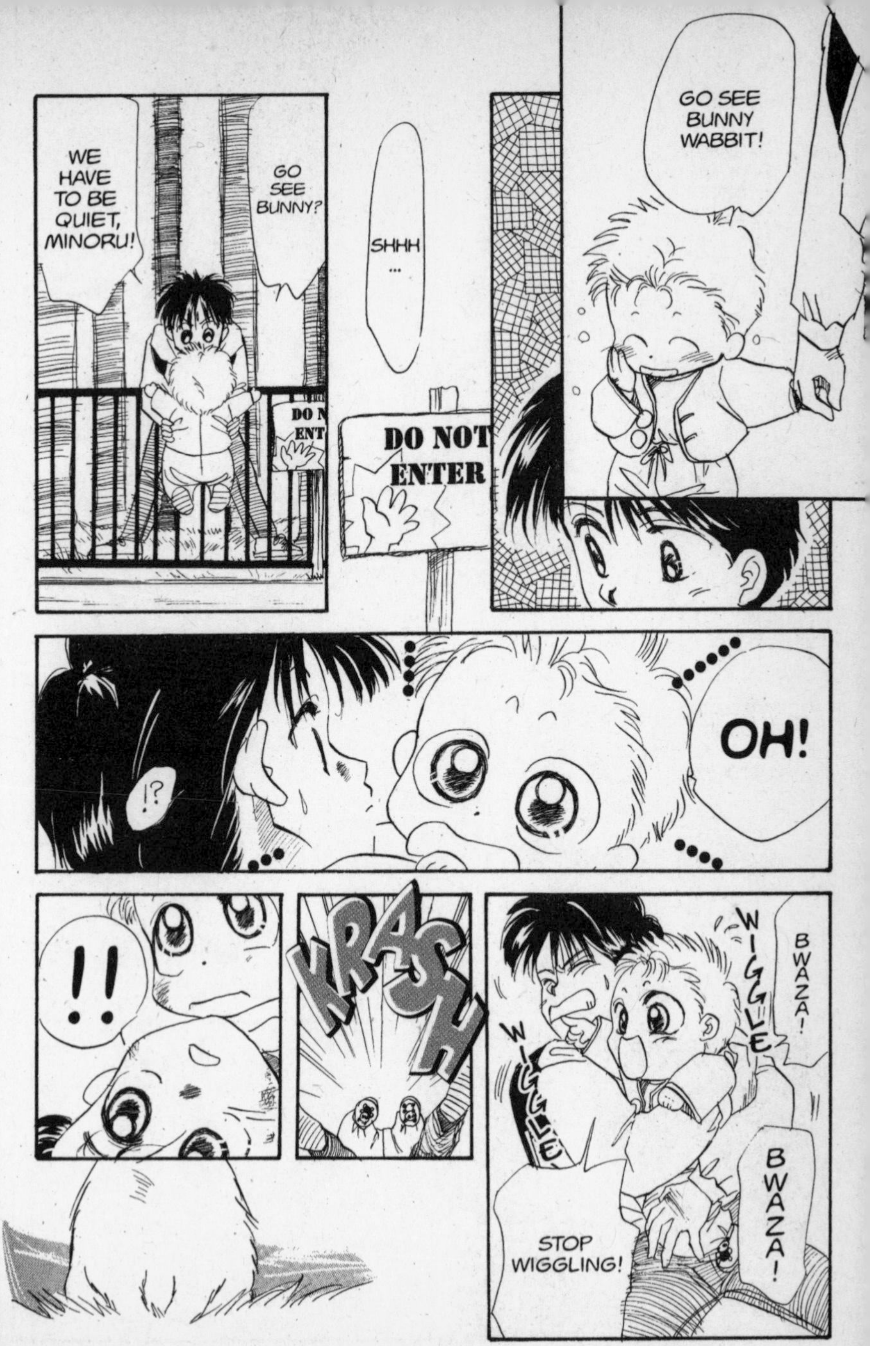
GO SEE BUNNY WABBIT!
SHHH ...
DO NOT ENTER
GO SEE BUNNY?
WE HAVE TO BE QUIET, MINORU!
DO NOT ENTER
OH!
!?
BWAZA!
WIGGLE
WIGGLE
BWAZA!
STOP WIGGLING!
KRASH
!!

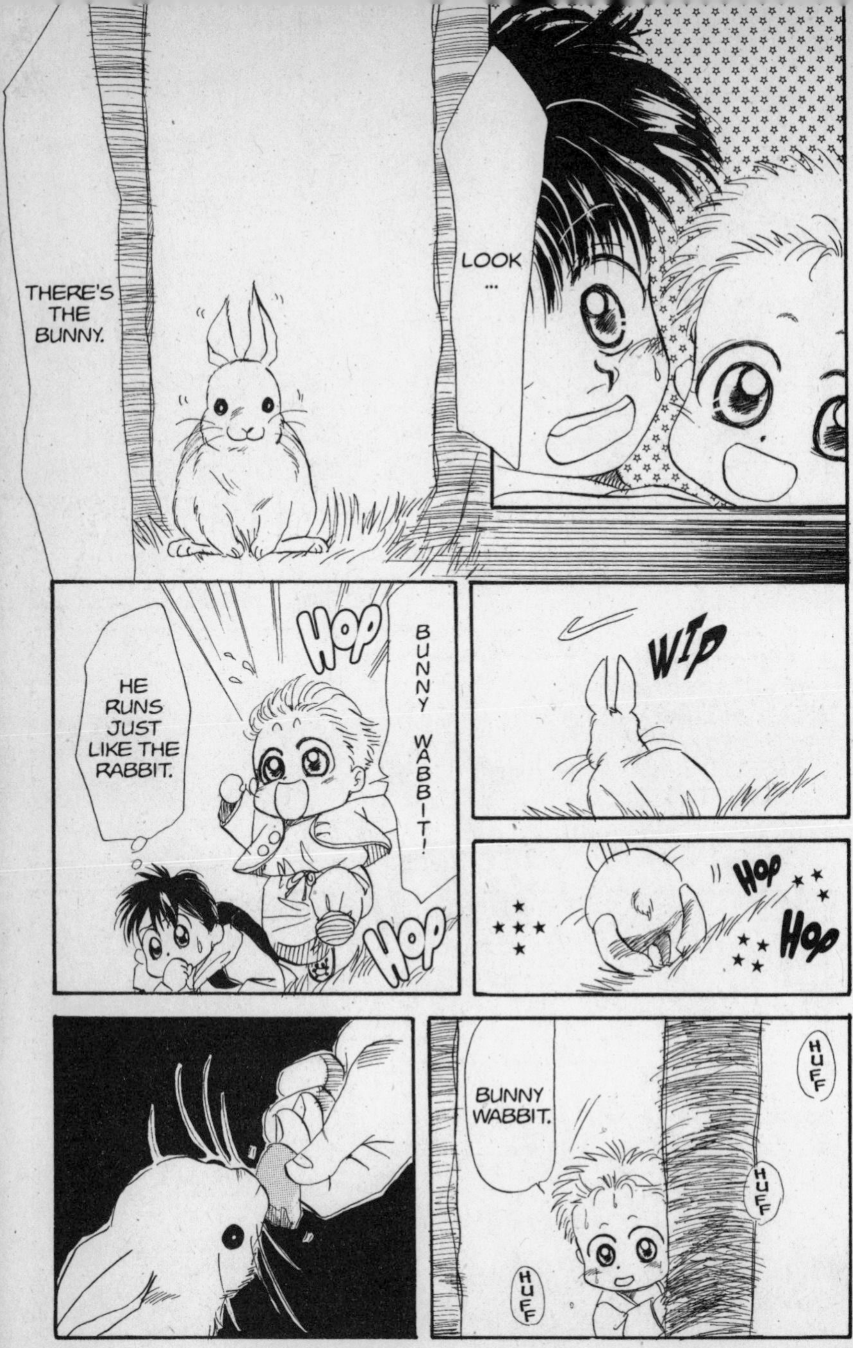
LOOK ...
THERE'S THE BUNNY.
WIP
HOP
HOP
HOP
BUNNY WABBIT!
HOP
HE RUNS JUST LIKE THE RABBIT.
HOP
HUFF
BUNNY WABBIT.
HUFF
HUFF

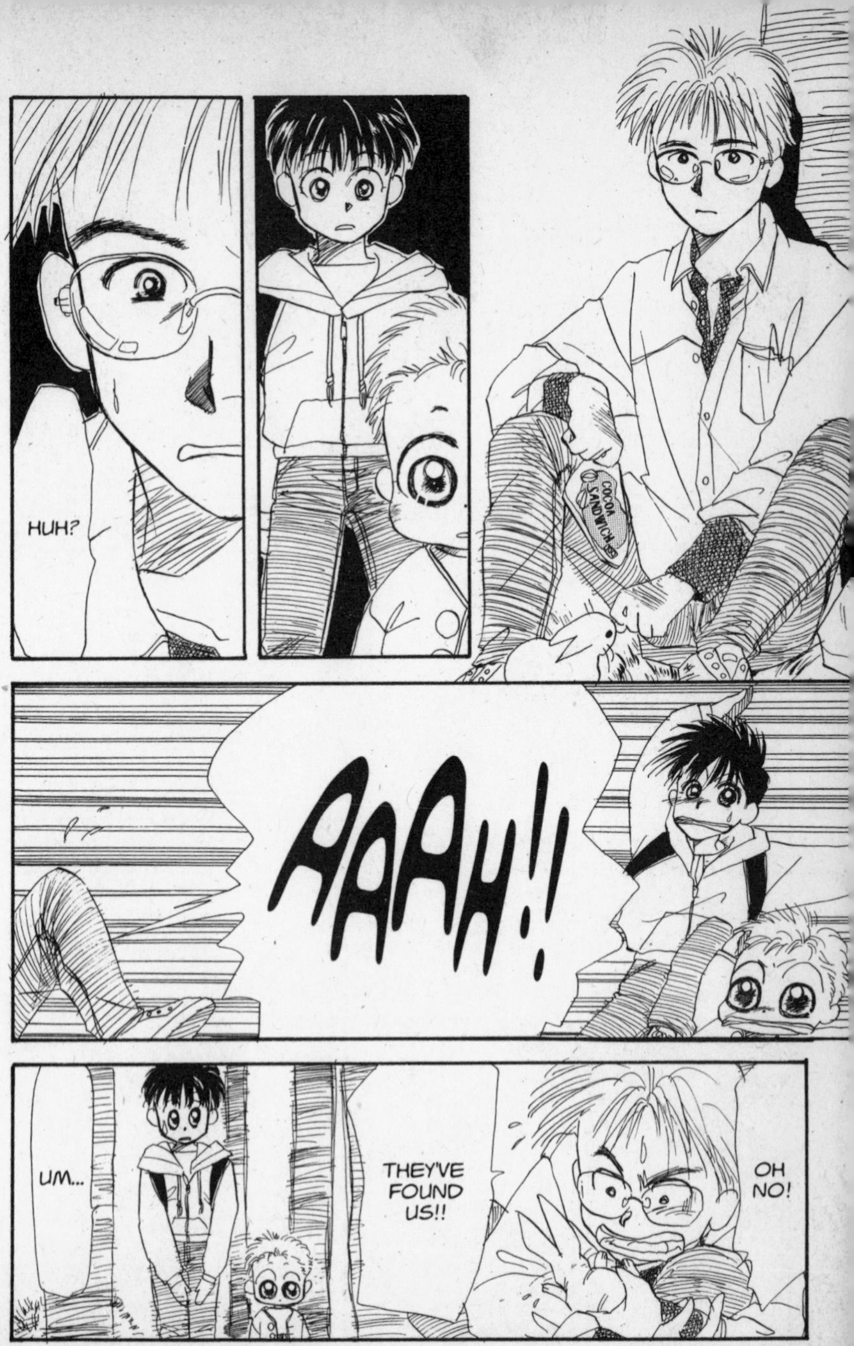
COCOA SANDWICH
HUH?
AAAH!!
OH NO!
THEY'VE FOUND US!!
UM...

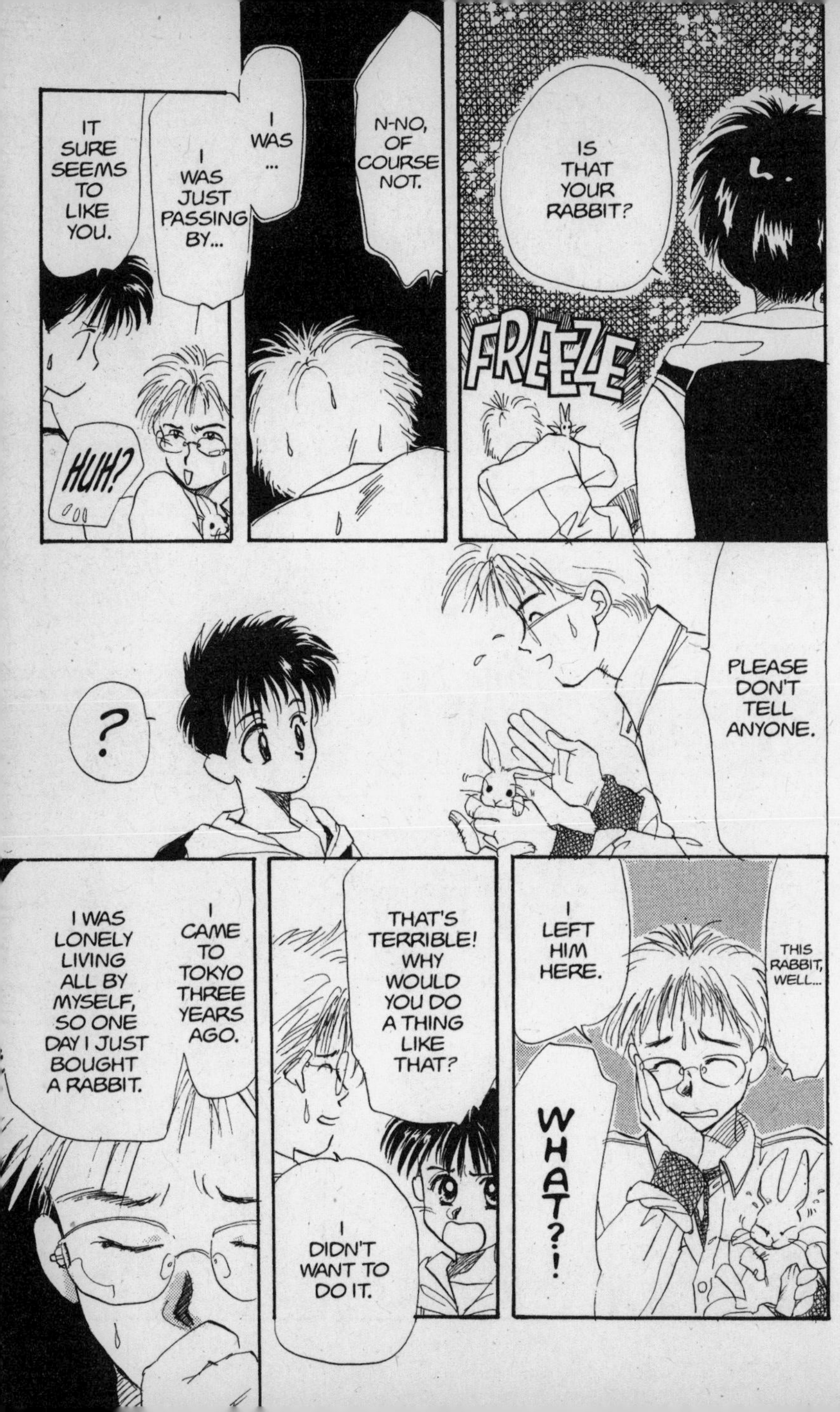
IS THAT YOUR RABBIT?
FREEZE
N-NO, OF COURSE NOT.
I WAS ...
I WAS JUST PASSING BY...
IT SURE SEEMS TO LIKE YOU.
HUH?
PLEASE DON'T TELL ANYONE.
?
THIS RABBIT, WELL...
I LEFT HIM HERE.
WHAT?!
THAT'S TERRIBLE! WHY WOULD YOU DO A THING LIKE THAT?
I DIDN'T WANT TO DO IT.
I CAME TO TOKYO THREE YEARS AGO.
I WAS LONELY LIVING ALL BY MYSELF, SO ONE DAY I JUST BOUGHT A RABBIT.

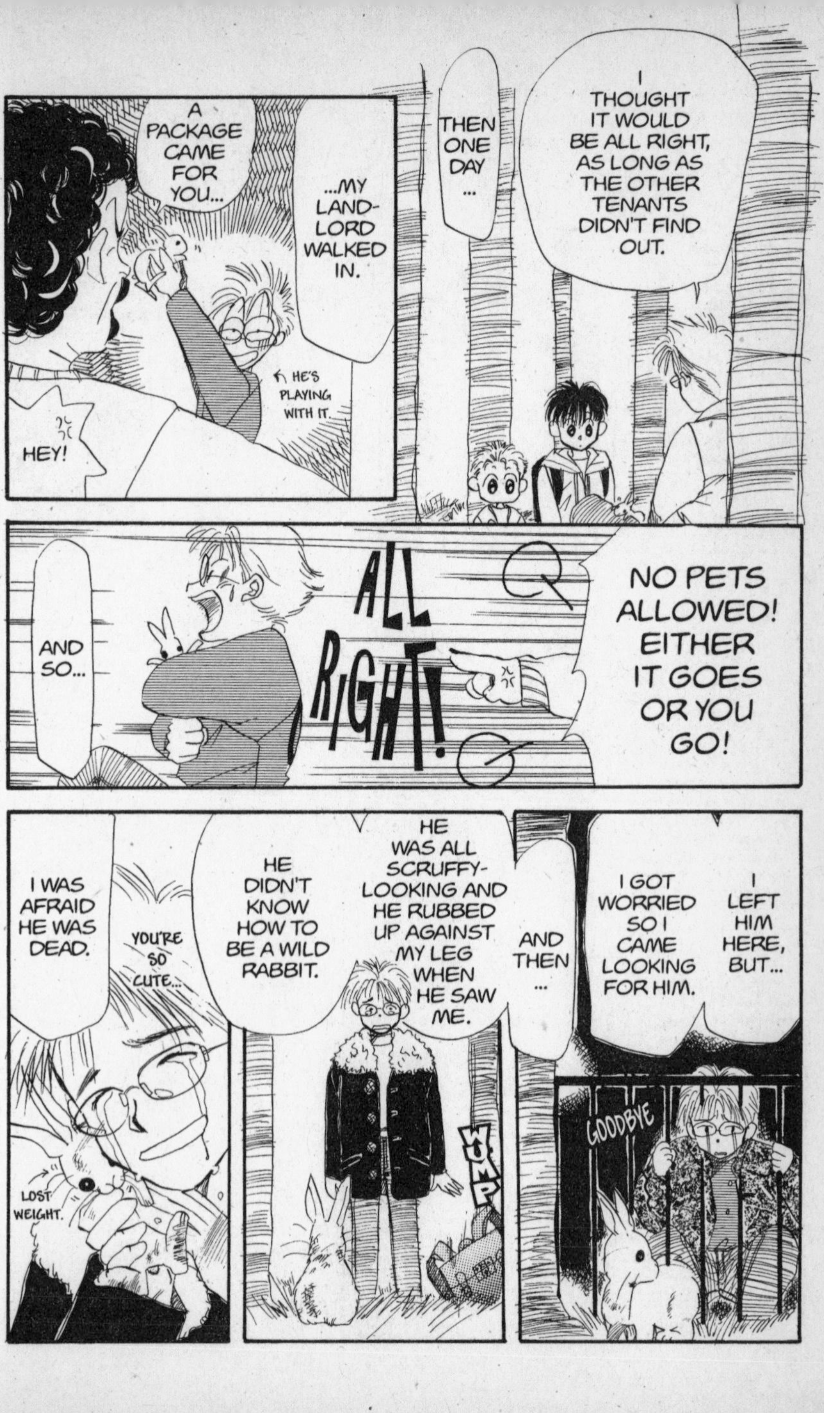
I THOUGHT IT WOULD BE ALL RIGHT, AS LONG AS THE OTHER TENANTS DIDN'T FIND OUT.
THEN ONE DAY ...
...MY LANDLORD WALKED IN.
A PACKAGE CAME FOR YOU...
HE'S PLAYING WITH IT.
HEY!
NO PETS ALLOWED! EITHER IT GOES OR YOU GO!
ALL RIGHT!
AND SO...
I LEFT HIM HERE, BUT...
I GOT WORRIED SO I CAME LOOKING FOR HIM.
GOODBYE
AND THEN ...
HE WAS ALL SCRUFFY-LOOKING AND HE RUBBED UP AGAINST MY LEG WHEN HE SAW ME.
HE DIDN'T KNOW HOW TO BE A WILD RABBIT.
WUMP
I WAS AFRAID HE WAS DEAD.
YOU'RE SO CUTE...
LOST WEIGHT.

I CAN'T KEEP HIM IN MY APARTMENT, SO I BRING FOOD TO HIM HERE EVERY DAY.
BUNNY...
OH, IT HAS A NAME.
IT'S SACHIKO.
IT'S A FEMALE?
MALE ...
SACHIKO IS THE NAME OF MY FIRST LOVE.
I'M KIND OF SENTIMENTAL.
...
SACHIKO !
BWAZA, WOOK ...
BUNNIES LOVE CARROTS.
A BUNNY.

A LOT OF PEOPLE HAVE TOLD ME THAT THIS STORY ABOUT SACHIKO REALLY MADE THEM CRY. I DREW IT DURING A TIME WHEN I WAS SQUIRMING AROUND, FEELING FRUSTRATED, AND WANTING TO DRAW ADULT CHARACTERS, SO THOSE COMMENTS MADE ME VERY HAPPY. BUT, AS ALWAYS, I HAD TO DO IT IN A HURRY, SO MY MANUSCRIPT WAS VERY MESSY.

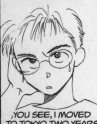

YOU SEE, I MOVED TO TOKYO TWO YEARS AGO, SO PARDON MY ACCENT.

(I RECEIVED LESSONS IN THE KANSAI DIALECT FROM A NATIVE SPEAKER, BUT I HAD TO GIVE AN EXCUSE.) I'D LIKE TO THANK MY SISTER WHO STAYED OVERNIGHT TO HELP ME PASTE THE TONE EVEN THOUGH SHE HAD TO WORK THE NEXT DAY. I'D ALSO LIKE TO THANK RIE ARAI, THE QUEEN OF FOUR-FRAME COMICS FOR GIRLS, FOR HELPING ME EVEN THOUGH SHE WAS REALLY BUSY HERSELF. I'LL RETURN YOUR CDS AS SOON AS POSSIBLE. THANKS ALSO TO LIVELY YOUNG NAHIRA YAMADA, WHO ALWAYS TALKS TO ME; TO MY EDITORS WHO HAVE NEVER GIVEN UP ON ME; AND MR. NAGASE AND THE CLUB MEMBERS; AND TO THE READERS WHO SEND ME SO MANY LETTERS EVERY MONTH; AND TO THE MEN WHO ARE READING THIS; AND TO ALL THOSE WHO HAVE SENT ME LETTERS AND GIFTS. I HOPE YOU'LL ALL CONTINUE TO SUPPORT ME.

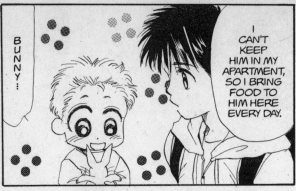

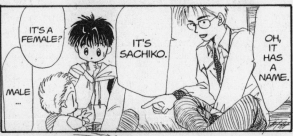

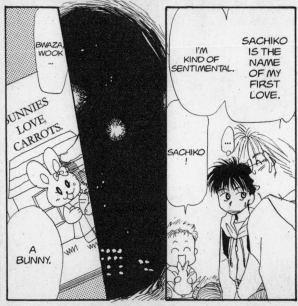

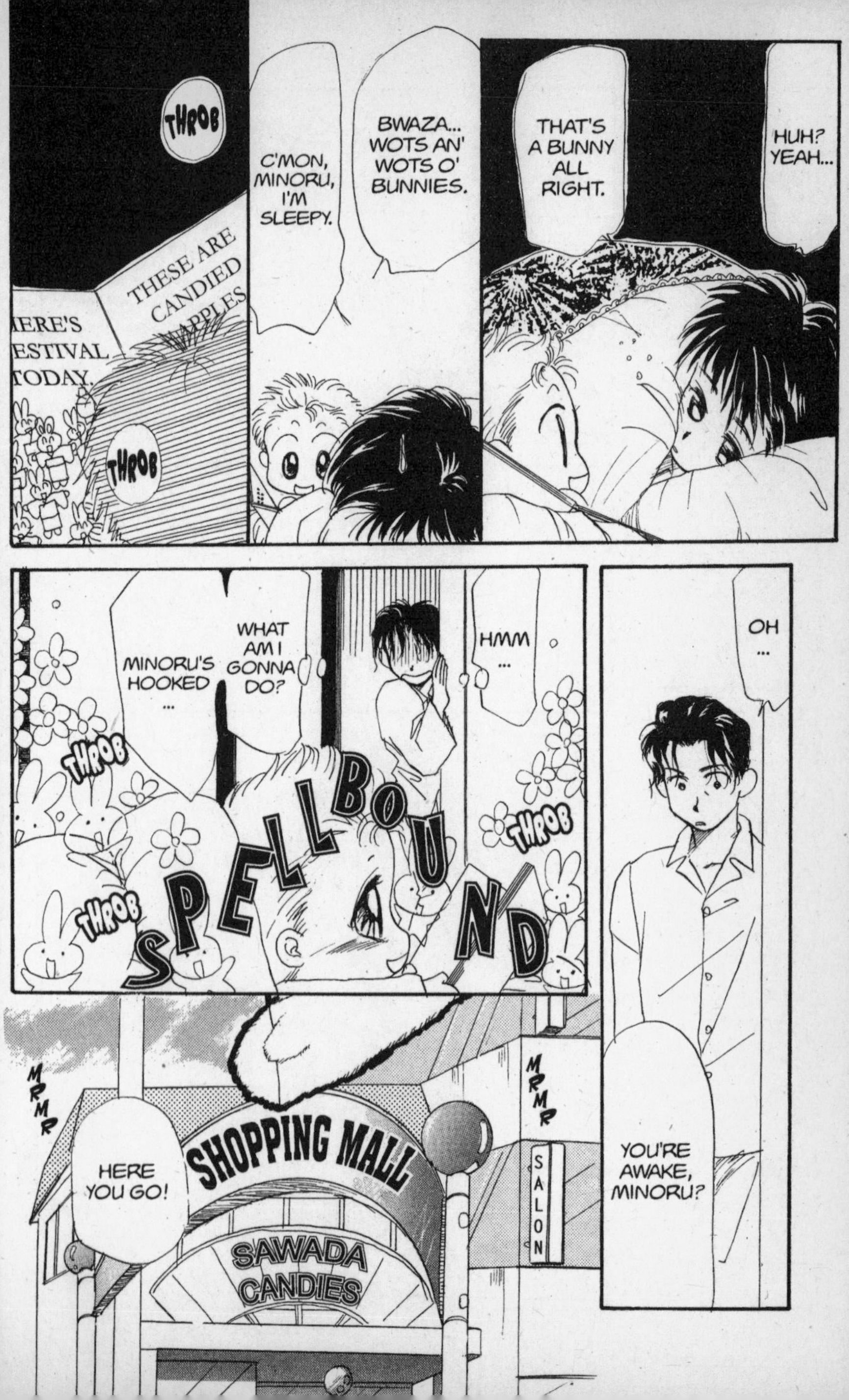
HUH? YEAH...
THAT'S A BUNNY ALL RIGHT.
BWAZA... WOTS AN' WOTS O' BUNNIES.
C'MON, MINORU, I'M SLEEPY.
THROB
THESE ARE CANDIED APPLES
THROB
OH ...
YOU'RE AWAKE, MINORU?
HMM ...
WHAT AM I GONNA DO?
MINORU'S HOOKED ...
THROB
SPELLBOUND
THROB
THROB
MRMR
SALON
SHOPPING MALL
HERE YOU GO!
SAWADA CANDIES
MRMR

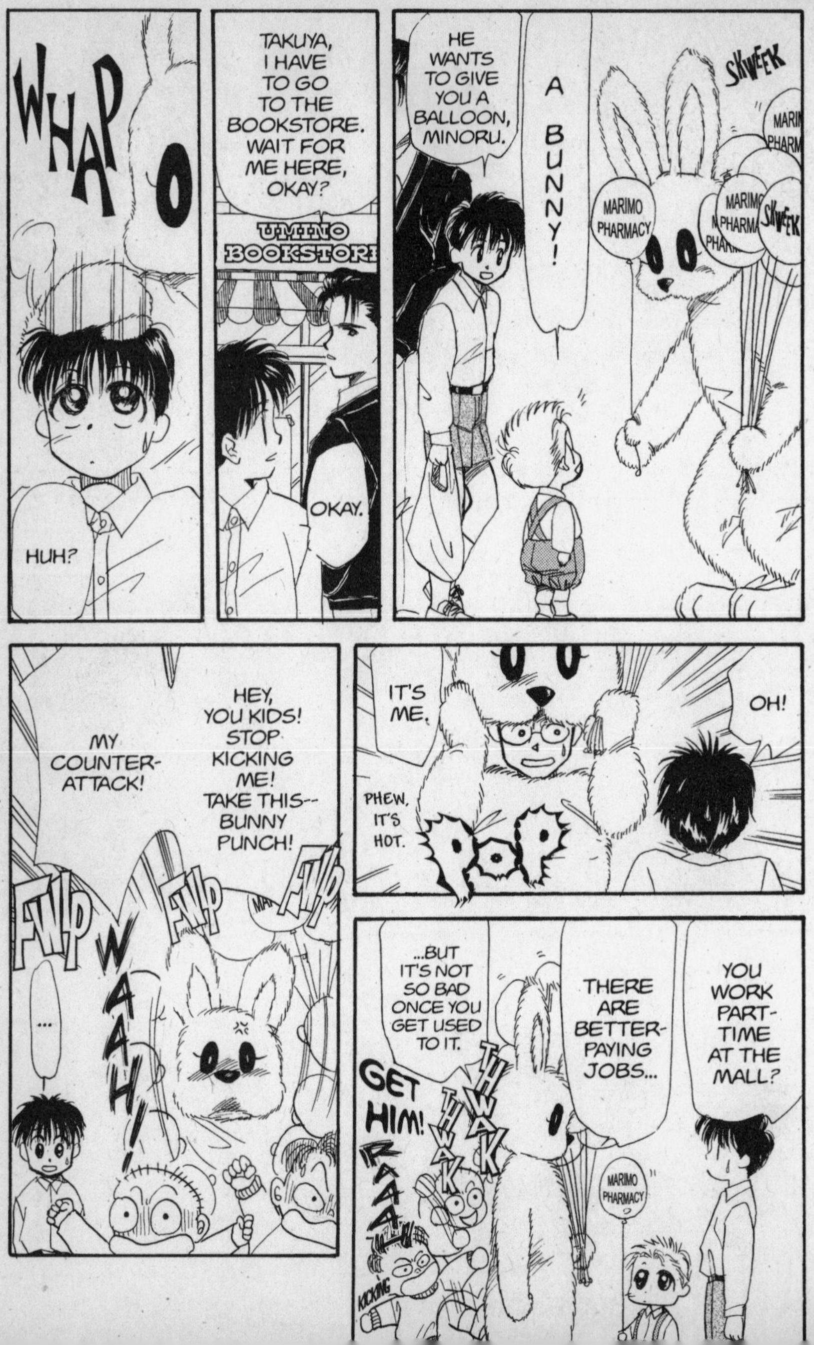
SKWEEK
MARIMO PHARMACY
SKWEEK
A BUNNY!
HE WANTS TO GIVE YOU A BALLOON, MINORU.
TAKUYA, I HAVE TO GO TO THE BOOKSTORE. WAIT FOR ME HERE, OKAY?
UMINO BOOKSTORE
OKAY.
WHAP
HUH?
OH!
IT'S ME.
PHEW, IT'S HOT.
POP
YOU WORK PART-TIME AT THE MALL?
THERE ARE BETTER-PAYING JOBS...
...BUT IT'S NOT SO BAD ONCE YOU GET USED TO IT.
THWAK
THWAK
GET HIM!
MARIMO PHARMACY
KICKING
HEY, YOU KIDS! STOP KICKING ME! TAKE THIS-- BUNNY PUNCH!
MY COUNTER-ATTACK!
FWIP
FWIP
FWIP
WAAH!!
...

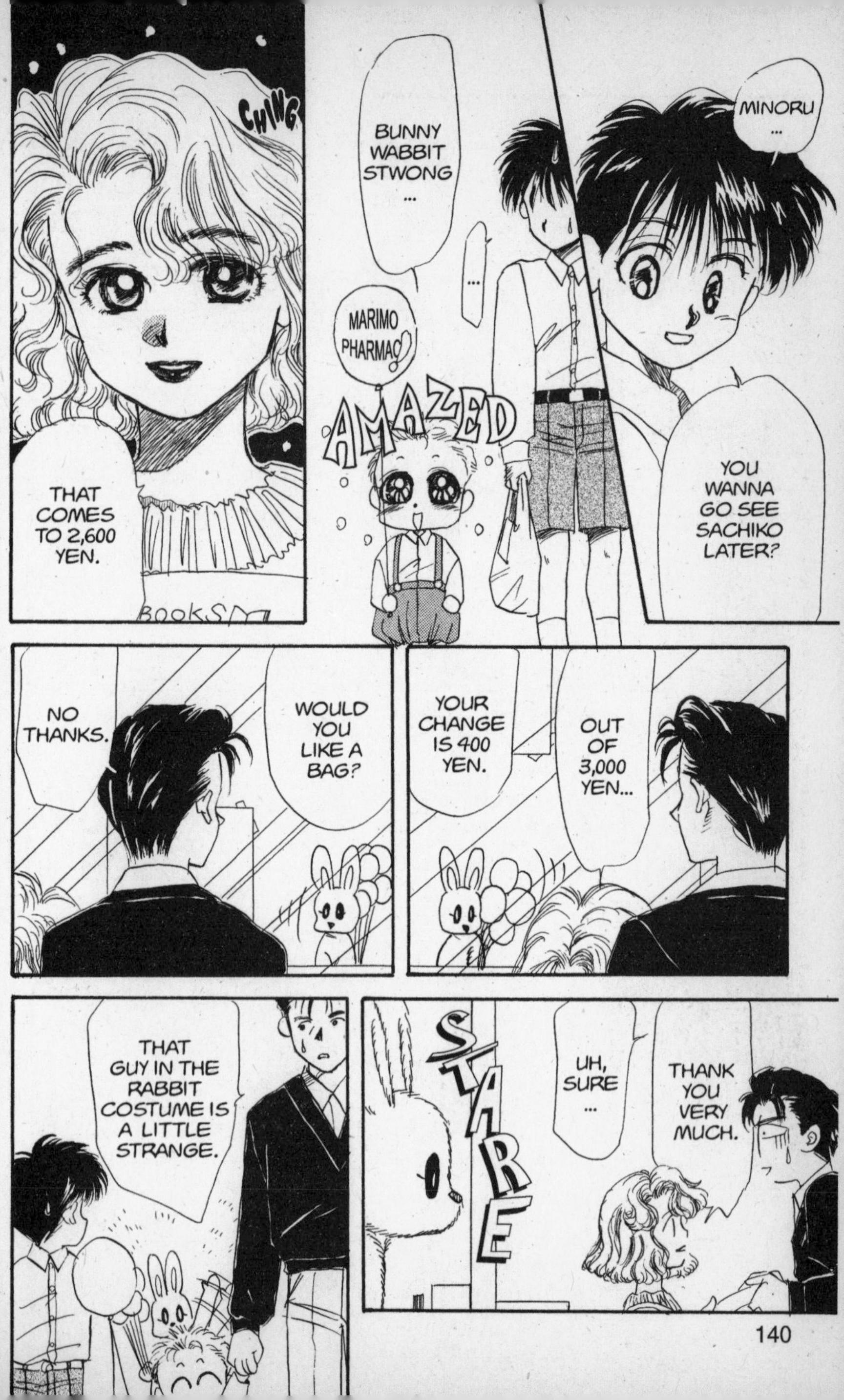
MINORU ...
YOU WANNA GO SEE SACHIKO LATER?
BUNNY WABBIT STWONG ...
...
MARIMO PHARMAC
AMAZED
CHING
THAT COMES TO 2,600 YEN.
OUT OF 3,000 YEN...
YOUR CHANGE IS 400 YEN.
WOULD YOU LIKE A BAG?
NO THANKS.
THANK YOU VERY MUCH.
UH, SURE ...
STARE
THAT GUY IN THE RABBIT COSTUME IS A LITTLE STRANGE.

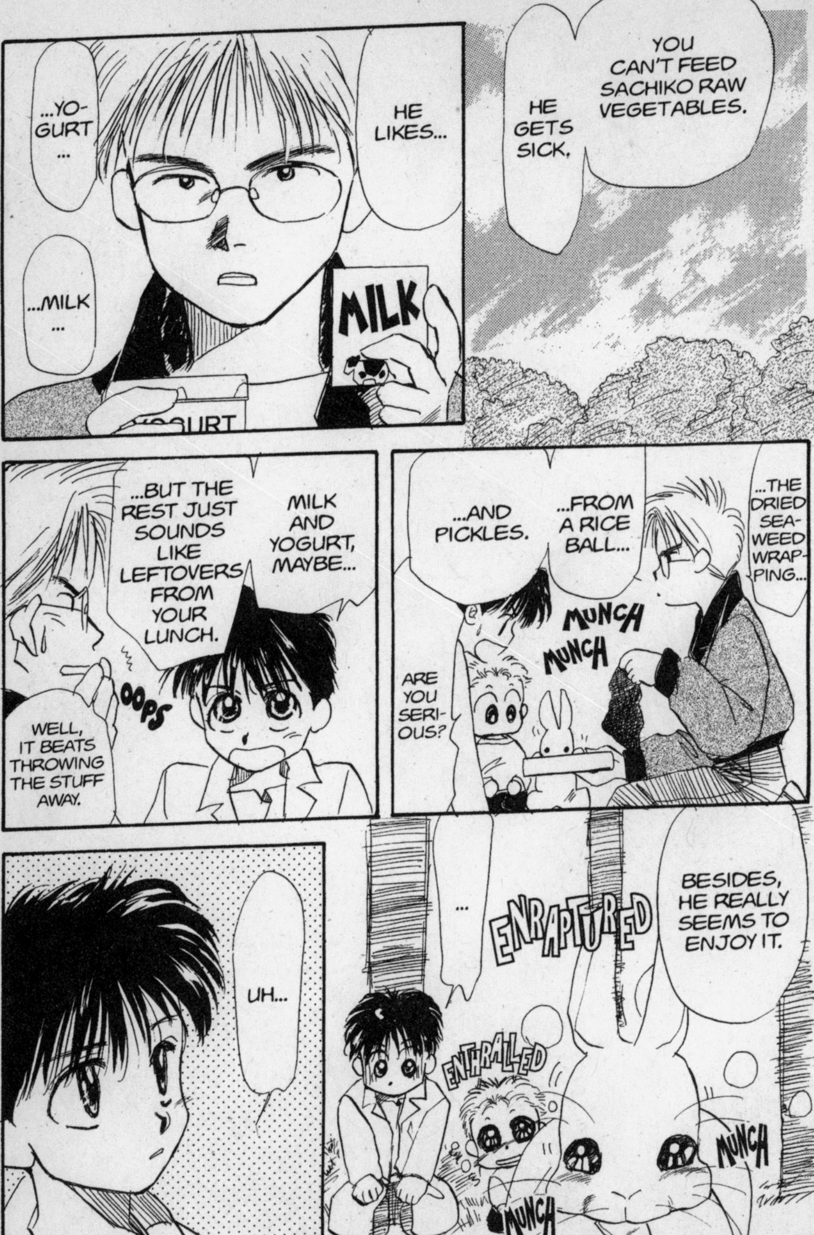
YOU CAN'T FEED SACHIKO RAW VEGETABLES.
HE GETS SICK.
HE LIKES...
...YO-GURT ...
...MILK ...
MILK
...THE DRIED SEA-WEED WRAP-PING...
...FROM A RICE BALL...
...AND PICKLES.
MUNCH
MUNCH
ARE YOU SERI-OUS?
MILK AND YOGURT, MAYBE...
...BUT THE REST JUST SOUNDS LIKE LEFTOVERS FROM YOUR LUNCH.
OOPS
WELL, IT BEATS THROWING THE STUFF AWAY.
BESIDES, HE REALLY SEEMS TO ENJOY IT.
ENRAPTURED
...
ENTHRALLED
MUNCH
MUNCH
UH...

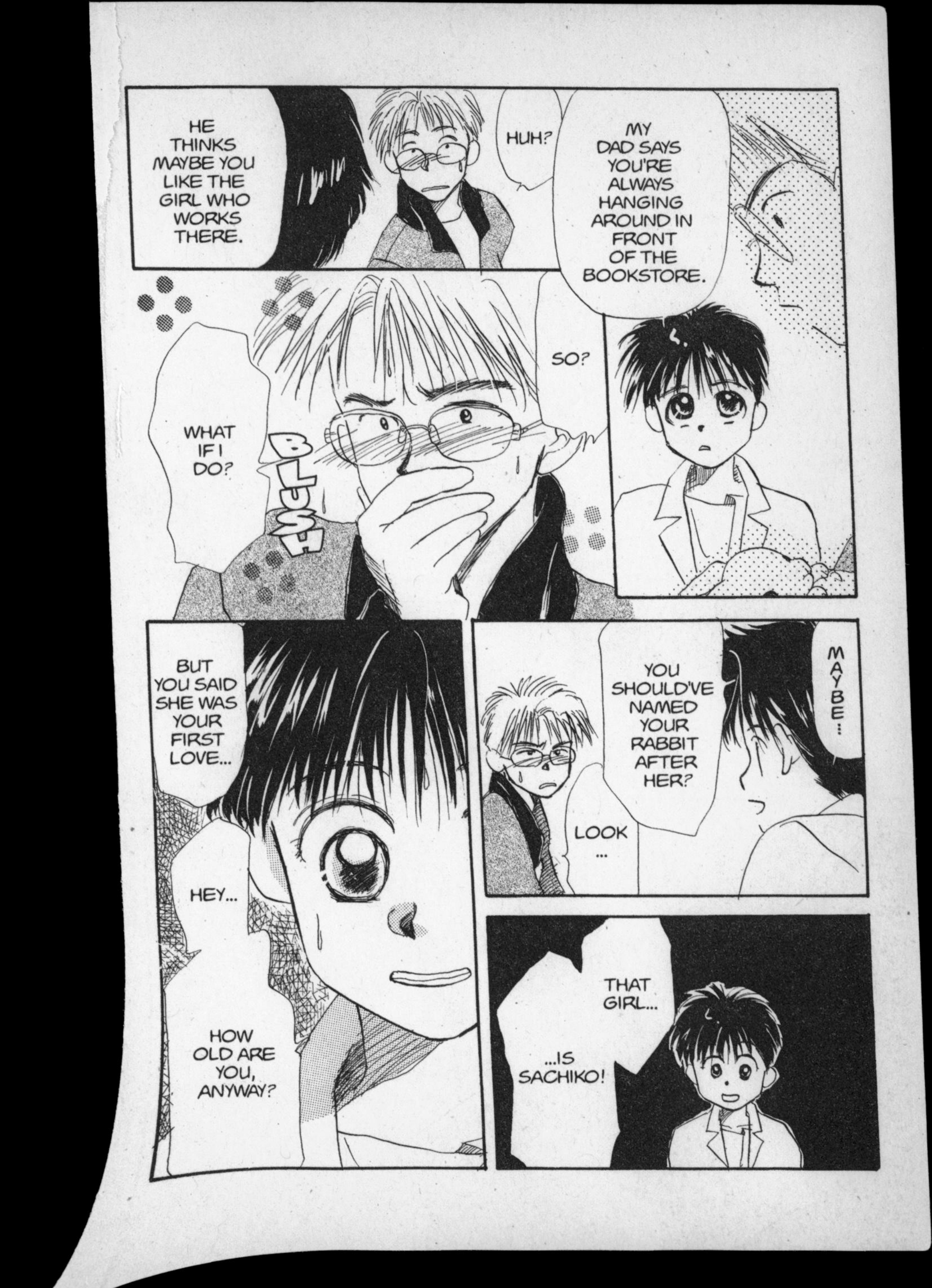
MY DAD SAYS YOU'RE ALWAYS HANGING AROUND IN FRONT OF THE BOOKSTORE.
HUH?
HE THINKS MAYBE YOU LIKE THE GIRL WHO WORKS THERE.
SO?
WHAT IF I DO?
BLUSH
MAYBE...
YOU SHOULD'VE NAMED YOUR RABBIT AFTER HER?
LOOK...
THAT GIRL...
...IS SACHIKO!
BUT YOU SAID SHE WAS YOUR FIRST LOVE...
HEY...
HOW OLD ARE YOU, ANYWAY?

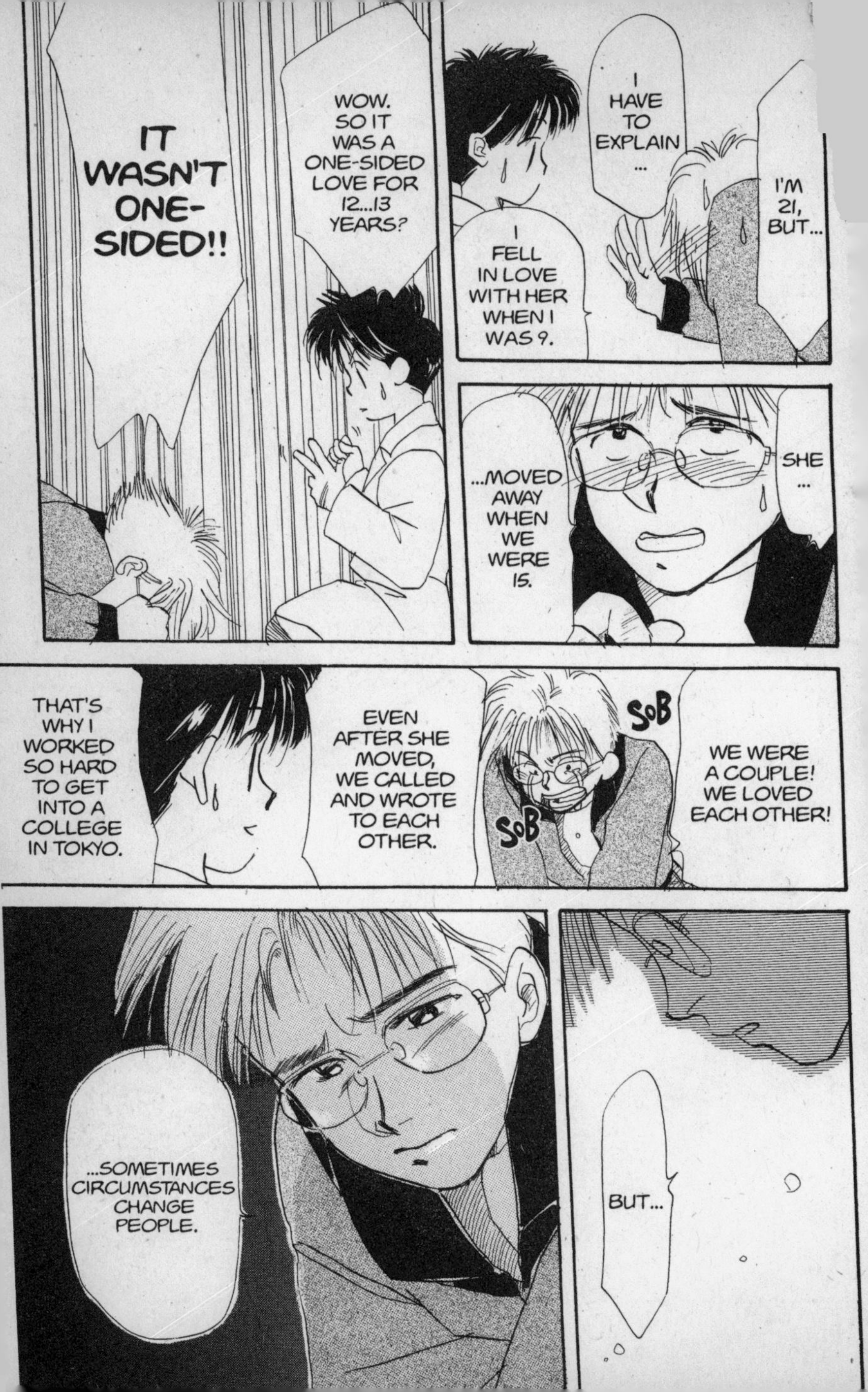
I HAVE TO EXPLAIN ...
I'M 21, BUT...
I FELL IN LOVE WITH HER WHEN I WAS 9.
SHE ...
...MOVED AWAY WHEN WE WERE 15.
WOW. SO IT WAS A ONE-SIDED LOVE FOR 12...13 YEARS?
IT WASN'T ONE-SIDED!!
WE WERE A COUPLE! WE LOVED EACH OTHER!
SOB
SOB
EVEN AFTER SHE MOVED, WE CALLED AND WROTE TO EACH OTHER.
THAT'S WHY I WORKED SO HARD TO GET INTO A COLLEGE IN TOKYO.
BUT...
...SOMETIMES CIRCUMSTANCES CHANGE PEOPLE.

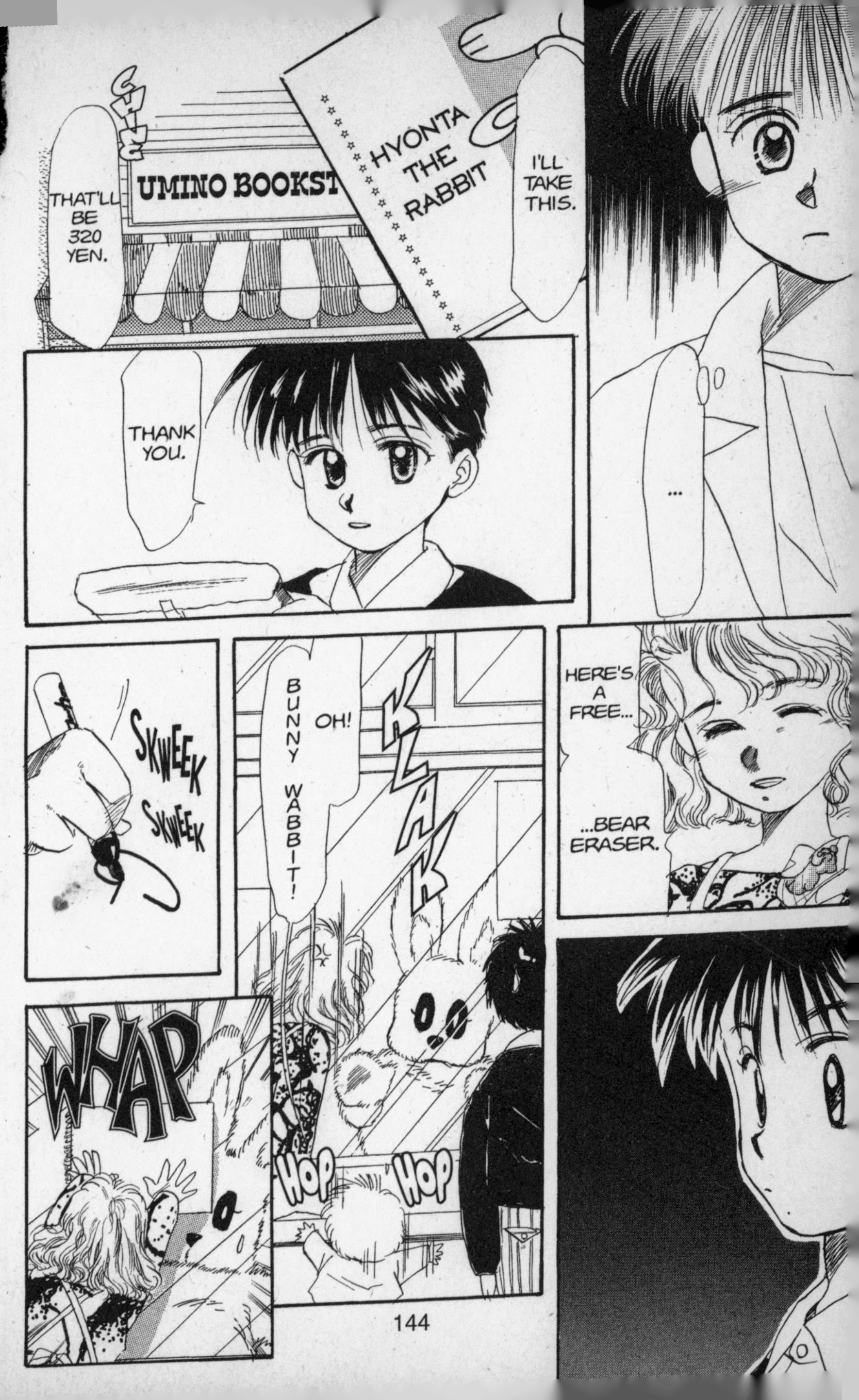
...
I'LL TAKE THIS.
HYONTA THE RABBIT
UMINO BOOKST
CHING
THAT'LL BE 320 YEN.
THANK YOU.
HERE'S A FREE...
...BEAR ERASER.
OH!
BUNNY WABBIT!
KLAK
HOP
HOP
SKWEEK
SKWEEK
WHAP

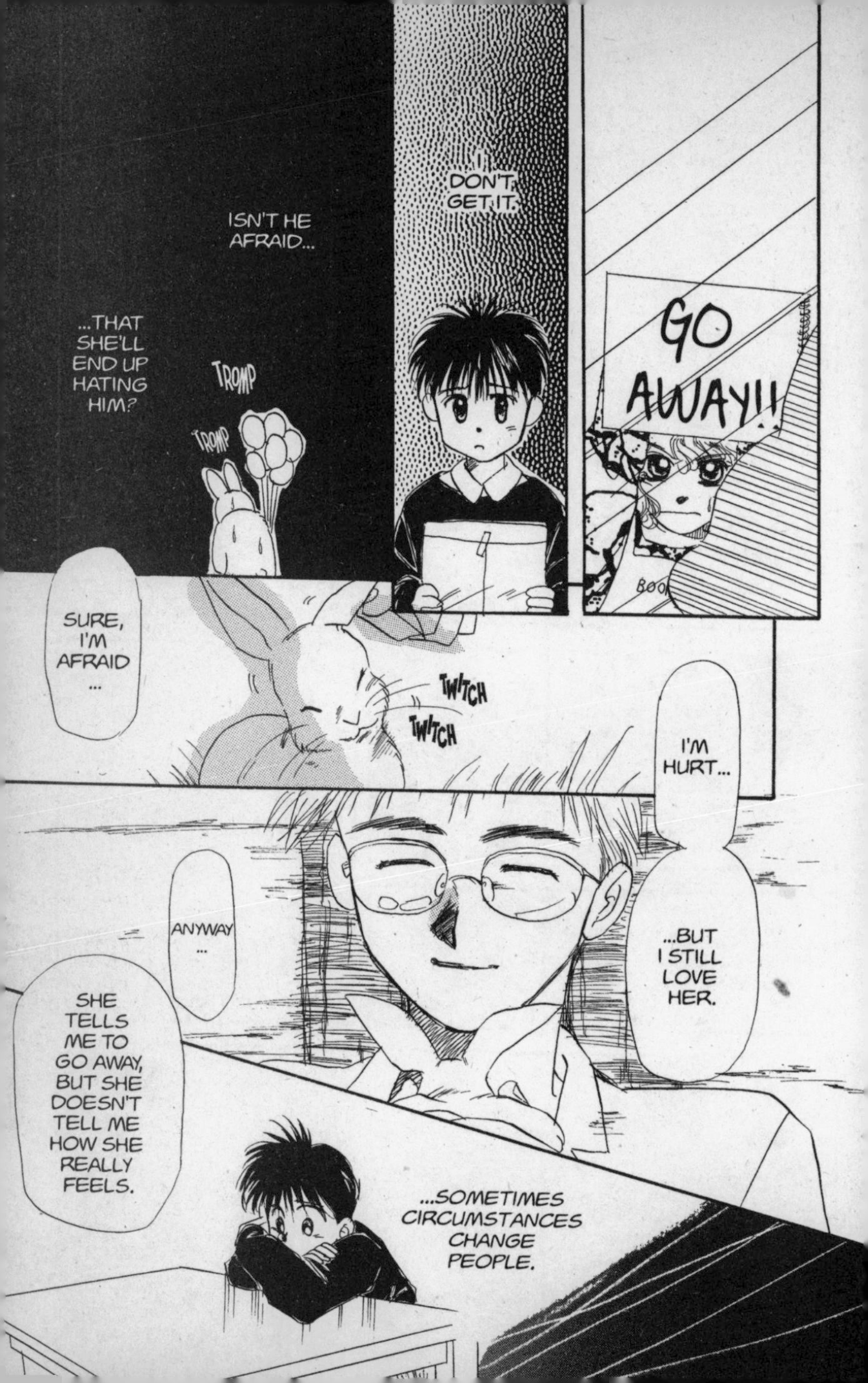
GO AWAY!!
I DON'T GET IT.
ISN'T HE AFRAID...
...THAT SHE'LL END UP HATING HIM?
TROMP
TROMP
TWITCH
TWITCH
SURE, I'M AFRAID...
I'M HURT...
...BUT I STILL LOVE HER.
ANYWAY...
SHE TELLS ME TO GO AWAY, BUT SHE DOESN'T TELL ME HOW SHE REALLY FEELS.
...SOMETIMES CIRCUMSTANCES CHANGE PEOPLE.

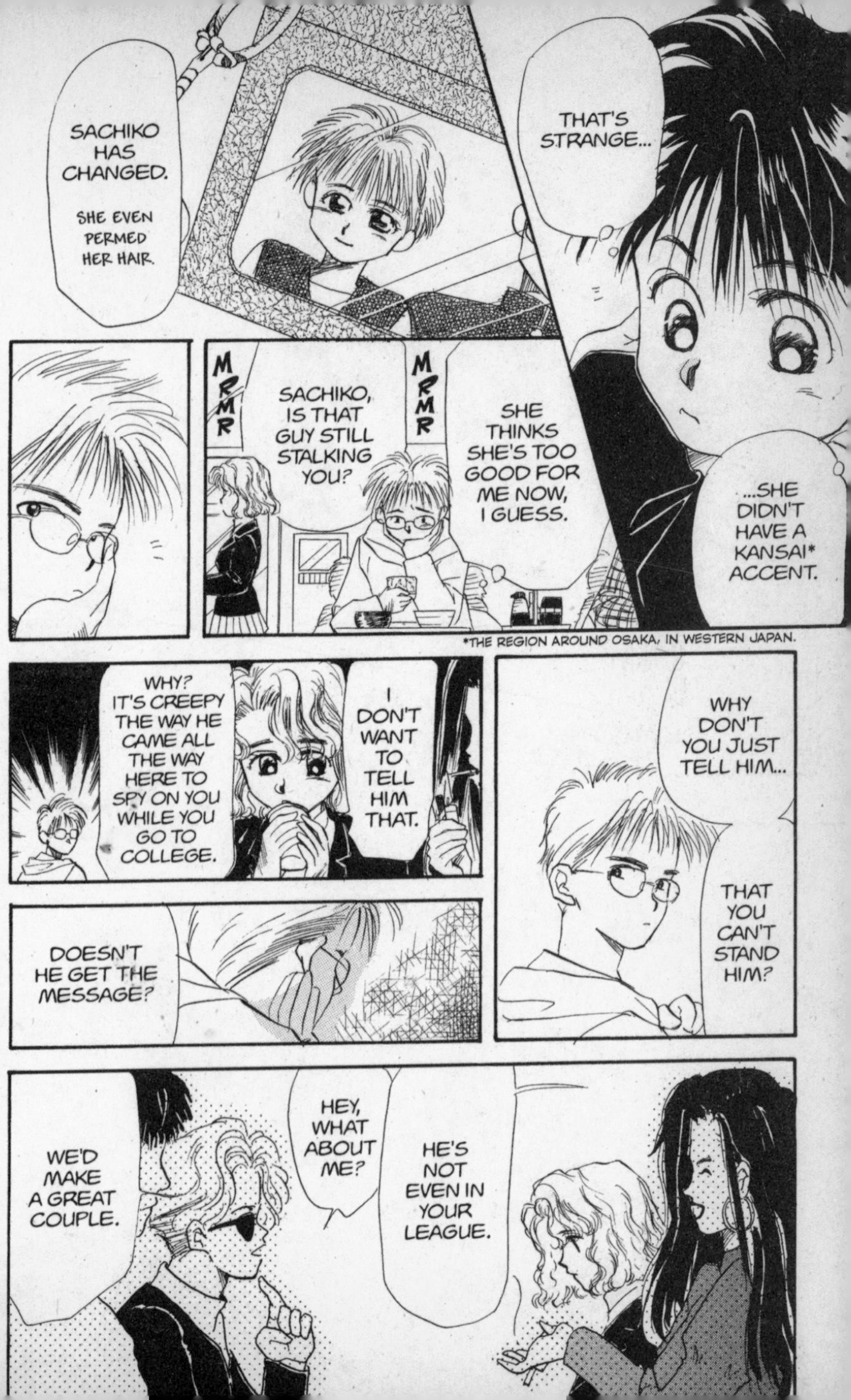
THAT'S STRANGE...
...SHE DIDN'T HAVE A KANSAI* ACCENT.
SACHIKO HAS CHANGED.
SHE EVEN PERMED HER HAIR.
MRMR
SHE THINKS SHE'S TOO GOOD FOR ME NOW, I GUESS.
MRMR
SACHIKO, IS THAT GUY STILL STALKING YOU?
WHY DON'T YOU JUST TELL HIM...
THAT YOU CAN'T STAND HIM?
I DON'T WANT TO TELL HIM THAT.
WHY? IT'S CREEPY THE WAY HE CAME ALL THE WAY HERE TO SPY ON YOU WHILE YOU GO TO COLLEGE.
DOESN'T HE GET THE MESSAGE?
HE'S NOT EVEN IN YOUR LEAGUE.
HEY, WHAT ABOUT ME?
WE'D MAKE A GREAT COUPLE.

*THE REGION AROUND OSAKA, IN WESTERN JAPAN.

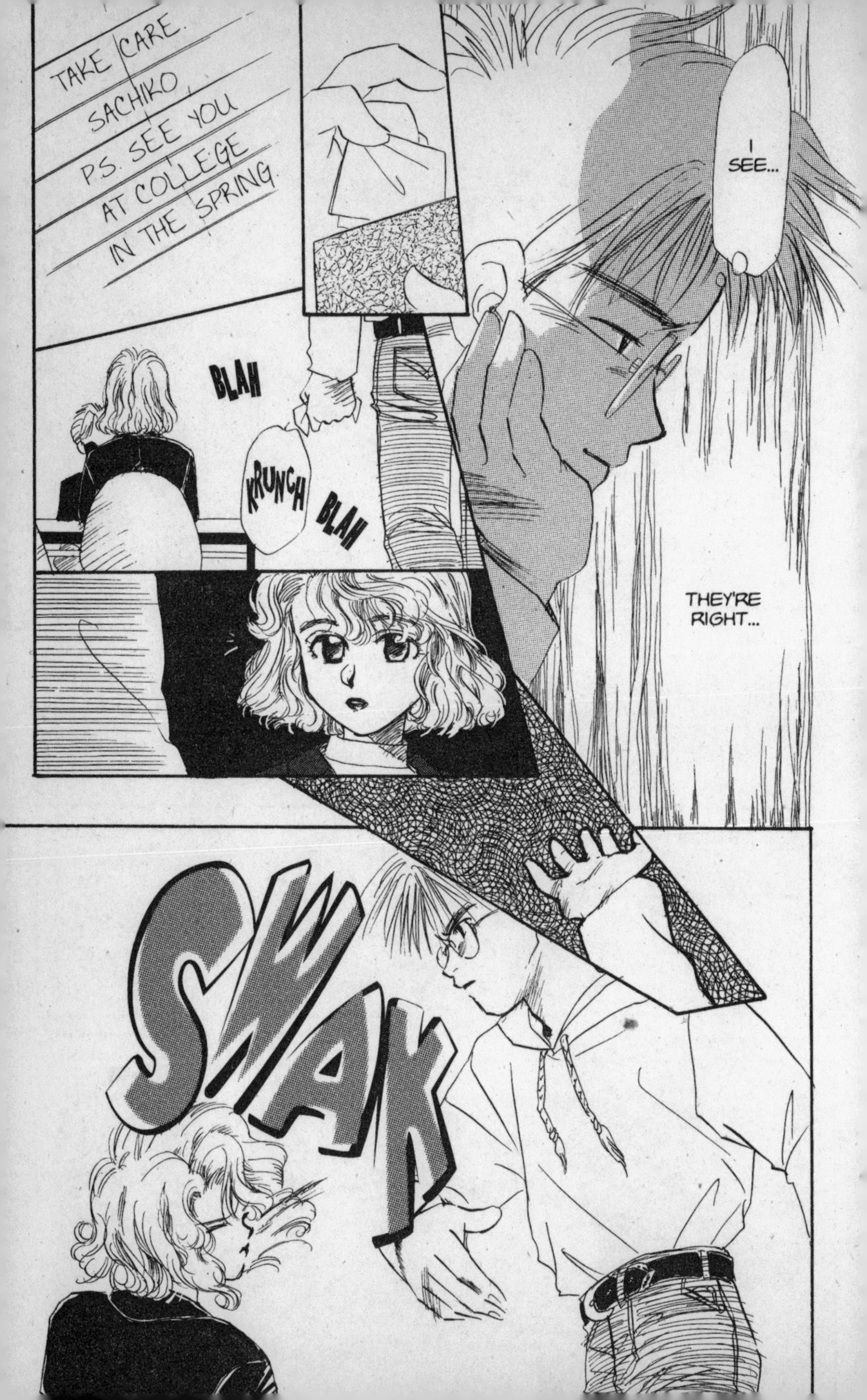
I SEE...
THEY'RE RIGHT...
TAKE CARE.
SACHIKO
P.S. SEE YOU AT COLLEGE IN THE SPRING
BLAH
KRUNCH
BLAH
SWAK

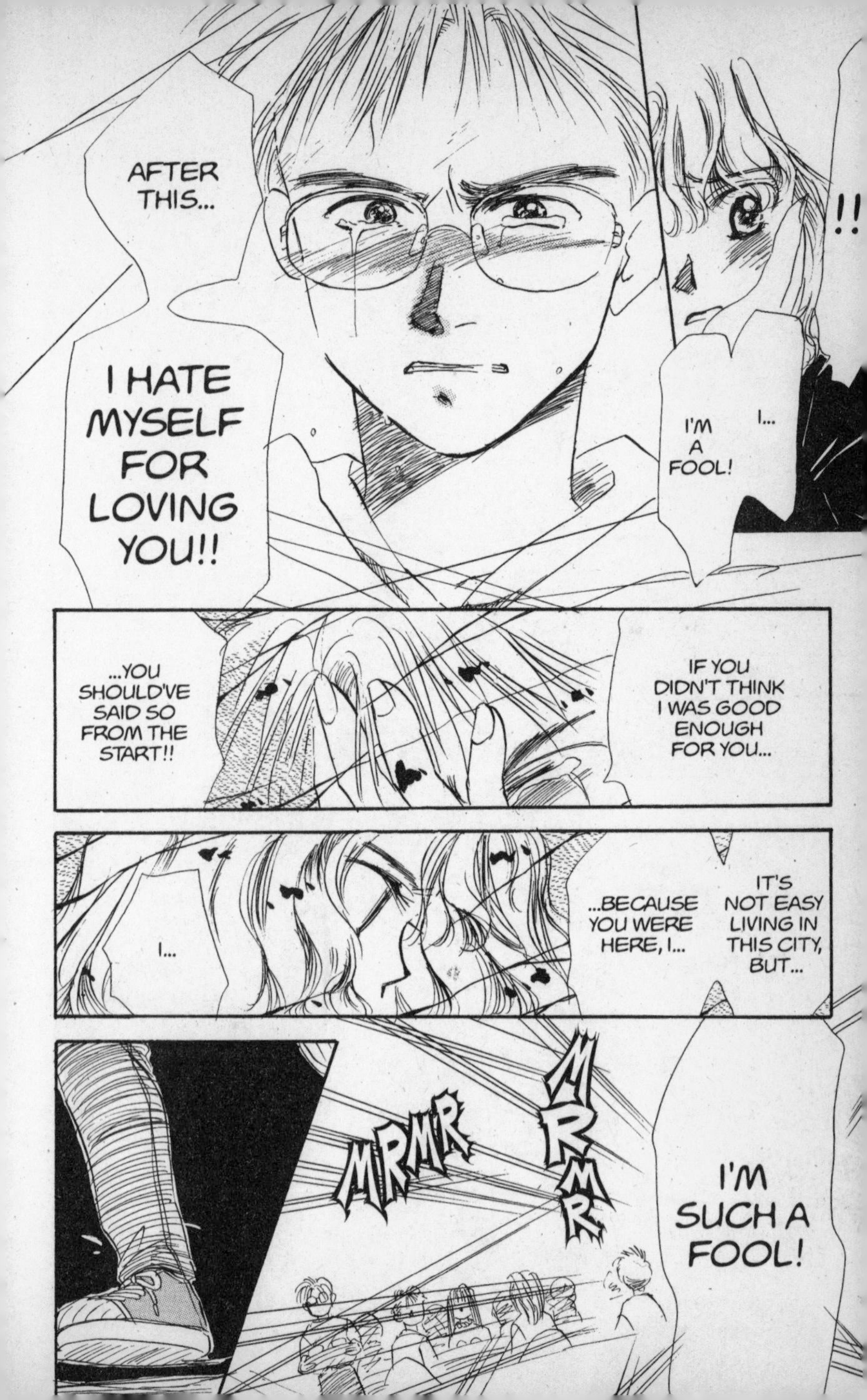
!!
I...
I'M A FOOL!
AFTER THIS...
I HATE MYSELF FOR LOVING YOU!!
IF YOU DIDN'T THINK I WAS GOOD ENOUGH FOR YOU...
...YOU SHOULD'VE SAID SO FROM THE START!!
IT'S NOT EASY LIVING IN THIS CITY, BUT...
...BECAUSE YOU WERE HERE, I...
I...
I'M SUCH A FOOL!
MRMR
MRMR

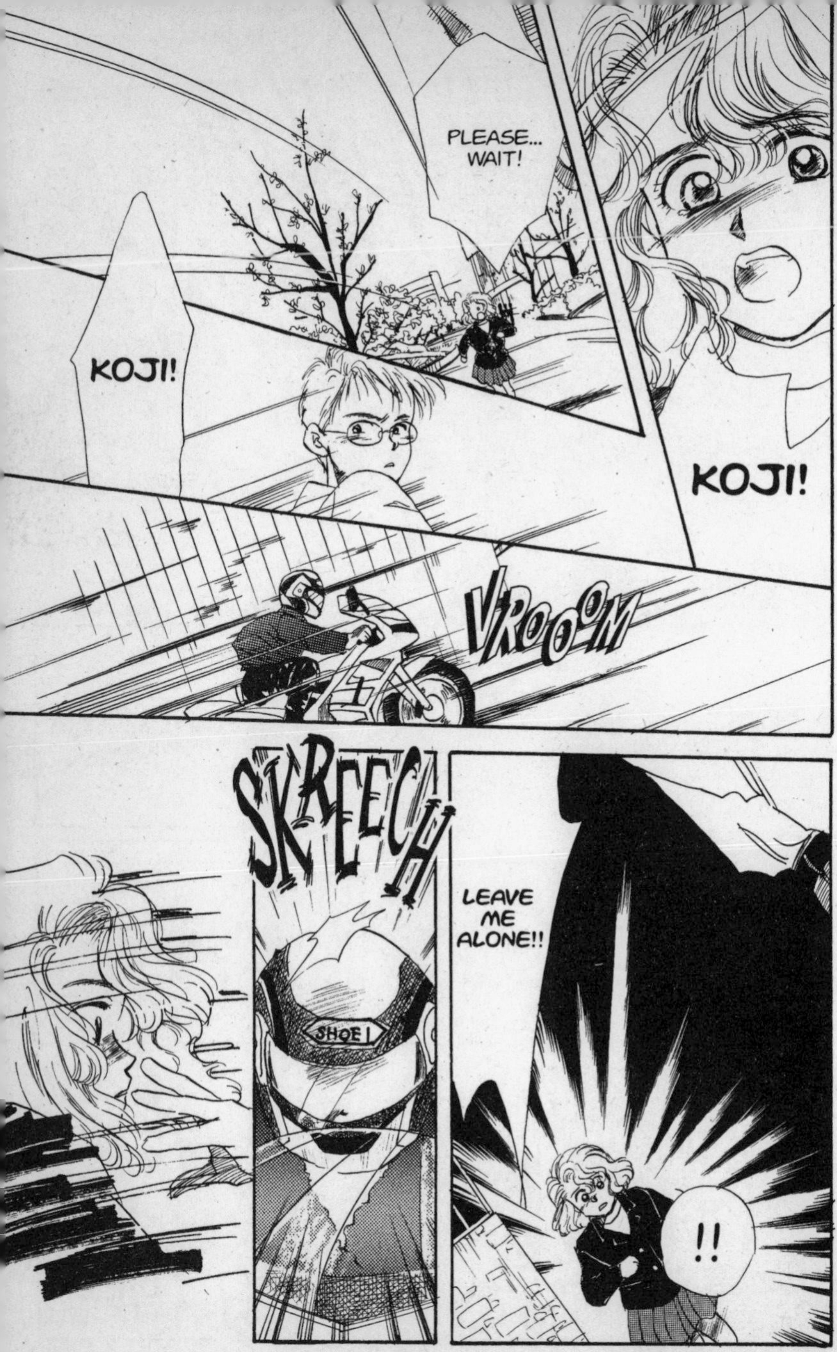
KOJI!
PLEASE... WAIT!
KOJI!
VROOOM
LEAVE ME ALONE!!
!!
SKREECH
SHOEI

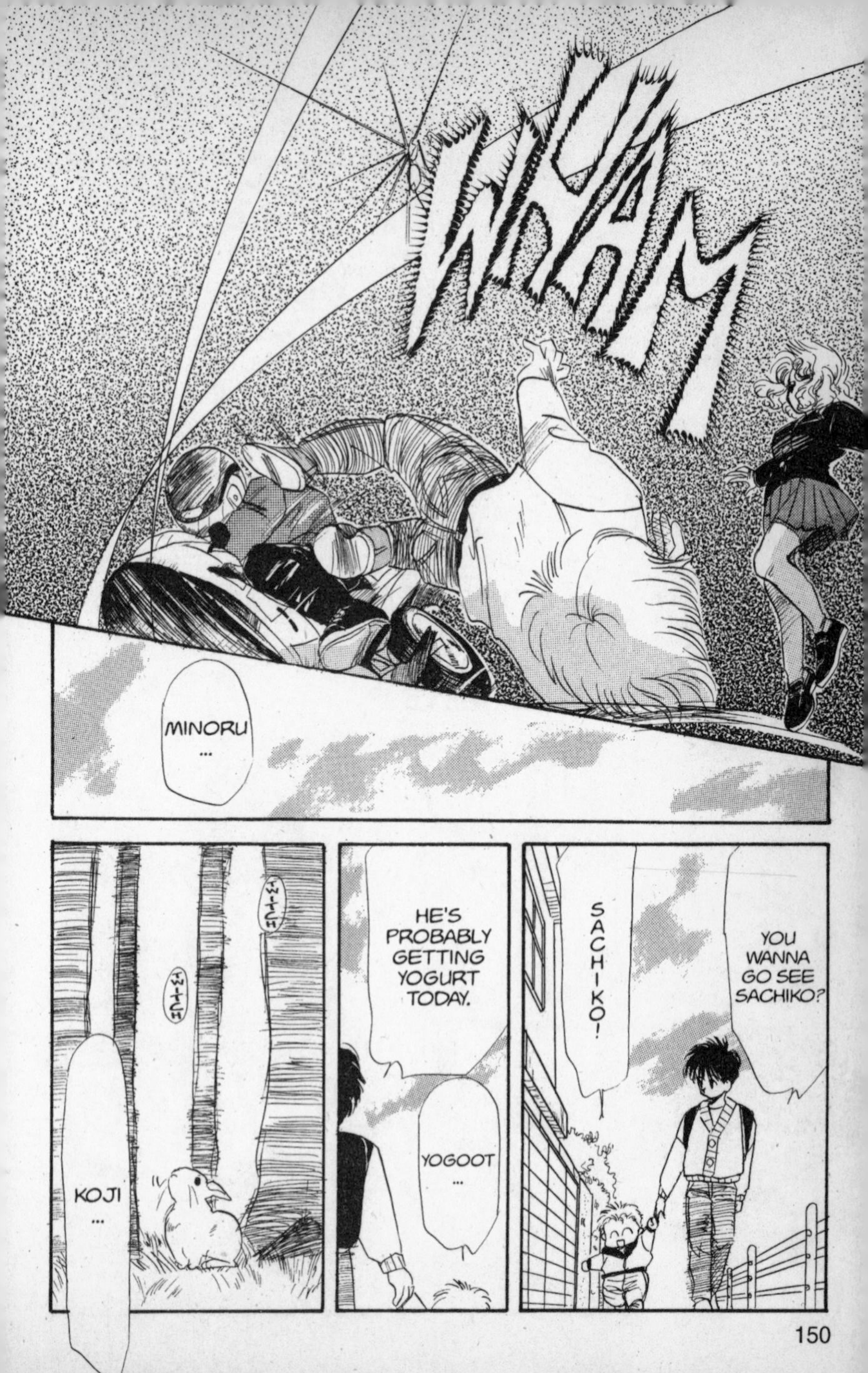
WHAM
MINORU ...
YOU WANNA GO SEE SACHIKO?
SACHIKO!
HE'S PROBABLY GETTING YOGURT TODAY.
YOGOOT ...
TWITCH
TWITCH
KOJI ...

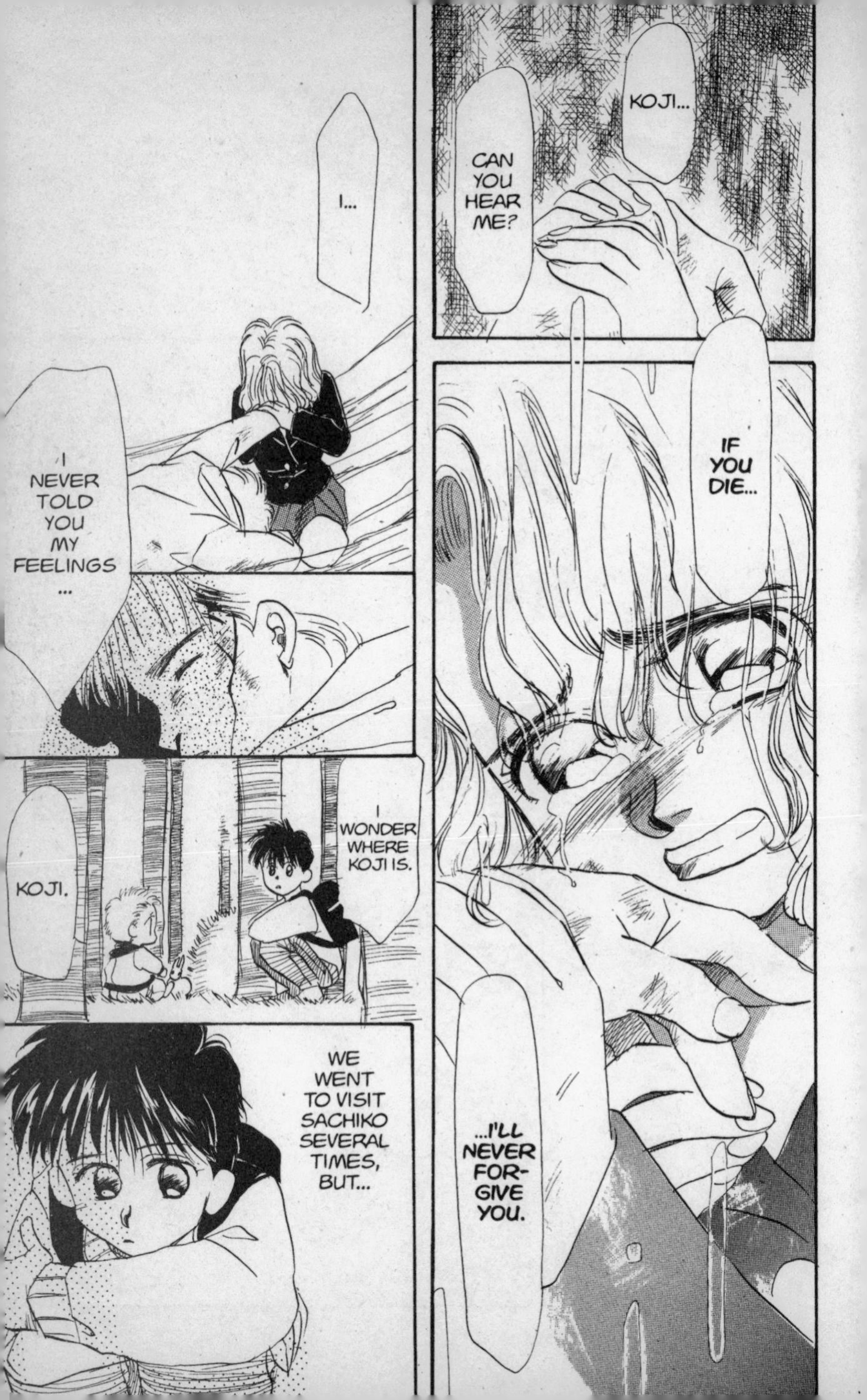
KOJI...
CAN YOU HEAR ME?
IF YOU DIE...
...I'LL NEVER FOR-GIVE YOU.
I...
I NEVER TOLD YOU MY FEELINGS...
I WONDER WHERE KOJI IS.
KOJI.
WE WENT TO VISIT SACHIKO SEVERAL TIMES, BUT...

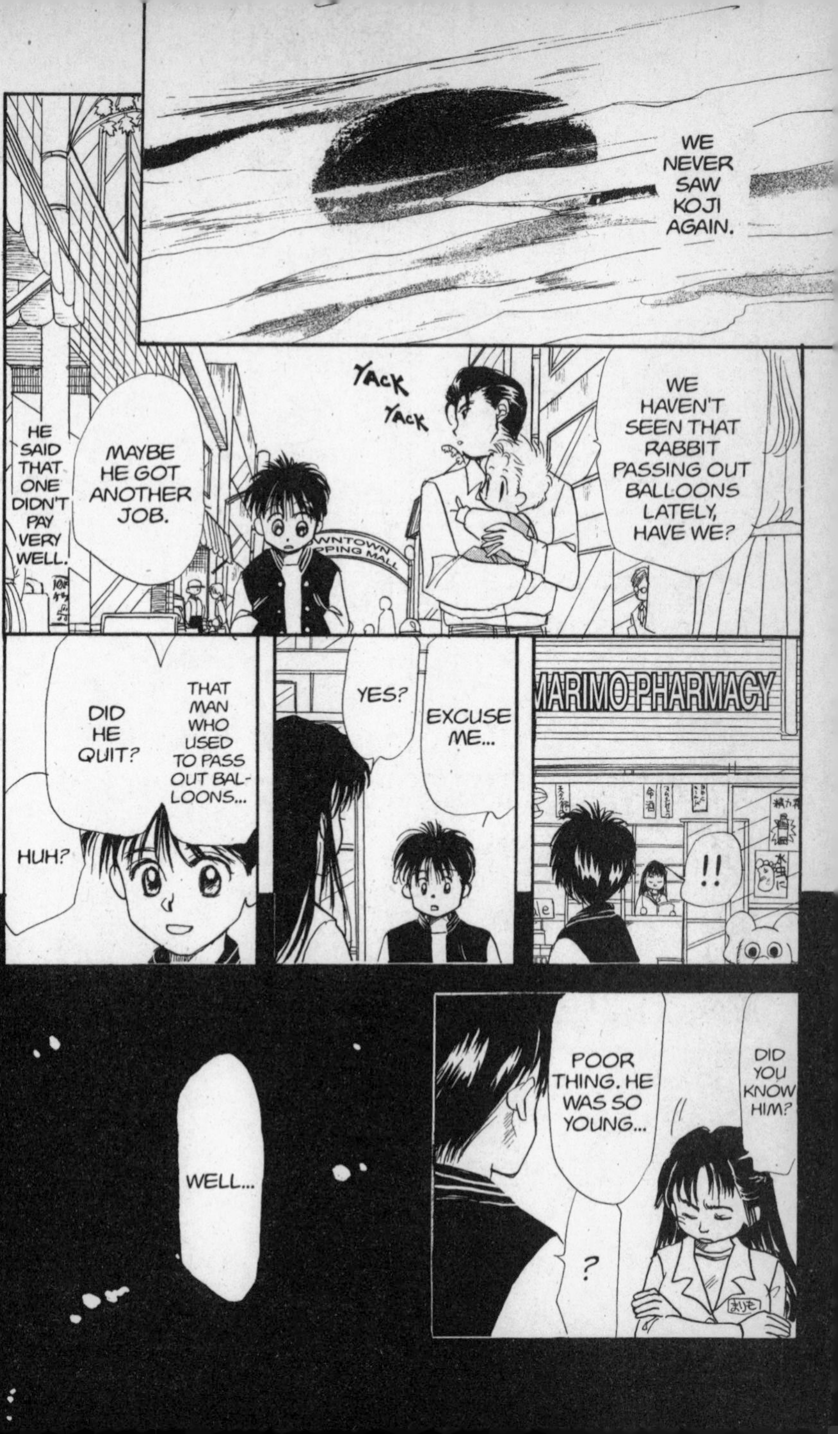
WE NEVER SAW KOJI AGAIN.
WE HAVEN'T SEEN THAT RABBIT PASSING OUT BALLOONS LATELY, HAVE WE?
YACK YACK
MAYBE HE GOT ANOTHER JOB.
HE SAID THAT ONE DIDN'T PAY VERY WELL.
MARIMO PHARMACY
!!
EXCUSE ME...
YES?
THAT MAN WHO USED TO PASS OUT BALLOONS...
DID HE QUIT?
HUH?
DID YOU KNOW HIM?
POOR THING. HE WAS SO YOUNG...
?
WELL...

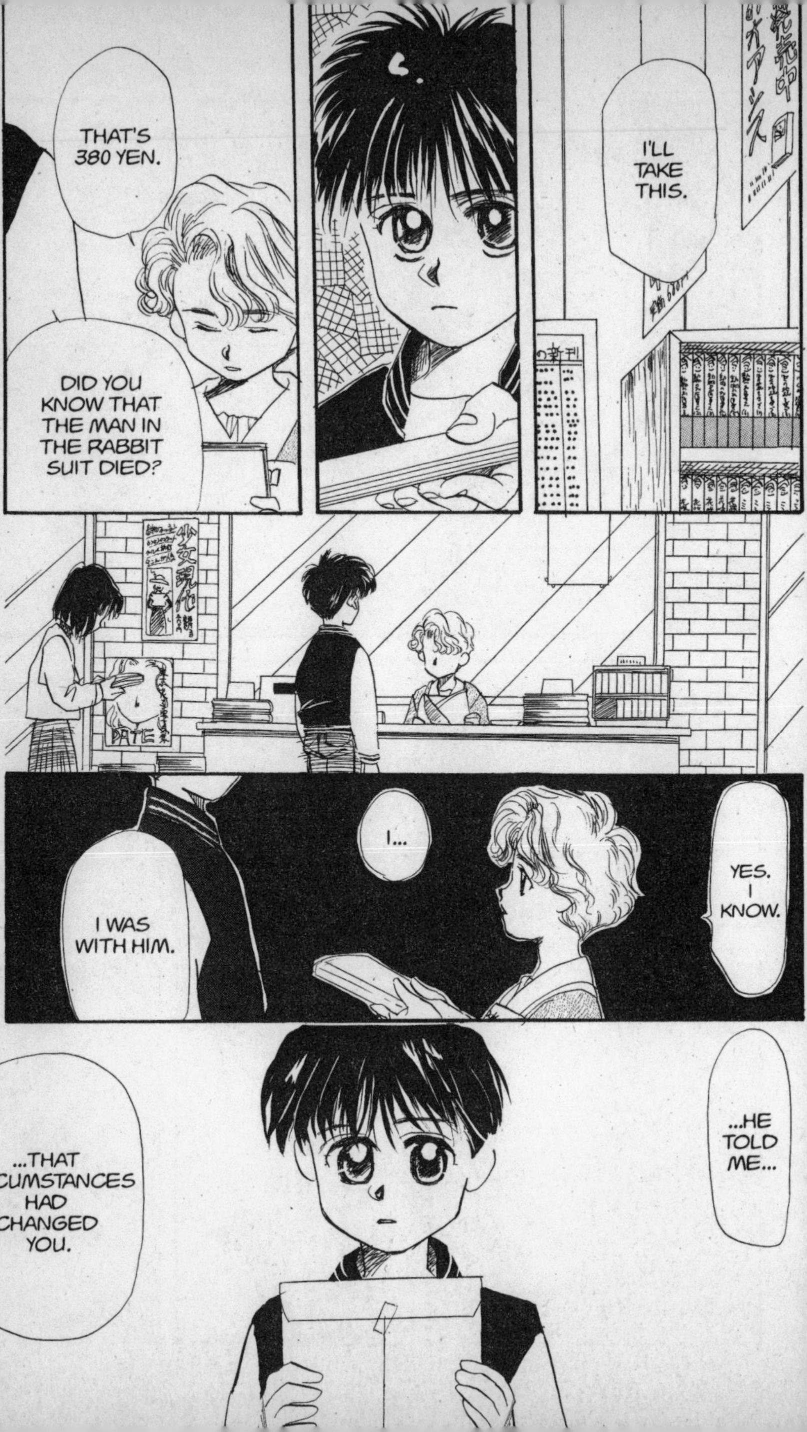
I'LL TAKE THIS.
THAT'S 380 YEN.
DID YOU KNOW THAT THE MAN IN THE RABBIT SUIT DIED?
YES. I KNOW.
I...
I WAS WITH HIM.
...HE TOLD ME...
...THAT CIRCUMSTANCES HAD CHANGED YOU.

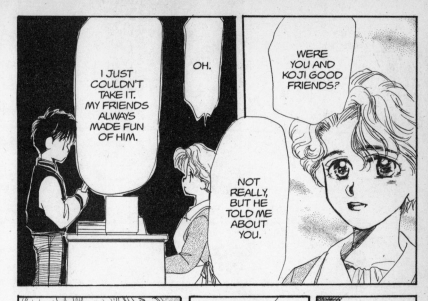

WERE YOU AND KOJI GOOD FRIENDS?
NOT REALLY, BUT HE TOLD ME ABOUT YOU.
OH.
I JUST COULDN'T TAKE IT. MY FRIENDS ALWAYS MADE FUN OF HIM.
I THOUGHT IF HE WASN'T AROUND ME, HE WOULDN'T GET TEASED.
BUT...
MAYBE YOU'D HAVE BEEN BETTER OFF...
...WITHOUT FRIENDS LIKE THOSE.
YOU'RE RIGHT.
I NEVER REALIZED HOW SHALLOW I WAS.

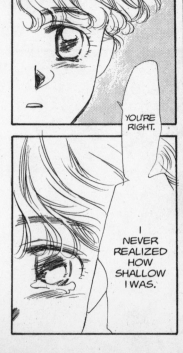

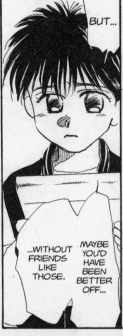

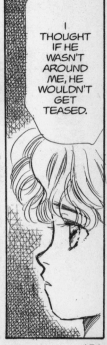

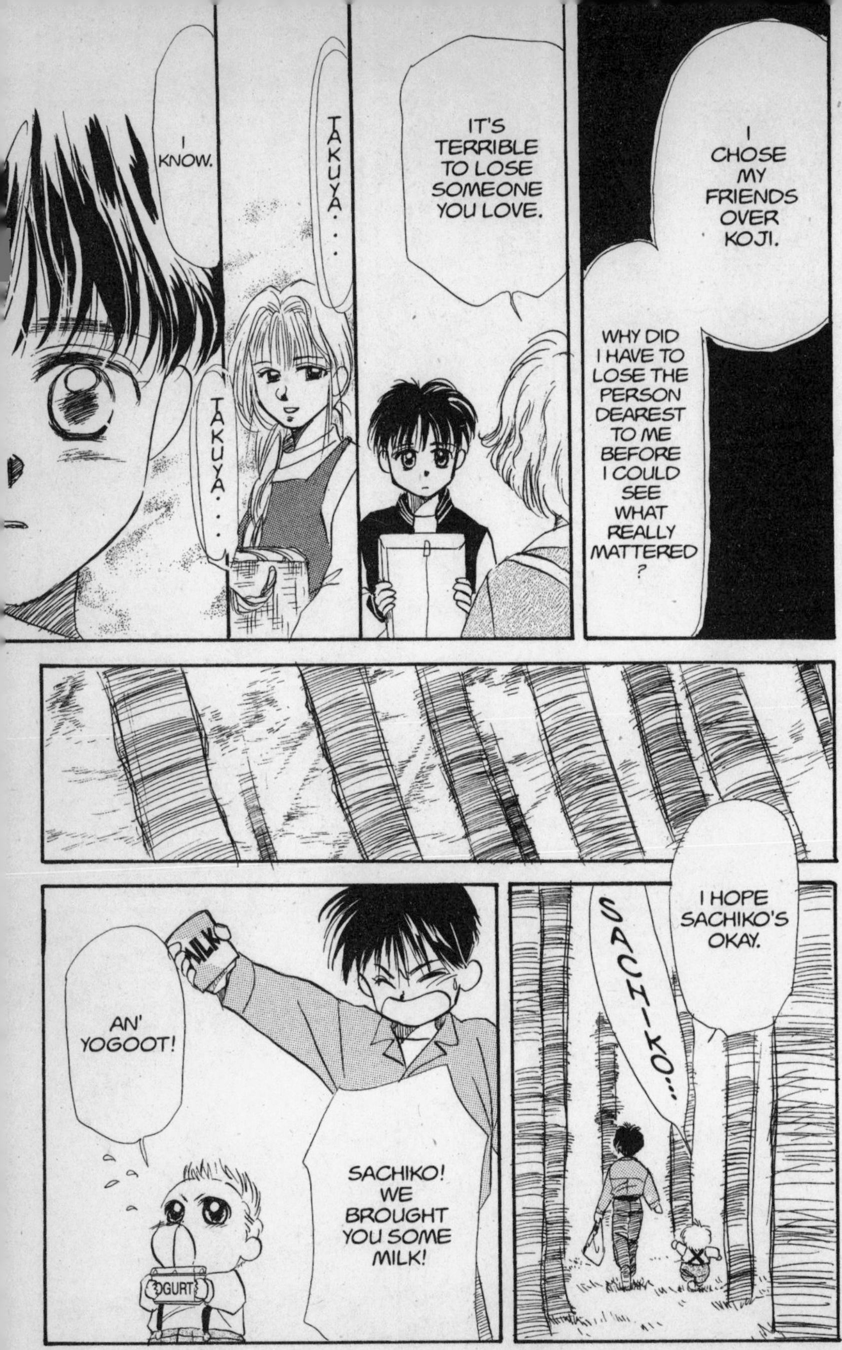
I CHOSE MY FRIENDS OVER KOJI.
WHY DID I HAVE TO LOSE THE PERSON DEAREST TO ME BEFORE I COULD SEE WHAT REALLY MATTERED?
IT'S TERRIBLE TO LOSE SOMEONE YOU LOVE.
TAKUYA...
TAKUYA...
I KNOW.
I HOPE SACHIKO'S OKAY.
SACHIKO...
MILK
SACHIKO! WE BROUGHT YOU SOME MILK!
AN' YOGOOT!

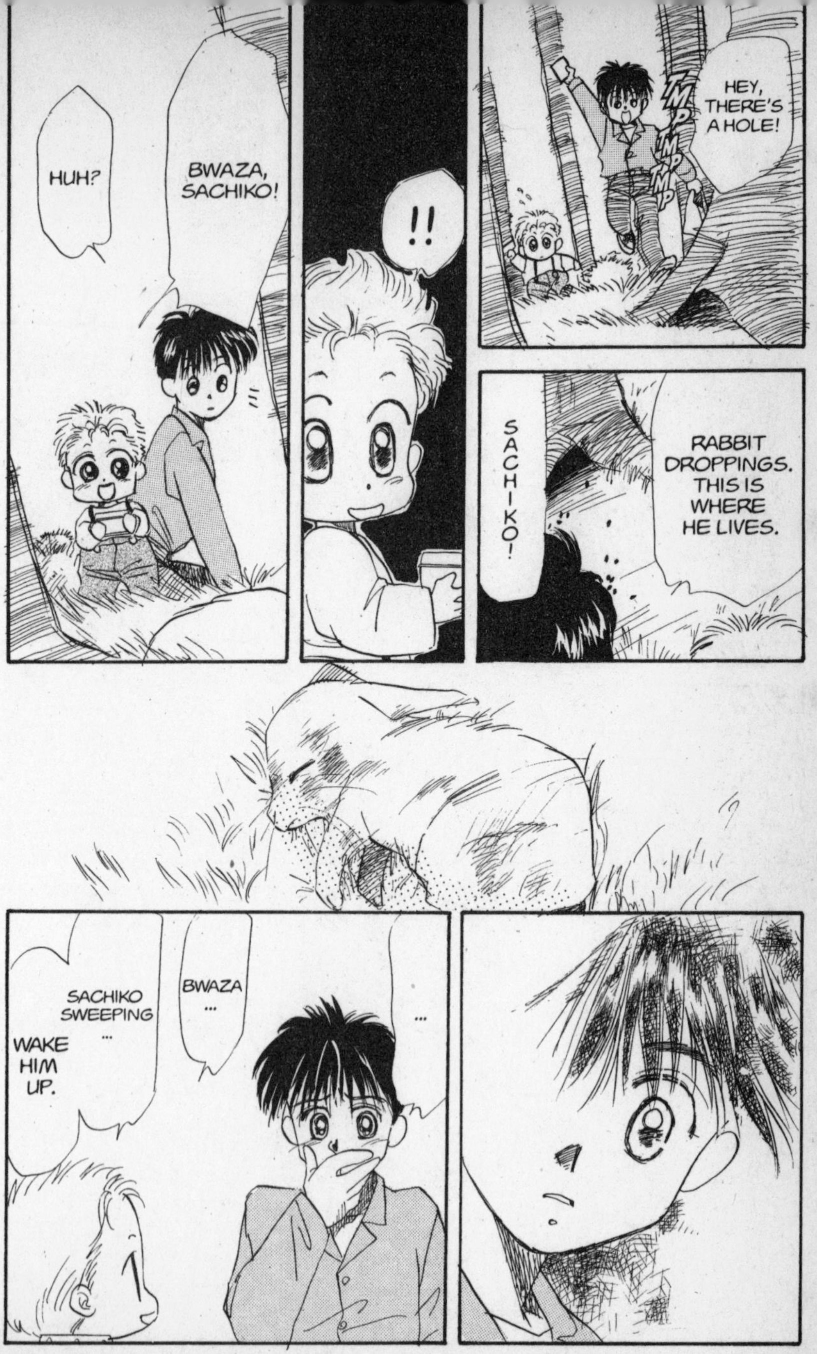
HEY, THERE'S A HOLE!
TMP TMP TMP
RABBIT DROPPINGS. THIS IS WHERE HE LIVES.
SACHIKO!
!!
BWAZA, SACHIKO!
HUH?
...
BWAZA ...
SACHIKO SWEEPING ...
WAKE HIM UP.

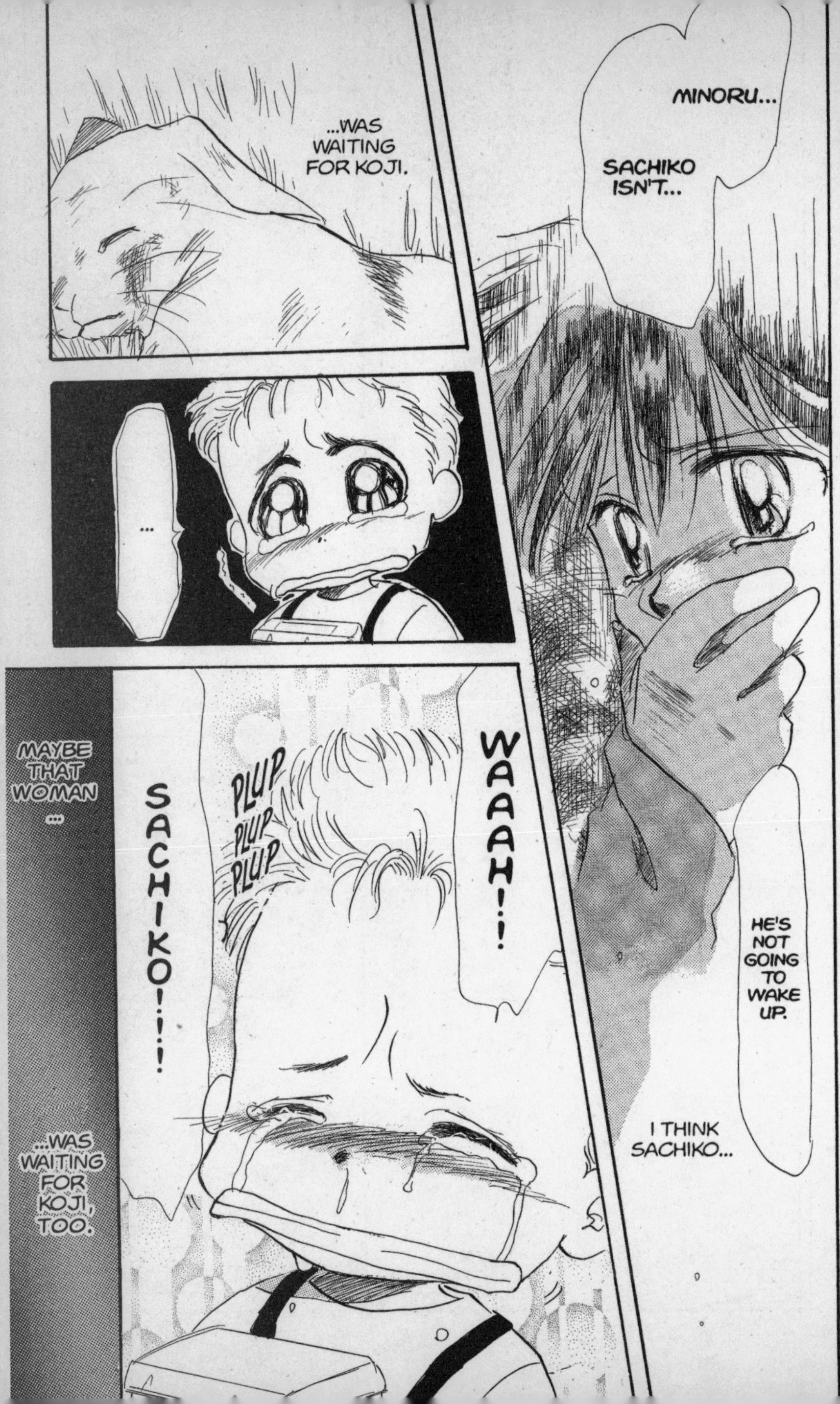
MINORU...
SACHIKO ISN'T...
I THINK SACHIKO...
HE'S NOT GOING TO WAKE UP.
...WAS WAITING FOR KOJI.
...
WAAAH!!
PLUP PLUP PLUP
SACHIKO!!!!
MAYBE THAT WOMAN ...
...WAS WAITING FOR KOJI, TOO.

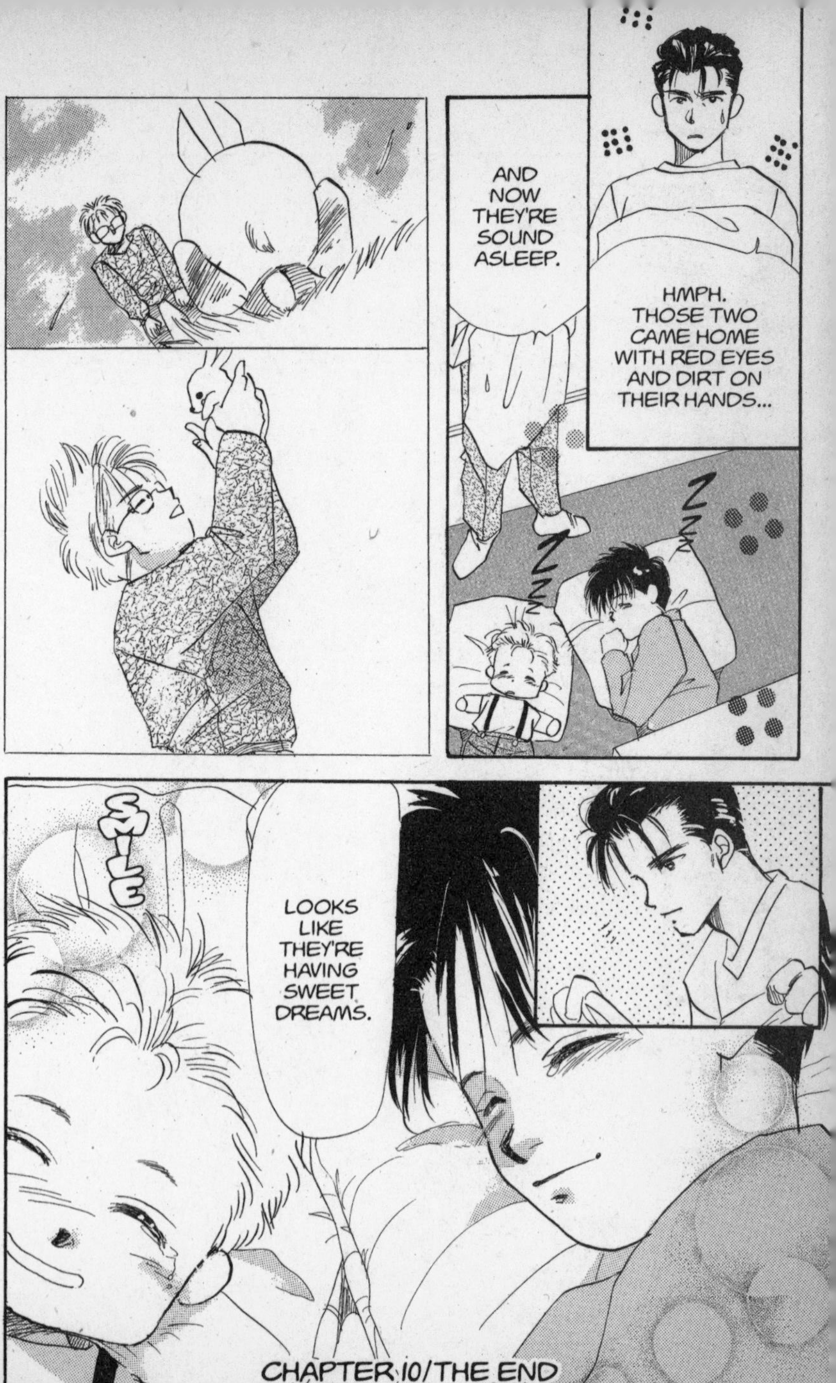
HMPH. THOSE TWO CAME HOME WITH RED EYES AND DIRT ON THEIR HANDS...
AND NOW THEY'RE SOUND ASLEEP.
ZZZ
ZZZ
SMILE
LOOKS LIKE THEY'RE HAVING SWEET DREAMS.
CHAPTER 10/THE END

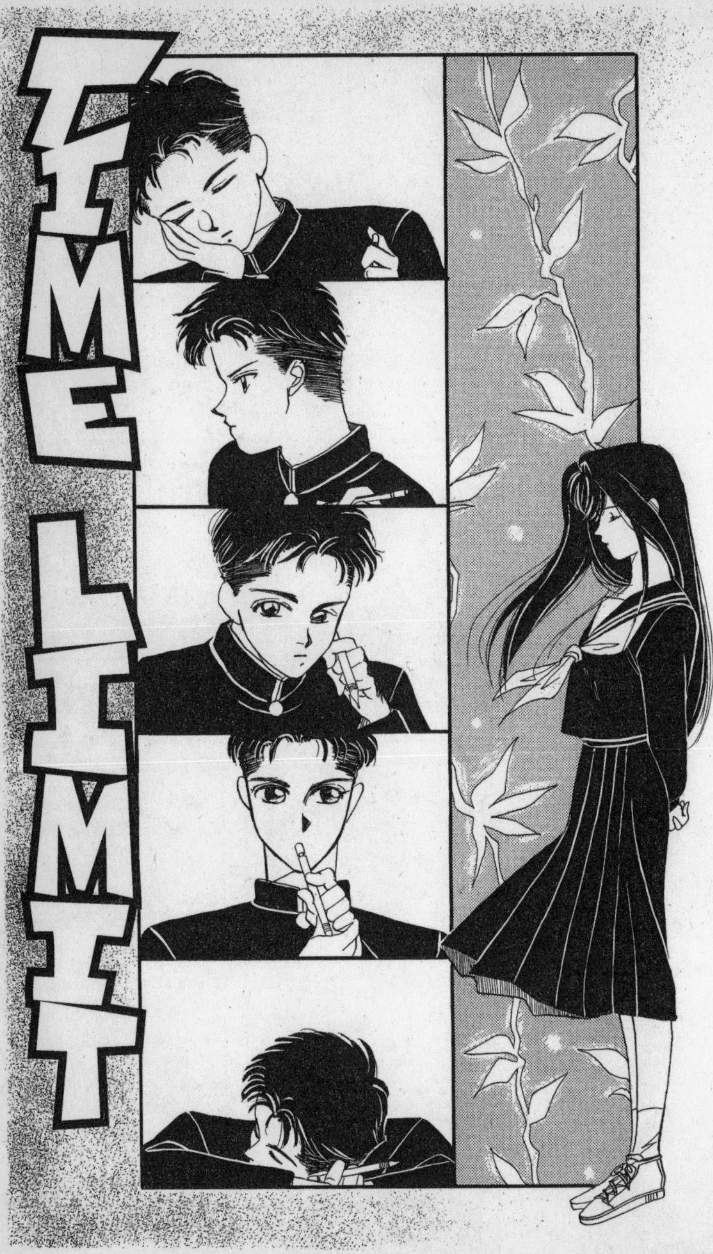
TIME LIMIT

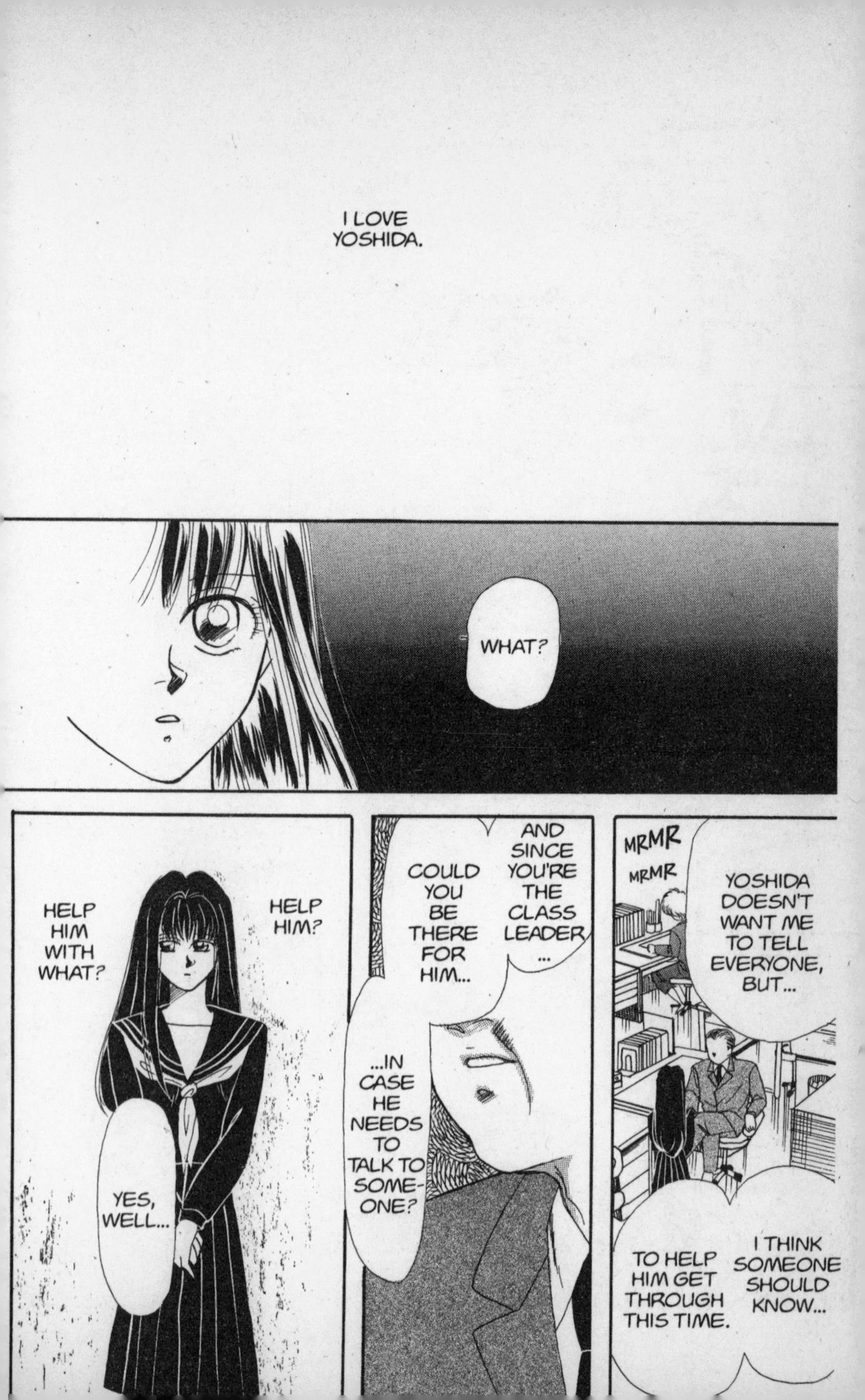
I LOVE YOSHIDA.
WHAT?
MRMR
MRMR
YOSHIDA DOESN'T WANT ME TO TELL EVERYONE, BUT...
I THINK SOMEONE SHOULD KNOW...
TO HELP HIM GET THROUGH THIS TIME.
AND SINCE YOU'RE THE CLASS LEADER...
COULD YOU BE THERE FOR HIM...
...IN CASE HE NEEDS TO TALK TO SOME-ONE?
HELP HIM?
HELP HIM WITH WHAT?
YES, WELL...

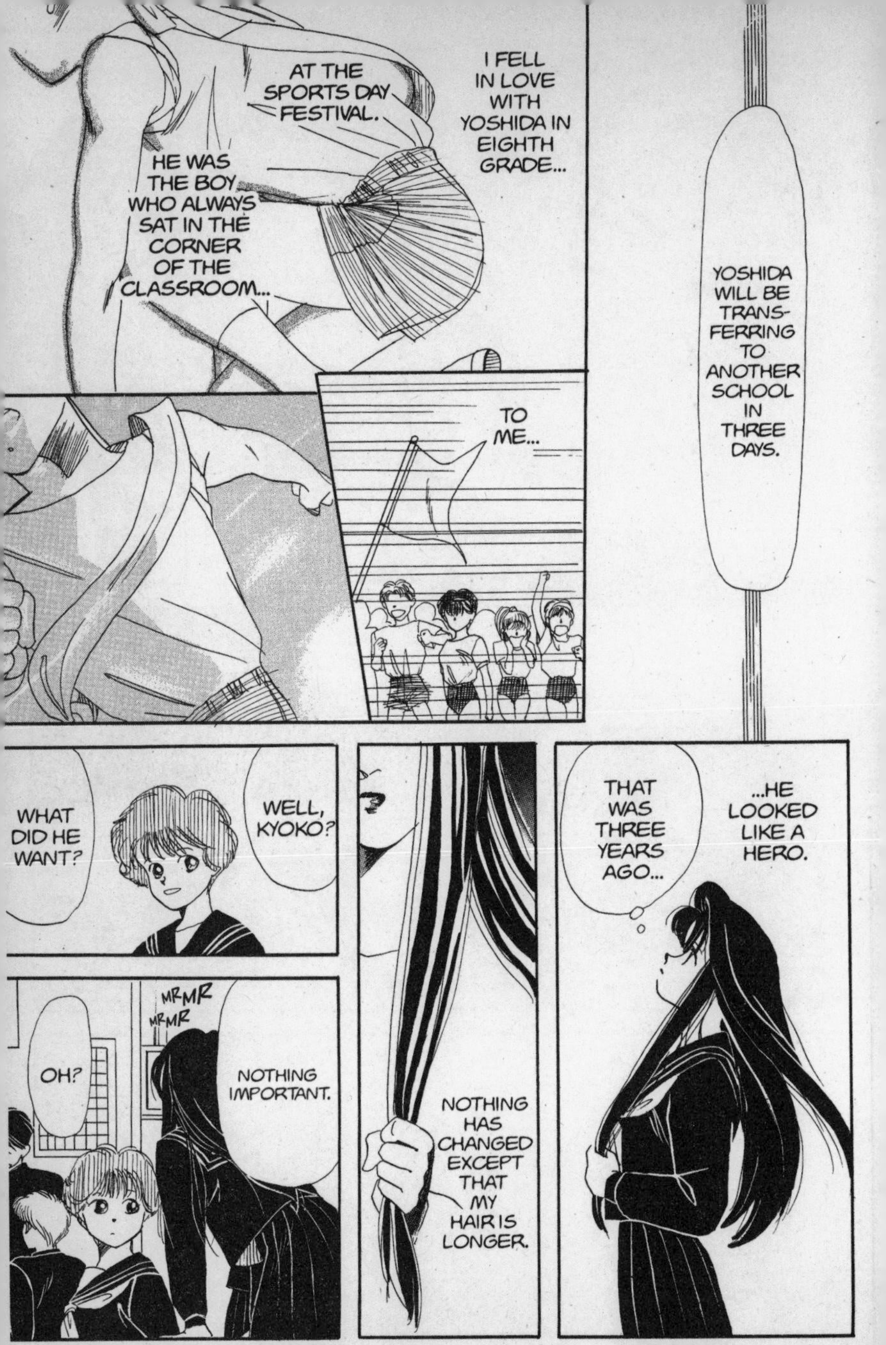
YOSHIDA WILL BE TRANSFERRING TO ANOTHER SCHOOL IN THREE DAYS.
I FELL IN LOVE WITH YOSHIDA IN EIGHTH GRADE...
AT THE SPORTS DAY FESTIVAL.
HE WAS THE BOY WHO ALWAYS SAT IN THE CORNER OF THE CLASSROOM...
TO ME...
...HE LOOKED LIKE A HERO.
THAT WAS THREE YEARS AGO...
NOTHING HAS CHANGED EXCEPT THAT MY HAIR IS LONGER.
WELL, KYOKO?
WHAT DID HE WANT?
NOTHING IMPORTANT.
MRMR MRMR
OH?

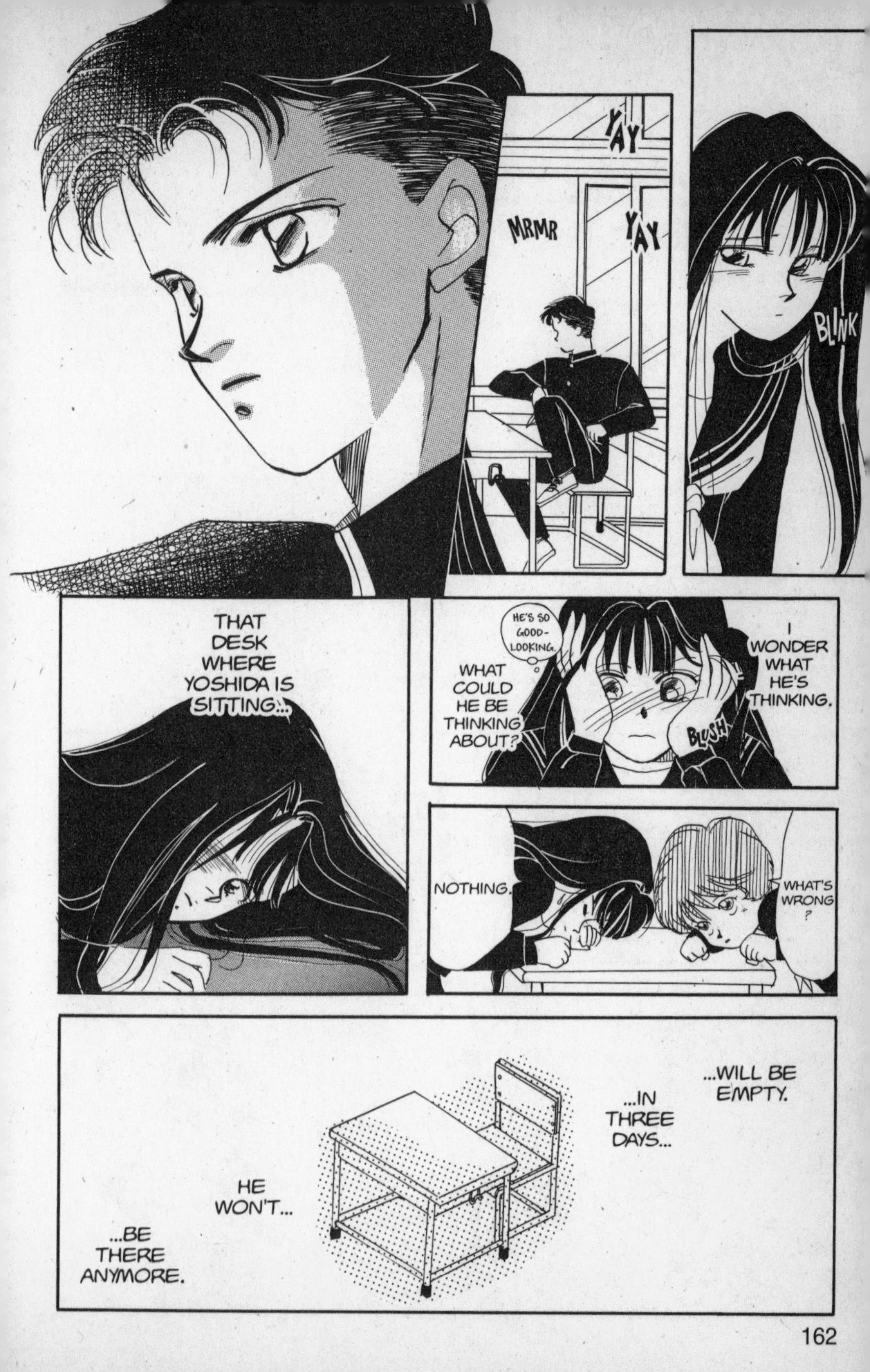
BLINK
YAY
YAY
MRMR
I WONDER WHAT HE'S THINKING.
HE'S SO GOOD-LOOKING.
WHAT COULD HE BE THINKING ABOUT?
BLUSH
WHAT'S WRONG?
NOTHING.
THAT DESK WHERE YOSHIDA IS SITTING...
...WILL BE EMPTY.
...IN THREE DAYS...
HE WON'T...
...BE THERE ANYMORE.

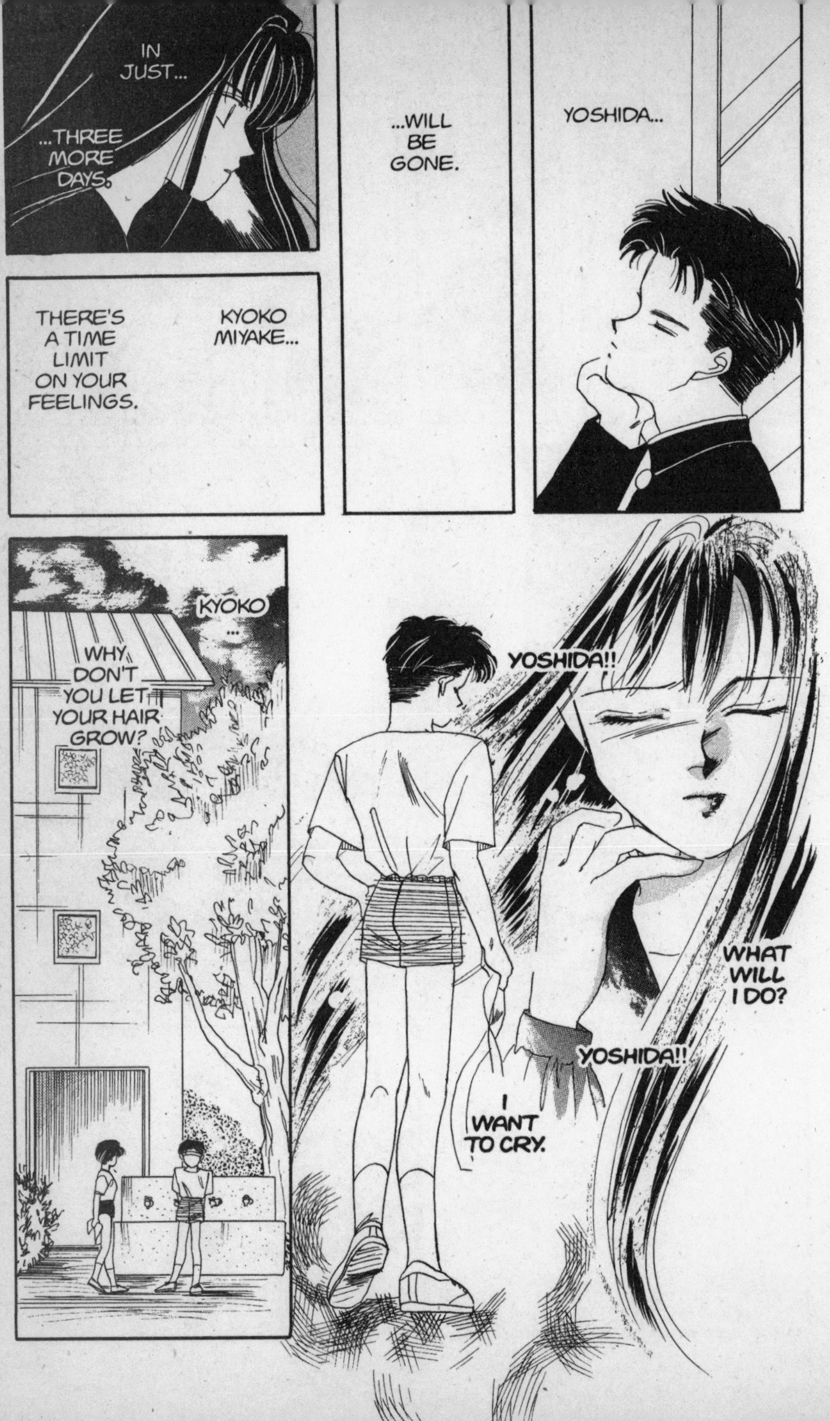
YOSHIDA...
...WILL BE GONE.
IN JUST...
...THREE MORE DAYS.
KYOKO MIYAKE...
THERE'S A TIME LIMIT ON YOUR FEELINGS.
YOSHIDA!!
WHAT WILL I DO?
YOSHIDA!!
I WANT TO CRY.
KYOKO...
WHY DON'T YOU LET YOUR HAIR GROW?

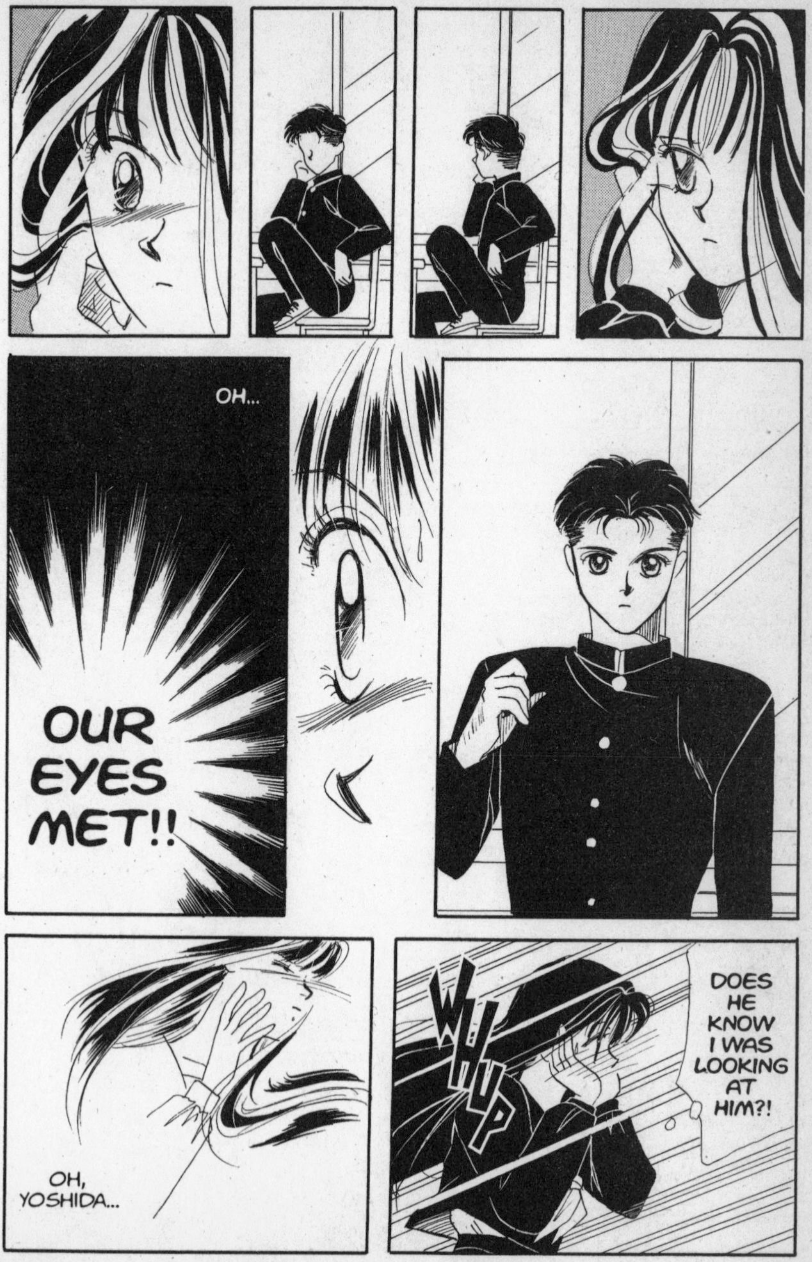
OH...
OUR EYES MET!!
WHUP
DOES HE KNOW I WAS LOOKING AT HIM?!
OH, YOSHIDA...

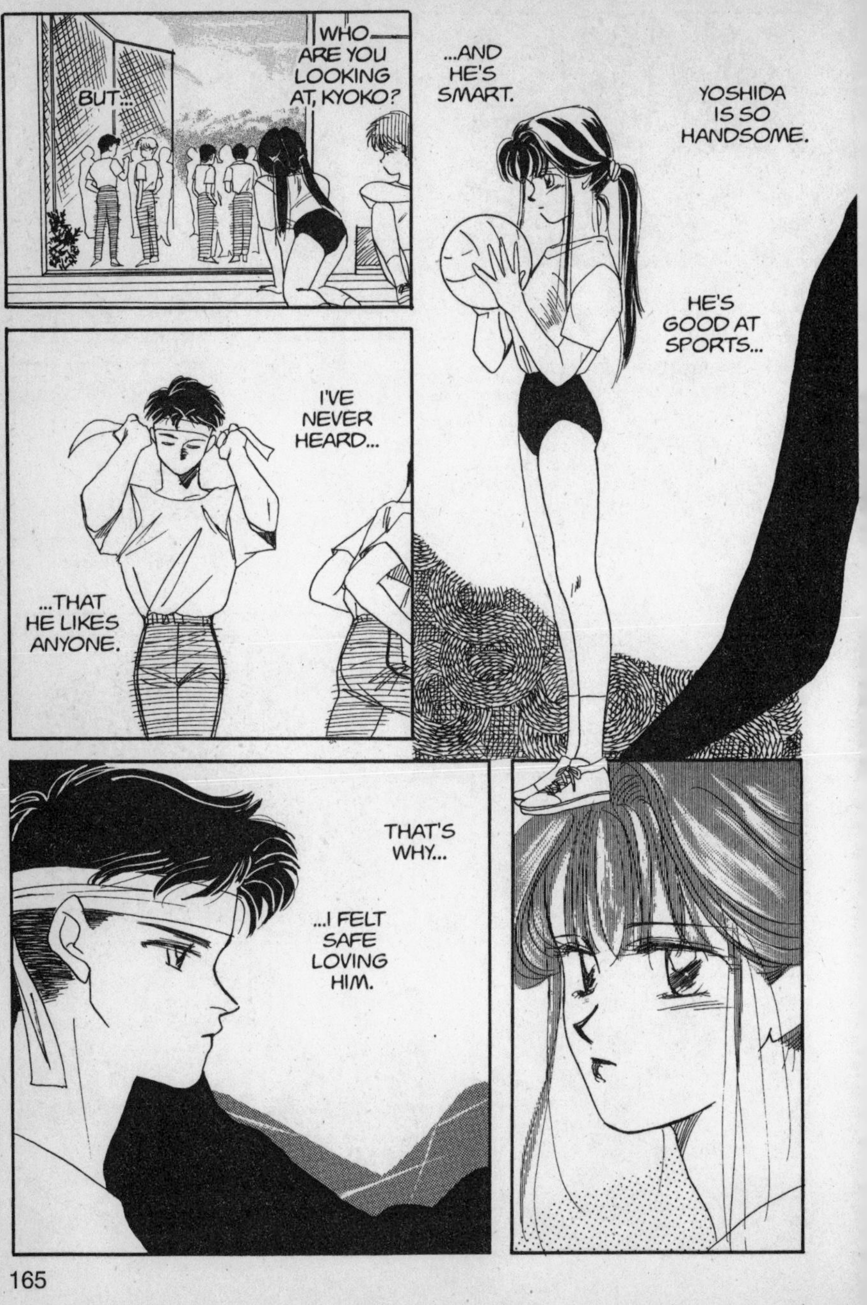
YOSHIDA IS SO HANDSOME.
HE'S GOOD AT SPORTS...
...AND HE'S SMART.
WHO ARE YOU LOOKING AT, KYOKO?
BUT...
I'VE NEVER HEARD...
...THAT HE LIKES ANYONE.
THAT'S WHY...
...I FELT SAFE LOVING HIM.

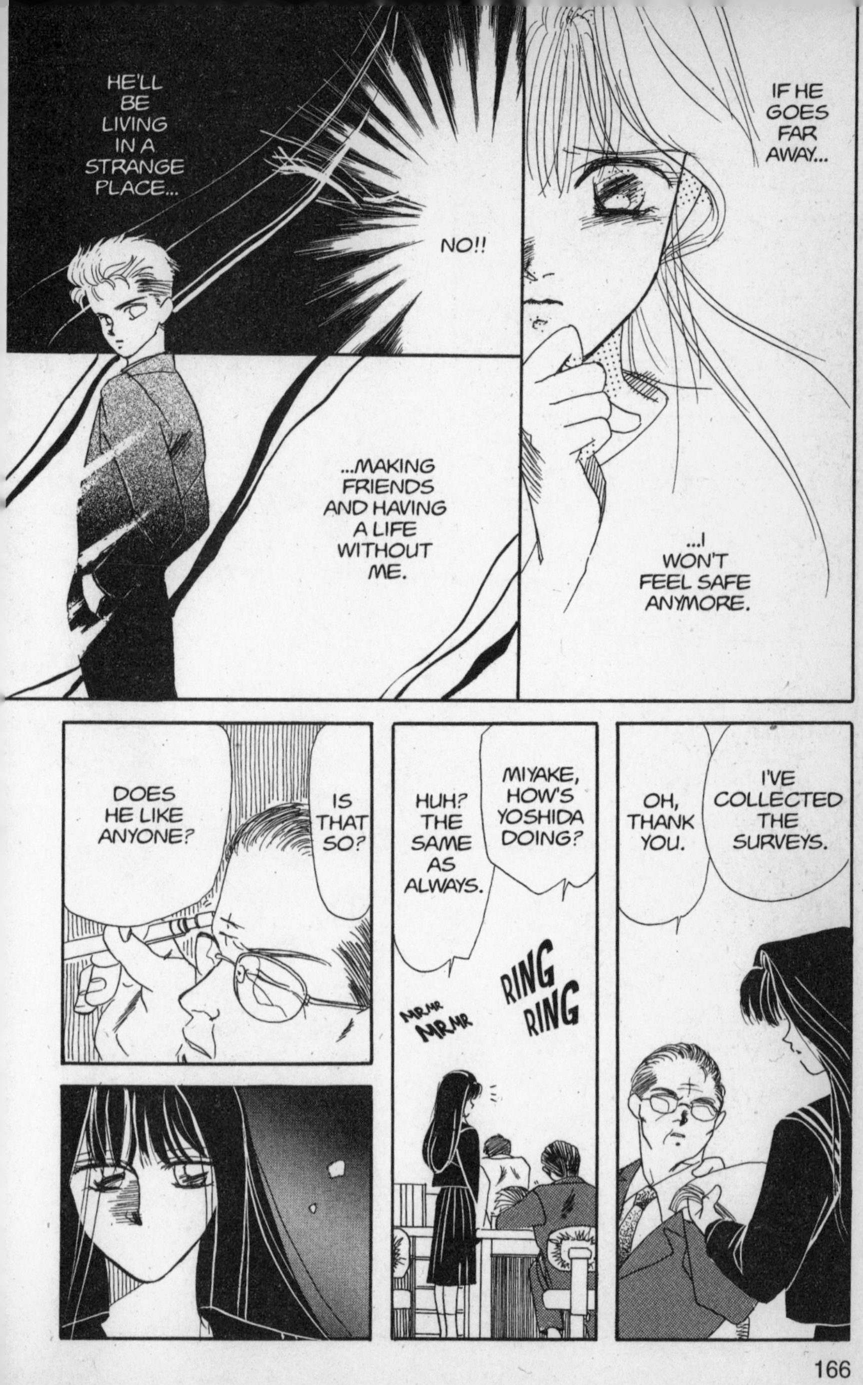
IF HE GOES FAR AWAY...
...I WON'T FEEL SAFE ANYMORE.
HE'LL BE LIVING IN A STRANGE PLACE...
NO!!
...MAKING FRIENDS AND HAVING A LIFE WITHOUT ME.
I'VE COLLECTED THE SURVEYS.
OH, THANK YOU.
MIYAKE, HOW'S YOSHIDA DOING?
HUH? THE SAME AS ALWAYS.
RING RING
MRMR MRMR
IS THAT SO?
DOES HE LIKE ANYONE?

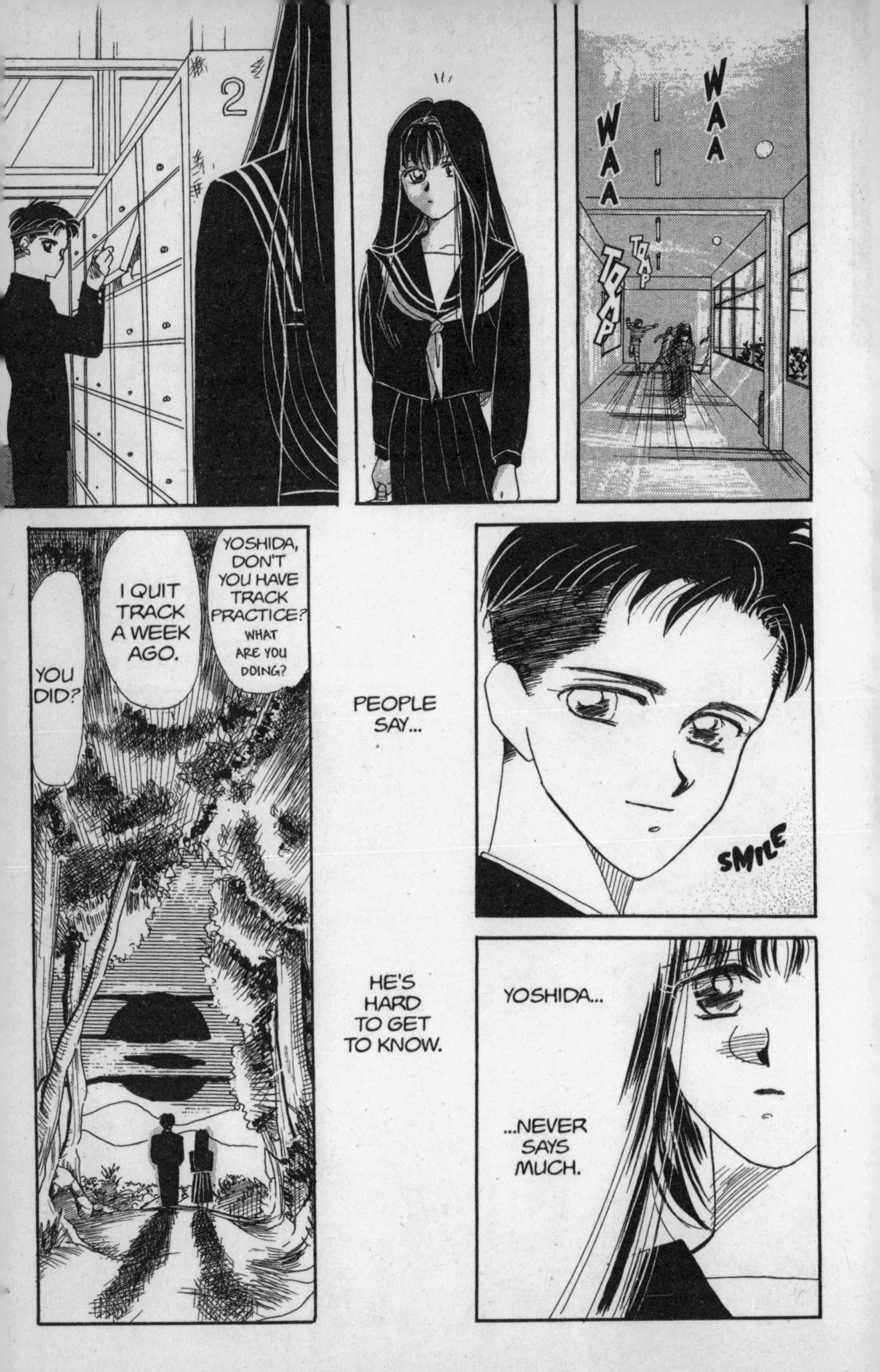
WAA
WAA
TOMP
TOMP
PEOPLE SAY...
SMILE
HE'S HARD TO GET TO KNOW.
YOSHIDA...
...NEVER SAYS MUCH.
YOSHIDA, DON'T YOU HAVE TRACK PRACTICE? WHAT ARE YOU DOING?
I QUIT TRACK A WEEK AGO.
YOU DID?

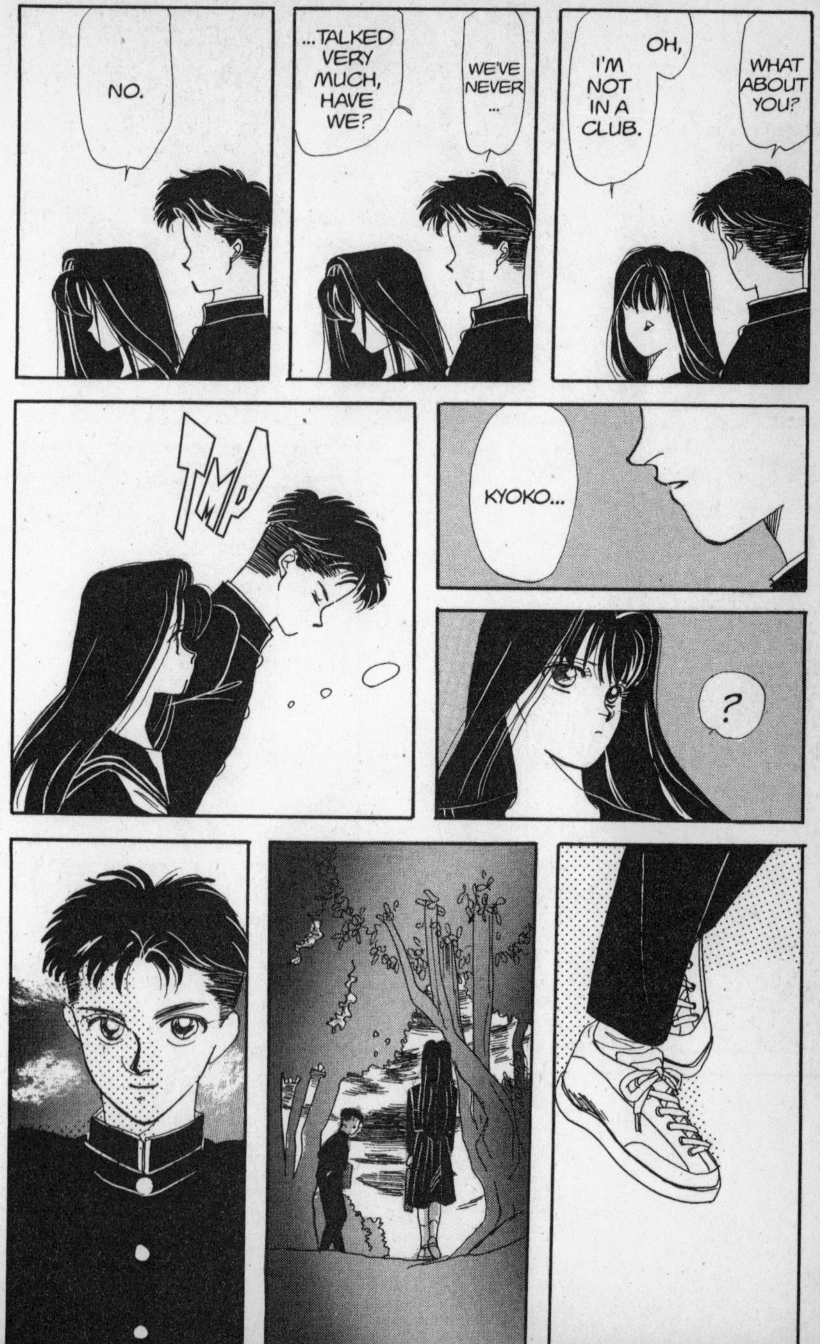
WHAT ABOUT YOU?
OH,
I'M NOT IN A CLUB.
WE'VE NEVER ...
...TALKED VERY MUCH, HAVE WE?
NO.
KYOKO...
?
TMP

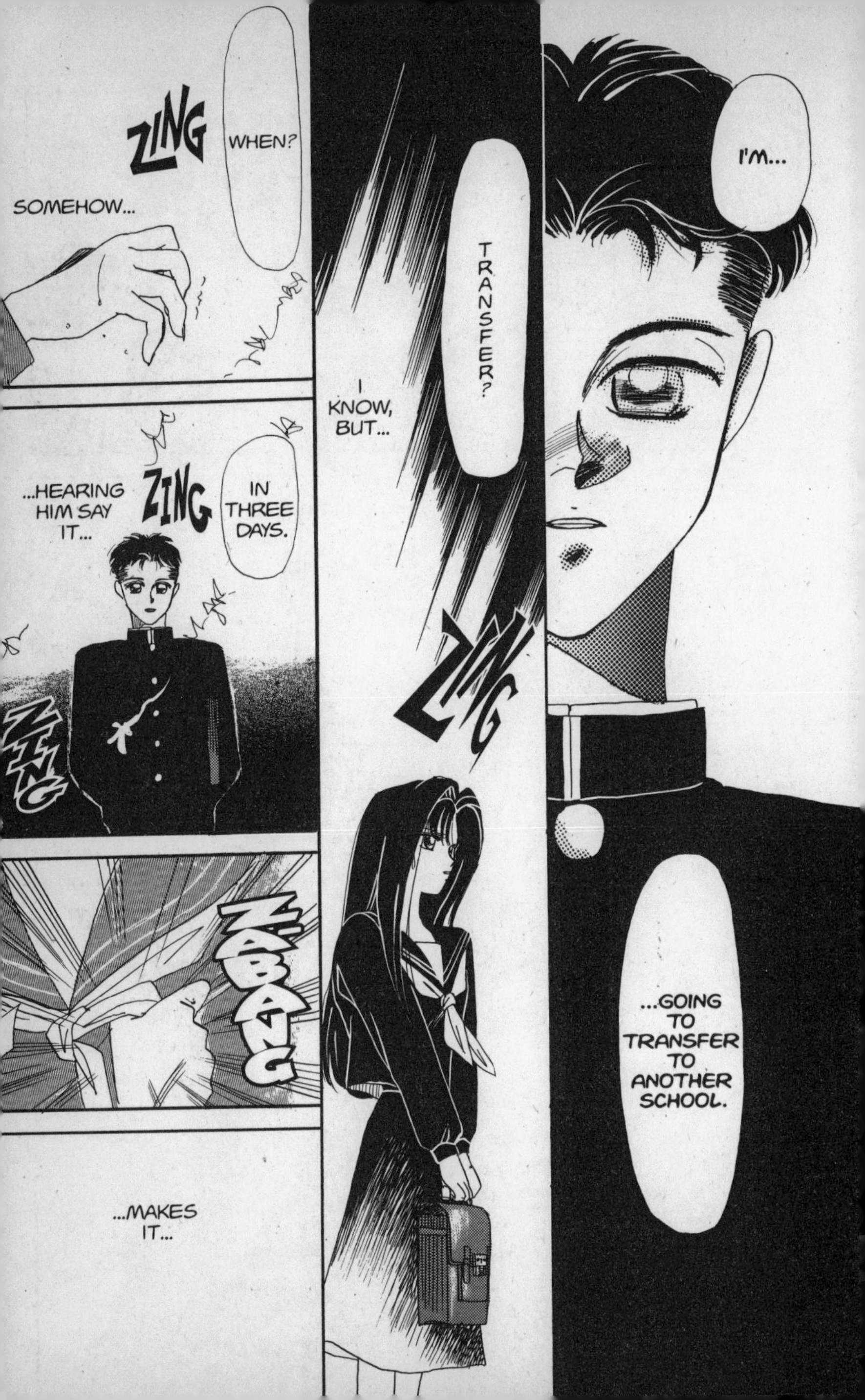
I'M...
...GOING TO TRANSFER TO ANOTHER SCHOOL.
TRANSFER?
I KNOW, BUT...
ZING
WHEN?
ZING
SOMEHOW...
IN THREE DAYS.
ZING
...HEARING HIM SAY IT...
ZING
ZABANG
...MAKES IT...

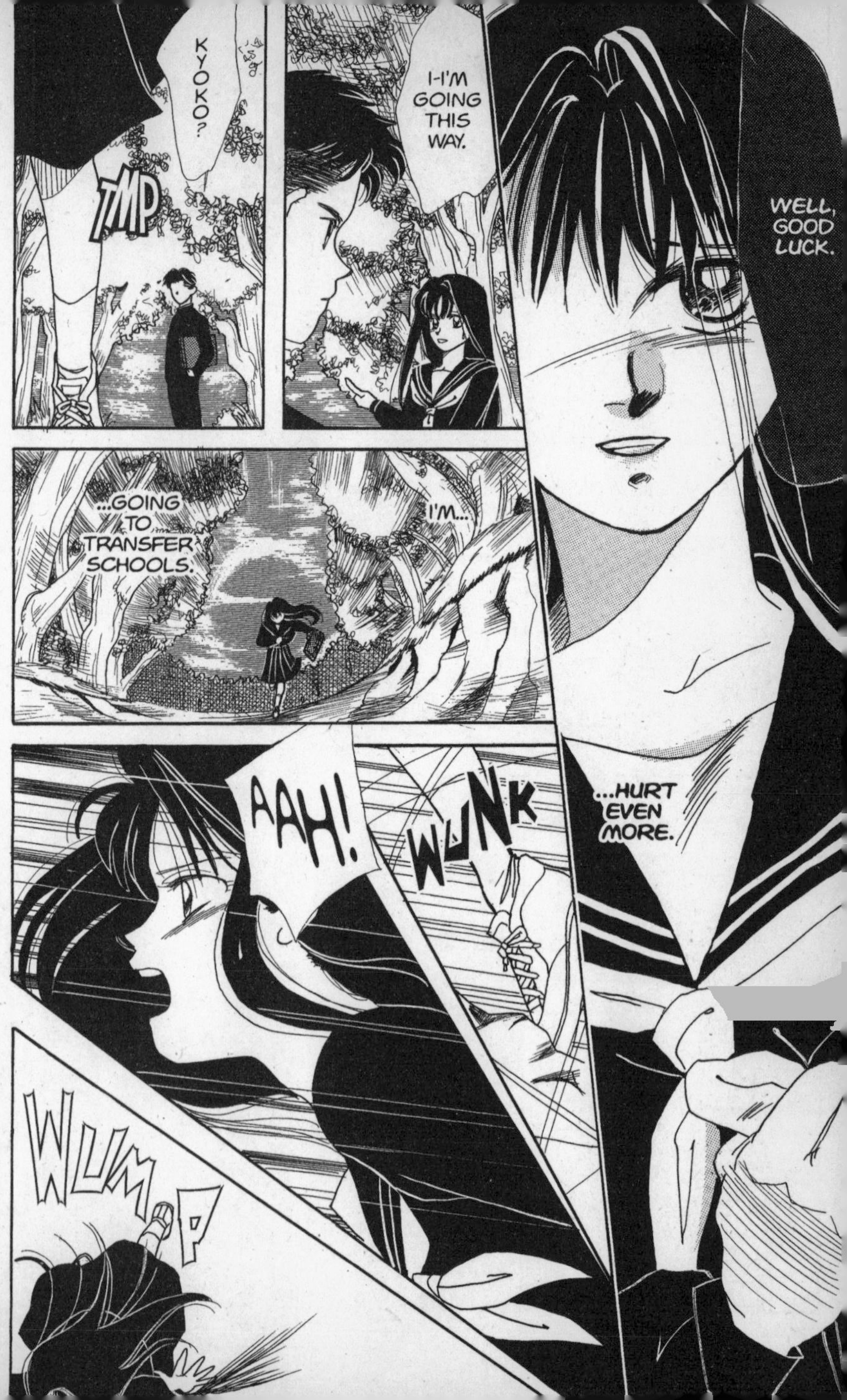
WELL, GOOD LUCK.
...HURT EVEN MORE.
I-I'M GOING THIS WAY.
KYOKO?
TMP
I'M...
...GOING TO TRANSFER SCHOOLS.
WUNK
AAH!
WUMP

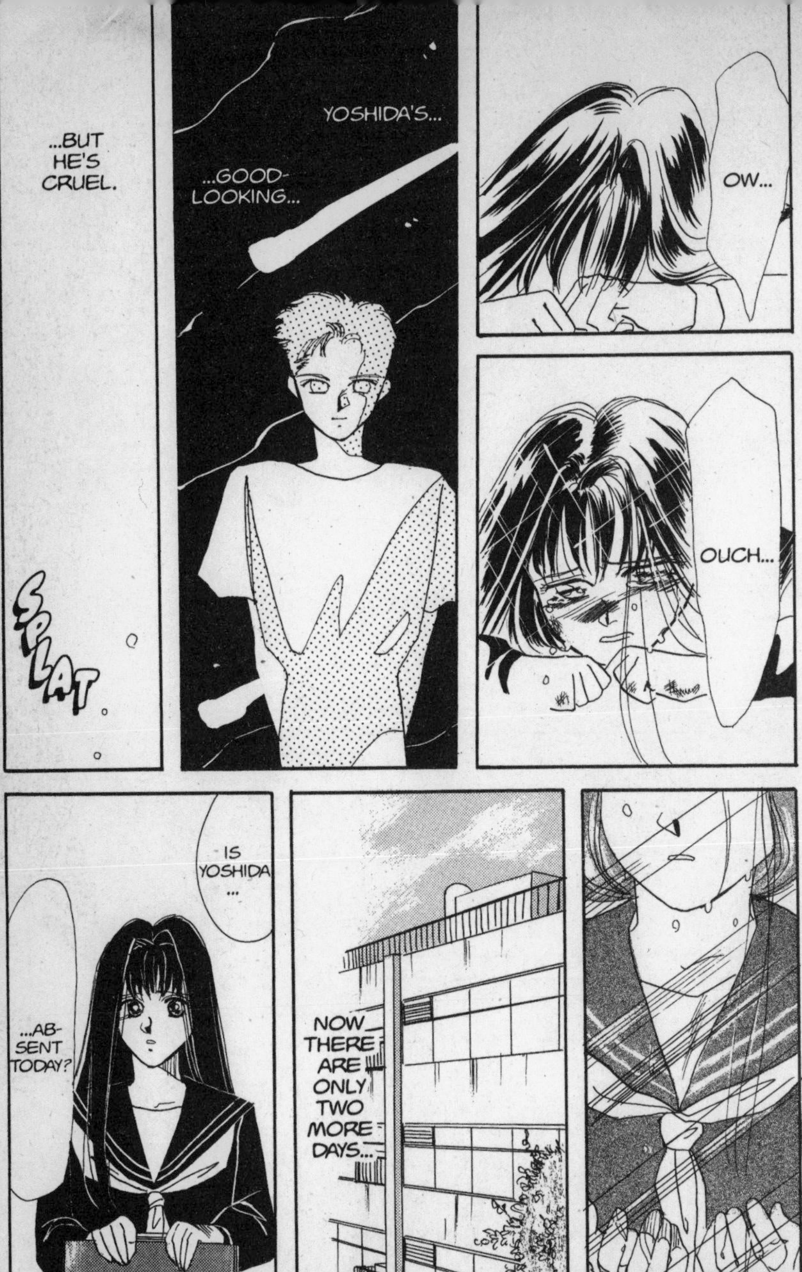
OW...
OUCH...
YOSHIDA'S...
...GOOD-LOOKING...
...BUT HE'S CRUEL.
SPLAT
NOW THERE ARE ONLY TWO MORE DAYS...
IS YOSHIDA ...
...ABSENT TODAY?

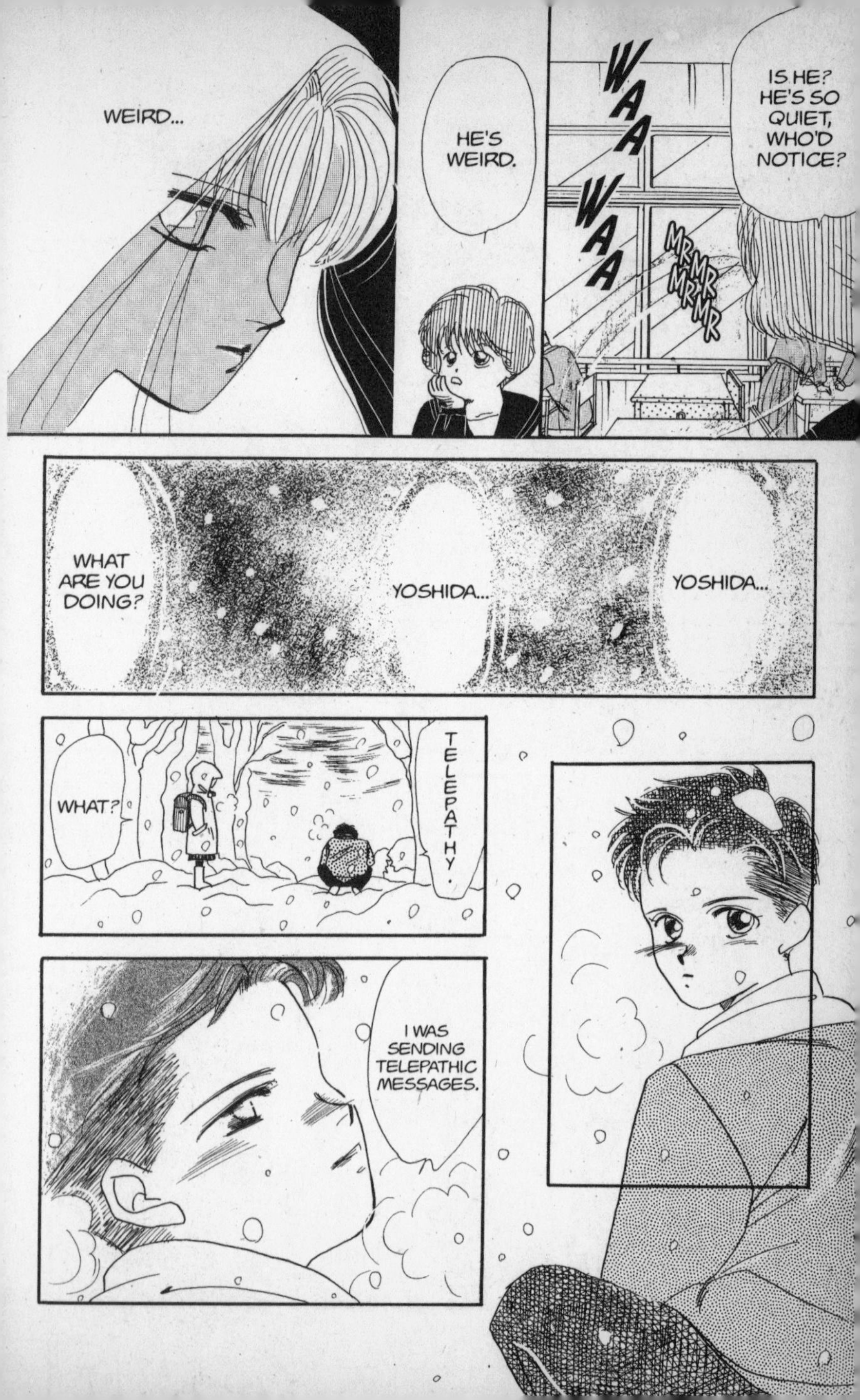
IS HE? HE'S SO QUIET, WHO'D NOTICE?
WAA WAA
MRMR MRMR
HE'S WEIRD.
WEIRD...
YOSHIDA...
YOSHIDA...
WHAT ARE YOU DOING?
TELEPATHY.
WHAT?
I WAS SENDING TELEPATHIC MESSAGES.

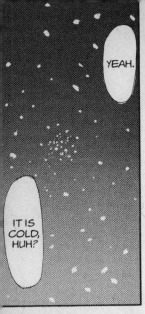

YEAH.

IT IS COLD, HUH?

FWOO

IT'S SNOW-ING...

IT'S COLD...

...WHEN YOSHIDA GOES AWAY?!

I...

WHAT WILL I DO...

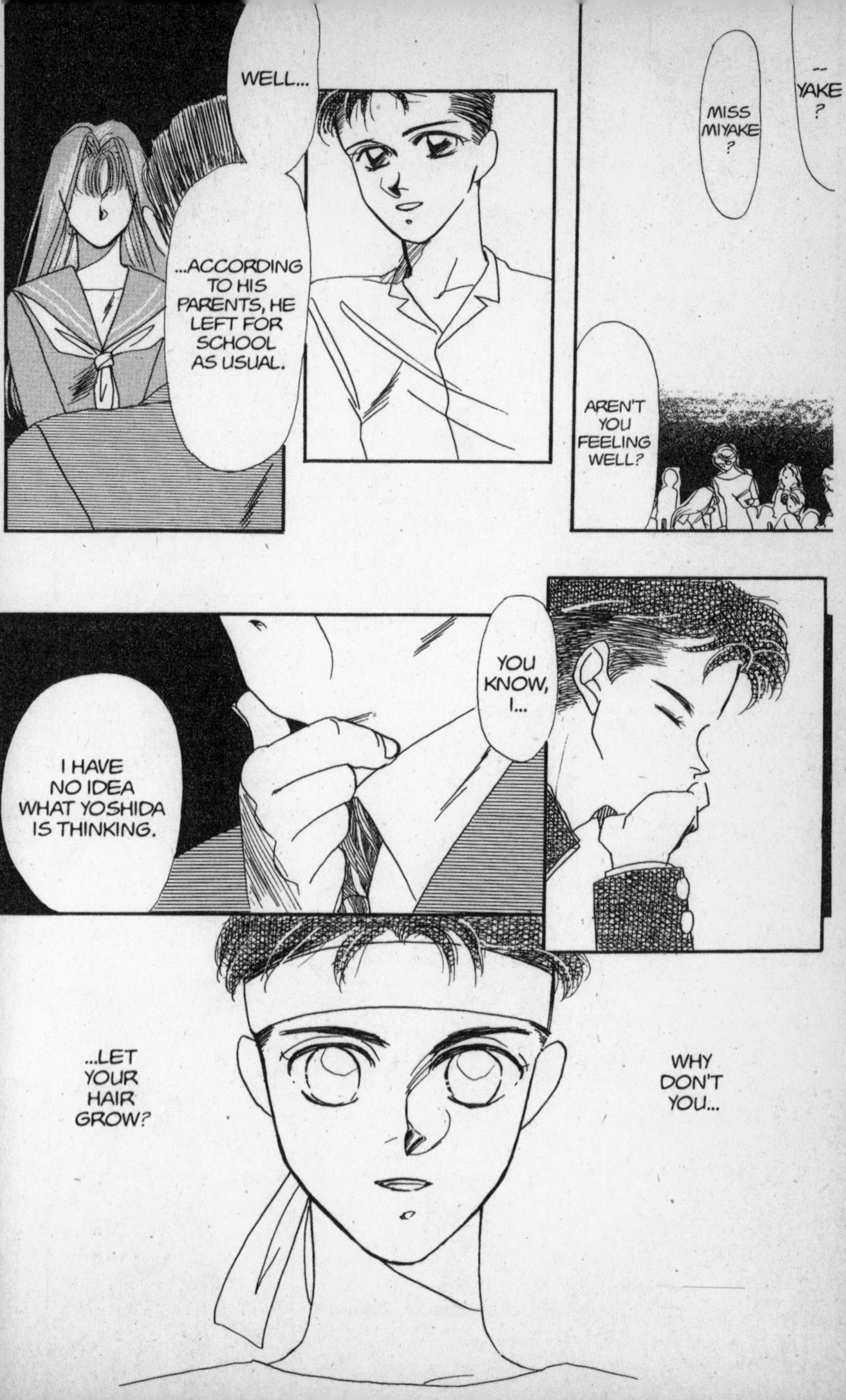

-- YAKE?
MISS MIYAKE?
AREN'T YOU FEELING WELL?
WELL...
...ACCORDING TO HIS PARENTS, HE LEFT FOR SCHOOL AS USUAL.
YOU KNOW, I...
I HAVE NO IDEA WHAT YOSHIDA IS THINKING.
WHY DON'T YOU...
...LET YOUR HAIR GROW?

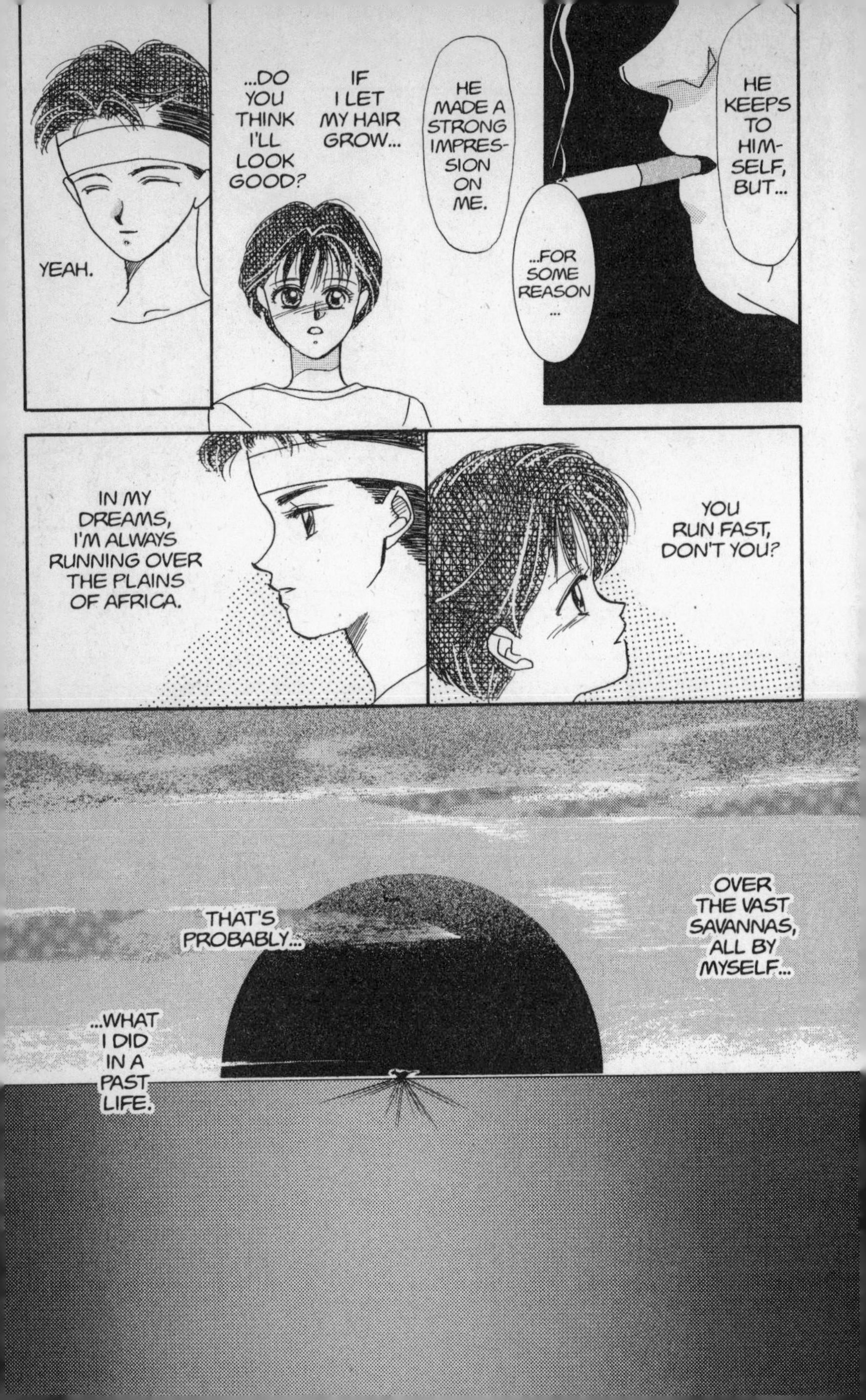
HE KEEPS TO HIM-SELF, BUT...
...FOR SOME REASON...
HE MADE A STRONG IMPRES-SION ON ME.
IF I LET MY HAIR GROW...
...DO YOU THINK I'LL LOOK GOOD?
YEAH.
YOU RUN FAST, DON'T YOU?
IN MY DREAMS, I'M ALWAYS RUNNING OVER THE PLAINS OF AFRICA.
OVER THE VAST SAVANNAS, ALL BY MYSELF...
THAT'S PROBABLY...
...WHAT I DID IN A PAST LIFE.

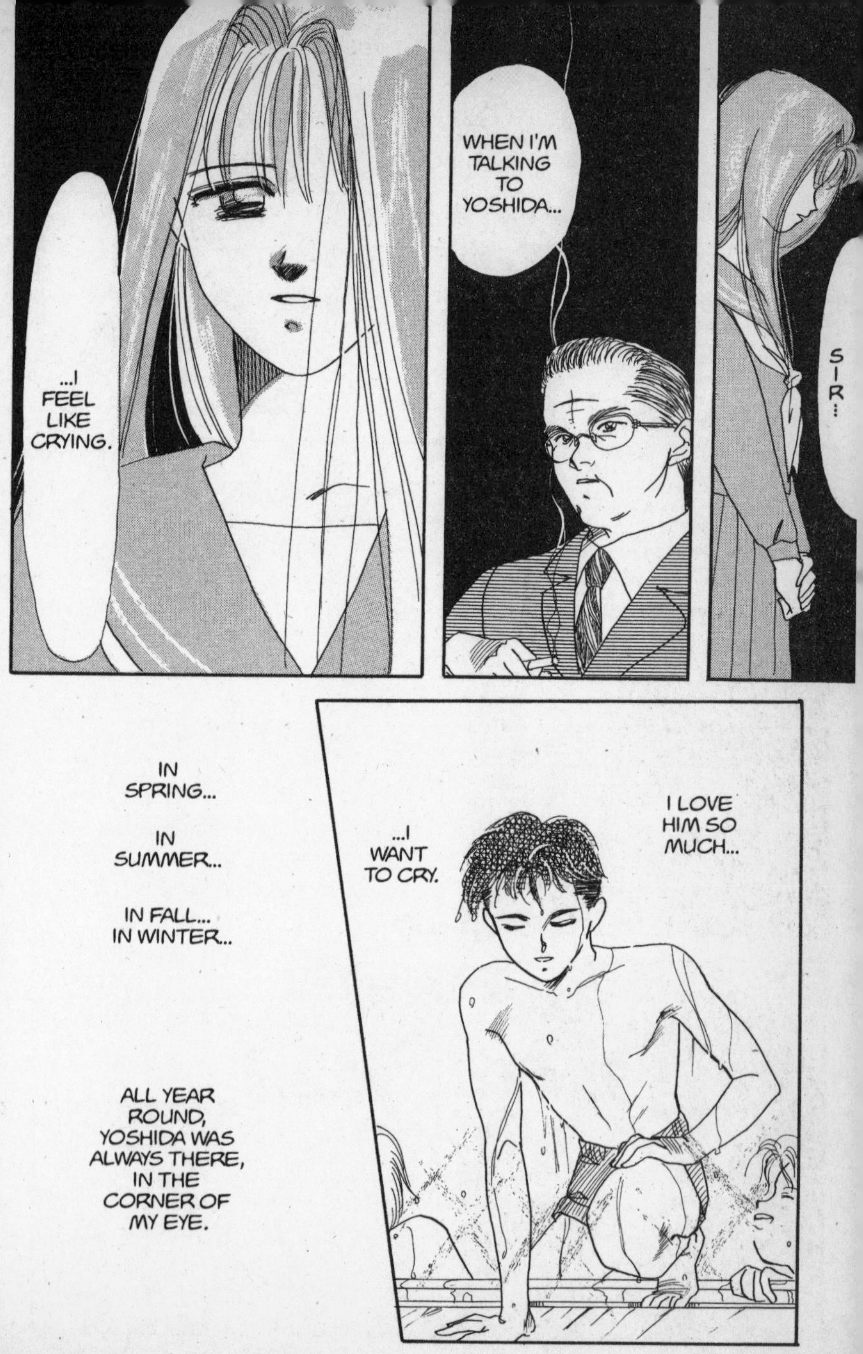
SIR...
WHEN I'M TALKING TO YOSHIDA...
...I FEEL LIKE CRYING.
I LOVE HIM SO MUCH...
...I WANT TO CRY.
IN SPRING...
IN SUMMER...
IN FALL... IN WINTER...
ALL YEAR ROUND, YOSHIDA WAS ALWAYS THERE, IN THE CORNER OF MY EYE.

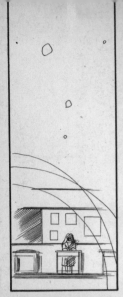

...HE'S NOT GOING TO BE THERE ANYMORE.

AND NOW...

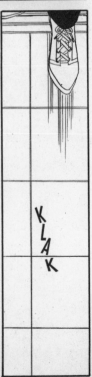

KYOKO...

KLAK

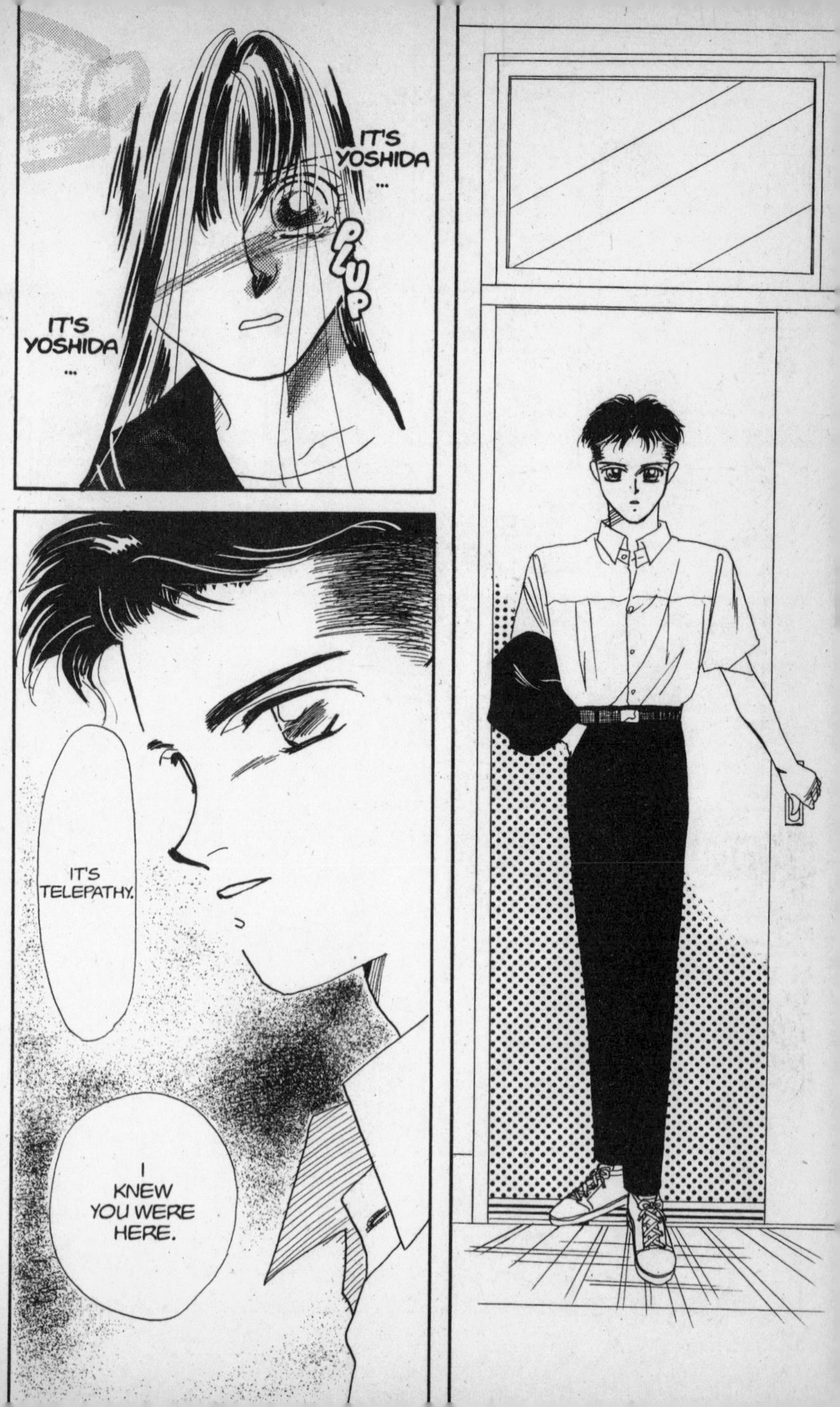
IT'S YOSHIDA ...
PLUP
IT'S YOSHIDA ...
IT'S TELEPATHY.
I KNEW YOU WERE HERE.

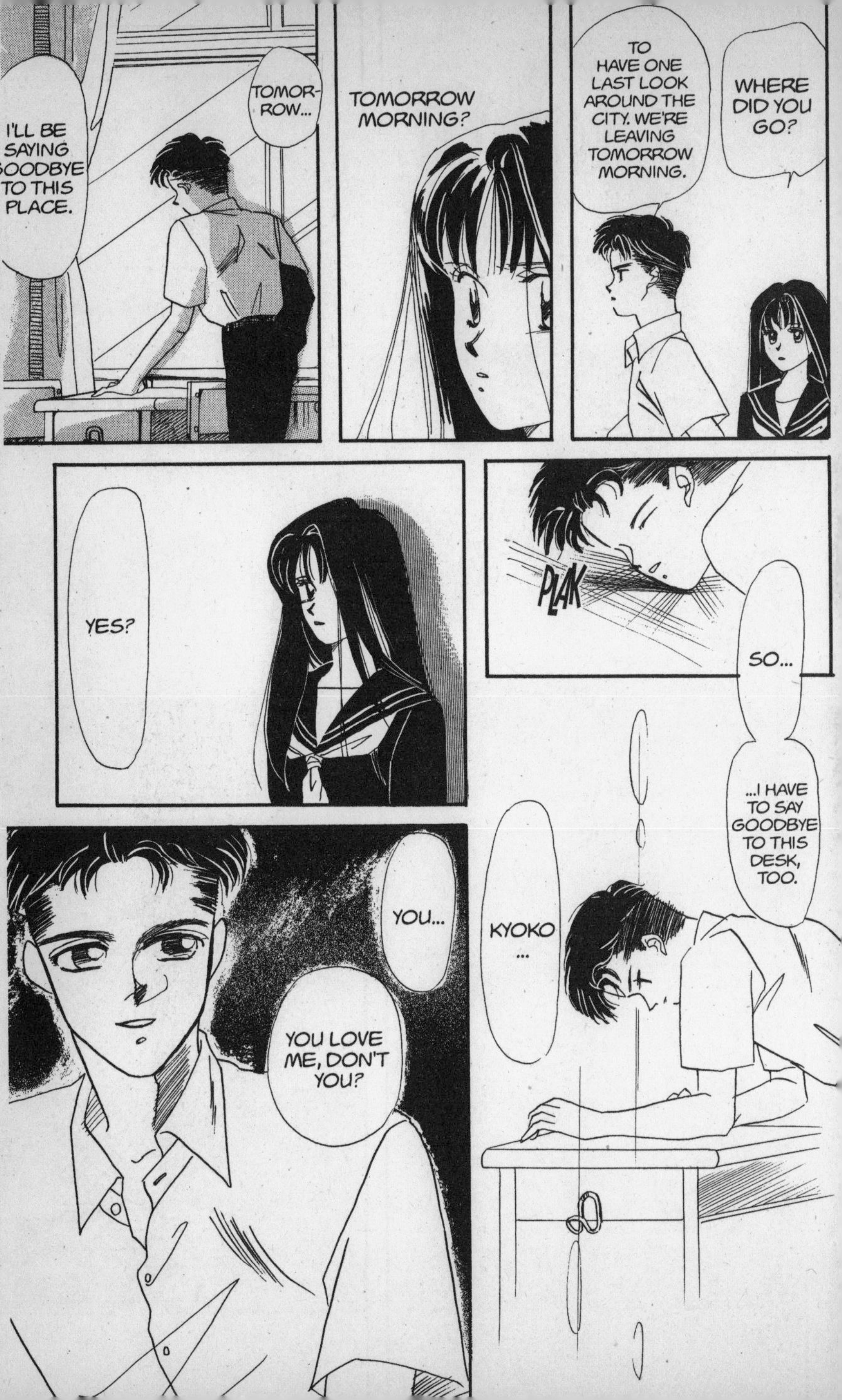
WHERE DID YOU GO?
TO HAVE ONE LAST LOOK AROUND THE CITY. WE'RE LEAVING TOMORROW MORNING.
TOMORROW MORNING?
TOMORROW...
I'LL BE SAYING GOODBYE TO THIS PLACE.
PLAK
SO...
...I HAVE TO SAY GOODBYE TO THIS DESK, TOO.
KYOKO...
YES?
YOU...
YOU LOVE ME, DON'T YOU?

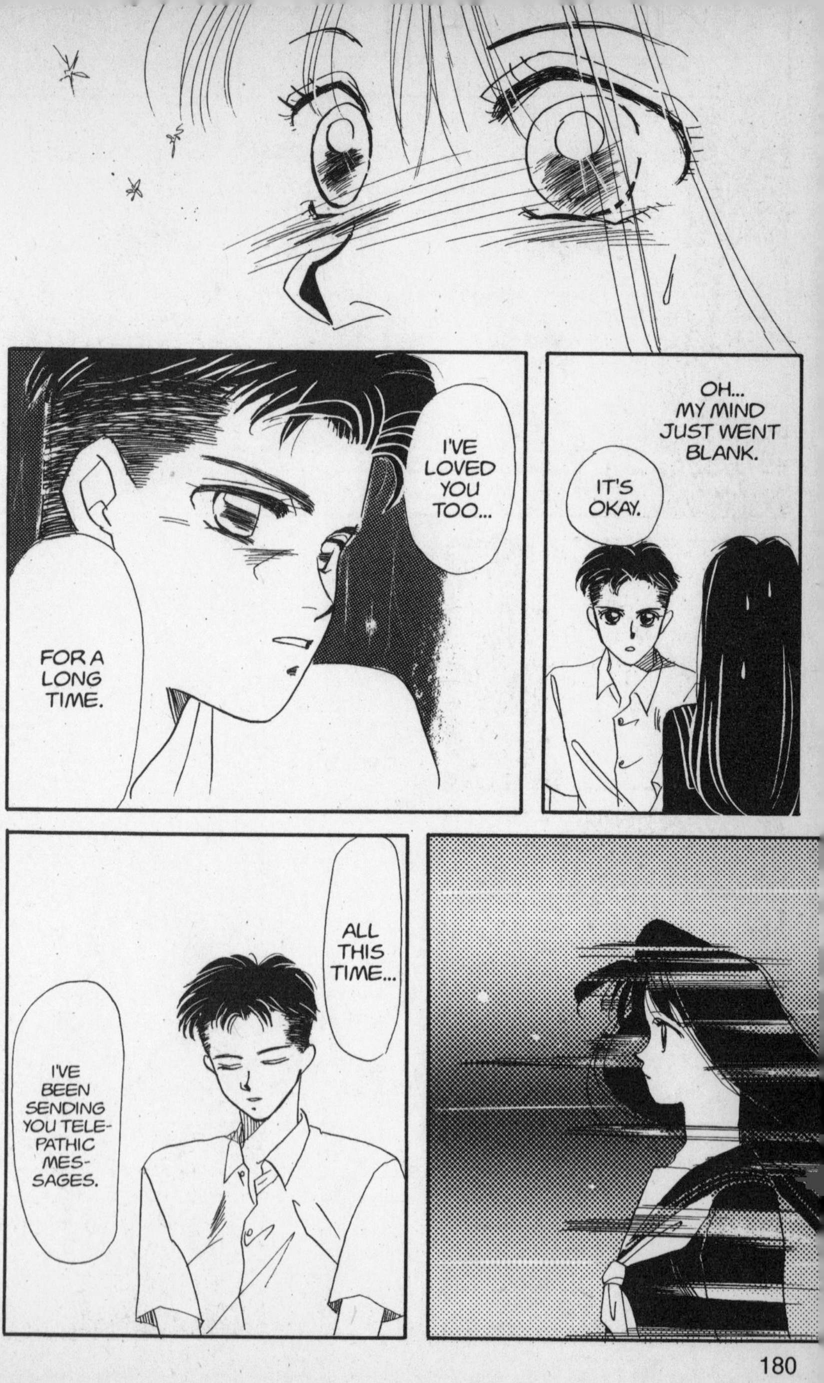
OH... MY MIND JUST WENT BLANK.
IT'S OKAY.
I'VE LOVED YOU TOO...
FOR A LONG TIME.
ALL THIS TIME...
I'VE BEEN SENDING YOU TELEPATHIC MESSAGES.

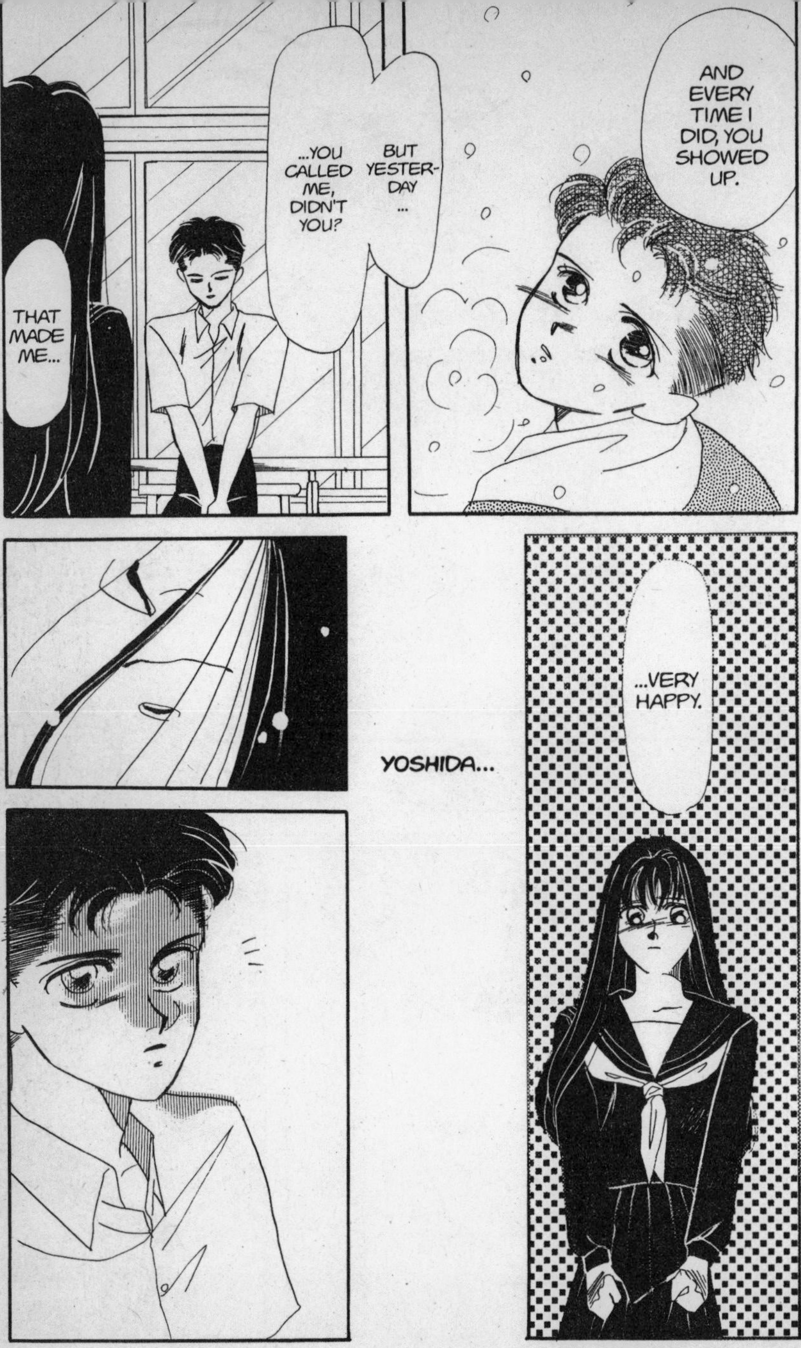
AND EVERY TIME I DID, YOU SHOWED UP.
BUT YESTER-DAY ...
...YOU CALLED ME, DIDN'T YOU?
THAT MADE ME...
...VERY HAPPY.
YOSHIDA...

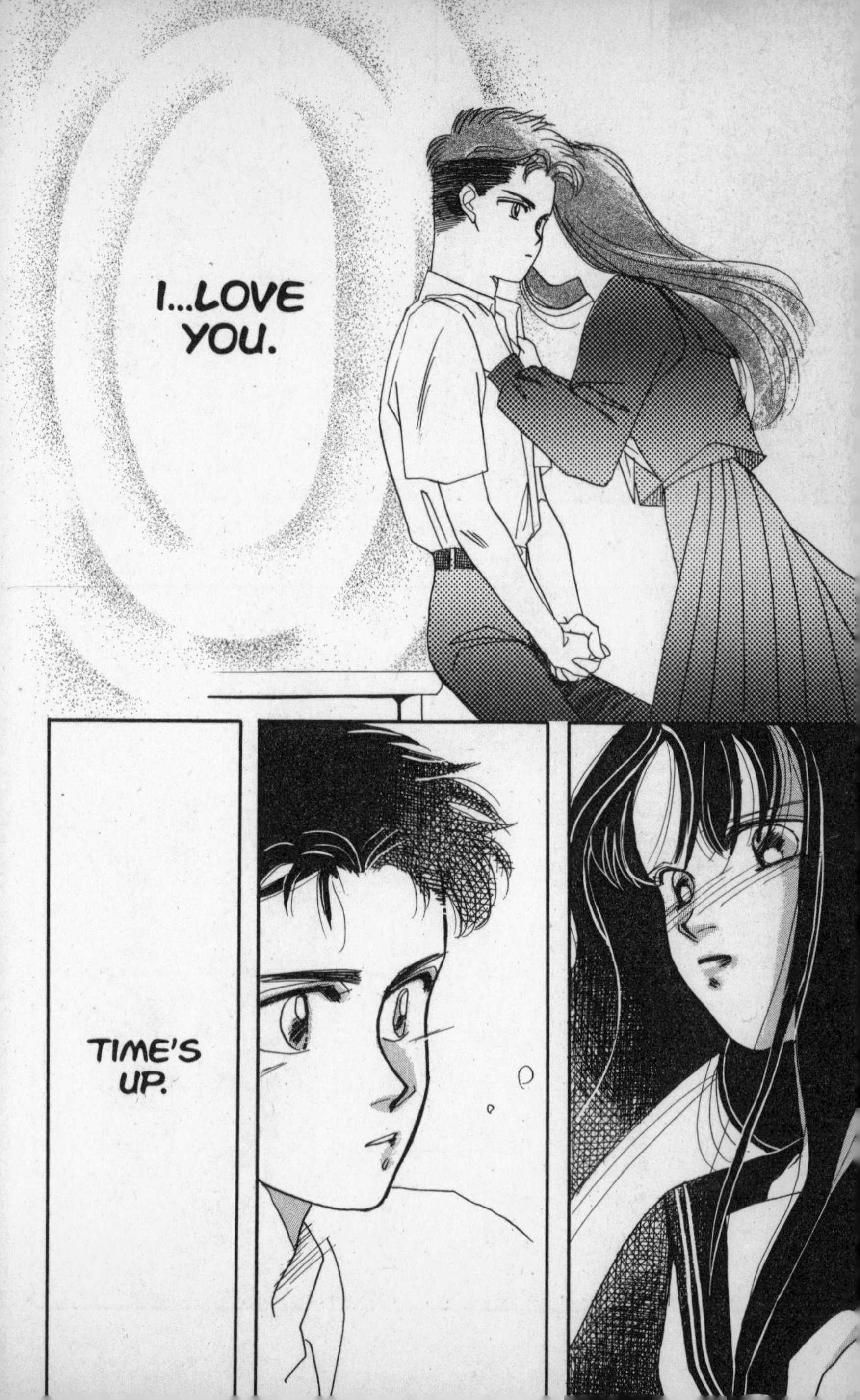
I...LOVE YOU.
TIME'S UP.

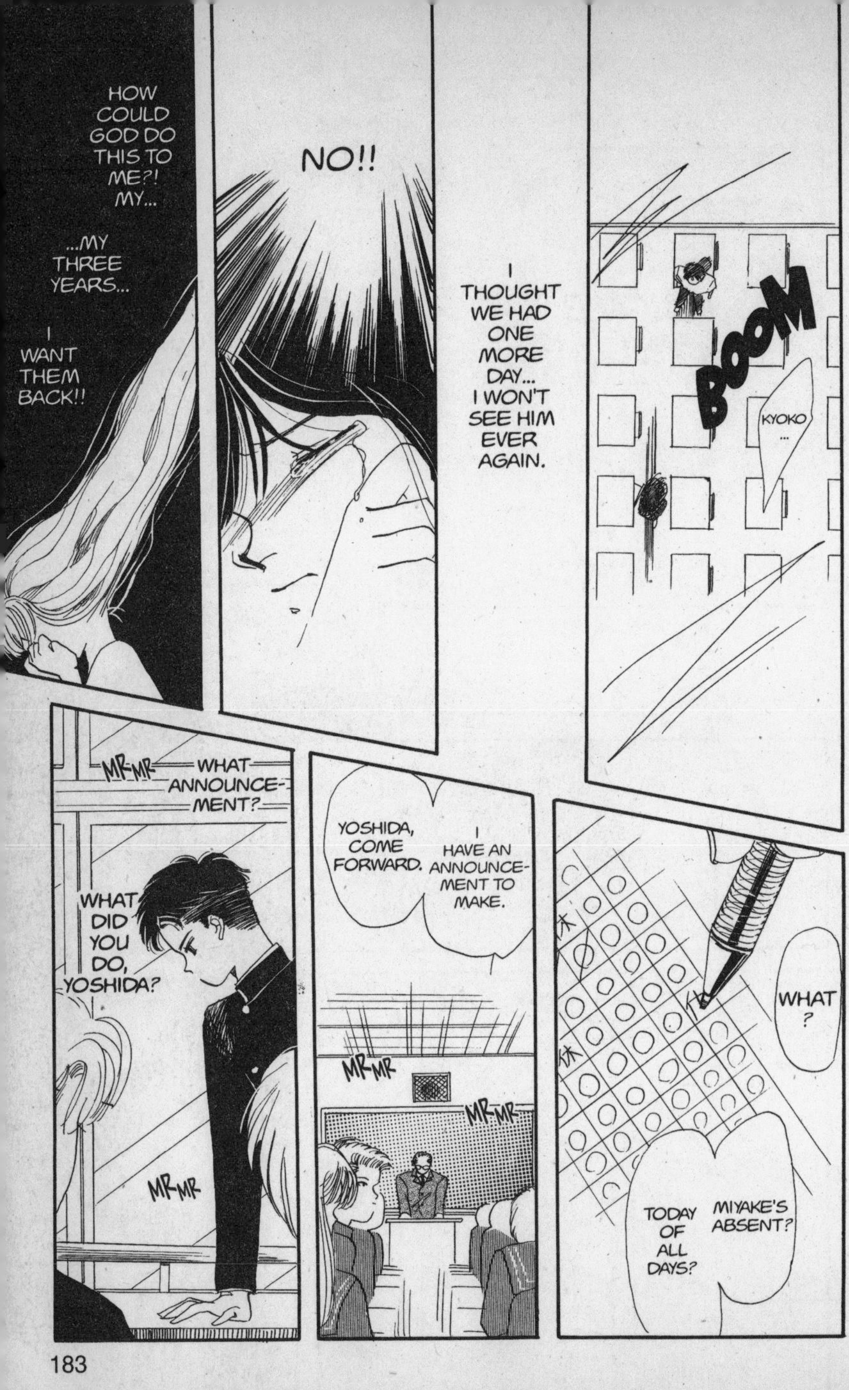
BOOM
KYOKO...
I THOUGHT WE HAD ONE MORE DAY... I WON'T SEE HIM EVER AGAIN.
NO!!
HOW COULD GOD DO THIS TO ME?! MY...
...MY THREE YEARS...
I WANT THEM BACK!!
WHAT?
MIYAKE'S ABSENT?
TODAY OF ALL DAYS?
I HAVE AN ANNOUNCEMENT TO MAKE.
YOSHIDA, COME FORWARD.
MR-MR
MR-MR
MR-MR
WHAT ANNOUNCEMENT?
WHAT DID YOU DO, YOSHIDA?
MR-MR

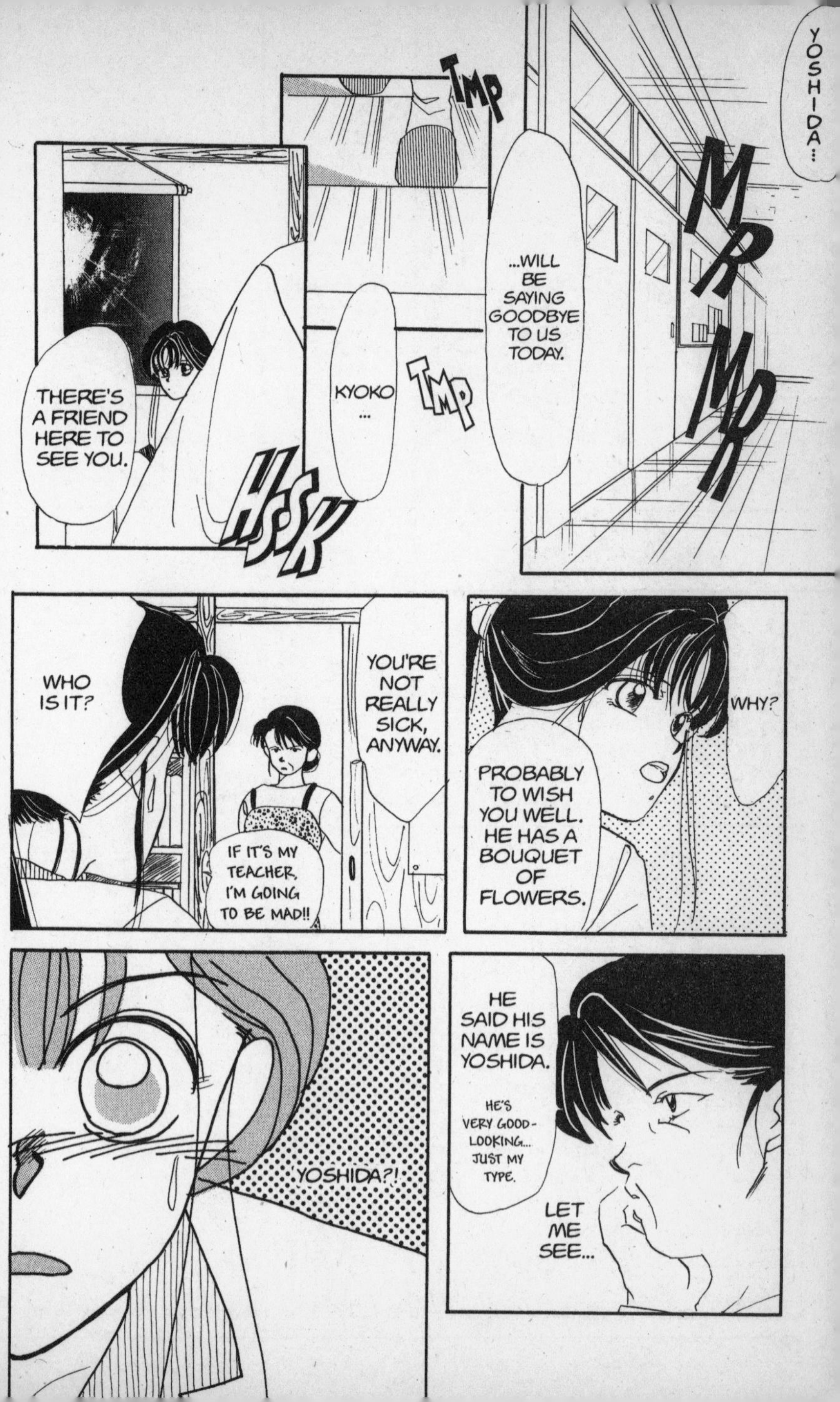
YOSHIDA...
MR
MR
...WILL BE SAYING GOODBYE TO US TODAY.
TMP
KYOKO ...
TMP
HSK
THERE'S A FRIEND HERE TO SEE YOU.
WHY?
PROBABLY TO WISH YOU WELL. HE HAS A BOUQUET OF FLOWERS.
YOU'RE NOT REALLY SICK, ANYWAY.
WHO IS IT?
IF IT'S MY TEACHER, I'M GOING TO BE MAD!!
HE SAID HIS NAME IS YOSHIDA.
HE'S VERY GOOD-LOOKING... JUST MY TYPE.
LET ME SEE...
YOSHIDA?!

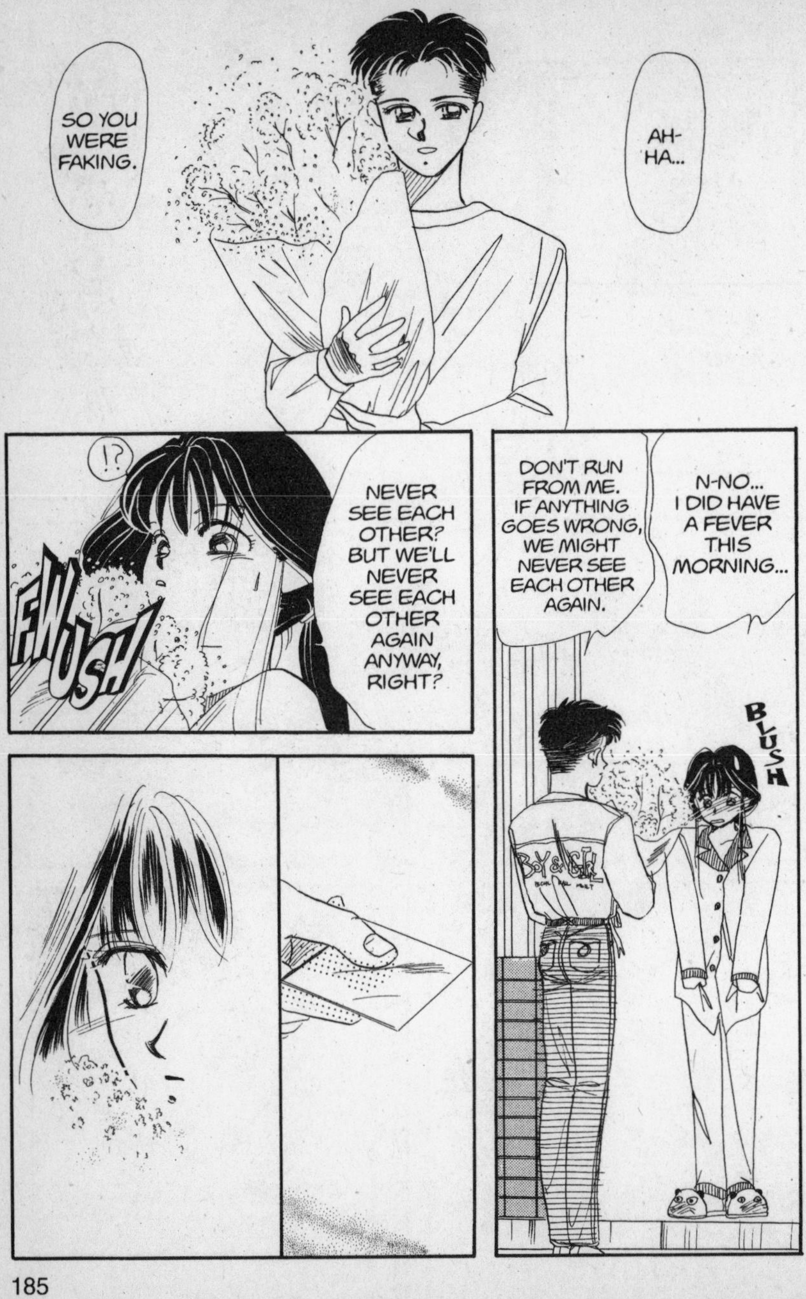
AH-HA...
SO YOU WERE FAKING.
N-NO... I DID HAVE A FEVER THIS MORNING...
DON'T RUN FROM ME. IF ANYTHING GOES WRONG, WE MIGHT NEVER SEE EACH OTHER AGAIN.
BLUSH
NEVER SEE EACH OTHER? BUT WE'LL NEVER SEE EACH OTHER AGAIN ANYWAY, RIGHT?
!?
FWUSH!

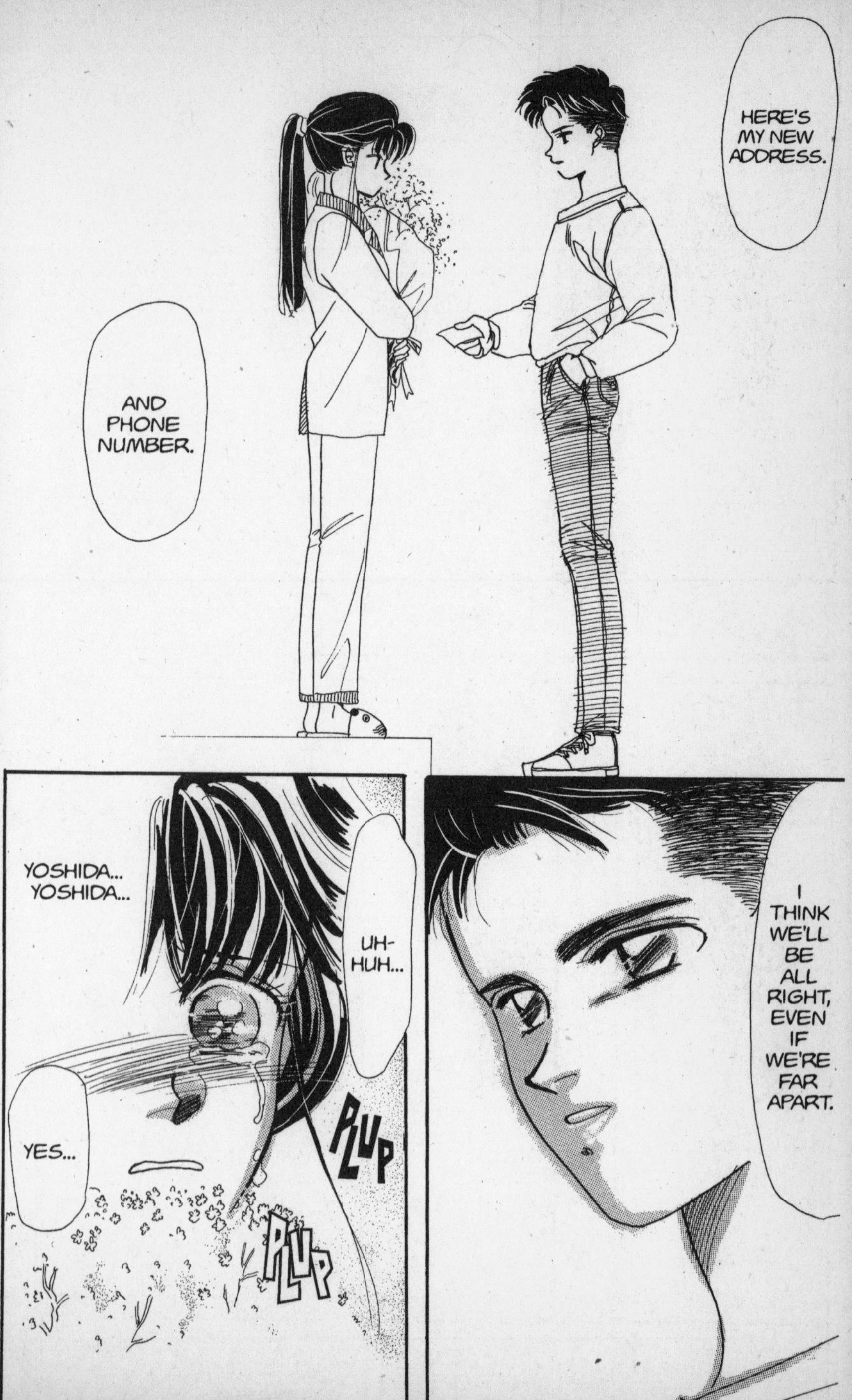
HERE'S MY NEW ADDRESS.
AND PHONE NUMBER.
I THINK WE'LL BE ALL RIGHT, EVEN IF WE'RE FAR APART.
UH-HUH...
YOSHIDA... YOSHIDA...
PLUP
YES...
PLUP

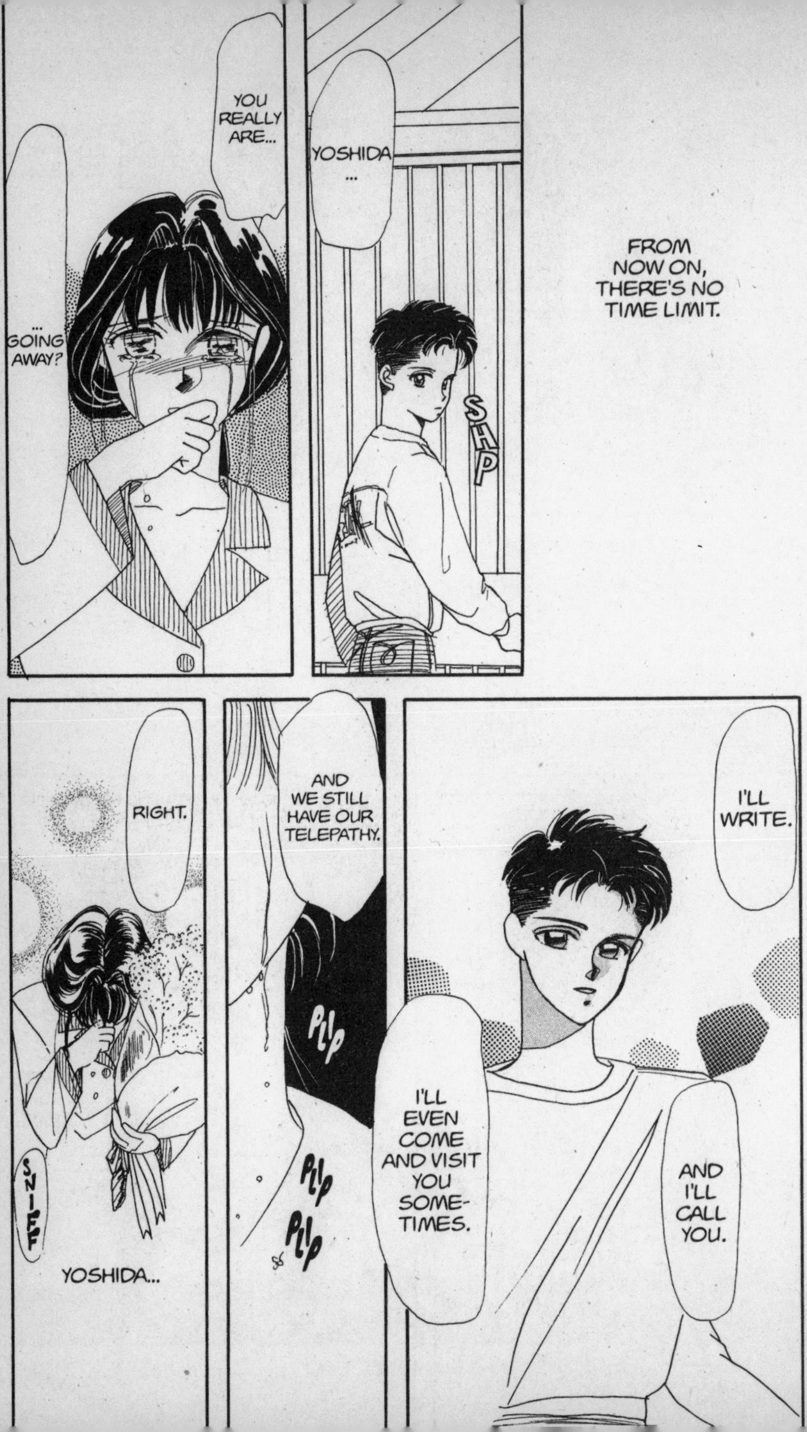
FROM NOW ON, THERE'S NO TIME LIMIT.
YOSHIDA ...
SHP
YOU REALLY ARE...
... GOING AWAY?
I'LL WRITE.
AND I'LL CALL YOU.
I'LL EVEN COME AND VISIT YOU SOME-TIMES.
AND WE STILL HAVE OUR TELEPATHY.
PLIP
PLIP
PLIP
RIGHT.
SNIFF
YOSHIDA...

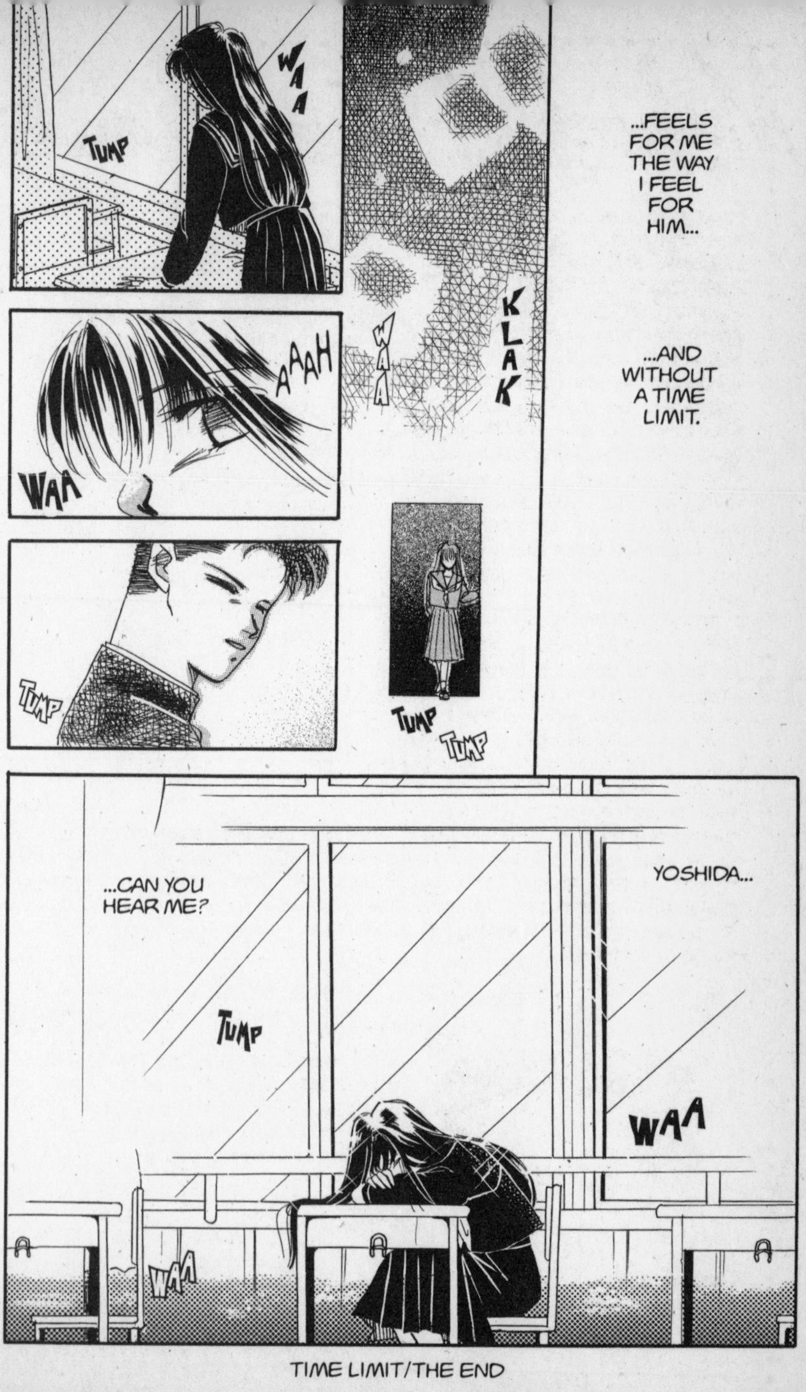
...FEELS FOR ME THE WAY I FEEL FOR HIM...
...AND WITHOUT A TIME LIMIT.
KLAK
WAA
WAA
TUMP
AAAH
WAA
TUMP
TUMP
TUMP
YOSHIDA...
...CAN YOU HEAR ME?
WAA
TUMP
WAA

TIME LIMIT/THE END

Making of Time limit.

メイキング　オブ　　　タイム　　リミット

"TIME LIMIT" WAS MY DEBUT PIECE. WHEN I READ IT AGAIN RECENTLY, I THOUGHT IT WAS LAUGHABLY BAD. (NOT THAT MY NEW STUFF IS SO MUCH BETTER...)

BEFORE MY DEBUT, I WAS EATING AT A RESTAURANT WITH MY EDITOR (IT WAS A BUSINESS LUNCH) WHEN TALK TURNED TO WRITING A LOVE STORY. I SAID, "SURE, OKAY," BUT TO TELL THE TRUTH, I'M NOT VERY GOOD AT WRITING LOVE STORIES. I'D BEEN WRITING STORIES ABOUT FRIENDS AND FAMILIES, AND COMEDIES, SO I HAD NO IDEA WHERE TO BEGIN WITH A LOVE STORY. INCIDENTALLY, THE AWARD I RECEIVED WAS FOR A LOVE STORY, BUT THAT WAS PRETTY MUCH THE FIRST ONE I'D EVER WRITTEN. SO WHEN I SAW THE STORY LINE THAT DEVELOPED, I THOUGHT IT WAS TOO MELODRAMATIC. IT WAS SO BAD THAT I DEVELOPED A TWITCH IN MY CHEEK. HOWEVER, THE DAY MY EDITOR AND I HAD AGREED WAS AT HAND, SO I PULLED MYSELF TOGETHER AND GAVE HIM "TIME LIMIT." THE EDITOR READ IT AND SAID, "NOT BAD," BUT I WAS SO EMBARRASSED THAT MY HEART WAS POUNDING. A FEW DAYS LATER THEY CALLED ME AND SAID, "WE'RE GOING TO

SKETCHES OF KYOKO THAT I FOUND AMONG MY NOTES.

PUBLISH IT IN OUR MAGAZINE." "WHAT?!" I SCREAMED. THIS IS VERY EMBARRASSING FOR ME TO SAY, BUT I WAS A RANK AMATEUR AS A CARTOONIST AT THE TIME. I DIDN'T EVEN KNOW WHAT KIND OF PAPER TO DRAW MY STORIES ON, SO I BORROWED SOME *FLOWERS AND DREAMS* CARTOON MANUSCRIPT PAPER FROM THE EDITORIAL STAFF. MY AWARD-WINNING PIECE HAD BEEN DRAWN ON SKETCH PAPER. I'M SURPRISED THAT *FLOWERS AND DREAMS* GAVE ME THAT AWARD. OH, IT'S ALL SO EMBARRASSING.

AND SO, THOSE WHO READ "TIME LIMIT" SEEMED TO THINK THAT IT WAS TYPICAL OF THE KIND OF STORIES I WRITE, AND WHEN THEY READ MY NEXT WORK, "HANDS OFF MY SECRET BOY!!" THEY WERE SURPRISED. IT SEEMS MY COMICS KEEP CHANGING. BUT I FEEL PRETTY GOOD ABOUT THAT.

CURRENTLY A FRESHMAN IN COLLEGE

I THINK

A SLIGHTLY OLDER YOSHIDA

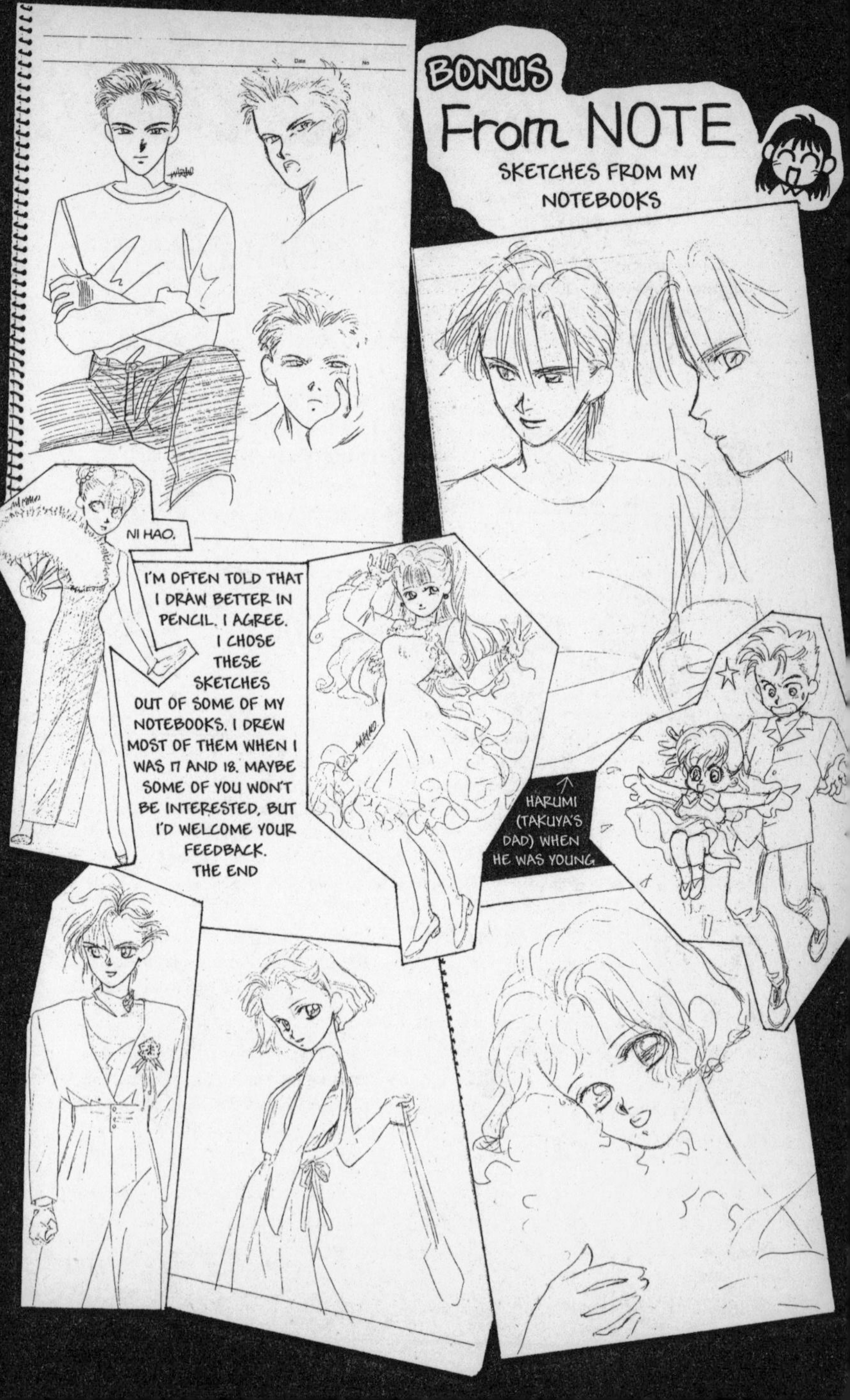
BONUS
From NOTE
SKETCHES FROM MY NOTEBOOKS
NI HAO.
I'M OFTEN TOLD THAT I DRAW BETTER IN PENCIL. I AGREE. I CHOSE THESE SKETCHES OUT OF SOME OF MY NOTEBOOKS. I DREW MOST OF THEM WHEN I WAS 17 AND 18. MAYBE SOME OF YOU WON'T BE INTERESTED, BUT I'D WELCOME YOUR FEEDBACK.
THE END
HARUMI (TAKUYA'S DAD) WHEN HE WAS YOUNG

BABY & Me ™

Creator: Marimo Ragawa

Date of Birth: September 21

Blood Type: B

Major Works: *Time Limit,
Baby & Me, N.Y. N.Y.,* and
Shanimuni-Go (Desperately—Go)

M arimo Ragawa first started submitting manga to a comic magazine when she was 12 years old. She kept up her submissions
for four years, but to no avail. She decided to submit her work
to the magazine *Hana to Yume*, where she received Top Prize in
the Monthly Manga Contest as well as an honorable mention (Kasaku) in the
magazine's Big Challenge contest. Her first manga was titled *Time Limit. Baby
& Me* was honored with a Shogakukan Manga Award in 1995 and was spun-
off into an anime.

Ragawa's work showcases some very cute and expressive line work along with
an incredible ability to depict complex emotions and relationships. Some of
her other works include *N.Y. N.Y.* and the tennis manga *Shanimuni-Go*.

Ragawa has two brothers and two sisters.

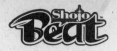

BABY & ME, Vol. 2
The Shojo Beat Manga Edition

This manga volume contains material that was originally published in English in *Shojo Beat* magazine, December 2005 – April 2006 issues.

STORY & ART BY
MARIMO RAGAWA

English Adaptation/Lance Caseleman
Translation/JN Productions
Touch-up Art & Lettering/Mark Griffin
Design/Courtney Utt
Editors/Ian Robertson & Pancha Diaz

Managing Editor/Megan Bates
Director of Production/Noboru Watanabe
Vice President of Publishing/Alvin Lu
Vice President & Editor in Chief/Yumi Hoashi
Sr. Director of Acquisitions/Rika Inouye
Vice President of Sales & Marketing/Liza Coppola
Publisher/Hyoe Narita

Printed in Canada

Published by VIZ Media, LLC.
P.O. Box 77010
San Francisco, CA 94107

Shojo Beat Manga Edition
10 9 8 7 6 5 4 3 2 1
First printing, July 2006

PARENTAL ADVISORY
BABY & ME is rated T for teen and is recommended for ages 13 and up. This volume contains adult situations.

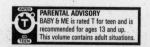

store.viz.com

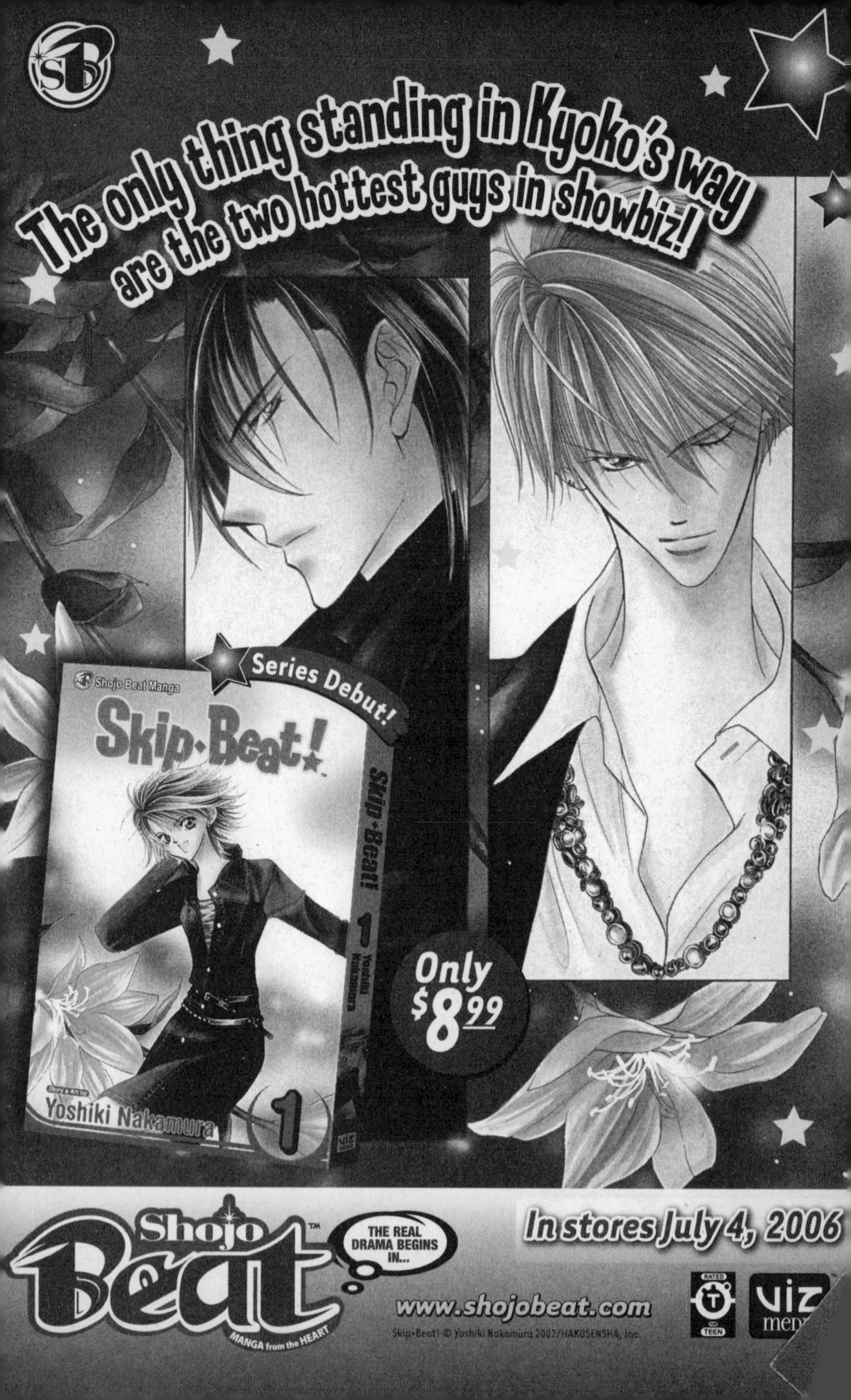

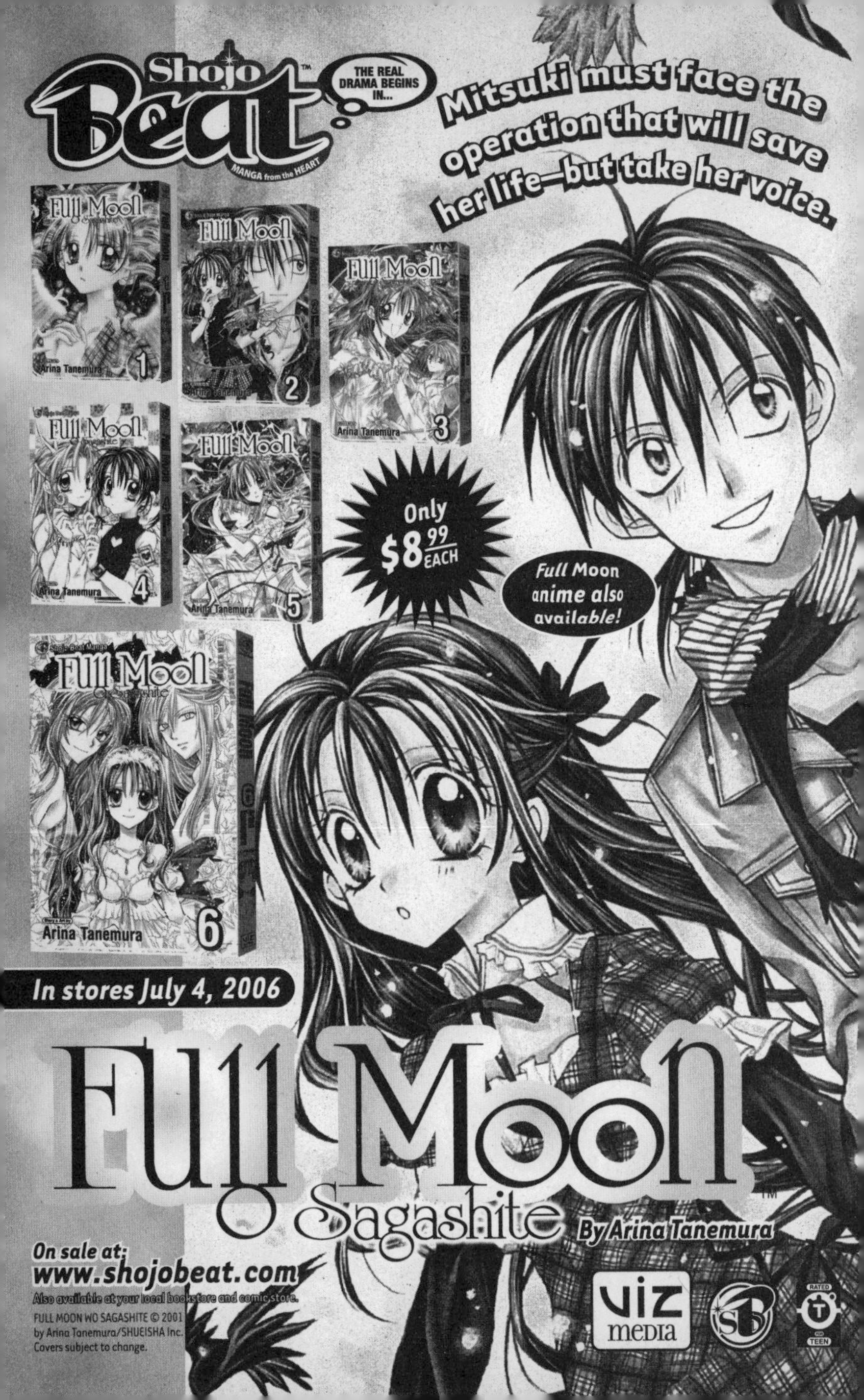
Shojo Beat™
THE REAL DRAMA BEGINS IN...
MANGA from the HEART
Mitsuki must face the operation that will save her life—but take her voice.
Full Moon
Arina Tanemura
1
Full Moon
Arina Tanemura
2
Full Moon
Arina Tanemura
3
Full Moon
Arina Tanemura
4
Full Moon
Arina Tanemura
5
Only $8.99 EACH
Full Moon anime also available!
Full Moon
Arina Tanemura
6
In stores July 4, 2006
Full Moon O Sagashite™
By Arina Tanemura
On sale at:
www.shojobeat.com
Also available at your local bookstore and comic store.
FULL MOON WO SAGASHITE © 2001 by Arina Tanemura/SHUEISHA Inc.
Covers subject to change.
viz media
RATED T FOR TEEN

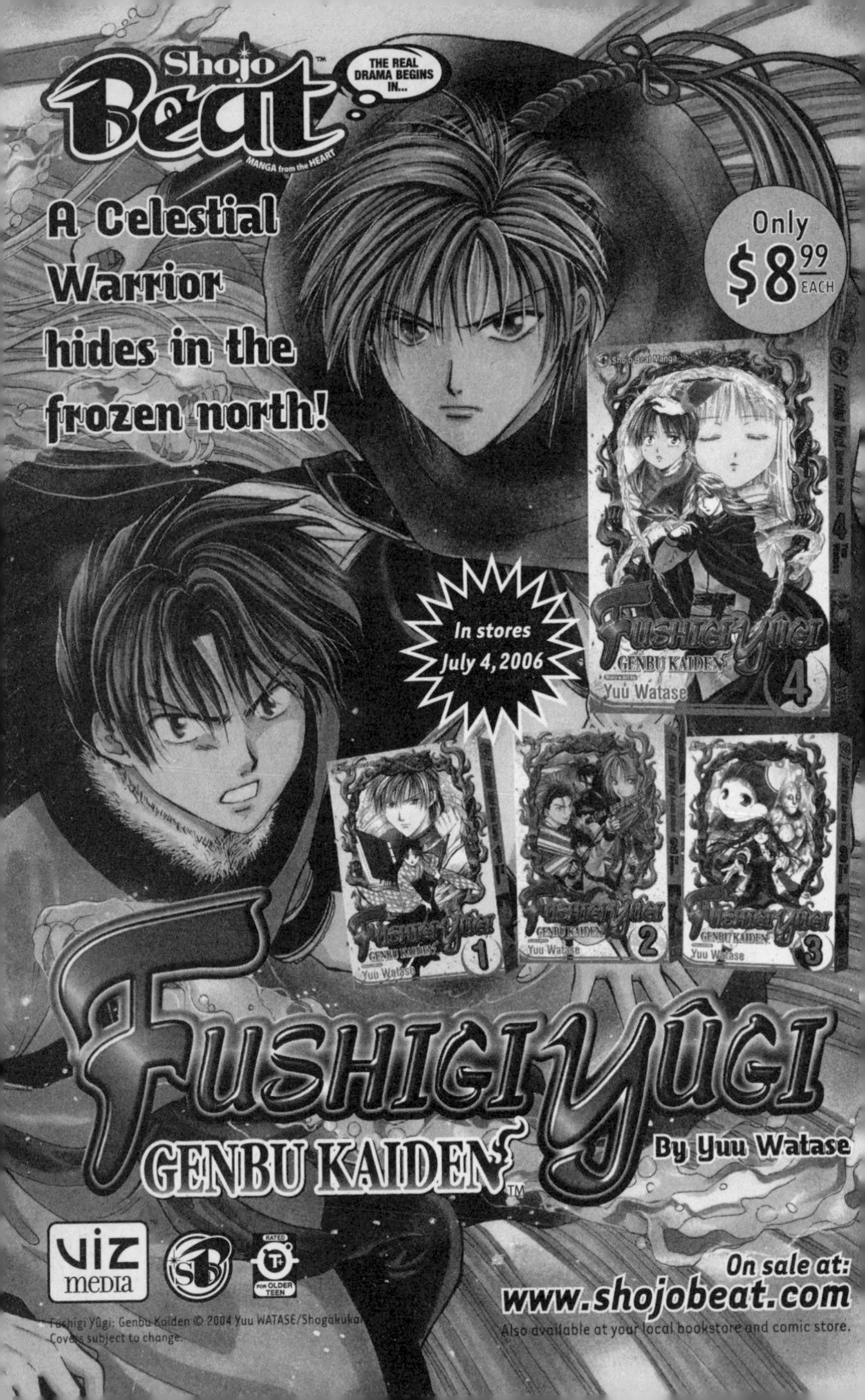
Shojo Beat™
THE REAL DRAMA BEGINS IN...
MANGA from the HEART
A Celestial Warrior hides in the frozen north!
Only $8.99 EACH
In stores July 4, 2006
FUSHIGI YÛGI
GENBU KAIDEN™
By Yuu Watase
VIZ media
RATED T+ FOR OLDER TEEN
On sale at:
www.shojobeat.com
Also available at your local bookstore and comic store.
Fushigi Yûgi: Genbu Kaiden © 2004 Yuu WATASE/Shogakukan
Covers subject to change.

Tell us what you think about Shojo Beat Manga!

Our survey is now available online. Go to:

shojobeat.com/mangasurvey

Help us make our product offerings better!

THE REAL DRAMA BEGINS IN...